"Finally a book convincingly and empirically demonstrates that Latin America serves as a model on how to best deal with human rights abuses from the past…." "…an original, sophisticated and nuanced interpretation."

Ariel Dulitzky, University of Texas School of Law/UN Working Group on Enforced Disappearances, USA

"The editors take on one of the key challenges in writing about transitional justice: establishing valid systematic comparisons without losing the context and particularity of each country's process." "…will add greatly to theoretical and practical discussions on the direction and future of transitional (and post-transitional) justice."

Naomi Roht-Arriaza, University of California, Hastings College of Law, USA

"This book presents the most ambitious and systematic attempt yet to provide an in-depth comparative analysis of transitional justice processes… an important step in shaping the development of empirical research in the transitional justice field."

Hugo van der Merwe, Centre for the Study of Violence and Reconciliation, Cape Town, South Africa

"A great contribution for our understanding of transitional justice in Latin America. It combines systematic comparative analysis with qualitative case studies and historical sequencing with synchronic assessments of policy outcomes. The challenge was great but the authors clearly succeeded!!!!"

Catalina Smulovitz, Universidad Torcuato Di Tella, Argentina

"The editors usefully establish a common framework with which to more systematically analyze the rich qualitative data collected by an impressive roster of country specialists. Some innovative data visualizations are used to illustrate outcomes in particular cases, and also to facilitate cross-national comparison across space and time."

Eric Wiebelhaus-Brahm, University of Arkansas at Little Rock, USA

Transitional Justice in Latin America

This book addresses current developments in transitional justice in Latin America – effectively the first region to undergo concentrated transitional justice experiences in modern times. Using a comparative approach, it examines trajectories in truth, justice, reparations, and amnesties in countries emerging from periods of massive violations of human rights and humanitarian law. The book analyses the cases of Argentina, Brazil, Chile, Colombia, Guatemala, El Salvador, Paraguay, Peru, and Uruguay, developing and applying a common analytical framework to provide a systematic, qualitative, and comparative analysis of their transitional justice experiences. More specifically, the book investigates to what extent there has been a shift from impunity towards accountability for past human rights violations in Latin America. Using 'thick', but structured, narratives – which allow patterns to emerge, rather than being imposed – the book assesses how the quality, timing, and sequencing of transitional justice mechanisms, along with the context in which they appear, have mattered for the nature and impact of transitional justice processes in the region. Offering a new approach to assessing transitional justice, and challenging many assumptions in the established literature, this book will be of enormous benefit to scholars and others working in this area.

Elin Skaar is at the Chr. Michelsen Institute, Bergen, Norway.

Jemima García-Godos is at the Department of Sociology and Human Geography, University of Oslo, Norway.

Cath Collins is at the Transitional Justice Institute, Ulster University, Northern Ireland, and Universidad Diego Portales, Chile.

Transitional Justice
Series Editor: Kieran McEvoy
Queen's University Belfast

The study of justice in transition has emerged as one of the most diverse and intellectually exciting developments in the social sciences. From its origins in human rights activism and comparative political science, the field is increasingly characterised by its geographic and disciplinary breadth. This series aims to publish the most innovative scholarship from a range of disciplines working on transitional justice-related topics, including law, sociology, criminology, psychology, anthropology, political science, development studies, and international relations.

Titles in this series:

Transitional Justice, Judicial Accountability and the Rule of Law
Hakeem O. Yusuf (2010)

The Era of Transitional Justice
The Aftermath of the Truth and Reconciliation Commission in South Africa and Beyond
Paul Gready (2010)

The Dynamics of Transitional Justice
International Models and Local Realities in East Timor
Lia Kent (2012)

Gender Politics in Transitional Justice
Catherine O'Rourke (2013)

Identity, Reconciliation and Transitional Justice
Overcoming Intractability in Divided Societies
Nevin T. Aiken (2013)

Corporate Accountability in the Context of Transitional Justice
Sabine Michalowski (2013)

Families of the Missing
A Test for Contemporary Approaches to Transitional Justice
Simon Robins (2013)

Transitional Justice Theories
Edited by Susanne Buckley-Zistel, Teresa Koloma Beck, Christian Braun, and Friederike Mieth (2014)

Truth, Denial and Transition
The Contested Past in Northern Ireland
Cheryl Lawther (2014)

Transitional Justice and the Arab Spring
Edited by Kirsten Fisher and Robert Stewart (2014)

The Art of Post-Dictatorship
Ethics and Aesthetics in Transitional Argentina
Vikki Bell (2014)

International Trials and Reconciliation
Assessing the Impact of the International Criminal Tribunal for the Former Yugoslavia
Janine Clark (2014)

The Concept of the Civilian
Legal Recognition, Adjudication and the Trials of International Criminal Justice
Claire Garbett (2014)

After Violence
Transitional Justice, Peace and Democracy
Elin Skaar, Camila Gianella, and Trine Eide (2015)

Transitional Justice and Reconciliation
Lessons from the Balkans
Edited by Martina Fischer and Olivera Simic (2016)

Forthcoming titles in the series:

The Judiciary and the Politics of Transition
Police Brutality Cases in Chile, Northern Ireland and South Africa
Marny Requa

The Trouble with Truth
Dealing with the Past in Northern Ireland
Kieran McEvoy

Violence, Law and the Impossibility of Transitional Justice
Catherine Turner

Transitional Justice in Latin America

The uneven road from impunity towards accountability

Edited by
Elin Skaar, Jemima García-Godos and Cath Collins

Routledge
Taylor & Francis Group
LONDON AND NEW YORK

First published 2016
by Routledge

2 Park Square, Milton Park, Abingdon, Oxfordshire OX14 4RN
711 Third Avenue, New York, NY 10017

a GlassHouse book

Routledge is an imprint of the Taylor & Francis Group, an informa business

First issued in paperback 2017

British Library Cataloguing in Publication Data
A catalogue record for this book is available from the British Library

Library of Congress Cataloguing in Publication Data
Skaar, Elin, editor. | García-Godos, Jemima, editor. | Collins, Cath, editor.
Title: Transitional justice in Latin America : The uneven road from impunity towards accountability / Edited by Elin Skaar, Jemima García-Godos and Cath Collins.
Description: New York : Routledge, 2016. | Series: Transitional justice |
Includes bibliographical references and index. Identifiers: LCCN 2015043553|
ISBN 9781138853249 (hbk) | ISBN 9781315722856 (ebk)
Subjects: LCSH: Transitional justice–Latin America. | Criminal justice, Administration of–Latin America. Classification: LCC KG574.T69 2016 | DDC 340/. 115–dc23
LC record available at http://lccn.loc.gov/2015043553

ISBN: 978-1-138-85324-9 (hbk)
ISBN: 978-0-8153-9292-7 (pbk)

Typeset in Baskerville by
Out of House Publishing

Impunity for international crimes and for systematic and widespread violations of fundamental human rights is a betrayal of our human solidarity with the victims of conflicts to whom we owe a duty of justice, remembrance, and compensation. To remember and to bring perpetrators to justice is a duty we also owe to our own humanity and to the prevention of future victimization.

– M. Cherif Bassiouni, 'Searching for Peace and Achieving Justice: The Need for Accountability'

Contents

Tables and figures

Tables

Figures

Contributors

Elin Skaar is a Senior Researcher and head of the research cluster on Rights and Legal Institutions at the Chr. Michelsen Institute in Bergen, Norway. Her research interests include human rights, transitional justice, and judicial reform. Publications include *Judicial Independence and Human Rights in Latin America: Violations, Politics, and Prosecution* (Palgrave Macmillan, 2011) and *After Violence: Transitional Justice, Peace, and Democracy* (Routledge, 2015). She holds a PhD in political science from the University of California, Los Angeles.

Jemima García-Godos is Associate Professor in the Department of Sociology and Human Geography, University of Oslo. Her broad research interest is state-society relations in post-conflict societies. Her research on transitional justice focuses on reparations programmes and land restitution, particularly in Colombia and Peru. She is co-editor of *Transitional Justice and Peacebuilding on the Ground: Victims and Ex-combatants* (Routledge, 2013). She holds a Dr.polit. degree in human geography from the University of Oslo.

Cath Collins is Professor of transitional justice at Ulster University, Northern Ireland, and Director of the Transitional Justice Observatory, Diego Portales University, Santiago, Chile. She has worked on transitional justice in Latin America since 1996. Her publications include *The Politics of Memory in Chile: From Pinochet to Bachelet* (Lynne Rienner, 2013) and *Post-transitional Justice: Human Rights Trials in Chile and El Salvador* (Pennsylvania State University Press, 2010). She holds a PhD in politics from the University of London.

Lorena Balardini is Assistant Professor in Social Sciences research and a PhD candidate at Buenos Aires University. She was formerly research coordinator at the Center for Legal and Social Studies (CELS) in Argentina. Her research focuses on measuring and monitoring human rights trials. She is co-author of 'Mapping Perpetrator Prosecutions in Latin America' (*International Journal of Transitional Justice*, 2012).

Elena Martínez Barahona is Professor of Political Science at the University of Salamanca, Spain. She specialises in Latin American comparative politics with a focus on the judiciary, transitional justice, and security issues. Publications include *Seeking the Political Role of the Third Governmental Branch: A Comparative Approach to High Courts in Central America* (VDM, 2009). She holds a PhD in Political Science from the European University Institute.

Martha Liliana Gutiérrez Salazar is Professor of Law and Human Rights at Jorge Tadeo Lozano University in Bogotá. Her interests are in Latin American comparative politics, especially the judiciary, human rights, and transitional justice. She has published in *América Latina Hoy* and other journals. She holds a PhD in Political Science from the University of Salamanca, Spain.

Boris Hau, a Lawyer, investigates memory and human rights policy at the Transitional Justice Observatory, Diego Portales University, Santiago, Chile. He worked as a researcher for two Chilean truth commissions (Valech I and Valech II) and contributed to Diego Portales University's 2015 annual report on human rights in Chile. He teaches classes on human rights at Alberto Hurtado University.

Francesca Lessa is a Post-Doctoral Researcher at the Latin American Centre, University of Oxford. Her interests include transitional justice in the Southern Cone, Operation Condor, and impunity for contemporary human rights violations in Latin America. She is the author of *Memory and Transitional Justice in Argentina and Uruguay: Against Impunity* (Palgrave Macmillan, 2013). She holds a PhD from the London School of Economics.

Glenda Mezarobba advised on the preparation of the draft bill that established the National Truth Commission in Brazil and subsequently served as a United Nations Development Programme consultant to the Commission. She has authored *Um acerto de contas com o futuro* (Humanitas/FAPESP, 2006). She holds a PhD in political science from São Paulo University.

Félix Reátegui is a Sociologist at the Institute for Democracy and Human Rights, Pontifical Catholic University of Peru. He has worked at the International Center for Transitional Justice in New York, advising truth-seeking initiatives in Côte d'Ivoire, Tunisia, Nepal, and Colombia. He edited *Transitional Justice: Handbook for Latin America* (Brazilian Amnesty Commission/ICTJ, 2011).

Luis Raúl Salvadó is a Researcher at the Latin American Faculty of Social Sciences (FLACSO) in Guatemala and has coordinated the organisation's curriculum on human rights. His interests focus on the rule of law in Guatemala. He holds a Master's degree in sociology from the University of Costa Rica.

Nelson Camilo Sánchez León is Research Coordinator at Dejusticia (Center for the Study of Law, Justice, and Society) in Colombia and Associate Professor at the National University of Colombia in Bogotá. He holds a JD degree from that university and an LLM degree in international legal studies from Harvard Law School.

Catalina Vallejo, a Lawyer, is a PhD candidate and Lecturer in administrative and environmental law at the University of Los Andes School of Law in Bogotá. Her research focuses on structural violence, peace and legal theory, global administrative law, and environmental regimes. Publications include *Plurality of Peaces in Legal Action* (LIT Verlag, 2012).

Acknowledgements

This book is the outcome of a three-year international research project funded by the Latin America Programme of the Research Council of Norway, entitled 'Reconceptualising Transitional Justice: The Latin American Experience'. The project, anchored at the Chr. Michelsen Institute (CMI) in Bergen, Norway, has been overseen by a three-part consortium consisting of the CMI, the University of Oslo, and the Universidad Diego Portales in Santiago, Chile. Four more Latin American institutional partners have been part of this project from the start: Centro de Estudios Legales y Sociales (CELS) in Argentina; Instituto de Democracia y Derechos Humanos, Pontificia Universidad Católica del Perú (IDEHPUCP); Facultad Latinoamericana de Ciencias Sociales (FLACSO) in Guatemala; and Dejusticia in Colombia. We have also been fortunate to work with individual researchers from Brazil, Colombia, Italy, and Spain.

All 13 authors contributing to this volume have experienced or encountered, directly or at one remove, the hardships of dictatorship and internal armed conflict and the challenges of transition to democracy and peace in Latin America. They bring different disciplinary backgrounds and country expertise to the project of examining developments in transitional justice. Using a comparative approach, they have tracked trajectories in truth-finding, justice, reparations, and amnesties in nine Latin American countries emerging from periods of massive violations of human rights and humanitarian law.

Completing this book has been a long journey, with many actors involved. In addition to the institutional partners and authors, the volume editors have worked closely with a vibrant and enthusiastic project reference group consisting of Leigh Payne, Catalina Smulovitz, Chandra Lekha Sriram, Hugo van der Merwe, and Eric Wiebelhaus-Brahm. The process started with a brainstorming session on the impact of transitional justice held at Solstrand outside Bergen, among fjords and mountains, in September 2011. During an exciting intellectual exchange over several days, we decided to move away from our original concern with the impact of transitional justice on democracy and peace in favour of a focus on the more immediate consequences of transitional justice. This led us to an 'accountability' approach, which we hope represents a novel way of understanding and comparing the depth and significance of transitional justice processes across countries and over time. We want to thank all the chapter authors, as well as our reference group members present at the Solstrand workshop, for valuable input in hammering out the concept of accountability used in this volume. We also thank Knut Andreas O. Lid and Stener Ekern, initially part of the project, for their input at the workshop. A big thank you to Natalia Flórez Mejía for helping us organise the Solstrand event.

After a year of collecting data and working on the nine country chapters, the authors gathered once again in Santiago in November 2012 to present empirical findings and analysis. The central question of concern was how to compare the very different country experiences. This is where the ideas arose for the transitional justice graphs and accountability triangles, two of the visual representations used in this volume. We warmly thank the Human Rights Observatory (now Transitional Justice Observatory) team at the Universidad Diego Portales, particularly Florencia González and Boris Hau, for their hospitality and for making the Santiago meeting a memorable experience.

Chapter drafts were presented at several conferences and benefited from participants' insightful comments. We thank panel members at the Latin American Studies Association congresses in San Francisco in 2012 and Chicago in 2014, as well as the European Consortium for Political Research conference in Bordeaux, France, in 2013.

Catalina Vallejo provided research assistance in preparing the section on the inter-American system in Chapter 1. For valuable comments on the theoretical framework, we are grateful to Juan Ochoa, Leigh Payne, Clara Sandoval, and Rachel Sieder. We would like to particularly thank Catalina Smulovitz and Eric Wiebelhaus-Brahm, who followed the project from its inception and provided critical input on several chapters, including the theoretical framework and the conclusions. We also thank three anonymous reviewers at Routledge for their constructive comments on the initial manuscript.

Many people helped us develop the country trajectories presented here, adding rigour and rich country detail. Heartfelt thanks to all who commented on drafts of the country chapters or worked as research assistants or translators: Mariel Alonso, Natalia Bermudez Qvortrup, Pelao Carvallo, Stener Ekern, Gabriela Fried, Boris Hau, Marcos Iglesias, Roberto Marcondes Cesar Jr., Soledad Pache, Leigh Payne, Andrea Rocha, Oliver Rogers, Luis Roniger, Elizabeth Salmón, Clara Sandoval, Rachel Sieder, Catalina Smulovitz, Catalina Vallejo, and Peter Winn.

We warmly thank the always helpful CMI administrative staff for providing important support functions throughout the project period: Steinar Hegre, Merete Leby, Reidunn Ljones, Guri Stegali, and Hong Kim Tran. CMI staff Marianne Skjold Ovaldsen, Pernille Jørgensen, and (especially!) Lars Ivar Høberg and Aksel Mjeldheim assisted us in the arduous task of preparing the accountability triangles and accountability graphs: thank you! Thanks to Howard Cooke for preparing the index. Our editorial assistant at Routledge, Laura Anne Muir and our project manager, Rebecca Willford have been helpful and accommodating in the process of preparing this book for publication. Our greatest gratitude is extended to our editorial magician, Cathy Sunshine, whose skill and professionalism helped us harmonise 13 different voices into a coherent publication. Any remaining errors are, of course, the authors' responsibility.

We hope the book will be useful to scholars and practitioners in the fields of human rights, transitional justice, area studies, and peacebuilding, and that the ideas presented here will help advance the debate on how transitional justice may contribute to accountability for past human rights violations.

Elin Skaar, Jemima García-Godos, and Cath Collins
Bergen, Oslo, Ulster, and Santiago
September 2015

Abbreviations

A	amnesties
ADPF	Argüição de Descumprimento de Preceito Fundamental (Allegation of Violation of Fundamental Precept, Brazil)
AJR	Asociación Justicia y Reconciliación (Association for Justice and Reconciliation, Guatemala)
ANM	Archivo Nacional de la Memoria (National Memory Archive, Argentina)
APDH	Asamblea Permanente por los Derechos Humanos (Permanent Assembly for Human Rights, Argentina)
ARENA	Alianza Republicana Nacionalista (Nationalist Republican Alliance, El Salvador)
AUC	Autodefensas Unidas de Colombia (United Self-Defence Forces of Colombia)
AVEMILGUA	Asociación de Veteranos Militares de Guatemala (Military Veterans' Association of Guatemala)
BDH	Bufete Jurídico de Derechos Humanos (Legal Bureau for Human Rights, Guatemala)
CAFCA	Centro de Análisis Forense y Ciencias Aplicadas (Centre for Forensic Analysis and Applied Sciences, Guatemala)
CALDH	Centro para la Acción Legal en Derechos Humanos (Centre for Human Rights Legal Action, Guatemala)
CBA	Comitê Brasileiro pela Anistia (Brazilian Committee for Amnesty)
CC	Constitutional Court
CEH	Comisión para el Esclarecimiento Histórico (Historical Clarification Commission, Guatemala)
CELS	Centro de Estudios Legales y Sociales (Centre for Legal and Social Studies, Argentina)

CEMDP	Comissão Especial sobre Mortos e Desaparecidos Políticos (Special Commission on the Dead and Disappeared for Political Reasons, Brazil)
CICIG	Comisión Internacional contra la Impunidad en Guatemala (International Commission against Impunity in Guatemala)
CIPAE	Comité de Iglesias para Ayudas de Emergencia (Churches' Committee for Emergency Assistance, Paraguay)
CJA	Center for Justice and Accountability, USA
CMAN	Comisión Multisectorial de Alto Nivel (High-Level Multisectoral Commission, Peru)
CMI	Chr. Michelsen Institute, Norway
CNAP	Consejo Nacional para el Cumplimiento de los Acuerdos de Paz (National Council for Implementation of the Peace Accords, Guatemala)
CNDDHH	Coordinadora Nacional de Derechos Humanos (National Human Rights Coordinating Committee, Peru)
CNMH	Centro Nacional de Memoria Histórica (National Centre for Historical Memory, Colombia)
CNR	Comisión Nacional de Resarcimiento (National Reparations Commission, Guatemala)
CNRR	Corporación Nacional de Reparación y Reconciliación (National Corporation for Reparations and Reconciliation, Chile)
CNRR	Comisión Nacional de Reparación y Reconciliación (National Commission for Reparation and Reconciliation, Colombia)
CNV	Comissão Nacional da Verdade (National Truth Commission, Brazil)
CNVR	Comisión Nacional de Verdad y Reconciliación (National Commission on Truth and Reconciliation, Chile)
CODEHUPY	Coordinadora de Derechos Humanos del Paraguay (Paraguayan Human Rights Coordinating Committee)
CONADEP	Comisión Nacional sobre la Desaparición de Personas (National Commission on the Disappearance of Persons, Argentina)
COPREDEH	Comisión Presidencial de Derechos Humanos (Presidential Commission for Human Rights, Guatemala)
CR	Consejo de Reparaciones (Reparations Council, Peru)
CVES	Comisión de la Verdad para El Salvador (Commission on the Truth for El Salvador)
CVJ	Comisión de Verdad y Justicia (Commission for Truth and Justice, Paraguay)

CVR	Comisión de la Verdad y Reconciliación (Truth and Reconciliation Commission, Peru)
DD	detained-disappeared
DNAT	Dirección Nacional de Asuntos Técnicos (National Technical Directorate of the national police, Paraguay)
DPS	Departamento para la Prosperidad Social (Department of Social Prosperity, Colombia)
EAAF	Equipo Argentino de Antropología Forense (Argentine Forensic Anthropology Team)
ELN	Ejército de Liberación Nacional (National Liberation Army, Colombia)
ENABI	Equipo Nacional para la Investigación, Búsqueda e Identificación Plena (National Team for Investigation, Search, and Full Identification, Paraguay)
ESMA	Escuela de Mecánica de la Armada (Navy Mechanics School, Argentina)
FAFG	Fundación de Antropología Forense de Guatemala (Forensic Anthropology Foundation of Guatemala)
FARC-EP	Fuerzas Armadas Revolucionarias de Colombia – Ejército del Pueblo (Revolutionary Armed Forces of Colombia – People's Army)
FASIC	Fundación de Ayuda Social de las Iglesias Cristianas (Social Aid Foundation of the Christian Churches), Chile
FCA	Federal Chamber of Appeals (Argentina)
FMLN	Frente Farabundo Martí para la Liberación Nacional (Farabundo Martí National Liberation Front, El Salvador)
GAM	Grupo de Apoyo Mutuo (Mutual Support Group, Guatemala)
GDP	gross domestic product
GMH	Grupo de Memoria Histórica (Historical Memory Group, Colombia)
HRO	human rights organisation
HRV	human rights violation
IACHR	Inter-American Commission on Human Rights
I/A Court HR	Inter-American Court of Human Rights
ICC	International Criminal Court
IDHUCA	Instituto de Derechos Humanos de la Universidad Centroamericana (Human Rights Institute of the Jesuit University, El Salvador)
IDP	internally displaced persons
MEDH	Movimiento Ecuménico por los Derechos Humanos (Ecumenical Movement for Human Rights, Argentina)

MINUSAL	United Nations Mission in El Salvador
MUME	Centro Cultural y Museo de la Memoria (Cultural Centre and Museum of Memory, Uruguay)
NGO	non-governmental organisation
OAS	Organization of American States
ONUSAL	United Nations Observer Mission in El Salvador
PAR	Programa de Apoyo al Repoblamiento y Desarrollo de Zonas de Emergencia (Repopulation Support Programme, Peru)
PCP-SL	Partido Comunista del Perú-Sendero Luminoso (Peruvian Communist Party-Shining Path)
PDI	Policía de Investigaciones (Investigations Police, Chile)
PIR	Programa Integral de Reparaciones (Comprehensive Reparations Programme, Peru)
PIT-CNT	Plenario Intersindical de Trabajadores – Convención Nacional de Trabajadores, Uruguay
PNR	Programa Nacional de Resarcimiento (National Reparations Programme, Guatemala)
PRAIS	Programa de Reparación y Atención Integral en Salud (Programme of Reparations and Comprehensive Health Care, Chile)
PRC	Programa de Reparaciones Colectivas (Collective Reparations Programme, Peru)
PREI	Programa de Reparaciones Económicas Individuales (Programme for Individual Economic Reparations, Peru)
R	reparations
REMHI	Proyecto Interdiocesano de Recuperación de la Memoria Histórica (Recovery of Historical Memory Project, Guatemala)
RUV	Registro Único de Víctimas (National Registry of Victims, Peru)
RUV	Registro Unificado de Víctimas del Terrorismo de Estado (Unified Register of Victims of State Terrorism, Argentina)
SC	Supreme Court
SERPAJ	Servicio Paz y Justicia (Peace and Justice Service)
SIE	Servicio de Inteligencia del Ejército (Army Intelligence Service, Peru)
SML	Servicio Médico Legal (Legal Medical Service, Chile)
STF	Supremo Tribunal Federal (Federal Supreme Court, Brazil)
STM	Superior Tribunal Militar (Superior Military Court, Brazil)
T	trials
TC	truth commission
TJ	transitional justice

TJM	transitional justice mechanism
UN	United Nations
URNG	Unidad Revolucionaria Nacional Guatemalteca (Guatemalan National Revolutionary Unity)

Chapter 1

Introduction

The accountability challenge

*Elin Skaar, Jemima García-Godos, and Cath Collins**

The Latin American region often evokes associations with turbulent politics, military regimes, fragile or patchy rule of law, and high levels of inequality. The Central American and Andean countries, including Colombia, are often characterised as riven by criminality linked to the drug trade and/or migration. The southern part of the region is known for brutal military dictatorships that used violence against guerrilla insurgencies, leftist activists, and members of social movements, casting a shadow of state terror over entire societies in the 1960s and 1970s.

Yet in recent decades, beginning in the 1980s, Latin America has been a pioneer in transitional justice mechanisms aimed at confronting the legacy of past military rule or internal armed conflict. As such, it was one of the first regions of the world to attract the sustained attention of transitional justice theorists and practitioners. Indeed, the term 'transitional justice' was coined by analysts whose attempts to construct a concept, and a field, drew in large part on the Latin American struggle in the 1980s and 1990s to deal with the terrible human cost of repressive dictatorships.

The course of transitional justice in the region has been uneven, both over time and between different countries. Initial efforts by Latin American states in transition from military rule or internal armed conflict were characterised by a strong emphasis on pragmatic or enforced accommodation around justice, combined with halting and incomplete programmes for truth-telling. Impunity through amnesties for past violations and concessions to elites were often considered essential to avoid the breakdown of the transition. Even large-scale, deliberate slaughter, such as the Guatemalan genocide of the 1980s, was rarely punished after transition to a new regime.

Nevertheless, on balance, Latin America is arguably the region of the world that has done the most to deal actively with serious crimes committed through the state apparatus and by non-state actors during past periods of military dictatorship or internal armed conflict. Why and how have some countries in the region been more able than others to address past political violence, sometimes more robustly than they deal with contemporary criminality? This question is the focus of our book.

We aim to describe and account for the recent transitional justice trajectory of Latin America by looking at the individual paths of nine countries. Although conventional analyses of transitional justice in the region focus primarily on the 1980s and 1990s and the initial transitions to democracy, this book extends the analysis into the first decades of the twenty-first century. It also focuses on specific transitional justice mechanisms rather than on the broad canvas of political transition.

We highlight complex patterns of changes over time with respect to impunity and accountability. Transitional justice trajectories that initially combined truth commissions with blanket amnesty for perpetrators, at the time of regime change or the signing of a peace agreement, have often later undergone substantial change in areas such as official and unofficial truth-telling, demand for and delivery of reparations, memory and counter-memory initiatives, and, most notably, persistent or resurgent demands for formal justice proceedings against perpetrators of historic crimes. What Geoffrey Robertson has called the 'age of human rights enforcement' (2013, xxxiii) has also been described as the 'age of accountability' (Sikkink 2012, 19). In the twenty-first century, in Latin America and beyond, transitional justice challenges are increasingly framed in the language of rights, entitlements, and obligations rather than of political bargaining, concessions, and expediency.

New patterns of transitional justice

In late 2015, as this book is completed, several examples of vibrant transitional justice activity are under way in the region. The 'Operation Condor' trials unfolding in courtrooms in Buenos Aires represent the largest and most extensive efforts to date in Latin America to systematically try military officials for cross-border crimes committed during the 1970s and 1980s.[1] Twenty-one defendants, all retired military officials, are facing charges of kidnapping and illicit association involving 106 victims and around 500 witnesses. The oral hearings are expected to last two years; a long prior investigation phase has already been completed. Such large-scale criminal investigations reinforce Argentina's current image as a protagonist of transitional justice.

Other Latin American countries have also seen recent justice activity over past violations such as forced disappearances, torture, extrajudicial killings, and crimes against humanity. This activity has been entirely home-grown, since no ad hoc or hybrid tribunals have operated in the region, and the International Criminal Court (ICC) has no temporal jurisdiction except, potentially, in the case of Colombia. In September 2012, Brazil opened its first state-sponsored criminal complaint against former military officials accused of torture during its last period of right-wing military rule, 1964–85. Only a few months earlier, President Dilma Rousseff had inaugurated the first official truth commission to examine a range of abuses committed during that regime.

As the first court case was under way in Brazil, prosecutors in Guatemala were preparing the trial of former general and ex-head of state Efraín Ríos Montt in a case that had bounced between Spanish and national courts. The Guatemalan Court for High Risk Crimes (Tribunal A de Mayor Riesgo) in May 2013 found Ríos Montt guilty of command responsibility for massacres against Ixil Maya indigenous people in Guatemala and sentenced to him to 80 years in prison. Although the Constitutional Court later set aside the judgment because of alleged procedural errors, this case marked the first time that a former head of state had been found guilty of genocide and crimes against humanity by the national justice system of his own country.

The unsuccessful battle to extradite former Chilean dictator Augusto Pinochet from the United Kingdom to Spain, which began in 1998, evoked the post-Nuremberg principle of universal jurisdiction. It became part of the back story to the founding of the ICC through the adoption of the Rome Statute in 1998 and its entry into force in 2002. The 2007 extradition of former Peruvian head of state Alberto Fujimori from Chile to Peru to face trial made him the first former head of state to be successfully prosecuted by a home-country court for gross human rights violations.

Developments in historical memory and truth-telling have been equally striking, fundamentally changing how violent events are remembered and retold (Atencio 2014; Hite 2013; Lessa 2013). Both in terms of formal judicial action and in terms of memory, the violent past is being remembered and acted upon.

Temporal distance from the violence and the levels of brutality involved vary significantly across countries. Gross human rights violations committed during dictatorships in Brazil and the Southern Cone (Chile, Argentina, Uruguay, Paraguay) in the 1970s and 1980s were matched, and even outstripped, by broad and intense fatal violence during internal armed conflicts in other parts of the region (Guatemala, El Salvador, Peru) from the 1960s to the 1990s. The conflict in Colombia continues, despite important strides in 2015 towards a peace agreement. Although it is an outlier in a temporal sense, the Colombian case is included here as a novel (for the region) example of efforts to consciously deploy transitional justice strategies and mechanisms even before completion of a peace settlement.

Gross violations, as well as early efforts to address or move beyond them, occurred in country contexts where impunity was part of the historical and social landscape. Elite actors and institutions generally expected, and usually secured, exemption from the legal, social, and political rules that applied to other members of society. This sense of being 'untouchable' inspired some of the worst expressions of state and paramilitary violence.

Given this reality, many of the transitional settlements of the 1980s and early 1990s focused on formal political change rather than substantive efforts to hold accountable those responsible for past violence. The motive was not always fear or incapacity. Sometimes there was a genuine belief that concessions providing impunity to former authoritarian regime figures or non-state combatants would, by securing peace and/or democracy, give rise to changes that would eventually weaken – or even overcome – such distorted patterns of privilege and of being 'above the law'. Even after successful transitions to peace or democratic government, full accountability was more the exception than the rule. Amnesty, whether written or unwritten, was the predominant response to past violations of human rights or of international humanitarian law.

Since the late 1990s, however, a different pattern has begun to emerge. In the more recent Latin American cases, that is, those countries embarking on transitional justice trajectories, truth commissions remain the most common policy response. However, they are much less likely than before to be accompanied by the introduction of blanket amnesty laws preventing criminal prosecution.[2] Today, more perpetrators are facing prosecution, domestic amnesty laws are being weakened or dismantled, and victims' rights have entered the public arena in a much more forceful way than previously. This suggests that the former picture of impunity in the formal judicial sphere is fading or at least changing. Reparations to victims and survivors have become a standard part of the post-violence repertoire, with more robust and internationally enshrined requirements for their scope.

What explains this observable shift from impunity towards accountability for past human rights violations? In order to explore when, how, under what conditions, and in response to whose agency accountability processes unfold, this book traces experiences since the 1980s in nine Latin American countries: Argentina, Brazil, Chile, Colombia, El Salvador, Guatemala, Paraguay, Peru, and Uruguay. The empirical description is framed by the spectrum ranging from impunity to accountability and by the role of transitional justice (TJ) and of specific transitional justice mechanisms (TJMs) in changing the level of accountability over time. We use the term 'transitional justice' to refer to processes and mechanisms for dealing with past atrocities in societies emerging from repressive regimes or internal armed conflicts. Although TJ encompasses a wide range of both formal and informal measures, this book's main focus is on truth-telling (including, but not limited to, truth commissions), criminal prosecution (for which we use the shorthand 'trials'), amnesties, and reparations. In particular, we explore how more recent democratic transitions[3] or peace settlements, as well as major changes in previously established settlements, may challenge traditional TJ thinking and practice.

This book makes three distinctive contributions to the TJ research literature. First, in evaluating the impact of TJ, it takes a step back from the broad goals often considered – such as peace, democracy, the rule of law, and reconciliation – to focus instead on more immediate indicators and outcomes of accountability. Throughout this volume, we define accountability as *an explicit acknowledgement by the state that grave human rights violations have taken place and that the state was involved in or responsible for them.*[4] Means of accountability can include, but are not limited to, the *recovery and diffusion of truth, criminal prosecution, reparations, and efforts to guarantee non-repetition.* This working concept of accountability incorporates, but also extends beyond, a minimal definition of accountability as the use of formal criminal justice mechanisms against perpetrators.

Second, the book offers a conceptual framework for exploring in depth how different TJMs play out in different contexts (Chapter 2), and how they may – or may not – contribute to increased accountability in the broad sense adopted here. Looking beyond the mere presence or absence of TJMs, we analyse their functioning, progress, consequences (intended and unintended), and limitations. We also consider other contextual factors that promote or inhibit accountability.

Third, the book provides detailed empirical evidence from nine Latin American countries, each featuring a systematic examination of a set of explanatory factors (Chapters 3–11). This allows the book to provide qualitative comparative analysis of TJ processes over time in a set of related countries. This approach differs from the single-country case studies that have dominated the TJ literature, as well as from the large-*n* quantitative studies that have also been prominent in recent years. Our focus is to carefully investigate to what extent there has been a shift from impunity towards accountability for human rights violations of the past in Latin America. Rather than the strict hypothesis-testing of large-*n* studies, the chapter authors use 'thick' narratives of multiple cases, guided by a common conceptual framework. The intention is to provide sufficient detail and nuance to account for variation among the cases, with a common structure to enable comparative analysis. Chapter 12 summarises such comparative judgments and assesses the weight of the evidence on theoretical questions of when, why, and how particular TJ measures come to constitute, or contribute to, accountability.

Explaining variations in shifts from impunity towards accountability for past human rights violations

Assessment of the impact of TJ mechanisms has often concentrated on macro-level changes, using indicators of broad societal phenomena such as peace or democracy. The results of such investigations are inconclusive, given the many difficulties in defining success. This is particularly the case with the trend of considering the 'transformative' potential of transitional justice interventions; strong claims are made for their ability to address long-term developmental goals along with socio-economic and gender injustice.[5] In Latin America, such ambitious agendas may give rise to tensions, given that the right-wing political violence with which transitional justice has historically been most concerned was largely a reaction to attempted revolutionary social change.

This book deliberately takes a less ambitious approach, focusing more narrowly on the effects of specific TJ mechanisms over time, both in the early paradigmatic transitions and in the subsequent trajectory in each country. Does transitional justice, after all, become just ordinary justice (Posner and Vermeule 2004), or do social, political, and legal responses to past violence continue to be identifiably special? In short, we focus on the distinctive goals of TJ mechanisms, namely to address, and ideally to ameliorate, the negative social and political legacy of past political violence.

Our guide to summarising the impact over time is the spectrum bounded by the ideal types of 'impunity' and 'accountability'. Although neither extreme exists in a pure form in the real world, the spectrum serves as a conceptual framework for comparing degrees of accountability or its absence (impunity). In the TJ field, accountability is generally associated with criminal accountability; impunity is considered to be its antithesis (Teitel 2000). The Inter-American Court of Human Rights has repeatedly defined impunity as a systematic failure to investigate, prosecute, arrest, adjudicate, and convict those responsible for violations of rights protected by the American Convention on Human Rights (Cassel 2007). We expand this minimal legalistic definition and employ impunity and accountability as end points of a wider spectrum that also includes the results of other forms of TJ, such as truth commissions, reparations, and informal mechanisms to deal with the memory of past violations.

Kathryn Sikkink (2012) distinguishes between three models of accountability: the immunity or impunity model (model 1), the state accountability model (model 2), and the individual criminal accountability model (model 3). She contends that impunity, that is, failure to allocate responsibility for serious human rights violations (model 1), can be erased by holding responsible either the state (model 2) or the individual(s) who allegedly committed the violations (model 3). As will become evident in our nine country chapters, most Latin American countries have moved in recent times from model 1 in the direction of model 2, model 3, or a combination of both.

Through a careful selection of country cases, this book attempts to map and then explain variations in accountability across time and across countries. We argue that mono-causal explanations fall short of capturing complex and frequently non-linear shifts from impunity towards accountability. Accordingly, we first track and explain such shifts within each country during the years that have elapsed between the initiation of transition (or signing of a peace agreement) and the end of 2014. Second, we compare and contrast observable levels of accountability at the time of writing across our nine country cases. The choice of cases from the Latin American region allows for comparison of countries that share a regional context, yet have a range of distinctive experiences in their transitional justice trajectories.

Why focus on Latin America?

There are good reasons why a study of transitional justice trajectories in Latin America is timely. First, this world region pioneered the use of TJ mechanisms. Latin America saw the origins of the official truth commission (TC) in the early 1980s; the region contains at least 12 of the 40 or so countries worldwide that have utilised TCs over the past three decades (Hayner 2011).[6] Latin America was also the pilot for the active involvement of the United Nations (UN) in peace processes in the post-Cold War period: the UN's involvement in El Salvador in 1991–92 and Guatemala in 1996–97 preceded its involvement in setting up the ad hoc tribunals in Rwanda and the former Yugoslavia. Nonetheless, in keeping with the prevailing wisdom of the time, the UN focused its role in Central America on peace mediation and truth-telling rather than on, as in the later cases, actively supporting criminal prosecution.

Second, Latin America is the world region that has seen the highest numbers of alleged human rights violators prosecuted in third-country courts. This has influenced international human rights law as well as domestic court practice (Skaar 2011). Since the 1980s, former members of Latin American armed forces and security services have been tried, sometimes *in absentia*, in the domestic courts of several Western European countries, including Spain, France, Italy, and Belgium. These cases, which include the 1998 Pinochet case in Spain, have contributed to advances in human rights jurisprudence and to the construction of limited enforceability for existing international human rights norms (Sikkink and Walling 2007).

Third, ongoing human rights trials in the region's domestic courts are, as we will see, probably the most extensive in the world today in both absolute and relative terms. They increasingly reach across borders, tracking intra-regional repressive networks such as Operation Condor but also drawing in US and Spanish courts. Parallel to this horizontal reach, domestic transitional justice dynamics have both stimulated and been stimulated by regional court activity. In the case of Colombia, they have led to the longest-running (since 2005) preliminary examination by the ICC and to the first contemplated theatre of ICC action outside Africa.

Finally, Latin America has also been a forerunner in reparation programmes for victims, survivors, their families, and sometimes others. Particularly in recent years, there has been an increased focus on bottom-up, victim-centred, and victim-driven reparation processes. Peru has emphasised the notion of collective reparations for indigenous communities, mirroring recent developments in acceptance of the principle of collective rights. The 2011 Victims' Law in Colombia is particularly notable for its historical extensiveness and for addressing land issues that lie at the heart of the decades-long conflict (García-Godos 2013). This exemplifies the socio-economic turn in transitional justice thinking. The victim-centred discourse surrounding reparations also requires attention to connections between state-initiated and bottom-up TJ processes.

This rich regional experience entails substantial variation in the way countries have dealt with their violent pasts. Some countries, like Argentina and Chile, may be considered world leaders in putting former military dictators and other alleged perpetrators on trial. Other countries, such as Brazil, have only very recently started to address their violent past, at least at the level of internationally visible public policy.

Thus, we can explore questions such as the following: What makes some countries apparently more able and willing than others to deal actively with past human rights violations? What affects the timing and depth of the debate when such issues are addressed nationally? Are the countries with less present-day activity simply those that satisfactorily resolved the issues at a previous juncture? Why have some countries seen more actions and initiatives that fall under our definition of accountability, and others less? Are patterns sufficiently explained by the relative intensity of violations? Is the key factor political will, level of judicial competence, judicial will, or culture? Is it a matter of the level of respect for human rights norms in general, or of elite and civil society actors pushing for or against particular transitional justice processes? What is the role and relative contribution of international actors?

In sum, Latin America can offer many useful lessons for transitional justice theory, and for practice in other parts of the world, due to its rich mix of types and time periods of transitional justice experience. Comparisons over recent decades allow insight into the extent to which 'international time' and trends in international scholarly and policy thinking on transitional justice may have operated alongside national and regional factors. Recent changes in formal justice outcomes, particularly the turn from amnesty to prosecutions in the south of the region, offer a unique chance to study the process and outcome of large-scale criminal trials for domestic atrocities. The special case of Colombia, meanwhile, serves as a bridge to active conflict settings in other regions.

Contextualising Latin American TJ development

To understand Latin America's recent trajectory in addressing past violations, it is important to keep in mind developments at the regional level that may have aided, or at least provided an enabling environment for, the shift from impunity towards accountability in specific countries. Here we focus on three: political developments, judicial developments, and normative development in the field of human rights.

Political developments

Two political trends in Latin America are particularly relevant: the endurance of formal democracy and an ideological shift to the left in the early 2000s, with moves from right-wing to centre-left, or to left-wing governments in some countries.

Democratic rule, for all its imperfections, now seems firmly rooted. Whereas military coups were almost routine in the 1970s and 1980s, since the year 2000 there have been, at most, half a dozen attempts, mostly unsuccessful, at forcible power transfer. No Latin American country is under military rule as of mid-2015, with Cuba generally considered the sole remaining authoritarian regime. Only Colombia is currently immersed in internal armed conflict, and peace talks are ongoing there. Some see the region as democratically consolidated. Even those who are concerned about deterioration, stagnation, or backsliding tend to agree that Latin America is 'enjoy[ing] its most democratic period ever' (Mainwaring and Pérez-Liñán 2013, 246). This means that elections are acceptably competitive, free, and fair; the military is back in the barracks; and there is heightened respect for the rule of law and the protection of basic citizenship rights. Increased efforts at democratic accountability (horizontal, vertical, and social)[7] in many Latin American countries can be expected, where successful, to also affect human rights compliance positively insofar as respect for human rights is intrinsic to democratic practices.

The second general political shift is ideological. Whereas right-wing dictatorships, frequently propped up by the United States, formerly dominated much of the continent, making common cause against a perceived 'communist threat', these regimes gave way in the 1980s and 1990s to elected governments of a more centrist hue. The decade beginning in 2000 then saw a leftward turn in, for example, Argentina, Brazil, Chile, Ecuador, El Salvador, Guatemala, Nicaragua, Uruguay, and Venezuela.[8] Though some left or centre-left governments did relatively little to address past human rights violations, several oversaw substantive changes in this respect. Current or recent heads of state in Chile (Michelle Bachelet, 2006–10 and 2014–), Brazil (Dilma Rousseff, 2011–), and Uruguay (José Mujica, 2010–15) were all personally victimised by authoritarian-era repression. In Argentina, left-wing presidents Nestor Kirchner (2003–7) and Cristina Fernández de Kirchner (2007–16) quickly adopted a strong pro-accountability stance. As detailed in the country chapters, both personal histories and state-level politics affected issues of human rights and transitional justice.

Judicial reform

Another development in the region that positively influenced formal criminal accountability for past crimes was a wave of judicial reforms in the 1980s and 1990s. These reforms, aided by external actors such as the World Bank and the Inter-American Development Bank, were encouraged by regional judicial experts and driven by institutional and citizen concern with the functionality of state institutions and the rule of law. Courts and other criminal justice institutions were overhauled in many countries (Dakolias 1996; Biebesheimer 2001; Buscaglia, Dakolias, and Ratliff 1995; Hammergren 1998; Jarquín and Carrillo 1998). Reforms aimed to increase the independence, accessibility, and efficiency of the courts. Many countries switched their criminal justice procedures from inquisitorial to accusatorial, with public prosecutors' offices redesigned and given more prominent roles.

Where successful, such reforms instigated a speedier, more democratic, judicial process more accessible than before to a range of citizens, including victims of human rights abuses. Where judges became more independent, they became, in principle, more able to take on human rights cases that in earlier times would have been rejected due to internal political pressure. Although the effectiveness of the reforms has been questioned (Hammergren 2010; Prillaman 2000), the bulk of the literature, including our own previous research, suggests that judicial reform measures have, on balance, aided the shift towards accountability for past crimes. Courts on the continent are now, on average, more accessible to victims, with judges more sensitive to human rights and hence more receptive to claims for truth, reparations, or justice than they were ten or 20 years ago (Skaar 2011).

Normative development

Finally, as part of an overall international trend, there has been a normative shift in Latin America towards acceptance of the validity of human rights framings. This is reflected in at least three areas: constitutional reform, treaties, and conventions that codify human rights protections, and the development of international human rights norms. Together, these point to the development of national iterations of a regional and international human rights culture.

First, constitutional reforms have rebalanced power relations within the state by increasing internal checks and balances and by reducing the relative power of presidents in a region with a strong tradition of presidentialism. The reforms have also improved protection of minority rights and women's rights (Sieder and McNeish 2012).

Second, a growing body of treaty law offers explicit protection of core human rights. Particularly relevant are the American Convention on Human Rights (which entered into force in 1978), the Inter-American Convention to Prevent and Punish Torture (1987), the Convention against Torture and Other Cruel, Inhuman or Degrading Treatment or Punishment (1987), and the Inter-American Convention on Forced Disappearance of Persons (1996). The Convention against Torture granted universal jurisdiction for torture. Significantly, the Inter-American Convention on Forced Disappearance explicitly classified disappearance as a crime against humanity, exempt from statutes of limitations, and as an ongoing or continuous crime (*delito permanente*) as long as the fate and whereabouts of the victim remain unknown. These concepts have been key in domestic court treatments of past Latin American crimes in Latin American and European courts, as detailed in the country chapters. The sequencing of regional followed by international treaties also demonstrates that Latin America has not only taken up, but also actively spearheaded, a change in international norms. Argentina, for example, was a key protagonist of the 2006 adoption of the International Convention for the Protection of All Persons from Enforced Disappearance.

Third, there has been further development of the concept of core atrocity crimes and common (universal) responsibility for prosecuting such crimes (Bassiouni 2001; Einarsen 2012). The 1998 Pinochet arrest and ensuing legal battle is the best-known example in which 'bystander' domestic courts have invoked this idea (Roht-Arriaza 2005). National prosecutions in third-country courts seem finally to be coming of age as a viable option alongside the emerging range of international venues for prosecution of atrocity crimes. This trend, running from Nuremberg and Tokyo through the ad hoc tribunals of the 1990s and later hybrid or mixed tribunals,[9] found its greatest expression in 2002 with the establishment of the International Criminal Court.

The interplay of these various domestic, regional, and international dynamics has given rise to Latin America's emerging 'age of accountability'. Growing concern for human rights in the region is intimately linked to the dual processes of democratic consolidation and judicial/constitutional reform briefly described above. This concern and an emphasis on transitional justice in particular, has been reinforced by the inter-American system for human rights protection. As this system forms an important institutional and legal backdrop to national TJ processes, it warrants discussion in greater detail.

The inter-American system of human rights protection

Latin America and Africa are the only two regions of the world that have both a court and a commission to deal with the promotion and protection of human rights.[10] The inter-American system dates back to the establishment of the Organization of American States (OAS) and the signing of the American Declaration of the Rights and Duties of Man in 1948, which became the first regional codification of human rights. The Inter-American Commission on Human Rights, created under the OAS Charter in 1959, is located in Washington, DC. The American Convention on Human Rights entered into force in 1978, and the Inter-American Court of Human Rights was set up in 1979 in San José, Costa Rica, to enforce and interpret provisions of the Convention.

Participation in this regional system of human rights protection has been widespread, excepting only the United States and Canada. At time of writing in mid-2015, 23 of the 35 independent states of the Americas – including all nine of the Latin American country cases examined in this book – are parties to the American Convention and subject to the contentious jurisdiction of the Inter-American Court (Table 1.1).[11]

The Inter-American Commission and Court

The Inter-American Commission on Human Rights has monitoring and advisory powers and acts as gatekeeper to the Inter-American Court of Human Rights. It advises member states of the OAS on improving human rights protection, conducts on-site visits, publishes country and annual reports, and investigates specific situations. Outcomes of investigations can include 'friendly settlements', the soliciting of an advisory opinion from the Court, or the referral of a case to the Court. According to its Rules of Procedure, the Commission can order a state to

Table 1.1 The nine country case studies and the inter-American system

Country	*Signed American Convention*	*Ratified American Convention*	*Accepted contentious jurisdiction of Inter-American Court*
Argentina	2 Feb 1984	5 Sep 1984	5 Sep 1984
Brazil	22 Nov 1969	25 Sep 1992	10 Dec 1998
Chile	22 Nov 1969	21 Aug 1990	21 Aug 1990
Colombia	22 Nov 1969	31 Jul 1973	21 Jun 1985
El Salvador	22 Nov 1969	23 Jun 1978	6 Jun 1995
Guatemala	22 Nov 1969	18 Jul 1978	9 Mar 1987
Paraguay	22 Nov 1969	24 Aug 1989	11 Mar 1993
Peru	27 Jul 1977	28 Jul 1978	21 Jan 1981
Uruguay	22 Nov 1969	19 Apr 1985	19 Apr 1985

Source: IACHR 2013.

adopt precautionary measures when 'serious and urgent situations [present] a risk of irreparable harm to persons or to the subject matter of a pending petition or case'.[12] Measures may be of a collective nature, that is, designed to protect people belonging to a particular group (the Convention on Forced Disappearance is one of the explicitly cited bases for this power).

The Inter-American Court has both advisory and adjudicatory functions. In the former capacity, it issues advisory opinions, solicited by the Inter-American Commission, agencies, and/or OAS member states, regarding the correct interpretation of the American Convention or other regional instruments. Its adjudicatory function involves hearing specific cases related to human rights violations allegedly committed by ratifying states that have accepted its jurisdiction (Pasqualucci 2013). The Court can also advise on the compatibility of domestic laws and bills with the state's duties under the regional human rights instruments.

The Court rules only on whether states have complied with treaty and other obligations. Since it is not a criminal court, it cannot decide on individual guilt. At most, it may rule that a state has infringed rights directly, by commission, or indirectly, such as by the denial of timely justice in a domestic criminal case. Complementarity also operates, as cases are only admissible if domestic remedies have been exhausted. Unlike in the single-tier European system, individuals do not have direct recourse to the Court but must first petition the Commission. Only states that have ratified the Convention and accepted the Court's contentious jurisdiction can be investigated and judged by the Court regarding individual alleged violations. Rulings of the Court are binding on the affected state and can involve pecuniary and non-pecuniary reparations for moral and physical damage of individual or collective character (Sandoval-Villalba 2009). The Court can also order a state to reopen a domestic case, offer a public apology to victims, publish details of a ruling in national media, and/or modify domestic legislation to bring it into line with Convention obligations. Both the Commission and the Court have mechanisms to follow up or supervise state compliance (Naddeo 2010), although the system's overall effectiveness in this respect is often questioned.

The contribution of the regional human rights system to transitional justice

It is widely agreed that the inter-American system of human rights protection has made a significant contribution to domestic accountability for past human rights violations. The system played a role in struggles for justice, truth, and reparations during times of repression and conflict as well as in the aftermath (Salazar and Antkowiak 2007; SLADI 2011). This had both symbolic and practical significance during the 1970s and 1980s, providing victims with a forum when national justice systems were inaccessible, compromised or actively hostile. The Commission's on-site visits and reports carried special significance at that time. Precautionary measures, especially in cases of enforced disappearance, protected lives (see González 2010), and the Commission's early assertion (1985) of the right to truth became central to individual and collective struggles for defence of human rights.

Indeed, the inter-American system can be considered a pioneer of the rights-based framing of transitional justice practice that is emerging in the region and beyond (IACHR 2014, para. 236). According to Alexandra Huneeus, the Court has played 'a leading role in developing international doctrine on disappearance, amnesties, the victim's right to the truth, the obligation of states to prosecute, and judicial guarantees' (2011, 500).[13] The inter-American system continues to play a key role in protecting individuals from human rights abuse, promoting awareness of human rights, creating space for democratic dialogue, and giving voice to victims and their families (Dulitzky 2007).

In the field of criminal accountability, Inter-American Court rulings have strongly supported access to justice[14] and have addressed dilemmas in prosecuting state and non-state agents for atrocity crimes. The Court's milestone ruling in *Velásquez Rodríguez v Honduras* (1988) clearly articulated that states parties have a general obligation to ensure Convention rights, which implies the obligation to investigate, prosecute, and punish gross violations of human rights and to provide reparation. A further series of judgments have been central in reinterpreting domestic amnesty laws, thus widening space for judicial proceedings against alleged human rights violators in national courts. In *Barrios Altos v Peru* (2001), the Court declared that the amnesty imposed by former president Alberto Fujimori violated victims' right to access to justice. In *Almonacid v Chile* (2006), the Court ruled that amnesty laws could not be allowed to contravene Convention obligations. This applied particularly to what the Court termed 'self-amnesty', that is, amnesty laws designed to principally or exclusively favour the regime or administration that instituted them. Forced disappearance was interpreted as prohibited by *jus cogens* (*Goiburú v Paraguay*, 2006) and was also declared a continuous crime (*Contreras et al. v El Salvador*, 2011). These principles, which can also be derived from domestic law principles, were previously and subsequently significant in national prosecutions in, among other countries, Chile, Argentina, Brazil, Uruguay, and Peru.[15]

Another central contribution to the struggle against impunity in the region has been the system's emphasis on the right to truth. Following the Commission's early lead, the Court accepted, in *Velásquez Rodríguez* and subsequently, that victims and relatives have the right to truth. The Court has also discussed truth as a social right and a form of reparation in, for example, *Gomes Lund (Guerrilha do Araguaia) v Brazil* (2010) and *Gelman v Uruguay* (2011) (IACHR 2014).

In spite of this substantial progress, there are also limitations to inter-American system influence on domestic TJ processes. First, temporal jurisdiction restrictions have most likely prevented a number of cases for past violations from being brought before the Court. In five of our nine case studies, systematic torture, killing, forced disappearance, and illegal imprisonment took place before the relevant state had ratified the Convention and/or accepted the jurisdiction of the Court, leaving it no competence to investigate the original alleged offence. However, this problem has been overcome in some recent cases by use of petitions that cite ongoing denial of truth or justice as, for example, in *Serrano-Cruz Sisters v El Salvador* (2005) and *García Lucero v Chile* (2013).

Second, levels of non-compliance suggest that there is still a fair amount of political and judicial resistance to Court rulings and Commission recommendations. A case in point is the reluctant implementation of the remedies ordered in the Gelman case, further discussed in the Uruguay chapter in this volume, or Chile's nine-year delay (as of September 2015) in complying with the 2006 Almonacid ruling by legislating on amnesty.

Third, some states have grown dissatisfied with the entire system. Trinidad and Tobago withdrew from ('denounced') the American Convention in 1998, in order to remove itself from the Court's jurisdiction, and Venezuela followed suit in 2012. Peru threatened to do so in 1999, under Fujimori. These withdrawals may herald attempts by other states to question or reduce the competence of the system, since tensions between national sovereignty and regional governance are as present in Latin America as in other parts of the world. However, the system's current significance for regional transitional justice is undeniable and is confirmed in the nine country cases.

Country studies: selection and grouping

Our nine case studies – Argentina, Brazil, Chile, Colombia, El Salvador, Guatemala, Paraguay, Peru, and Uruguay – share a number of important features, explored in more depth in Chapter 2. While it is important not to overstate the similarities, the existence of roughly homologous formal state and legal systems and two mutually comprehensible official languages (Spanish and Portuguese) has undoubtedly facilitated intra-regional exchanges and the diffusion of transitional justice practices at both official and grassroots levels. Nevertheless, these nine countries also differ significantly with respect to the implementation of TJ measures. On the basis of conflict and transition type, we can divide them into three clusters or groups of cases. The variations between and within groups provide opportunities to examine, first, how transitional justice has evolved over time within national settings, and second, how the transitional justice menu itself now reflects the regional and international realities of the new millennium rather than those of the 1980s.

Group 1, which we call 'post-authoritarian' cases, consists of countries in which the state was responsible for an overwhelming proportion of the most serious abuses. This group includes the Southern Cone countries plus Brazil, which were linked not only by geographic proximity but also by Operation Condor. In both of the remaining two groups, state violence was accompanied by significant violations of international humanitarian law by non-state armed actors. Group 2, the 'post-conflict' group, includes the Central American countries and Peru. Group 3

Table 1.2 Groups of country cases according to type of transition

Group	*Characteristics*	*Transition type*	*Countries*
Group 1	Military authoritarian regime, state mainly responsible for violations; effective self-amnesty; subsequent significant tensions in civil-military relations; elite reaction against challenges to impunity in the courts; justice system reform as an independent variable producing or facilitating post-transitional accountability.	Post-authoritarian	Argentina Brazil Chile Paraguay Uruguay
Group 2	Civil/internal wars followed by peace processes and/or amnesties intended to secure peace; higher perceived legitimacy of amnesty given contribution of non-state armed actors to fatal violence; varied levels of subsequent social pressure for accountability; historically low levels of justice system functionality; potentially demobilising effect of high levels of rurality and relatively low human development index and income per capita scores when compared to Group 1 (except Paraguay).	Post-conflict	El Salvador Guatemala Peru[a]
Group 3	Ongoing and long-lasting armed conflict; equal and/or greater responsibility of non-state armed actors for fatalities; TJMs currently considered as contributing to, as well as resulting from, a transition to peace; possible external (international) justice intervention (ICC preliminary examination); cumulative intra-regional learning and explicit appropriation of transitional justice idiom and norms.	Ongoing conflict	Colombia

a. Peru has experienced multiple transitions: from military rule to democracy in 1980, from armed conflict in the mid-1990s, and from civilian authoritarian rule in 2000. It is thus a hybrid case for purposes of our taxonomy, yet, on balance, it lies closer to the Central American contexts of Group 2 than to the post-authoritarian cases of Group 1.

consists of Colombia, which is distinct in being the only case where political violence is still ongoing. Although an active peace process was under way as of 2015, with transitional justice questions on the table as an agreed part of the agenda, no conclusion had been reached at time of writing. Table 1.2 provides details on significant characteristics reflecting differences between these three broad contexts.

The subdivision of the nine cases into three groups is designed to maximise, for control and comparison purposes, similarities within groups and differences between groups along the following: (a) timing of and time elapsed since transition (domestic and international timing); (b) type of conflict and transition (post-authoritarian, post-conflict, or ongoing conflict); (c) type and scale of violations (low/high) and victims' political and sociological profiles; (d) number and sequencing of TJMs (few/many, early/late); and (e) drivers of justice (local/state/international). See Table 1.3 for a summary comparison of some of these basic data. Within each of the three groups, the countries are listed chronologically by year of formal initiation of transition away from authoritarian rule or internal armed conflict, paralleling the order of the country chapters in this book.

In addition to the distinctions outlined above, our cases also vary with respect to their rates of compliance with verdicts, settlements, and remedies required by the Inter-American Commission and Court (Basch et al. 2010). To consider Court and Commission influence over domestic TJ processes, each country chapter will examine the levels, content of, and domestic receptivity to major inter-American system activity regarding transitional justice matters – including, where relevant, domestic court citation of rulings by the regional system in relation to other states.

The special case of Colombia

Colombia has been selected as a special case for three reasons. First, as already discussed, it is the only case where TJ mechanisms are being implemented *before* the end of an internal armed conflict. This provides a unique opportunity for a baseline study of what can happen when TJMs are employed at an early stage in the peacebuilding process (rather than after the conflict has ended, as in Guatemala, El Salvador, and Peru).

Second, whereas most of the other cases are characterised by significant sequencing and spacing of TJMs, Colombia has been able to learn from almost three decades of accumulated TJ experience in the rest of the region. Thus, it has chosen to attempt simultaneous implementation of all four of the TJMs on which this study focuses.[16] Third, Colombia's current process is unfolding in a climate of substantially more complete and stringent regional and international norms and presumptions regarding victims' rights to truth, justice, and reparations.

Methods and data collection

In developing our framework, we first define 'impunity' and 'accountability' as ideal types representing the opposite ends of a spectrum. Chapter 2 elaborates

Table 1.3 Nine Latin American cases of transitional justice

Group	*Country*	*Year of formal transition*	*Conflict or regime type before transition*	*Number of dead, detained-disappeared (DD), and displaced (all figures are contested estimates)*	*Primary actor(s) in transition/early TJ*	*Type and sequencing of official TJMs*	
						Under transitional government	*Later (post-transition)*
Group 1	Argentina	1983	Military dictatorship	10,000–30,000 dead and DD; extensive torture	National actors	TC, trials, amnesty, reparations	Large-scale trials from 2000
	Uruguay	1984	Military dictatorship	190 dead and DD; 200,000 tortured	National actors	TC, amnesty	Trials; 2nd TC; reparations
	Brazil	1985	Military dictatorship	420 dead and DD; extensive torture	National actors	Amnesty	TC established 2011
	Chile	1991	Military dictatorship	3,200 dead and DD; 40,000 tortured	National actors	TC, amnesty, reparations	2nd TC; large-scale trials from 1998
	Paraguay	2003 milestone[a]	One-man/one-party military rule	400 dead and DD; 20,000 tortured	National actors	No amnesty; TC later	Reparations

Table 1.3 (cont.)

Group	*Country*	*Year of formal transition*	*Conflict or regime type before transition*	*Number of dead, detained-disappeared (DD), and displaced (all figures are contested estimates)*	*Primary actor(s) in transition/early TJ*	*Type and sequencing of official TJMs*	
						Under transitional government	*Later (post-transition)*
Group 2	El Salvador	1991	Internal armed conflict	50,000 killed and DD	International actors (UN) and national actors (warring parties)	TC, amnesty	
	Guatemala	1996	Internal armed conflict	200,000 killed, some in genocide	International actors (UN) and national actors (warring parties)	TC, limited amnesty	Trials for Guatemala
	Peru	2000 milestone[b]	Authoritarian regime and internal armed conflict	69,000 dead and DD; 600,000 internally displaced	National actors	TC, trials reparations	Fujimori conviction 2009; other high-level trials ongoing
Group 3	Colombia	Ongoing (2005 milestone[c])	Internal armed conflict	Large-scale killings; 4 million internally displaced	National actors, with high levels of international consultation; ICC active in formal justice discussion	Conditional amnesties, trials, reparations, truth-seeking	N/A

a. Dictator Alfredo Stroessner was ousted in a palace coup in 1989, but his Colorado Party remained in power until 2008. The Paraguayan TC investigated human rights violations from 1954 up to the time of its establishment in 2003.

b. The year 2000 marks the end of the authoritarian civilian Fujimori presidency (1990–2000) and the beginning of discussion of TJMs.

c. The Justice and Peace Law (Law 975), enacted in 2005, established the legal framework for implementation of TJ mechanisms in Colombia.

this conceptual framework and identifies elements we will examine to provide thick descriptions of specific instances in the case studies. Our methodological approach entails application of a common set of variables to all country cases, with a focus on social actors and surrounding dynamics. We apply process-tracing techniques to produce nuanced accounts of how particular TJMs and processes have evolved over time. This longitudinal approach contrasts with the more common approach of comparative studies, which focus mainly on the formal decisions taken at the initial transitional 'moment'.

The empirical studies provide detailed descriptions of specific transitional justice processes in each of the nine countries, as well as, where available, some indication of how national populations, or at least key domestic actors, evaluate and perceive them. These descriptions, including interpretation of particular political and legal phenomena as constituting or contributing towards impunity or accountability, benefit from the on-the-ground expertise of the country case authors. The mere presence or absence of a specific TJM does not in itself constitute a shift towards or away from accountability. Rather, a society will be classified as moving closer to one extreme or the other through a nuanced decoding of the meaning and quality of each TJ action as well as the sum of its TJ actions at a given point in time. Chapter 2 also explains in more detail our methodology for aggregating, comparing, and graphically representing the outcomes of these assessments.

Primary data for the case studies were collected principally during fieldwork carried out by the chapter authors in 2012–13 in each of the nine countries, supplemented subsequently by additional field data and input by the in-country chapter authors. All authors consulted and collaborated closely with national institutions and organisations working on TJ issues, and some were aided by local field assistants. Each country chapter draws upon a mix of primary and secondary sources. The former include extensive interviews with a variety of actors in the TJ field, including judges, prosecutors, relatives and survivors, staff of human rights organisations, public officials, journalists, academics, and other experts.

Closing remarks

We have argued that a systematic structured comparison of selected Latin American cases is timely for two reasons. First, it provides new comparative empirical information on how a selection of transitional justice mechanisms can combine over time to provide accountability for grave human rights violations committed during authoritarian rule or internal armed conflict. Second, this empirical analysis can inform our theoretical and conceptual framework for thinking about transitional justice trajectories over time – both in and beyond the Latin American context.

Chapter 2, covering the conceptual and methodological framework, defines the impunity–accountability spectrum and introduces the four specific TJ mechanisms considered in the case studies. The case studies then appear in Chapters 3–11 in the order explained above: Argentina, Uruguay, Brazil, Chile, Paraguay, El Salvador, Guatemala, Peru, and Colombia. The concluding chapter draws overall comparative conclusions on the trajectory of shifts along the impunity–accountability spectrum, including the factors affecting the adoption and contribution to accountability of specific TJ mechanisms.

Notes

* The authors are grateful to Catalina Vallejo for valuable research assistance in preparing the section on the inter-American system. We also thank Juan Ochoa, Clara Sandoval, Catalina Smulovitz, Eric Wiebelhaus-Brahm, and three anonymous readers for constructive comments on earlier drafts.

1 Operación Cóndor refers to a semi-clandestine network of coordination for repression that operated between the armed forces of Argentina, Chile, and Uruguay in 1973–74, formalised in 1975. Military intelligence agencies in these three countries plus Bolivia, Brazil, and Paraguay collaborated to hunt down, execute, or forcibly 'disappear' purported subversives, conducting joint operations and rendition across national borders. Peru and Ecuador also became peripherally involved. See McSherry (2005).

2 In Latin America, Guatemala's 1993 amnesty law was the first to explicitly respect the international prohibition of amnesty for crimes against humanity. Subsequent transitions in Paraguay and Peru abandoned amnesty laws altogether. On the gradual decline of attempts to enshrine impunity in domestic Latin American legislation since the 1990s, see Collins (2012).

3 We use the term 'transition' here, and throughout, in its widest sense to denote the process of a society moving from one set or type of formal political arrangements to another.

4 State responsibility is foregrounded here, as it is in the relevant international instruments, by virtue of the state's direct responsibility for its own actions and omissions and its related duties to prevent and protect with regard to the actions of non-state actors. In general terms, of course, transitional justice, like human rights thinking and practice in general, is extremely deficient in its current treatment of the state/non-state actor divide.

5 See, among others, Posner and Vermeule (2004), de Greiff and Duthie (2009), Waldorf (2012), O'Rourke (2013), Sharp (2014), and García-Godos (2013).

6 We adopt here Hayner's classic definition of truth commissions as 'bodies set up to investigate a past history of violations of human rights in a particular country – which can include violations by the military or other government forces or by armed opposition forces' (1994, 598).

7 Scholarship on democracy and the role of courts addresses, variously, 'horizontal' and 'vertical' accountability (O'Donnell 1999) and 'social' accountability (Peruzzotti and Smulovitz 2006), and identifies courts as a key agent of each type (Gloppen, Gargarella, and Skaar 2004). In essence, accountability operates when certain institutions, agencies, or collectivities successfully hold responsible other institutions, agencies, or individuals when they break established rules or overstep constitutionally or otherwise mandated powers. Institutions with an explicit horizontal accountability mandate are entrusted with overseeing, from an equivalent position in the hierarchy, the actions of parts of the state. Such institutions may include human rights commissions, ombudspersons, electoral tribunals and commissions, national audit institutions,

and anti-corruption bodies (Gloppen et al. 2010, 2). Vertical accountability is exercised by the state towards society through the criminal justice system, and by society towards the state through elections. The distinctive contribution of the notion of social accountability is to consider the multiple additional ways in which citizens' groups and a free media can demand transparency and probity from state institutions independently of electoral cycles.

8 The change in Guatemala was later reversed when centre-left President Álvaro Colom, elected in 2007, was replaced in 2011 by a right-wing former general, Otto Pérez Molina.

9 The ad hoc tribunals are the International Criminal Tribunal for the former Yugoslavia, established in 1993, and the International Criminal Tribunal for Rwanda, established in 1994. Hybrid tribunals have included those for Cambodia, Sierra Leone, and Lebanon.

10 Africa has the African Court on Human and Peoples' Rights (2006) and the African Commission on Human and Peoples' Rights. Europe has the European Court on Human Rights, but the corresponding commission was abolished in 1998. Asia has had a commission since 1986, but no equivalent court.

11 Recent criticism of the system by some countries has led to threats of withdrawal, but only Venezuela has withdrawn from the Convention as of mid-2015. Withdrawal does not, however, automatically remove a state from the purview of the Inter-American Commission, given its dual status as a Treaty-based and Charter-based body.

12 Rules of Procedure of the Inter-American Commission on Human Rights, Art 25.

13 On the duty to punish rather than only to investigate and prosecute, however, see the recent *El Mozote v El Salvador* ruling (2012), in which the Court seems to soften its previously strong assertion.

14 Based on Arts 8 and 25 of the American Convention; see Cassel (2007).

15 On Peru, see Sandoval (2008). Regarding the now widespread positive citation of this and other inter-American jurisprudence on international crimes, see work by the Due Process of Law Foundation (DPLF 2010, 2013, 2015).

16 While there is no formal amnesty in place, the Justice and Peace Law offers conditional amnesties. Some observers also consider capped maximum sentencing for grave crimes to be an attempt at a norm-compliant version of amnesty principles.

References

Atencio, Rebecca J. 2014. *Memory's Turn: Reckoning with Dictatorship in Brazil*. Madison: University of Wisconsin Press.

Basch, Fernando, Leonardo Filippini, Ana Laya, Mariano Nino, Felicitas Rossi, and Bárbara Schreiber. 2010. 'The Effectiveness of the Inter-American System of Human Rights Protection: A Quantitative Approach to Its Functioning and Compliance with Its Decisions.' *SUR: International Journal of Human Rights* 7(12): 9–35.

Bassiouni, M. Cherif. 2001. 'Universal Jurisdiction for International Crimes: Historical Perspectives and Contemporary Practice.' *Virginia Journal of International Law* 42(1): 81–162.

Biebesheimer, Christina. 2001. 'Justice Reform in Latin America and the Caribbean: The IDB Perspective.' In *Rule of Law in Latin America: The International Promotion of Judicial Reform*, edited by Pilar Domingo and Rachel Sieder, 99–141. London: Institute of Latin American Studies, University of London.

Buscaglia, Edgardo Jr., Maria Dakolias, and William Ratliff. 1995. *Judicial Reform in Latin America: A Framework for National Development*. Stanford, CA: Stanford University Press.

Cassel, Douglass. 2007. 'The Inter-American Court of Human Rights.' In *Victims Unsilenced: The Inter-American Human Rights System and Transitional Justice in Latin America*, edited by Katya Salazar and Thomas Antkowiak, 151–66. Washington, DC: Due Process of Law Foundation.

Collins, Cath. 2012. 'The End of Impunity? "Late Justice" and Post-Transitional Prosecutions in Latin America.' In *Critical Perspectives in Transitional Justice*, edited by Nicola Palmer, Philip Clark, and Danielle Granville, 399–423. Antwerp: Intersentia.

Dakolias, Maria. 1996. *The Judicial Sector in Latin America and the Caribbean: Elements of Reform*. Washington, DC: World Bank.

de Greiff, Pablo, and Roger Duthie, eds. 2009. *Transitional Justice and Development: Making Connections*. New York: Social Science Research Council.

DPLF (Due Process of Law Foundation). 2010. *Digest of Latin American Jurisprudence on International Crimes, Volume I*. Washington, DC: DPLF.

——2013. *Digest of Latin American Jurisprudence on International Crimes, Volume II*. Washington, DC: DPLF.

——2015. *Digest of Latin American Jurisprudence on the Rights of Victims*. Washington, DC: DPLF.

Dulitzky, Ariel E. 2007. 'The Inter-American Commission on Human Rights.' In *Victims Unsilenced: The Inter-American Human Rights System and Transitional Justice in Latin America*, edited by Katya Salazar and Thomas Antkowiak, 129–50. Washington, DC: Due Process of Law Foundation.

Einarsen, Terje. 2012. *The Concept of Universal Crimes in International Law*. FICHL Publication Series No. 14. Oslo: Torkel Opsahl Academic EPublisher.

García-Godos, Jemima. 2013. 'Victims' Rights and Distributive Justice: In Search of Actors.' *Human Rights Review* 14(3): 241–55.

Gloppen, Siri, Roberto Gargarella, and Elin Skaar, eds. 2004. *Democratization and the Judiciary: The Accountability Function of Courts in New Democracies*. London: Frank Cass.

Gloppen, Siri, Bruce Wilson, Roberto Gargarella, Elin Skaar, and Morten Kinander. 2010. 'Introduction: Power and Accountability in Latin America and Africa.' In *Courts and Power in Latin America and Africa*, by Siri Gloppen, Bruce Wilson, Roberto Gargarella, Elin Skaar, and Morten Kinander, 1–9. New York: Palgrave Macmillan.

González, Felipe. 2010. 'Urgent Measures in the Inter-American Human Rights System.' *SUR: International Journal of Human Rights* 7(13): 51–73.

Hammergren, Linn A. 1998. *The Politics of Justice and Justice Reform in Latin America: The Peruvian Case in Comparative Perspective*. Boulder, CO: Westview.

——2010. *Envisioning Reform: Improving Judicial Performance in Latin America*. University Park: Pennsylvania State University Press.

Hayner, Priscilla B. 1994. 'Fifteen Truth Commissions – 1974 to 1994: A Comparative Study.' *Human Rights Quarterly* 16(4): 597–655.

——2011. *Unspeakable Truths: Transitional Justice and the Challenge of Truth Commissions*. 2nd ed. New York: Routledge.

Hite, Katherine. 2013. *Politics and the Art of Commemoration: Memorials to Struggle in Latin America and Spain*. Abingdon, UK: Routledge.

Huneeus, Alexandra. 2011. 'Courts Resisting Courts: Lessons from the Inter-American Court's Struggle to Enforce Human Rights.' *Cornell International Law Journal* 44(493): 493–533.

IACHR (Inter-American Commission on Human Rights). 2013. 'Reconocimiento de la Jurisdicción de la Corte.' Washington, DC: OAS.

——2014. *The Right to Truth in the Americas.* OEA/Ser.L/V/II.152, Doc. 2. Washington, DC: OAS.

Jarquín, Edmundo, and Fernando Carrillo, eds. 1998. *Justice Delayed: Judicial Reform in Latin America.* Washington, DC: Inter-American Development Bank.

Lessa, Francesca. 2013. *Memory and Transitional Justice in Argentina and Uruguay: Against Impunity.* New York: Palgrave Macmillan.

Mainwaring, Scott, and Aníbal Pérez-Liñán. 2013. *Democracies and Dictatorships in Latin America: Emergence, Survival, and Fall.* Cambridge: Cambridge University Press.

McSherry, J. Patrice. 2005. *Predatory States: Operation Condor and Covert War in Latin America.* Lanham, MD: Rowman and Littlefield.

Naddeo, Cecilia Cristina. 2010. *The Inter-American System of Human Rights: A Research Guide.* New York: Hauser Global Law School Program, New York University School of Law.

O'Donnell, Guillermo. 1999. 'Horizontal Accountability in New Democracies.' In *The Self-Restraining State: Power and Accountability in New Democracies*, edited by Andreas Schedler, Larry Diamond, and Marc F. Plattner, 29–51. Boulder, CO: Lynne Rienner.

O'Rourke, Catherine. 2013. *Gender Politics in Transitional Justice.* London: Routledge.

Pasqualucci, Jo M. 2013. *The Practice and Procedure of the Inter-American Court of Human Rights.* Cambridge: Cambridge University Press.

Peruzzotti, Enrique, and Catalina Smulovitz, eds. 2006. *Enforcing the Rule of Law: Social Accountability in the New Latin American Democracies.* Pittsburgh, PA: University of Pittsburgh Press.

Posner, Eric, and Adrian Vermeule. 2004. 'Transitional Justice as Ordinary Justice.' *Harvard Law Review* 117(3): 761–825.

Prillaman, William C. 2000. *The Judiciary and Democratic Decay in Latin America: Declining Confidence in the Rule of Law.* Westport, CT: Praeger.

Robertson, Geoffrey. 2013. *Crimes Against Humanity: The Struggle for Global Justice.* New York: New Press.

Roht-Arriaza, Naomi. 2005. *The Pinochet Effect: Transnational Justice in the Age of Human Rights.* Philadelphia: University of Pennsylvania Press.

Salazar, Katya, and Thomas Antkowiak, eds. 2007. *Victims Unsilenced: The Inter-American Human Rights System and Transitional Justice in Latin America.* Washington, DC: Due Process of Law Foundation.

Sandoval, Clara. 2008. 'The Challenge of Impunity in Peru: The Significance of the Inter-American Court of Human Rights.' *Essex Human Rights Review* 5(1): 1–20.

Sandoval-Villalba, Clara. 2009. 'The Concepts of "Injured Party" and "Victim" of Gross Human Rights Violations in the Jurisprudence of the Inter-American Court of Human Rights: A Commentary on Their Implications for Reparations.' In *Reparations for Victims of Genocide, War Crimes and Crimes against Humanity: Systems in Place and Systems in the Making*, edited by Carla Ferstman, Mariana Goetz, and Alan Stephens, 243–82. Leiden, Netherlands: Brill.

Sharp, Dustin N., ed. 2014. *Justice and Economic Violence in Transition.* New York: Springer.

Sieder, Rachel, and John-Andrew McNeish, eds. 2012. *Gender Justice and Legal Pluralities: Latin American and African Perspectives.* London: Routledge.

Sikkink, Kathryn. 2012. 'The Age of Accountability: The Global Rise of Individual Criminal Accountability.' In *Amnesty in the Age of Human Rights Accountability: Comparative and International Perspectives*, edited by Francesca Lessa and Leigh A. Payne, 19–41. New York: Cambridge University Press.

Sikkink, Kathryn, and Carrie Booth Walling. 2007. 'The Impact of Human Rights Trials in Latin America.' *Journal of Peace Research* 44(4): 427.

Skaar, Elin. 2011. *Judicial Independence and Human Rights in Latin America: Violations, Politics, and Prosecution*. New York: Palgrave Macmillan.

SLADI (Sociedad Latinoamericana para el Derecho Internacional). 2011. *Justicia transicional en América Latina: Primer informe del grupo de trabajo 'Justicia Transicional' de la SLADI*. Geneva: SLADI.

Teitel, Ruti G. 2000. *Transitional Justice*. New York: Oxford University Press.

Waldorf, Lars. 2012. 'Anticipating the Past: Transitional Justice and Socio-Economic Wrongs.' *Social & Legal Studies* 21(2): 171–86.

Chapter 2

Analytical framework

*Elin Skaar, Cath Collins, and Jemima García-Godos**

Why and how have some countries in Latin America shifted over the last two decades from widespread impunity for past human rights violations towards the implementation of various forms of specific accountability measures?

This chapter lays out the analytical and methodological framework applied to the nine Latin American case studies in this volume. The framework provides a tool for (a) documenting the shift from impunity towards accountability in each country and (b) assessing the relative achievements in accountability across countries. Although the framework is applied here to Latin America, it could be adapted and extended to transitional justice (TJ) processes elsewhere in the world. The empirical focus of our case studies is on four transitional justice mechanisms (TJMs): truth-telling (particularly truth commissions), trials, amnesties, and reparations. We pay close attention to the specific contexts in which transitional justice plays out, discussing a range of institutional and non-institutional factors, including both actors and structures that may affect the establishment and implementation of TJMs.

The framework should be understood as exploratory rather than fully explanatory. The book is not intended as a testing ground for hypotheses about causality. Instead, we opt for thick description, letting the rich, comparative empirical studies speak for themselves. It may be best to think of the framework as a matrix that can be overlaid on particular country experiences in order to illuminate common patterns and allow differences to emerge. Thus, we seek to discern patterns in the data rather than to advance specific hypotheses for testing. By comparing and contrasting findings from the nine case studies, we arrive at conclusions that are presented in the last chapter of the book.

This chapter starts with an overview of recent scholarship on the impact of transitional justice, after which we explain why we have chosen to organise our analysis around the concept of accountability. We then define and discuss the four TJMs selected for this study. We propose that impunity and accountability can usefully be understood as ideal types, at two ends of a continuum, and we present a scheme for assessing the contribution of particular TJMs to accountability or impunity based on their combination, timing and sequencing, and quality.

Transitional justice and impact assessment: a critical review

When the notion of transitional justice was first developed in the 1980s, it focused mainly on questions of criminal accountability. The academic TJ literature has grown enormously over the last two decades, and its scope and scholarly concerns have expanded. Much of the early TJ literature dealt with state-level decisions about truth commissions, criminal prosecutions, perpetrator amnesty, or lustration, and with potential tensions between institutional reform and transitional stability (Barahona de Brito, González-Enríquez, and Aguilar 2001; Hayner 2001; Kritz 1995; Minow 1998; Roht-Arriaza 1995; Rotberg and Thompson 2000; Teitel 2000). Scholars later widened their focus to take the issue of reparations more seriously (de Greiff 2006b; De Feyter et al. 2005; Du Plessis and Pete 2007; Rubio-Marín 2006; Torpey 2006). They also sought to take better account of the pivotal role long exercised by civil society actors in international, national, and subnational (informal, local) spaces (Stover and Weinstein 2004; Fletcher and Weinstein 2002; Huyse and Salter 2008; Shaw, Waldorf, and Hazan 2010; Waldorf 2006).

In the 1990s, the scholarly debate also shifted to include questioning of early heuristic definitions of key concepts such as 'truth' and 'justice' and to examine more carefully the mix of short-term and medium-term aims and claims assigned to particular mechanisms. More recently, concerns have turned towards impact measurement (Duggan 2010; van der Merwe, Baxter, and Chapman 2009) and the relationships, if any, between TJMs and rule of law, conflict transformation, and democratisation (Skaar, Gianella Malca, and Eide 2015). There has been a proliferation of large-*n* studies investigating the relationship between transitional justice and peace and democracy, but these studies have come to mixed conclusions, as we will see below.

Drawing heavily on early Latin American experiences, but also on those from Eastern Europe, the early TJ literature tended to regard formal state-level initiatives such as truth commissions, prosecutions, reparations, and amnesties as important contributors to democratisation and (later) to peacebuilding. It was claimed, for example, that TJ measures undertaken by new authorities could help create a break with the past, establish the rule of law and respect for human rights, deter further violence, encourage democratisation, and promote peace, justice, and reconciliation (Bassiouni 2002; de Greiff 2006b; Hayner 2001; Roht-Arriaza and Mariezcurrena 2006). Yet the empirical evidence to support such ambitious claims is contested and inconclusive (Hazan 2006). Although international development cooperation initiatives increasingly include transitional justice issues in their governance and rule of law packages, broadly encouraged by the United Nations (2004, 2010) and by international donors, there is a need to substantiate or revise claims concerning the positive contributions of these mechanisms to long-term peace and democratic governance.

The need for such an assessment is particularly apparent now that conflict or post-conflict contexts are replacing post-authoritarian contexts as the most common settings for TJ application. In a post-conflict situation, the ongoing 'truth versus justice' debate (Rotberg and Thompson 2000; Sriram 2004) often poses these two desired outcomes as contradictory alternatives, although some claim this debate has been superseded (Bissett 2012).

An assumption that is still unduly prevalent in the TJ literature – although questions have been raised recently (Mutua 2015) – is that more TJ is better TJ, and that, by extension, more TJMs should produce more or better democracy or peace. However, empirical evidence is, at best, inconclusive. Since these assumptions can be explored but not strictly tested in single-case studies, we refer here to a few large-*n* studies. Analysing 187 post-conflict cases between 1946 and 2003, Lie, Binningsbø, and Gates (2007) found that transitional justice had only a weak impact on the duration of peace. They found war crimes trials to be associated with longer periods of peace, but only in states they classify as non-democracies. For democratic countries, the effect of trials on peace was found to be negligible. Sikkink and Walling (2007), in an analysis of all Latin American countries for the period 1979–2004, argue that trials for past human rights violations neither undermined formal democracy nor led to detectable exacerbation of ongoing human rights violations or conflict. Expanding the universe of cases to include 100 transitional countries around the world for the period 1980–2004, Kim and Sikkink (2010) found transitional countries with human rights prosecutions to be less repressive in the present day than countries without such prosecutions. Contrary to the findings of Snyder and Vinjamuri (2003), they found that prosecutions carried out during active conflict did not have a lesser impact on subsequent violations when compared to those carried out in peacetime, and might, in fact, have had a greater one. They also found that the holding of a formal (state) truth commission was positively correlated with improved human rights protection.

Olsen, Payne, and Reiter (2010), covering 161 countries over almost 40 years (1970–2007), investigated interaction effects and found that single TJ mechanisms when deployed alone did not have statistically significant positive effects on democracy and human rights. Rather, only certain combinations – trials plus amnesties, or trials, amnesties, and truth commissions together – were associated with improvements in indicators of democracy and human rights compliance. Notably, they found support for a positive effect from the combined adoption of two TJ mechanisms, trials and amnesties, which were previously often considered incompatible.[1] They also found truth commissions deployed in isolation to have a negative rather than the expected positive impact on democracy and human rights indicators.

Such diversity of findings suggests the usefulness of a bounded set of country studies offering a range of combinations and sequencing. However, a number of existing cross-country analyses focusing on a small number of countries (and, often, on a single TJ mechanism) come to equally disparate conclusions regarding whether or not TJ 'works' in relation to some external horizon or dependent variable (Brahm 2007; Wiebelhaus-Brahm 2010). Most existing impact assessment studies fall into this category. Many single-case studies either do not set out to produce generalisable findings or fail to present plausible cases for generalising their findings. Larger-scale statistical analyses, for their part, may suggest, but do not provide sufficient detail to identify, the intermediate causal mechanisms that might explain observed correlations. There is thus a strong case to be made for an intermediate approach with a small number of countries and greater attention to nuance and detail, attempting to play upon the strengths of the two contrasting research strategies.

Scope of this study

In this volume we step back from the broad meta-goals of transitional justice and concentrate on its mid-level or endogenous objectives, tracing the observable empirical dynamics that connect specific TJMs to the truth, justice, and reparation goals that they were overtly designed to pursue – goals that we jointly denominate as 'accountability'. This apparently limited scope is appropriate and productive, given how little is known about the inner workings of TJ processes and their interactions in particular national trajectories (Hazan 2006; Mendeloff 2004; Thoms, Ron, and Paris 2008). In particular, although few countries have employed only a single transitional justice mechanism in isolation, the existing literature rarely considers interaction effects explicitly. Another key issue, often flagged but rarely explored fully in the literature, is precisely how, rather than simply whether, timing and sequencing in the adoption of TJMs affects medium- and long-term outcomes. The application of a single qualitative framework, using shared key indicators, to a group of related cases, promises to help fill these gaps in the research literature.

We, therefore, opted in this project to study four specific TJMs, in a delimited but substantial number of cases (nine countries), with a certain degree of qualitative depth. This method allows for more nuanced conclusions and a fuller exploration of causal connections than is possible in large-*n* studies, although the generalisability of the conclusions is correspondingly more modest.

Four TJMs, many forms

Transitional justice has been promoted as being necessary to bring closure to past violations and facilitate long-term, forward-looking processes such as national reconciliation, democratisation, and peacebuilding. As noted, there is an ever-expanding toolbox of transitional justice mechanisms, formal as well as informal. Given the empirical focus of this volume on Latin America, we concentrate on four of the region's most commonly employed formal TJMs: truth-telling (especially truth commissions), trials, amnesties, and reparations. Since each term covers a category or group of measures rather than denoting a singular, clearly defined mechanism, we explore some of the definitional complexities below.

Truth-telling, including truth commissions

Periods of violence or authoritarianism are often characterised by active deception, denial, concealment, or lack of openness regarding violations committed and actors involved. Accurate factual knowledge about political violence or repression is frequently scarce. Individuals and groups often have conflicting perceptions of what the violence consisted of, why it happened, and who is or was responsible. Some kind of formal accounting for the past in terms of truth-seeking, truth recovery, or truth-telling is often held to be an essential component of a successful transition, democratisation, or peacebuilding process. Truth is variously assumed to encourage social healing and reconciliation; restore the dignity of victims by rectifying previous official denial or silence; promote – or sometimes replace – justice; allow for the establishment of an official historical record; serve public education; aid institutional reform; promote democracy; and pre-empt or deter future atrocities (Mendeloff 2004). Measures to recover or acknowledge truth should, it is often believed, not only establish facts but also address presumed causes of violence and suggest non-violent ways of dealing with social conflict in the future. But in reality, perceptions about the need for truth and how best to achieve it vary widely, both within a society and between countries.

In this volume we focus principally on truth commissions (TCs) and other (mainly state-level) truth recovery activities, in line with Priscilla Hayner's classic definition of TCs as 'bodies set up to investigate a past history of violations of human rights in a particular country – which can include violations by the military or other government forces or by armed opposition forces' (1994, 558). This, unlike many subsequent definitions, potentially encompasses commissions set up by civil society actors, something particularly significant in Latin America, where commissions linked to or sponsored by the Catholic Church have often rivalled state-level initiatives in reach, depth, and reliability.[2] Whether state-sponsored or not, a truth commission's contribution to accountability is affected by who sets it up, who serves on the commission, and who endorses, disputes, or disseminates its findings. Even official commissions vary widely in type, scope, and perceived legitimacy, as will be evident in our country chapters. The follow-up and implementation of recommendations, whether these are intended to be binding or merely advisory, is also particularly important when considering the contribution of commissions to accountability. The focus in this volume on state-sponsored versions of such initiatives is a heuristic one, and does not blind us to the importance or consequences of non-state actions where these have a demonstrable effect on public demand and/or state policy.

Trials

Historically, as well as in the existing transitional justice scholarship, the core understanding of accountability has referred to criminal accountability for human rights violations or atrocity crimes committed by state agents or other actors. Indeed, TJ theorist and jurist Ruti Teitel commented a decade and a half ago that 'punishment dominates our understandings of transitional justice' as it is 'emblematic of accountability and the rule of law' (Teitel 2000, 27). Although the TJ field has diversified since then, action by the formal criminal or civil justice system against individual perpetrators is still widely held to be essential for establishing or re-establishing the rule of law. Some also argue the need for action against institutional and/or corporate perpetrators believed to have actively colluded with or knowingly benefited from gross abuses of human rights.

Justice in the form of prosecution for past violations of human rights or international humanitarian law has been considered instrumental in avoiding cycles of extrajudicial or vigilante justice, establishing future respect for human rights, and deterring future abuse (Nino 1996). Retributive criminal justice, which includes appropriate punishment, may, it is claimed, pre-empt and deter future atrocities by making individual (and, by implication, institutional) responsibilities explicit. Civil claims, whose use has grown in Latin America in recent times, may similarly spur perpetrators and/or institutions, including the state, to change their behaviour in order to limit future liability. Trials for past atrocity crimes may also support democratisation by demonstrating that the law applies equally to everyone, including the formerly powerful, and by fostering respect for the courts and other justice system institutions, which are an essential part of democratic governance. While these claims are usually based on a universal legal concept of justice, they do not necessarily address issues of historical or structural injustice, which may significantly expand the range of possible claims in particular settings.[3] Finally, prosecutions can also contribute to truth-finding.[4]

In this book, we distinguish between accountability of individuals and accountability of the state. Individual accountability may be achieved through fair trials in domestic, third-country, or international courts. Some level of proportionality of remedy, in the form of penalties reflecting the gravity of the offence where perpetrators are found guilty, is also essential, in our view, if such processes are to be considered fully contributory to accountability. Such an expansive interpretation of the duty of remedy is largely restricted to the Americas and is still considered controversial, even within the region.

State-level accountability, for the actions and omissions of past and present authorities, is also available in the Americas through the inter-American human rights system. As noted in Chapter 1, the Inter-American Court of Human Rights and the Inter-American Commission on Human Rights can officially declare a state to be in contravention of its obligations under the American Convention on Human Rights or other applicable regional instruments, and can require remedial action in truth-telling, justice, attenuation of amnesty, or provision of reparations. As a result, the regional system also contributes to enhanced accountability at the country level. Increasingly, the Court also emphasises that state duties to prosecute are not fully satisfied by the mere toleration of private suits. This is significant in a region whose civil code-based systems generally allow space for victims to initiate criminal investigations. Recent waves of case-bringing in Latin America may, therefore, represent significant accountability advances without necessarily signalling the active compliance of states with their justice obligations.

In this volume, we focus on the evolution of domestic-level trials, which are proliferating throughout Latin America and indeed constitute a growing proportion of trials for atrocity crimes globally. No ad hoc or mixed tribunals have yet been held or mooted in the region, and the International Criminal Court has jurisdiction only over crimes occurring after 2002. This means that for most of Latin America, justice for past crimes will happen domestically and regionally or not at all.[5]

Amnesty

In the peace-versus-justice debate, a central argument has been that pursuing prosecutions during an active conflict can delay or otherwise interfere with the negotiation of peace (Kim and Sikkink 2010; Snyder and Vinjamuri 2003). This perceived dilemma has brought another mechanism to the forefront: amnesty, which guarantees participants immunity from *ex post facto* criminal prosecution and/or civil liability for past crimes. We use Louise Mallinder's (2008) definition of amnesties as laws or executive policies designed to remove criminal and/or civil sanctions from specified categories of offenders or offences. According to this definition, amnesties can be enshrined in law (*de jure* amnesties) or can take the form of informal agreements (*de facto* amnesties). Amnesties can include all or some crimes, all perpetrators (blanket amnesties), or only some perpetrators (partial amnesties).[6]

Prosecutions and amnesty are treated in some early literature as binary opposites and mutually exclusive options: in this framing, amnesty is considered largely synonymous with impunity. Here, however, we deal with prosecutions and amnesty as separate but increasingly coexistent realities. This partly reflects the gradual shift of Latin American TJ from post-authoritarian to conflict resolution modes. However, it also recognises the fact that as post-authoritarian societies have revisited initial TJ settlements, amnesty has often been attenuated or even overturned, at least for core atrocity crimes. Thus, separate treatment better reflects the initial conflict transformation and transitional catalyst role that amnesty laws, properly understood, can, and arguably have, played. It is consistent with another striking reality in the evolution of TJ worldwide, namely that recent growth in prosecutions has not impeded a concurrent rise in the deployment of new amnesties. While counterintuitive, this is explained by an increasing tendency to enact amnesty laws that do not provide blanket impunity, but instead grant conditional and partial amnesties that are compatible with the prosecution of core crimes (Mallinder and McEvoy 2011).

Where early conditions make trials or the threat of future trials politically difficult or potentially destabilising, amnesty has been seen as a possible solution. The combination of truth recovery with some form of amnesty became almost routine in the early Latin American experiences. Transitional settlements that followed this initial recipe are among those facing the most sustained pressure in recent years, suggesting that the gap between factual acknowledgement and formal accountability is closing. Blanket amnesties in particular – those that take little or no account of the type or severity of the crime, 'amnestying' entire episodes or periods of history – were clearly not compatible with the emergence of an internationally recognised right to truth and with the long-standing right of access to justice, to which relatives, survivors, and arguably, societies as a whole are entitled. The Inter-American Court has repeatedly declared blanket amnesties to be incompatible with international obligations, and the early Southern Cone examples come in for particular criticism (Thoms, Ron, and Paris 2008). By contrast, Central American amnesties were applied to both guerrillas and authoritarian regimes, albeit unequally, and were undeniably key to ending long-running civil conflicts.

Latin America offers a unique opportunity to construct more sophisticated comparative analyses of amnesty that include a longitudinal element rather than focusing only on initial transitional settlements. Early amnesty laws in the region, in Argentina, Brazil, Chile, El Salvador, and Uruguay, were particularly broad and are today under serious challenge. Later amnesties, for example in Guatemala, tended to be more nuanced, respecting internationally mandated exclusions of atrocity crimes (war crimes, crimes against humanity, and genocide). The most recent transitions, in Peru and Paraguay, dispensed with *de jure* amnesties altogether. Colombia, still in the midst of an armed conflict, has used partial and conditional amnesties as an incentive to the demobilisation of paramilitary and guerrilla groups (García-Godos and Lid 2010). Our study, therefore, explores conditions under which amnesty has and has not persisted and the factors affecting its social and political legitimacy. The country chapters go into more depth on these issues, making distinctions between self-amnesties, blanket amnesties, and conditional amnesties.

Reparations

Reparations to those who suffer wrongs are part of any domestic justice system. In a tort model, reparation in the form of restitution or awards for damages can result from findings of civil liability suits; it can also be part of criminal sentencing, where a party found guilty is required to compensate the victim. In a TJ context, reparations can take administrative or judicial forms and are increasingly considered part of the responsibilities of states in an emerging rights-based framing of transitional justice.[7] Even where non-state perpetrators are the origin of the specific harm, state responsibilities are invoked via the 'failure to prevent'.[8]

The provision of reparations, to victims, survivors, their relatives, and sometimes others, is generally held to have a positive impact on truth (through acknowledgement), justice, and/or reconciliation (Laplante 2014). Also noted, however, is the potentially counterproductive impact of selective reparations in setting individuals or communities at odds with one another. Moreover, the provision of reparations to former perpetrators who are also victims has caused controversy in recent years.

Forms of reparation vary widely but fall into two broad categories: material reparations and symbolic reparations. Material reparations can include cash transfers, pension or tax credits, and health or welfare services designed to ameliorate or reverse specific harm. Here the empirical challenge is often to distinguish reparations from health care or other public spending that is, or ought to be, part of the delivery of basic socio-economic entitlements to victims and non-victims alike. Symbolic reparations, such as official memorials and state museums, can restore the good name and social standing of victims and emphasise the current repudiation of past abuse.

The underlying assumption of reparations policy is that physical, psychological, and social harm must be both acknowledged and addressed. A wide range of both ameliorative and compensatory measures have accordingly been attempted (García-Godos 2008; de Greiff 2006a). Restoration of the status quo ante, a common standard in civil tort law, is hardly feasible in contexts of massive human rights violations. We might also question whether the tort model obfuscates questions of state or institutional responsibility by constructing reparations as a private payment from a guilty to an injured party (Gray 2010). Most states in our study have implemented administrative reparations programmes, for which international standards increasingly require active participation of survivors and relatives in the reparations process. Justice efforts increasingly produce Inter-American Commission settlements or Inter-American Court rulings awarding economic and symbolic reparations. Latin America has recently seen a wave of memorialisation activities framed as symbolic reparation, many of them privately sponsored initiatives. Concerning symbolic reparations, this book focuses on officially initiated and/or officially funded initiatives only: thus, a state-sponsored memorial to victims might count as reparations, whereas a plaque placed by private subscription or grieving relatives would not.

Accountability and impunity as ideal types

Throughout this volume, we define accountability as *an explicit acknowledgement by the state that grave human rights violations have taken place and that the state was involved in or responsible for them*. Means of accountability can include, but are not limited to, the *recovery and diffusion of truth, criminal prosecution, reparations, and efforts to guarantee non-repetition*. We define impunity as the absence or active negation of accountability in any or all of the aspects mentioned in this definition. In general terms, TJMs as public policy decisions are adopted, combined, and set in motion at the time of a transition or peace agreement to either promote or avoid explicit assignment of responsibility for acknowledged wrongdoing to some or all perpetrators of past atrocities. In cases where mechanisms, including amnesty, are initially selected precisely to avoid this kind of public accounting, we can speak of impunity.[9] By contrast, where the state adopts TJMs to allocate responsibility and, in some cases, add specific justice, reparations, and truth-telling activities, we can properly speak of accountability.

In this book, we consider impunity and accountability to occur along a continuum. At one end of this spectrum, full accountability suggests the most complete imaginable level of official and social repudiation of past abuses. This would probably imply comprehensive and not significantly contested truth-telling; a holistic reparations package for direct and indirect victims, and at least the possibility of specific attribution of responsibility to individual and/or institutional perpetrators through prosecutions, accompanied by proportionate penalties. At the opposite end of the spectrum, a situation of complete impunity might include official silence about, denial or justification of past atrocities; non-existent, incomplete, or significantly contested official truth-telling; and application of *de jure* or *de facto* blanket amnesties for perpetrators. In between, we find situations of more or less impunity and accountability, reflecting variations in the number, scope, and quality of TJMs that have been implemented. Table 2.1 summarises the characteristics of accountability and impunity as ideal types in relation to each TJM.

The impunity–accountability spectrum can be applied to each TJM separately, empirically locating countries along the range according to the extent to which they have or have not deployed each measure. Preferably, in our view, the spectrum can be used to locate countries relative to one another according to an aggregate assessment of the combined effect of various TJMs. The ideal types of impunity and accountability are thus, in one important sense, descriptive rather than explanatory. It is also important to note that a country's movement along the impunity–accountability continuum cannot be explained solely as a result of TJMs. The adoption, presence, absence, and extent of TJMs can be both contributors to and indicators of these shifts. Explanations for particular changes or configurations are to be found not in the concepts of impunity or accountability themselves – since this would lead to a circular logic – but in the structural forces and the institutional and individual actors responsible for the decisions and outcomes that situate a society on the spectrum. Accordingly, we go on to identify a number of variables that, taken together, indicate the predominance of impunity or accountability in a specific place.

There are a number of contextual factors, in addition to the TJMs discussed in this volume, which may have a direct or indirect impact on accountability. We group these factors into four main categories: power holders or state institutions; government policies and prevailing norms; legal-institutional factors; and other factors (see Appendix 1). We suggest how each set of factors can be identified or observed on the ground, thereby creating indicators of impunity and accountability as ideal types. We do not, of course, expect any society to be a perfect fit with either ideal type.

Some power constellations are more conducive than others to accountability. Continuation in office of the same set of political power holders and/or the high command of the security forces, power-sharing between former warring parties, and continuity in public administration are likely to impede accountability.

Table 2.1 The four TJMs and the impunity–accountability spectrum

TJM	*Impunity* ⟵	⟶ *Accountability*
Truth-telling, particularly truth commissions	Official truth-telling mechanisms are absent, and offences are explicitly divorced from consequences, e.g. by secrecy laws or bans on naming of perpetrators. Atrocities are denied, forgotten, or incorrectly attributed exclusively to non-state actors or to losers in the conflict. State dismisses or discredits civil society sources and archives. Strong discipline, hierarchy, and loyalty within perpetrator ranks prevents confessions.	Comprehensive or incremental official truth-telling mechanisms are established with a mandate to allocate responsibilities and/or recommend reforms. Access to information is provided through laws and/or opening of official archives. Active investigative journalism or other forms of investigation progressively reveal details about atrocities. Significant anniversaries attract public attention and media coverage. Regional developments include extradition requests or document discovery in neighbouring countries.
Justice, including trials and other judicial processes	No individual or institutional criminal responsibility or civil liability for atrocities is assigned or accepted.	Victims and survivors are free to bring criminal or civil claims; state fulfils duty to prosecute.
Amnesties	*De facto* or *de jure* blanket amnesty is granted to some or all perpetrators of politically motivated crimes, disregarding internationally mandated exclusions of atrocity crimes (war crimes, crimes against humanity, and genocide).	Domestic amnesty is absent or limited (compliant with international law).
Reparations	There are no reparations measures and no acknowledgement of victims.	Specific, comprehensive forms of symbolic and material reparations are offered to victims, survivors, their families, and sometimes others. Access to reparations does not exclude the possibility of pursuing criminal or civil liability. Public apologies are made.

Conversely, political alternation, lustration, and the vetting or replacement of officials involved in repression is likely to contribute to accountability (see Appendix 1, Table A.1). Accountability is also strongly influenced by how the transitional or subsequent government perceives the need for dealing with past atrocities, by the government discourse (if any) on human rights, and by the ideological distance between the government and former perpetrators. The international environment, both normatively and through institutions, including financial and economic, may also influence TJ policy and policy discourse (see Appendix 1, Table A.2).

Legal-institutional frameworks may be more or less conducive to accountability according to whether there is constitutional reform; whether and how rights are framed and guaranteed in new constitutions; the strength, independence, and resource base of the justice system (directly affecting how the criminal justice dimension of accountability is implemented); and whether or not permanent structures to oversee and promote human rights are created (see Appendix 1, Table A.3).

A host of other factors may contribute to accountability or preserve impunity. At the time of transition, demands by civil society for more or less accountability can be crucial in determining the place of TJ on the agenda of politicians and perhaps also of the courts. These demands are linked to the type and scope of violations that have taken place and to the profiles of perpetrators, victims, and survivors. The residual strength of military networks and economic elites may weigh heavily, but there may also be some level of public sympathy for former authoritarian power holders (or for former combatants). Regional and global civil society networks may have influence, and unforeseen events may irrupt dramatically into domestic TJ processes: the arrest of Pinochet in London and that of Fujimori in Chile are two well-known examples (see the country chapters on Chile and Peru and Appendix 1, Table A.4).

In sum, this flexible understanding of impunity and accountability as a continuum allows us to consider a variety of measures as indicative (or not) of impunity or accountability. Post-conflict or transitional societies are located along this spectrum according to the configuration, at any given moment, of measures, actions, and attitudes regarding past violence and atrocity. The location of a society on the spectrum is, therefore, dynamic and changing. Change may come gradually with the passage of time, but specific events may also propel a society towards either end of the spectrum. Although we contend that most of the Latin American societies studied here have moved, in recent years, towards the accountability pole, this direction of change is not inevitable. Changes are reversible and complex. That is, there may be movement towards accountability at the aggregate level, taking into account all dimensions, but this may include stagnation or counter-change along one or more of the four dimensions – truth-telling, justice, amnesties, and reparations. Changes in the trajectory of specific TJMs may be both indicators of the current situation and causes of further changes along one or more dimensions. Only a textured, in-depth exploration of each country case can illuminate the specific drivers of change for each setting. In this sense, the specific independent variables driving change in TJ settings emerge from field data rather than being pre-defined.

Empirically, most countries in our study are located closer to the midpoint than to either end point of the spectrum. This leaves the question of what methodology we can use to deal with this complexity without simplifying the picture to the point of distortion. How can we identify, measure, weigh, or assess signs of impunity and accountability in real-life settings? The next section lays out our approach to this quandary.

The impunity–accountability spectrum: a qualitative approach for assessing accountability

This book assesses the place of TJMs in a process of societal movement between the primacy of impunity and the prevalence of accountability for past atrocity. We look at various stages of the transitional justice process: the establishment of TJMs, their implementation, and their estimated impact on accountability. For each of these stages we carry out a detailed empirical analysis, paying close attention to the actors who drive or oppose the TJ processes; the official policies, norms, and discourses that frame TJ policies; and the legal-institutional framework in which the TJ process takes place. Appendix 1 presents a summary of how each of these sets of factors can contribute to either impunity or accountability.

The time frame for the empirical studies extends from the time of transition (i.e. the first free and fair democratic elections held after a period of military rule or the signing of a lasting peace agreement after the end of civil war or armed conflict) to the end of 2014, which marks the end of data collection. We also take into account the period immediately preceding the transition to gauge the level of violence committed and the balance of power between central actors such as political parties, the military, and paramilitary groups, which create the context for TJ action (see Appendix 1, Table A.1). In other words, we are looking at long, complex historical trajectories.

While the principal focus of analysis is the four TJMs identified above, we know that accountability is more than the sum of these mechanisms. Our chapter authors analyse each TJM separately, discussing the empirical trajectory of its implementation as well as the related debates, facilitating factors, and obstacles. The order in which the TJMs are presented follows the chronology of TJ implementation in each country and thus varies somewhat from chapter to chapter. One chapter, on Colombia, treats trials and amnesties together since they are intrinsically linked. Each chapter includes both an assessment of each TJM's contribution to accountability (or to impunity) and an overall evaluation of their joint contribution. Some contextual variables may strongly affect the final evaluation of the current status of accountability in each country.

Our study starts with the premise that each of the four TJMs matters for accountability – positively or negatively. Our second premise is that it is necessary to investigate *how* the TJMs, singly and in combination, affect accountability. In particular, we explore the assumptions made in recent TJ literature that the combination, timing and sequencing, and quality of TJMs all have consequences for their impact on accountability. In order to investigate these effects and consequences, we need to find some way to assess the impact of TJMs on accountability (a) across time within each country, and (b) between countries. We propose to do this in a stepwise fashion.

Basic premise: the presence of TJMs in a country matters for accountability

We presume that states that have established TJMs have made at least some conscientious effort to address violations of the past. Other things being equal, we therefore expect these countries to achieve more in terms of accountability than countries that have not established TJMs, except in cases where the only measure adopted is amnesty (as discussed below). The first step in our analysis is thus to record the presence or absence of each of the four TJMs. Each country chapter documents this through an historical analysis, using the definitions of TJMs provided earlier in this chapter. The findings are recorded in Table 2.2, where *x* indicates the presence of a given TJM in the period from the time of transition through the end of 2014.

As the table shows, all nine of the countries have employed at least three of the four TJMs. Measured solely in terms of the number of TJMs present, then, there is little variation among the countries. This is where a limited statistical analysis, using binary variables, might stop: by recording the presence/absence of a TJM without any reference to its scope, type, or quality. However, a much more nuanced approach is needed to say anything sensible about the potential links between the four TJMs and accountability levels in different countries. Having similar independent variables (truth-telling, trials, amnesties, reparations) and different outcomes for the dependent variable (location on the impunity–accountability spectrum) allows us to dig deeper into the features of each TJM – its qualities, the motivations driving it, the actors who push for or obstruct it, etc. – and see how this affects accountability.

Table 2.2 Presence of TJMs in nine Latin American countries since transition

TJM	*Argentina*	*Brazil*	*Chile*	*Paraguay*	*Uruguay*	*Peru*	*Guatemala*	*El Salvador*	*Colombia*
Truth-telling	x	x	x	x	x	x	x	x	x
Trials	x		x	x	x	x	x		x
Amnesties	x	x	x		x	x	x	x	x
Reparations	x	x	x	x	x	x	x	x	x

Note: An x indicates that the measure was in use for some, though not necessarily all, of the period since transition.

Hypotheses: the combination, timing and sequencing, and quality of TJMs matter for accountability

In our empirical analysis, we investigate three hypotheses that come out of recent scholarship on transitional justice but remain underexamined:

H1: The combination of TJMs matters for accountability.
H2: The timing and sequencing of TJMs matters for accountability.
H3: The quality of TJMs matters for accountability.

H1: the combination of TJMs matters for accountability

Our first hypothesis is that the state's commitment to TJ processes (and indeed, to accountability) is reflected not only in the number of TJMs but also in the way they are combined. Some combinations are arguably more potent than others in achieving positive effects. For instance, Olsen, Payne, and Reiter (2010) find that, statistically speaking, amnesty in combination with trials is associated with improvements in indicators of democracy and respect for human rights (implying a positive impact on accountability levels), whereas truth commissions in isolation are reported to have no effect on these indicators (implying no impact on accountability levels). They also find that no TJM in isolation has a measurable impact on democracy. Apart from the Olsen et al. study, however, we are not aware of any scholarship that has systematically examined all possible combinations of the four TJMs that we investigate in this volume. Attempting more depth and detail than statistical studies can offer, albeit over a restricted number of cases, we consider how various combinations of TJMs may or may not contribute to accountability. Our aim, and therefore our findings, on this question differ in evident ways from those of Olsen, Payne, and Reiter (2010) and similar works: although single TJMs may not have measurable impacts on democracy, they clearly affect accountability, either positively or negatively.

Below we consider combinations of the four TJMs: truth commissions (TC, here used as shorthand for all truth-telling activities), trials (T), amnesties (A), and reparations (R). Combining them may, in theory, result in 16 different scenarios: one with nothing (no TJMs); four with only one TJM (A only, TC only, T only, R only); six combinations of two TJMs (A+TC, A+R, A+T, TC+R, TC+T, R+T); four combinations of three TJMs (A+TC+R, A+TC+T, A+R+T, TC+R+T), and one combination featuring all four TJMs (A+T+TC+R).

These possible combinations are presented in Table 2.3, along with their most likely rankings along the impunity–accountability spectrum. For the purpose of determining the rankings, we take it as likely that (a) a combination of TJMs excluding amnesty is more conducive to accountability than one with amnesty; (b) a combination including trials is more conducive than one without trials; and (c) truth commissions are more important for accountability than are reparations.

We thus suggest that criminal prosecution of alleged perpetrators through courts is the measure that contributes most strongly to accountability, followed, in order, by the potential contributions of truth commissions and reparations.

This relative valuation is often reflected empirically in the level of domestic contention surrounding the adoption of these TJMs and what this is taken to imply about the recognition of the role and responsibility of the state in particular. Whether or not to prosecute those responsible for violations has invariably been the most contentious issue, politically as well as legally, in Latin American countries undergoing transitions from military rule to democratic rule or from armed conflict to peace. While truth commissions can be controversial and even bitterly disputed, assigning individual guilt to perpetrators of human rights violations has been considered more politically sensitive than documenting patterns of abuse. Movement along the amnesty–prosecution axis may be particularly likely, therefore, to bring a society closer to (full) accountability. Truth commissions have generally been regarded as less of a threat to current or previous authorities, while reparations in general have been seen as the least controversial of the three measures that advance accountability. To express this in a simple manner, we can evaluate the positive contributions of TJMs to accountability in the following order: T>TC>R>A.

As Table 2.3 shows, the worst-case scenario is amnesty only. This would, by definition, effectively preclude trials, with no other measures in place to compensate for the absence of criminal justice by revealing the truth or making compensation to victims. The second-poorest option, nothing at all, is slightly better than amnesty because there is no law in place to specifically hinder trials. Accountability must be achieved by some means other than TJMs. At the other end of the scale, the best-case scenario is the combination of trials, truth commissions, and reparations, with no amnesty laws imposing restrictions on criminal prosecutions. All the other combinations fall in between the two extremes; ranking them requires a judgment call.

H2: the timing and sequencing of TJMs matters for accountability

The effect of a combination of TJMs may depend not only on which measures are included, but also on their timing and sequencing. In the immediate aftermath of a political transition or the end of an armed conflict, violations are fresh in people's minds. Demands for truth and justice may, therefore, be passionate, at least in some sectors, but may be accompanied by fears as to possible repercussions. State responses are often perceived by all parties as inadequate. Depending on the balance of power between different forces in the society, it may not be politically possible (or even desirable to a significant majority) to address human rights violations at such an early stage (Correa Sutil 1997). The first TJMs that are established in response to strong domestic or international demands are thus likely to evoke high expectations among their proponents, but may have limited chances of success. However, the balance of power between actors may change over time,

Table 2.3 Combinations of TJMs and levels of accountability

Combination of TJMs	*Comment*	*Accountability level*
A	Amnesty precludes trials. No other TJMs are in place to enhance accountability. The type of amnesty matters, but in general, amnesty alone is associated with the lowest level of accountability.	Lowest level
Nothing	No TJMs at all are better than amnesty alone, because there is no law in place hindering trials. Accountability can potentially be achieved through means other than TJMs.	
A+R	Reparations signal state recognition that violence has taken place, though the truth about violence remains undocumented.	
A+TC	Documentation of human rights violations by a truth commission is likely to provoke demands for justice. These demands will not be met if a broad amnesty law is in place, so the type of amnesty matters.	
A+T	A partial amnesty law may allow for some kinds of trials.	
R	Reparations can be a separate state policy, not linked to court process or the recommendations of truth commissions.	
TC	Documentation of human rights violations by a truth commission is likely to provoke demands for justice. These demands can, in theory, be met later since there is no amnesty law precluding prosecution.	
T	Trials (without truth-telling) are possible in the absence of an amnesty law.	
A+TC+R	An amnesty law precludes trials, but not truth commissions or reparations.	
A+R+T	A partial amnesty law may allow for some kinds of trials and reparations.	
A+TC+T	A partial amnesty law may allow for some kinds of trials and truth-finding.	
TC+R	Reparations may be recommended by a truth commission, but could also be a separate state policy undertaking.	
R+T	Reparations may be linked to trials, but could also be a separate state policy undertaking.	
TC+T	Truth commissions and trials are likely to produce different kinds of 'truth'.	
A+TC+R+T	Certain types of trials may be precluded by the amnesty law.	
TC+R+T	A combination of all measures except amnesty is likely to produce greatest accountability.	Highest level

as will other aspects of the domestic context (Hunter 1998; Skaar 1999). What was initially deemed impossible may eventually (in some cases years later) become possible. It is an open question, of course, whether it also remains, or becomes, desirable.

There is an assumption in recent TJ literature that not only timing but also sequencing of TJMs matters: that is, that the order of occurrence of specific TJMs makes a difference (Olsen, Payne, and Reiter 2010). Since TJMs have multiple, divergent, and even counterproductive goals (Leebaw 2008), the sequence in which they are attempted or implemented may be more or less successful in leading to the impacts that were envisaged or desired by their proponents and supporters. Deliberate sequencing might be intended to enhance positive synergy. For instance, if a truth commission is set up before trials are held, information gathered may be used as evidence in the trials. As Juan Méndez argues, 'With respect to domestic prosecutions ... some reasonable sequencing can be helpful because the state needs time to restore the credibility and legitimacy of its judiciary, and a period of truth-telling can lay the groundwork for later prosecutions' (2012, xxvii). If a truth commission strongly recommends reparations programmes, this may increase the likelihood that the government will make a commitment to reparations. Some scholars maintain, in a similar vein, that early-stage amnesties can usefully pave the way for later truth and justice.

In terms of evidence on the importance of sequencing, however, there is not much scholarly work to draw on. In a recent article, Dancy and Wiebelhaus-Brahm (2015) test whether combinations such as A+TC would differ from TC+A. They also test whether the establishment of a particular TJM increases the likelihood that this TJM will be attempted or implemented more than once in the same country – so-called 'path-dependency'. However, based on a qualitative comparative analysis of Latin American countries, the authors find little evidence for path-dependency owing to the chronological order of TJMs. There is thus still a gap in the TJ literature regarding the observable effects of both timing and sequencing. This is a gap that our nine case studies help to fill, inasmuch as each tells an actual story of the unfolding of a set of interrelated TJ measures in one place over time.

H3: the quality of TJMs matters for accountability

The fact that a state implements a TJ mechanism (other than amnesty) signals some degree of commitment to accountability. Yet the significance of this commitment varies, depending, in part, on a range of variables that can be revealed through empirical investigation. They include the intentions driving a particular TJM as well as its design, establishment, and implementation on the ground – a group of factors we refer to collectively as 'quality'.

To capture some of the nuances concerning the quality of TJMs while avoiding purely subjective evaluations, we asked our chapter authors to address a predefined set of questions when examining specific TJMs in the country cases (see

Appendix 2). The answers to these questions were scored numerically when we developed the accountability graphs, principally as a way to facilitate comparison across country cases. A fair amount of subjective judgment is involved in the assignation of scores such as these, especially where authors are asked to give an 'overall' score to a dimension that may have proceeded through a series of measures – more than one truth-telling instance, various forms of reparation – or through advances and regressions, such as where amnesty is followed by renewed prosecution or vice versa. The questions and scoring guide allow us to go beyond existing qualitative studies, using common standards to increase the rigour of comparative case analysis without falling into the trap often imposed by more rigid kinds of statistical study, where context cannot be adequately captured due to the need for binary yes/no definition.

The indicators of quality are different for each TJM. For example, a truth commission with trusted commission members, an ample budget, numerous, highly trained personnel, and a broad mandate is likely to have more clout than a commission where the members are perceived as political appointees, the budget is inadequate, the personnel are few and untrained, and the mandate is narrow. Likewise, a truth commission report that is officially launched, supported, and widely disseminated will arguably contribute to higher levels of accountability than a report that is neither made public nor endorsed by the government and not widely disseminated, perhaps not even written in a language accessible to most inhabitants of the country. Moreover, a truth commission that issues a wide range of recommendations that are taken seriously and implemented by the government (for instance, with respect to reparations or legal and institutional reforms) will contribute to more accountability than a truth commission that issues a few recommendations that are largely ignored by the government.

State-sponsored reparations may be directed to individuals or collectivities. Programmes that are both material and symbolic and extensive in scope – in terms of who is eligible for reparations, and for what kinds of crimes – contribute more to accountability than limited reparations programmes that are inaccessible to most survivors and victims' kin. Another important point is whether the reparations have a symbolic and reparatory value that goes beyond citizens' existing socio-economic entitlements to, for example, pensions or health care.

To assess the contribution of criminal prosecution for past wrongs, we not only count the number of trials (as may be done in large-*n* studies) but also consider who is on trial for what crimes, what kinds of verdicts and sentences are handed down, what sentences are actually served, and under what conditions (e.g. in special prisons or under house arrest). Extensive trials against a large number of perpetrators from all ranks of the military or perpetrating institutions, conducted in a free, fair, and efficient manner, represent a greater contribution to accountability than trials of a small number of alleged perpetrators, prosecuted for a very limited number of atrocities, with lenient sentences and very short times actually served.

Finally, trials are closely linked to the presence and status of amnesties. The type, scope, and timing of amnesties are important factors to consider when assessing to what extent amnesties are conducive to impunity. Limited amnesties allow accountability for core atrocity crimes. They can have a politically stabilising effect by facilitating transitions to democracy or the signing of peace accords, which may pave the way for justice later. amnesty laws are, however, generally designed to limit or prevent criminal prosecution for human rights violations. The country chapters pay particular attention to the type of amnesty laws introduced and whether or not they have been seriously challenged or defended by the judiciary, the legislature, or the executive branch at the behest of external or in-country, non-state actors. They also consider whether domestic amnesty laws have been challenged by the Inter-American Commission or the Inter-American Court, and whether the scope for prosecution of perpetrators has broadened as a result.

Documenting and assessing TJM trajectories

The next step, based on the considerations above, is to operationalise the shift or movements from impunity towards accountability in the nine Latin American countries. Examining the establishment and implementation of TJMs over time in each country provides the basis for assessing the shift from impunity towards accountability at the country level, by documenting and evaluating the transitional justice trajectory.

We do this by ranking the contribution to accountability of each of the four TJMs on a scale from 0 to 10, where 0 marks no contribution to accountability and 10 marks maximum contribution to accountability. Using the questions listed in Appendix 2 as a point of departure for each TJM, the chapter authors identify eight to ten events or markers that, in their opinion, signalled particular milestones in either accountability or impunity. Drawing on their detailed knowledge of the country context, supplemented by interview material and data collection, the authors make a qualitative judgment regarding each TJM's contribution to accountability. Both the extent of the contribution and the direction (pro-accountability or pro-impunity) are considered. The main period examined starts with the year of transition for each country and ends, for the most part, in December 2014, when fieldwork and most desk work for the nine country studies was concluded.[10] If any measures that affect accountability (such as amnesty laws) were in place before the transition, the years immediately preceding the transition are also included in the time frame. The chapter authors construct individual graphs for each TJM, showing movement along an impunity–accountability spectrum from a low of 0 to a high of 10. We refer to these graphs as 'TJM trajectories'.

Scoring the amnesties component requires particular care. We pay particular attention to two aspects: (a) the type of amnesty law, and (b) the seriousness of efforts to overcome the amnesty laws. Amnesties generally aim to preclude or limit criminal accountability, as we have seen. They may also hamper truth-finding by mandating silence on key facts. It is, therefore, essential to distinguish between different types of amnesties. The presence of a *de facto* or *de jure* blanket amnesty would yield an accountability score of 0. A limited amnesty law, precluding only certain kinds of prosecutions, for certain kinds of crimes or certain categories of perpetrators, would receive a slightly higher accountability score. An amnesty law that is annulled or revoked, thus allowing, at least in theory, prosecutions to take place, attracts a higher overall accountability score. The annulment of amnesty provisions would earn the highest score, 10, on this dimension. In essence, the amnesty dimension measures the space defining the *possibility* of criminal trials taking place. Whether trials actually take place or not is captured by the trial's dimension.

In order to fully evaluate the relative openness of a country to trials for past serious crimes, it is insufficient to assess in a simplistic binary fashion the presence or absence of specific amnesty legislation. An informal *de facto* amnesty without explicit legal underwriting can be at least as potent as a formal law, yet is less susceptible to overt challenge. Keeping in mind the findings of Mallinder (2012a, 2014) and Olsen, Payne, and Reiter (2010) about the possible coexistence of amnesty with prosecutions, we evaluate not just the presence or absence of amnesty legislation but also (a) its quality, scope, and real-life application where it does exist and (b) actual justice practice (diligence or not, and respect for due process, in pursuing prosecutions) where it does not. Country study authors accordingly consider the text, spirit, date, and proximate cause of domestic amnesties, paying particular attention to whether they exclude internationally recognised human rights crimes from their ambit of application. Only then is it possible to determine whether a particular amnesty law is, on balance, positive, negative, or neutral for an anti-impunity agenda.

All the country chapters conclude with presentation of an overall trajectory from impunity towards accountability over time, based on the authors' assessment of the combined effect of the four TJMs under study.

Conclusions

This chapter has mapped out the analytical framework to be systematically applied to the nine country studies featured in this volume. Using thick description and qualitative comparative analysis, we study transitional justice in terms of possible shifts from impunity towards accountability, introducing a longitudinal dimension to each country study and to the project as a whole. We strive for a balanced appreciation of TJ as a dynamic and long-term process – a perspective that has often been missing from comparative studies, which have focused primarily on official decisions taken at the initial moment of transition. Latin America, effectively the first region to undergo concentrated TJ experiences in modern times, today offers a unique opportunity to see how these national experiences have evolved and interacted with one another over time in a geographically delimited and culturally/linguistically related area.

Notes

* For valuable input in developing this framework, the authors thank panel participants at the Latin American Studies Association congresses in San Francisco and Chicago, USA, in 2012 and 2014, and at the European Consortium for Political Research conference in Bordeaux, France, in 2013, as well as country case authors at the project workshop held in Santiago, Chile, in November 2012. We are also grateful to Rachel Sieder, Catalina Smulovitz, and Eric Wiebelhaus-Brahm for helpful comments on earlier drafts.

1 These findings are compatible with recent work by Louise Mallinder (2012a, 2012b, 2014), suggesting that worldwide, amnesties and prosecution are increasingly coexistent and mutually limiting.
2 Examples of truth commissions set up by the Catholic Church or non-governmental organisations include Nunca Mais in Brazil, Nunca Más in Uruguay, and the Recovery of Historical Memory Project (REMHI) in Guatemala (see the country chapters for details). Wiebelhaus-Brahm (2009) offers a more detailed analysis of definitional discrepancies in discussion of truth commissions.
3 Recent debates over transformative justice and the socio-economic dimension of TJ are discussed by Winter (2013), Lambourne (2014), de Greiff and Duthie (2009), Sharp (2014), and Gready and Robins (2014).
4 Prosecution potentially produces cumulative 'legal truths' that may win broader adherence than the essentially administrative truths produced by a one-off commission. Informal truth-telling by survivors, journalists, artists, and even perpetrators and their sympathisers can also have significant impact, but our concern here is principally with the portion of these 'truths' that are taken up and validated by the state.
5 Third-country prosecutions or civil claims in domestic courts in other regions are also an alternative and were significant in the 1990s. But with respect to this option, Latin America increasingly has become a venue as well as an object of third-country justice, with cases brought in Argentina over Spanish civil war crimes, as detailed in the Argentina country chapter.
6 For a comprehensive overview of how amnesties differ from other leniency measures, such as pardons, reduced sentence measures, statutes of limitations, status-based legal immunities, and prosecutorial immunities, see Freeman (2009, 14–15). For another discussion of amnesties in comparative and international perspectives, see Lessa and Payne (2012).
7 See UN General Assembly Resolution 60/147, 'Basic Principles and Guidelines on the Right to a Remedy and Reparation for Victims of Gross Violations of International Human Rights Law and Serious Violations of International Humanitarian Law', 21 March 2006.
8 In Peru and Colombia, the moral, legal, or financial liabilities of non-state perpetrators are also included.
9 In contrast, some appropriately restricted forms of amnesty – excluding core atrocity crimes – could be compatible with our definition of accountability.
10 Particularly significant shifts in individual country trajectories during 2015 were sometimes incorporated in the qualitative (narrative) sections of country chapters.

References

Barahona de Brito, Alexandra, Carmen González-Enríquez, and Paloma Aguilar, eds. 2001. *The Politics of Memory: Transitional Justice in Democratizing Societies*. Oxford: Oxford University Press.

Bassiouni, M. Cherif. 2002. *Post-Conflict Justice*. Ardsley, NY: Transnational.
Bissett, Alison. 2012. *Truth Commissions and Criminal Courts*. Cambridge: Cambridge University Press.
Brahm, Eric. 2007. 'Uncovering the Truth: Examining Truth Commission Success and Impact.' *International Studies Perspectives* 8(1): 16–35.
Correa Sutil, Jorge. 1997. '"No Victorious Army Has Ever Been Prosecuted ...": The Unsettled Story of Transitional Justice in Chile.' In *Transitional Justice and the Rule of Law in New Democracies*, edited by A. James McAdams, 123–54. Notre Dame, IN: University of Notre Dame Press.
Dancy, Geoff, and Eric Wiebelhaus-Brahm. 2015. 'Timing, Sequencing, and Transitional Justice Impact: A Qualitative Comparative Analysis of Latin America.' *Human Rights Review*: 1–22.
De Feyter, Koen, Stephan Parmentier, Marc Bossuyt, and Paul Lemmens, eds. 2005. *Out of the Ashes: Reparation for Victims of Gross and Systematic Human Rights Violations*. Antwerp: Intersentia.
de Greiff, Pablo, ed. 2006a. *The Handbook of Reparations*. Oxford: Oxford University Press.
——2006b. 'Repairing the Past: Compensation for Victims of Human Rights Violations.' In *The Handbook of Reparations*, edited by Pablo de Greiff, 1–18. Oxford: Oxford University Press.
de Greiff, Pablo, and Roger Duthie, eds. 2009. *Transitional Justice and Development: Making Connections*. New York: Social Science Research Council.
Du Plessis, Max, and Stephen Pete, eds. 2007. *Repairing the Past? International Perspectives on Reparations for Gross Human Rights Abuses*. Antwerp: Intersentia.
Duggan, Colleen, ed. 2010. 'Transitional Justice on Trial: Evaluating Its Impact.' Special issue, *International Journal of Transitional Justice* 4(3).
Fletcher, Laurel E., and Harvey M. Weinstein. 2002. 'Violence and Social Repair: Rethinking the Contribution of Justice to Reconciliation.' *Human Rights Quarterly* 24(3): 573–639.
Freeman, Mark. 2009. *Necessary Evils: Amnesties and the Search for Justice*. New York: Cambridge University Press.
García-Godos, Jemima. 2008. 'Victim Reparations in Transitional Justice – What Is at Stake and Why.' *Nordic Journal of Human Rights* 26(2): 111–30.
García-Godos, Jemima, and Knut Andreas O. Lid. 2010. 'Transitional Justice and Victims' Rights before the End of a Conflict: The Unusual Case of Colombia.' *Journal of Latin American Studies* 42(3): 487–516.
Gray, David C. 2010. 'A No-Excuse Approach to Transitional Justice: Reparations as Tools of Extraordinary Justice.' *Washington University Law Review* 87(5): 1043–1103.
Gready, Paul, and Simon Robins. 2014. 'From Transitional to Transformative Justice: A New Agenda for Practice.' *International Journal of Transitional Justice* 8(3): 339–61.
Hayner, Priscilla B. 1994. 'Fifteen Truth Commissions – 1974 to 1994: A Comparative Study.' *Human Rights Quarterly* 16(4): 597–655.
——2001. *Unspeakable Truths: Confronting State Terror and Atrocity*. New York: Routledge.
Hazan, Pierre. 2006. 'Measuring the Impact of Punishment and Forgiveness: A Framework for Evaluating Transitional Justice.' *International Review of the Red Cross* 88(861): 19–47.
Hunter, Wendy. 1998. 'Negotiating Civil-Military Relations in Post-authoritarian Argentina and Chile.' *International Studies Quarterly* 42(2): 295–317.
Huyse, Luc, and Mark Salter, eds. 2008. *Traditional Justice and Reconciliation after Violent Conflict: Learning from African Experiences*. Stockholm: International IDEA.

Kim, Hunjoon, and Kathryn Sikkink. 2010. 'Explaining the Deterrence Effect of Human Rights Prosecutions for Transitional Countries.' *International Studies Quarterly* 54(4): 939–63.

Kritz, Neil, ed. 1995. *Transitional Justice: How Emerging Democracies Reckon with Former Regimes.* 3 vols. Washington, DC: United States Institute of Peace Press.

Lambourne, Wendy. 2014. 'Transformative Justice, Reconciliation and Peacebuilding.' In *Transitional Justice Theories*, edited by Susanne Buckley-Zistel, Teresa Koloma Beck, Christian Braun, and Friederike Mieth, 19–39. New York: Routledge.

Laplante, Lisa J. 2014. 'The Plural Justice Aims of Reparations.' In *Transitional Justice Theories*, edited by Susanne Buckley-Zistel, Teresa Koloma Beck, Christian Braun, and Friederike Mieth, 66–84. New York: Routledge.

Leebaw, Bronwyn Anne. 2008. 'The Irreconcilable Goals of Transitional Justice.' *Human Rights Quarterly* 30(1): 95–118.

Lessa, Francesca, and Leigh A. Payne, eds. 2012. *Amnesty in the Age of Human Rights Accountability: Comparative and International Perspectives.* New York: Cambridge University Press.

Lie, Tove Grete, Helga Malmin Binningsbø, and Scott Gates. 2007. *Post-Conflict Justice and Sustainable Peace.* Post-Conflict Transitions Working Paper 5/World Bank Policy Research Working Paper 4191. Washington, DC: World Bank.

Mallinder, Louise. 2008. *Amnesty, Human Rights and Political Transitions: Bridging the Peace and Justice Divide.* Portland, OR: Hart.

——2012a. 'Amnesties' Challenge to the Global Accountability Norm? Interpreting Regional and International Trends in Amnesty Enactment.' In *Amnesty in the Age of Human Rights Accountability: Comparative and International Perspectives*, edited by Francesca Lessa and Leigh A. Payne, 69–96. New York: Cambridge University Press.

——2012b. 'Beyond the Courts? The Complex Relationship of Trials and Amnesty.' In *International Criminal Law*, edited by William A. Schabas, 758–75. Cheltenham, UK: Edward Elgar.

——2014. 'Amnesties in the Pursuit of Reconciliation, Peacebuilding, and Restorative Justice.' In *Restorative Justice, Reconciliation and Peacebuilding*, edited by Jennifer J. Llewellyn and Daniel Philpott, 138–73. Oxford: Oxford University Press.

Mallinder, Louise, and Kieran McEvoy. 2011. 'Rethinking Amnesties: Atrocity, Accountability and Impunity in Postconflict Societies.' *Contemporary Social Science* 6(1): 107–28.

Mendeloff, David. 2004. 'Truth-Seeking, Truth-Telling, and Postconflict Peacebuilding: Curb the Enthusiasm?' *International Studies Review* 6(3): 355–80.

Méndez, Juan E. 2012. Foreword to *Amnesty in the Age of Human Rights Accountability: Comparative and International Perspectives*, edited by Francesca Lessa and Leigh A. Payne, xvii–xxix. New York: Cambridge University Press.

Minow, Martha. 1998. *Between Vengeance and Forgiveness: Facing History after Genocide and Mass Violence.* Boston: Beacon.

Mutua, Makau, ed. 2015. 'Does Transitional Justice Have a Future?' Special issue, *International Journal for Transitional Justice* 9(1).

Nino, Carlos Santiago. 1996. *Radical Evil on Trial.* New Haven, CT: Yale University Press.

Olsen, Tricia D., Leigh A. Payne, and Andrew G. Reiter. 2010. *Transitional Justice in Balance: Comparing Processes, Weighing Efficacy.* Washington, DC: United States Institute of Peace Press.

Roht-Arriaza, Naomi. 1995. *Impunity and Human Rights in International Law and Practice.* Oxford: Oxford University Press.

Roht-Arriaza, Naomi, and Javier Mariezcurrena, eds. 2006. *Transitional Justice in the Twenty-First Century: Beyond Truth versus Justice.* Cambridge: Cambridge University Press.

Rotberg, Robert I., and Dennis Thompson, eds. 2000. *Truth v. Justice: The Morality of Truth Commissions.* Princeton, NJ: Princeton University Press.

Rubio-Marín, Ruth, ed. 2006. *What Happened to the Women? Gender and Reparations for Human Rights Violations.* New York: Social Science Research Council.

Sharp, Dustin N., ed. 2014. *Justice and Economic Violence in Transition.* New York: Springer.

Shaw, Rosalind, Lars Waldorf, and Pierre Hazan, eds. 2010. *Localizing Transitional Justice: Justice Interventions and Priorities after Mass Violence.* Stanford, CA: Stanford University Press.

Sikkink, Kathryn, and Carrie Booth Walling. 2007. 'The Impact of Human Rights Trials in Latin America.' *Journal of Peace Research* 44(4): 427.

Skaar, Elin. 1999. 'Truth Commissions, Trials – or Nothing? Policy Options in Democratic Transitions.' *Third World Quarterly* 20(6): 1109–28.

Skaar, Elin, Camila Gianella Malca, and Trine Eide. 2015. *After Violence: Transitional Justice, Peace, and Democracy.* Abingdon, UK: Routledge.

Snyder, Jack, and Leslie Vinjamuri. 2003/4. 'Trials and Errors: Principle and Pragmatism in Strategies of International Justice.' *International Security* 28(3): 5–44.

Sriram, Chandra Lekha. 2004. *Confronting Past Human Rights Violations: Justice vs. Peace in Times of Transition.* New York: Frank Cass.

Stover, Eric, and Harvey M. Weinstein, eds. 2004. *My Neighbor, My Enemy: Justice and Community in the Aftermath of Mass Atrocity.* Cambridge: Cambridge University Press.

Teitel, Ruti G. 2000. *Transitional Justice.* New York: Oxford University Press.

Thoms, Oskar N. T., James Ron, and Roland Paris. 2008. *The Effects of Transitional Justice Mechanisms: A Summary of Empirical Research Findings and Implications for Analysts and Practitioners.* CIPS Working Paper. Ottawa: Centre for International Policy Studies, University of Ottawa.

Torpey, John. 2006. *Making Whole What Has Been Smashed: On Reparations Politics*: Cambridge, MA: Harvard University Press.

United Nations. 2004. *The Rule of Law and Transitional Justice in Conflict and Post-Conflict Societies: Report of the Secretary-General.* S/2004/616. New York: United Nations.

——2010. *Guidance Note of the Secretary-General: United Nations Approach to Transitional Justice.* New York: United Nations.

van der Merwe, Hugo, Victoria Baxter, and Audrey Chapman, eds. 2009. *Assessing the Impact of Transitional Justice: Challenges for Empirical Research.* Washington, DC: United States Institute of Peace Press.

Waldorf, Lars. 2006. 'Mass Justice for Mass Atrocity: Rethinking Local Justice as Transitional Justice.' *Temple Law Review* 79(1): 1–88.

Wiebelhaus-Brahm, Eric. 2009. 'What Is a Truth Commission and Why Does it Matter?' *Peace and Conflict Review* 3(2): 1–14.

——2010. *Truth Commissions and Transitional Societies: The Impact on Human Rights and Democracy.* New York: Routledge.

Winter, Stephen. 2013. 'Towards a Unified Theory of Transitional Justice.' *International Journal of Transitional Justice* 7(2): 224–44.

Chapter 3

Argentina

Regional protagonist of transitional justice

Lorena Balardini[*]

An undisputed regional protagonist of transitional justice over the past 30 years, Argentina has explored the full menu of transitional justice mechanisms (TJMs) in its efforts to address gross human rights violations committed during its last period of military rule (1976–83). These have included a truth commission, restitution of rights, reparations, criminal and 'truth' trials, and lustration – barring of officials culpable under the previous regime from further influence (Smulovitz 2012).

This chapter explores the specific contributions of four mechanisms – trials, truth-finding, reparations, and amnesty – to accountability for past human rights violations. It argues that Argentina did not follow a linear path but traced an erratic trajectory, especially through the first two decades of transition (1983–2003). After 2003, the policy preferences of state authorities gradually converged with civil society demands for accountability, which strengthened the accountability process. While this process still presents challenges, it can be considered mostly consolidated as of 2015.

The analysis that follows traces the role of different actors in pushing for or obstructing the implementation of TJMs. They included state agents from various government agencies, national human rights organisations, survivors' and relatives' associations, some international actors, and the armed forces and security services. The debates, confrontations, and alliances among these actors, taking place within shifting national and international contexts, together shaped Argentina's accountability outcomes.

Authoritarian rule, regime collapse, and transition to democracy

Argentina's accountability process emerged in response to the human rights crimes committed by the country's most recent – and most cruel – dictatorship.[1] The military seized power on 24 March 1976, installing a dictatorship that was distinguished in several ways from previous periods of military rule. For the first time, all three branches of the armed forces held power, forming a government junta that enacted a series of laws and statutes to award itself constitutional powers. This emergency legislation coexisted with parallel secret norms that regulated repressive operations, a system of dual governance that has been described as a 'doctrine of global parallelism' (Mignone and Conte 1981, 2).

Repression was arguably more brutal and more widespread than in the other Southern Cone countries, even considering the shorter duration of the Argentine regime. It was targeted mainly at pre-existing left-wing armed movements such as the Montoneros and the Ejército Revolucionario del Pueblo, perceived as threats to the state. Limited armed resistance from these groups was quickly overpowered, and the vast majority of political violence was carried out by the state.

Professionals, students, workers, and activists not affiliated with armed groups but considered political opponents were also victims of repressive violence. Kidnapping, forced disappearance, and torture were central features. Detainees were forcibly disappeared, freed under surveillance, or held as long-term political prisoners. The regime cooperated with other Southern Cone dictatorships in Operation Condor, a repressive cross-border alliance that carried out abductions, rendition, torture, and disappearances of suspected subversives (see Chapter 1). In Argentina, the majority of the 8,961 officially acknowledged victims of forced disappearance were young men living in urban areas.[2] One-third of the victims were women, some of whom were pregnant when abducted. After they gave birth, their newborns were appropriated – abducted – by military or military-linked families and brought up under false identities.[3]

The transition to democracy in Argentina began with the abrupt collapse of this regime. Severe economic crisis, coupled with Argentina's military defeat in the Malvinas/Falklands War with the United Kingdom in 1982, drove the dictatorship to call elections. Radical Party candidate Raúl Alfonsín won the vote, somewhat unexpectedly, and took office in December 1983. Although he left office five months before his term expired, again due to a severe economic crisis, his mandate marked the beginning of a sustained period of uninterrupted democracy – 31 years, as of December 2014.

Each government since the transition has given a different emphasis to human rights policy. Immediately after the election, the question of how to resolve past gross violations was high on the new government's agenda (Nino 1991). Alfonsín (1983–89) pursued a variety of truth, justice, and reparations measures. Military pressure, however, led him to introduce two laws that halted ongoing trials of alleged perpetrators. His successor, Peronist politician Carlos Menem (1989–99), took a right-wing turn once in office: he pardoned junta members and others who had been convicted or prosecuted.[4] Congress, nonetheless, passed several reparations laws. 'Truth trials' (*juicios por la verdad*), which used the judicial process to investigate and document the truth about past crimes at a time when amnesty still prevented the sentencing of perpetrators, also started just before the end of Menem's mandate.

The next president, Fernando De la Rúa of the Radical Party (1999–2001), also placed obstacles to accountability. Though the truth trials continued, extradition requests for Argentine military officers investigated abroad under universal jurisdiction were refused. The first court ruling to annul amnesty provisions came during De la Rúa's term,[5] but in December 2001 he resigned during an economic meltdown. During the ensuing crisis, several caretaker presidents were designated by Congress. The last of these was Peronist Eduardo Duhalde (January 2002–May 2003), who acted in favour of impunity, pardoning junior officers who had led 1989 rebellions against Alfonsín's government. Duhalde also attempted to restore military power, prerogatives, and oversight over internal security functions.

The turning point in transitional justice came in 2003 with the election of Peronist Néstor Kirchner (2003–7). This positioned Argentina within the 'new left' movement then prevalent in the region (see Chapters 1 and 2). Kirchner established a very strong pro-accountability line, supporting legislative annulment of amnesty and renewed prosecution of military perpetrators. Cristina Fernández de Kirchner, his wife and later widow, succeeded him as president in 2007. Her government deepened the previous policy of active support for trials. She was succeeded on 10 December 2015 by the right-wing Mauricio Macri.

The Kirchner and Fernández presidencies turned the discourse and demands of human rights organisations into official policy, and both presidents appointed members of the human rights community to public office. This shift has had some consequences for the human rights movement, elevating its profile while also diminishing its ability to retain critical distance from government policy. This has led, in some cases, to contradictions or disagreements within the movement. For example, in 2013, the Fernández administration decided to name General César Milani as army commander-in-chief, even though documentary evidence and the recollections of survivors linked Milani directly to 1970s repression crimes. While many human rights organisations supported the government on Milani's appointment, others attempted unsuccessfully to veto his promotion (*La Nación* 2013).

State and civil society responses during and after repression

The push to address past military human rights violations has come principally from a strong network of domestic human rights organisations (HROs), several of which are active in the legal field. Some, particularly relatives' associations, emerged during the dictatorship: they include Mothers of the Plaza de Mayo (Madres de Plaza de Mayo), Grandmothers of the Plaza de Mayo (Abuelas de Plaza de Mayo), Relatives of Persons Detained-Disappeared for Political Motives (Familiares de Desaparecidos y Detenidos por Razones Políticas), and the Centre for Legal and Social Studies (Centro de Estudios Legales y Sociales, CELS). Many groups, however, predated the onset of military rule, a pattern unusual for the region.[6] During the dictatorship, all these organisations attempted to lobby the authorities to secure the release of disappeared persons. When this proved fruitless and dangerous, many turned to international reporting and denunciation (Brysk 1994). In the post-dictatorship era, these same HROs have generally pushed consistently for criminal accountability.

Argentina has deployed each of the TJMs considered in this book, and this chapter reviews separately the contributions to accountability of each mechanism. The importance of feedback processes between mechanisms means that their interactions must also be addressed (Smulovitz 2012).

Truth-finding

Truth-finding in Argentina has taken place in several stages, beginning during the dictatorship, when human rights organisations made the first major attempt to systematise and publicise information on the crimes. This occurred in 1979, in the context of an Inter-American Commission on Human Rights (IACHR) visit to Argentina.[7] HROs presented the IACHR with accounts of kidnapping and disappearances, producing an initial sketch of repressive patterns (Balardini 2015). Next, when the armed forces released a self-justificatory report just before the end of the dictatorship (Junta Militar 1983), HROs demanded a bicameral parliamentary commission to investigate state terrorism once the elected government took office. To pave the way, in August 1983, the main HROs formed the Technical Commission for Data Collection to pool the information they held in their respective archives.[8] These activities became the building blocks of the truth commission's methodology and also led HROs to perfect their in-house research and documentation practices.

National Commission on the Disappearance of Persons (CONADEP)

State-driven transitional truth initiatives in Argentina have received extensive scholarly attention from Emilio Crenzel and others, so we give only a brief summary here. Alfonsín had made human rights investigations a campaign promise, and shortly after taking office he established a truth commission 'to shed light on […] the disappearance of persons'.[9] This exclusive focus on disappearance, striking in retrospect, reflected what was believed at the time to be the principal mode of repression. There was also a sense of urgency arising from the hope that some of the disappeared might yet be alive. The National Commission on the Disappearance of Persons (Comisión Nacional sobre la Desaparición de Personas, CONADEP) was mandated to receive denunciations and evidence and pass them to the judiciary, reveal the fate of disappeared persons, locate abducted children, report any attempt to conceal or destroy evidence, and submit a final report within 180 days.

CONADEP took its first steps amid high political tension. Although it challenged high-ranking military perpetrators who still defended the struggle against 'subversion', it was also mistrusted by some HROs (Hayner 2011, 64–5). Those who had been part of the Technical Commission, however, cooperated fully, placing archives and even personnel at CONADEP's disposal (Balardini 2015). CONADEP received 7,000 testimonies and documented 8,961 cases of enforced disappearance. It obtained proof of the existence of 340 clandestine detention centres (Crenzel 2012, 85).

CONADEP produced a 5,000-page report, submitted to the president in September 1984. A summary was published by the Universidad de Buenos Aires under the title *Nunca Más* (Never Again) (CONADEP 1984). The report declared that forced disappearances should be considered a crime against humanity and insisted that comprehensive judicial investigation was needed. It also recommended financial, social, and educational assistance to victims' relatives.

Widely regarded as the first comprehensive truth commission of modern times, CONADEP became a model for subsequent commissions around both the region and the world. It also played an important role in promoting domestic accountability, as it provided valuable evidence in the 1985 trial of nine junta members (known as the Juicio a las Juntas, or Juntas Trial; see below). It was, however, decided that the names of an estimated 1,000 perpetrators mentioned in testimonies could not be published (Hayner 2011, 155–58).

Forensic anthropology and genetics

Another truth technique pioneered in Argentina is the use of forensic anthropology to identify remains and reconstruct the circumstances surrounding the deaths, as well as to identify abducted children using DNA. This is both an exercise in truth and justice, as such information may constitute judicial proof in ongoing court proceedings. This work began even before Argentina's transition, when representatives of Abuelas requested the US-based American Association for the Advancement of Science to provide assistance in finding abducted grandchildren (Abuelas de Plaza de Mayo 2008). In 1984, CONADEP officially requested the Association's assistance, and a team led by US forensic anthropologist Clyde Snow worked with Argentine professionals to establish the Argentine Forensic Anthropology Team (Equipo Argentino de Antropología Forense, EAAF). This non-governmental organisation today works throughout Latin America and elsewhere in the world, an example of international networking that began during the dictatorship and later proved invaluable for accountability.[10] EAAF's early work in Argentina, at the behest of the judiciary, led to the identification of numerous disappeared persons. Geneticist Mary-Claire King developed a 'grandparenthood index' that Abuelas could use to identify abducted children even when their parents remained disappeared. The state-funded National Genetic Databank was created in 1987 to store samples for future identification.[11]

Individual revelations: Scilingo and the death flights

A set of 'unofficial' truths revealed by memoirs, films, and investigative journalism has also contributed to truth-finding in Argentina. One incident had a particularly dramatic impact because the testimony came from a former perpetrator. In 1995, former navy captain Adolfo Scilingo approached journalist Horacio Verbitsky and gave him a tortuous confession about his time at the notorious clandestine detention centre at the Navy Mechanics School in Buenos Aires (Escuela de Mecánica de la Armada, ESMA). Thousands of detainees were held at the site, many of whom later disappeared.[12] Scilingo confirmed the survivors' statements of the existence of death flights, when victims were thrown alive into the sea from planes (Verbitsky 2004). He revealed that the technique had been sanctioned by military chaplains, who reassured perpetrators that they were acting in accordance with Christian values. The revelations reinforced existing knowledge of high-level connections between the Church hierarchy and the juntas (Mignone 1986).

Trials as producers of truth: the value of testimonies

Trials both produce and make use of different kinds of truth, including survivor testimony. 'Judicial truths' produced by such processes constitute a particular contribution to accountability. During the 1980s, survivor testimony was solicited and used by both CONADEP and by the Juntas Trial, mainly to prove the existence of a systematic plan of repression and to legally frame the concept of disappearance. Understanding the personal experiences of survivors was considered less important than clarifying the master plan. The 1990s saw the truth trials, another Argentine innovation, described further below. These helped to reconstruct the likely fate of the disappeared, allowed the gathering of evidence that would prove useful later, and kept accountability on the public agenda.

In the current period, since 2001, full criminal trials have been reactivated; their scope has widened from disappearance to include kidnapping and torture endured by the survivors, whose testimony has begun to focus for the first time on their own experiences. Particularly in the case of women, these include gender-based crimes. Another notable change is in the treatment of the political affiliations and activism of victims and survivors. During the 1985 Juntas Trial, the prosecutor had warned witnesses against mentioning their political affiliation, fearing possible accusations against them. CONADEP, meanwhile, presented a sanitised notion of 'innocent', apolitical victims. However, in the framework of the new trials, many victims acknowledge their past political activism, giving a more complete picture.

Unified Register of Victims of State Terrorism

The state-run National Memory Archive (Archivo Nacional de la Memoria, ANM) was created in 2003 to preserve and update the CONADEP archive. The ANM corrected original CONADEP data and established the Unified Register of Victims of State Terrorism (Registro Unificado de Víctimas del Terrorismo de Estado, RUV) in 2012. The RUV includes victims of political execution and survivors as well as potential new cases of disappearance. To date, however, it has not made public the cumulative totals of victims. It has stated only that according to its registers, about 63 per cent of presently acknowledged victims are disappeared persons, 12 per cent are victims of political execution, and 24 per cent are survivors. Although the RUV is an important tool, the fact that victim lists and totals are not made fully public and are still contested is an obstacle to full accountability.[13] Also, the RUV data have not been cross-referenced with other sources, such as trial testimonies and reparations records.

Reparations

Reparations has probably been the TJM implemented most consistently in Argentina. However, it has also been the most contested within the human rights movement. Reparations have been both material and symbolic, as detailed in this section.

Economic reparations and the restitution of rights

The first reparation laws were approved during the mid-1980s (Guembe 2006). They partially followed CONADEP recommendations, reversing authoritarian-era suspensions of nationality or citizenship, restoring labour rights for blacklisted workers, and annulling spurious administrative actions and judicial processes against victims.[14] Spouses and dependent children of disappearance victims were awarded pensions and medical coverage, equivalent to what the disappeared person would have been entitled to upon retirement.

Under Menem's government, reparations were obtained through vigorous lobbying of Congress, given the executive's conciliatory position towards the military. The provisions focused on financial reparations for former detainees and for relatives of victims of fatal violence.[15] Some HROs opposed economic reparations, arguing that their acceptance implied forgoing justice in exchange for money (Guembe 2006). The government's policy thus exposed and exacerbated divisions within the human rights movement. The most significant consequence was the split of the relatives' association Madres de Plaza de Mayo into two factions (Gorini 2008).

Under Néstor Kirchner's government, Congress approved economic reparations for children who had been born in illegal detention or abducted with their parents. This established a broader notion of victim, recognising the intergenerational transmission of harm and the wider social consequences of repression.

Symbolic reparations

The construction of historical memory is at the core of symbolic reparations. During the Alfonsín administration, the *Nunca Más* report and the Juntas Trial became the principal vehicles of collective testimony about the past. To counter Menem's policy of oblivion, HROs actively promoted street activities and commemorations. They also redirected advocacy work towards the legislative branch and other organs of state, lobbying for the construction of an official memory that would repudiate past crimes. This persistence paid off: the first law that can be classified as providing symbolic reparations was enacted in 1994.[16] It created the legal category of 'missing as a result of enforced disappearance'. During Menem's administration, the Buenos Aires City Legislature also approved the building of a monument to victims of state terrorism in a specially designated Memory Park.

During the 2000s, archives, museums, monuments, and civil society memory commissions proliferated around the country. Under the Kirchner government, Congress declared 24 March a national holiday, the Day of Remembrance for Truth and Justice, in commemoration of the 1976 coup.

Former clandestine detention centres were recovered by neighbourhood organisations and HROs, which transformed them into memory sites. One such site was inaugurated in 2007 in the place where the notorious ESMA detention centre had once stood. The project had been agreed in principle between the national government and Buenos Aires city authorities in 2004, but had faced delays. The navy continued to occupy part of the site for three years after the agreement was signed, and major repairs were needed once they left. There were also disagreements among HROs and with the authorities on how to develop and manage the site. In the end, the remodelled ESMA contains a mosaic of official entities, including the National Memory Archive, the human rights institute of the regional trading bloc Mercosur, an arts centre, and buildings given over to historical and newer HROs. A memory museum at the exact part of the extensive site where the former detention centre operated was inaugurated by Cristina Fernández in May 2015 (Dandan 2015b).

In all, these symbolic measures have helped express and build a social discourse that repudiates past atrocities, prevents historical amnesia, and extends public recognition to victims of state terrorism.

Amnesties

The first amnesty measure of the period examined in this chapter was a blanket self-amnesty, which established immunity for crimes committed by members of the armed forces between 1973 and 1982.[17] Enacted in September 1983, it was overturned by Congress and the Supreme Court three months later,[18] allowing the Juntas Trial and many other criminal investigations for serious human rights violations. This provoked several military revolts, leading the government to change course and design measures to contain, and eventually halt, trials.

The first of these was the Full Stop Law (Ley de Punto Final), enacted on 23 December 1986. It established a 60-day period after which federal courts would no longer admit new criminal complaints against military perpetrators.[19] The measure produced results opposite to its intentions, sparking 'frenetic activity' in the courts (Nino 1998, 150). As hundreds of claims were presented nationwide, the number of cases in court tripled during the allowed period. Tensions between the government and the military increased as a result. After military revolts that threatened democracy, Alfonsín submitted to Congress the Due Obedience Law

(Ley de Obediencia Debida). Approved in 1987, it limited the criminal liability of subordinates based on the presumption that they were following orders.[20] The immediate effect of these two laws was the withdrawal of charges against 431 existing defendants, bringing most ongoing investigations to a definitive halt (CELS et al. 1988). The only criminal sanctions that remained in effect were those imposed on junta members and other high-ranking officials in 1985–86, but these were dissolved through Menem's presidential pardons in 1989–90.[21]

Menem's 'pro-reconciliation' transitional justice line might appear to be merely pragmatic rather than actively pro-military. But in the Argentine context, where reconciliation is considered a synonym for impunity, his discourse was clearly reactionary in both intent and effect.[22] He also completed the neo-liberalisation project initiated by the military regime, setting the country on course for the political, social, and economic meltdown of 2001. His presidential pardons are remembered as the final blow to early justice pretensions in Argentina. Together with amnesty, they succeeded in halting criminal trials for almost a decade, despite the efforts of HROs.

Judicial and political challenges to amnesty

The national context at the turn of the millennium was not conducive to restarting criminal processes against perpetrators. The years leading up to 2001 were ones of unprecedented political and economic crisis, which had shifted the focus of public and policy attention to social problems such as violent public order policing, poverty, and unemployment.

Despite this unfavourable political context, as the wave of accountability began to roll across Latin America, opposition to amnesty in Argentina gradually took root in different sectors of society.[23] At the same time, military veto power over accountability actions had been weakened by various reforms during the Menem and Kirchner administrations. HROs and others had insisted since transition that if the bad habit of military intervention in politics was to be broken for good, the military must be definitively subordinated to civilian control (CELS 2006). This dismantling of the armed forces as an influential political actor involved a substantial revision of military training, regulations, and education in an effort to eradicate totalitarian ideologies.[24] Overall, therefore, a favourable international context for prosecuting grave offences,[25] a weakened military, political will at high levels of the state, and the considerable strength of the HRO lobby facilitated the onset of a new era of trials.

Strategic litigation against amnesty: the Simón case

The landmark Simón case signalled the beginning of the definitive dismantling of amnesty and the restarting of criminal justice for dictatorship crimes in Argentina. It began with a complaint filed in 2000 by CELS and Abuelas in the case of Claudia Poblete, abducted at the age of eight months in 1978.[26] The case laid bare the paradox at the heart of the amnesty laws: Claudia's case was already under judicial investigation, because child abduction was excluded from amnesty. However, amnesty prevented investigation of the forced disappearance of her parents, the proximate cause of the whole crime. In a first instance ruling in 2001, then federal judge Gabriel Cavallo used international human rights standards to argue that states must prosecute serious human rights violations. He charged two former police officers with crimes against Claudia and her parents. The respective Federal Chamber of Appeals (FCA) confirmed the ruling, arguing that 'in the current context of constitutional development of human rights, repealing and declaring these [amnesty] laws unconstitutional is not just an alternative, it is a duty' (CELS 2012, 32; my translation).

This was the first time the judiciary had used arguments based on international human rights law to declare the amnesty laws null and void. This change has explanations at both macro and micro levels. In the broader scheme, a 1994 constitutional reform had explicitly given constitutional status to international human rights treaty law. This led to the inclusion of the topic in traditional law school curricula, despite opposition from conservative jurists. Since that time, lawyers, jurists, and future judicial personnel have been trained in international human rights law as well as domestic law. More specifically, HRO legal teams who filed the Simón case took a strategic decision to stress the international law arguments before the various judicial operators who considered the case.[27]

The definitive annulment of amnesty

The Supreme Court and the National Congress each played a key role in annulment of the amnesty laws. In Congress the initial impulse came from representatives of left-wing parties, who presented a draft bill and called for its debate. Only a few members of the Radical Party voted in favour of annulment, although former president Alfonsín gave support (*Página*/12 2003). Peronist party deputies mostly voted in favour, while President Kirchner promised to abide by the legislature's decision. In what was surely a signal of intent, while the debate was under way the president signed a decree that ratified the UN Convention on the Non-Applicability of Statutory Limitations to War Crimes and Crimes against Humanity.[28] Congress then approved the annulment of the amnesty laws on 2 September 2003.[29] This was a clear signal that the principal legal obstacles to prosecution of past atrocity crimes, that is, statutes of limitations and amnesty, were no longer underwritten by the political branch.

The Supreme Court (SC) put a definitive end to the amnesty in 2005, following up on signals it had sent a year earlier when, in the Arancibia Clavel extradition case, it ruled that crimes against humanity were not subject to statutes of limitations.[30] In 2005, in its final verdict in the Simón case, the Court argued that amnesty laws were contrary to international human rights law. The Supreme Court drew heavily on opinions and jurisprudence from the inter-American human rights system. It cited the Inter-American Court of Human Rights verdict in *Barrios*

Altos v Peru, from 2001, which argued that state obligations to prosecute and punish precluded amnesty, as well as Inter-American Commission Report 28/92, on Argentina, which underlined the state's duty to investigate dictatorship-era crimes (IACHR 1992; see also CELS 2005, 51). The immediate effect of the Simón decision was that HROs, victims, and prosecutors actively asked courts to reopen cases closed in the 1980s, presenting hundreds of new claims. Some groups from the armed forces felt threatened, but the three commanders-in-chief publicly signalled their acquiescence (*La Nación* 2005; Schurman 2005).

Even though amnesty laws continued to be invoked by the defendants in each of the 134 trials completed by December 2014, the courts each time have cited the Supreme Court's Simón verdict and others that followed and made a similar finding of unconstitutionality.[31]

Thus, the combination of political and legal strategising pursued by HROs, both nationally and internationally, plus clear political will in the various branches of the state, led eventually to a full reopening of trials against perpetrators.

Trials

The large-scale trials currently unfolding in Argentine courts are a result of the prolonged struggle for justice waged by human rights organisations. Three different periods can be identified, each linked to the changing status of amnesty. The focus here is mainly on the most recent developments, as they have received less scholarly attention to date.

Phase 1: going after the juntas in national courts (1985–1986)

Argentina is the only country in Latin America, and one of only a few in the world, where military high commanders were prosecuted during transition. Prosecution, however, required a complex struggle between state authorities, HROs, and the military. Alfonsín's initial retributive justice plan allowed for both state terrorists and non-state armed actors to be brought to justice, although responsibility would be limited to those ordering the crimes.[32] This strategy was a soft response to HRO demands: it was intended to strengthen democratic institutions but prevent an open confrontation with serving military (Acuña and Smulovitz 1991, 11–12).

Congress approved a set of measures that included repealing the military's attempted self-amnesty, modifying the Military Justice Code to give the civilian appeal courts power to review military court decisions, and implementing judicial reform to improve impartiality (Nino 1998, 122). The Supreme Council of the Armed Forces was given 180 days to act on human rights cases, a deadline it proved unwilling to meet. The FCA, therefore, submitted cases against former junta members to civilian public prosecutor Julio Strassera (Nino 1998, 128).

The Juntas Trial, as it came to be known, started in April 1985 and lasted for eight months. All nine members of the three military juntas that had operated between 1976 and 1983 were prosecuted. They were charged under the existing Argentine criminal code with unlawful deprivation of liberty, torture, theft, and murder committed against 711 victims, representing less than 8 per cent of the total disappearances recorded by CONADEP (Crenzel 2012, 103). Generals Emilio Massera and Jorge Rafael Videla were sentenced to life imprisonment, while Roberto Viola, Armando Lambruschini, and Orlando Agosti were sentenced to 17, 8, and 4.5 years respectively. The other four defendants were acquitted, as the Court found a lack of specific proof relating to crimes committed during their time in charge.

Another important trial during this first phase saw General Ramón Camps and four police officers convicted of torture against disappeared persons held at clandestine detention centres in Buenos Aires. The five were sentenced to between four and 25 years' imprisonment. These rulings promoted the filing of additional judicial claims all over the country, which helped prompt the enactment of the amnesty laws, as noted in the preceding section. Thus, although the military failed at first to stop investigations, they ultimately succeeded in derailing prosecutions reaching down the chain of command by threatening democratic stability (Acuña and Smulovitz 1991, 15).

Phase 2: child abduction and truth trials in domestic courts; criminal trials in third-country courts (1987–2000)

As noted above, the Due Obedience Law of 1987 contained a loophole that enabled the criminal investigation of child abduction, rape, sexual abuse, and theft. HROs then focused on child abduction cases, and judicial activity dropped dramatically: only 12 criminal trials were held between 1987 and 2000.[33] However, after Scilingo's confession, HROs began the first 'right to truth' actions before domestic courts. The first two came from Emilio Mignone and Carmen Lapacó, founding members of CELS.[34] The Supreme Court invoked presidential pardons to deny the claims, attempting to close the door on future actions of this nature (IACHR 2000).

HROs therefore resorted to the inter-American system.[35] The Lapacó case, submitted in 1998, reached a friendly settlement before the IACHR in 1999. It established that the right to truth is not subject to statutes of limitations, prompting the initiation of truth trials in several cities. Premised on the fact that the right to truth is indivisible from the right to justice in international human rights law, and on the assertion that relatives and society as a whole have a right to know the fate of the disappeared, this form of trial, particular to Argentina, was an innovative use of legal tools to reveal the truth in times of impunity.

Meanwhile, some Argentine officers were being investigated by courts in Europe invoking universal jurisdiction.[36] In response to requests for their extradition, on 5 December 2001, President De la Rúa issued Decree 1581/2001, which blocked extraditions in such cases, arguing double jeopardy.[37] This became another part of the legal scaffolding of impunity, disregarding the fact that while the decision to extradite constitutes a state's sovereign right, when it comes to crimes against humanity, the state has obligations under the 'extradite or prosecute' principle. Despite the blocking of extradition, trials abroad became an alternative route to seeking justice for crimes against humanity, exerting pressure for those responsible to be tried in Argentina. This international pressure plus the annulment of domestic amnesty opened up a new legal scenario, leading to domestic trials on a scale that is perhaps unique in Latin America.

Phase 3: large-scale trials in domestic courts (2001 to present)

Once the legal barriers were removed, cases formerly suspended under amnesty began to reopen all around the country.[38] This burst of activity, plus Argentina's federal structure, made it difficult to know exactly how many cases were active against how many defendants at a given moment. Also, as HROs pointed out, neither the government nor the Supreme Court had designed a clear prosecutorial strategy for organising the trials (CELS 2007).

The criminal justice system

As a federal state, Argentina has a two-tier criminal justice system. Each Argentine province has its own provincial justice system that deals with regular crimes. At the national level, a federal justice system oversees major and complex crimes such as drug trafficking, tax evasion, or money-laundering. Offences against human rights are dealt with at this level. In this federal system, cases may be heard at four levels: first instance courts; appeal courts (FCAs), one per region; a Court of Cassation (an intermediate review body, only for criminal cases, that provides a second level of appeal of convictions or acquittals); and the Supreme Court, which is the definitive instance.

Most accountability cases today are investigated within the framework of a reformed criminal procedural code, introduced in 1991, which establishes a mixed system using both written and oral procedures. A small number of cases are being prosecuted under the old, written, inquisitive criminal procedure. When this occurs, it is because defendants have so requested. Criminal investigations in the new system pass through various phases. The instruction or investigation phase constitutes the initial, written phase of proceedings, conducted by a judge. In this phase, the appeal courts are responsible for confirming or rejecting the prosecutions. Next comes the trial phase, which starts once the judge in charge of the first phase closes the investigation and submits his or her findings to the corresponding oral court. The trial phase uses oral hearings, conducted before a panel of three judges (*tribunal oral*), and concludes by determining guilt or innocence. After sentencing, appeals can be made to the Court of Cassation and may eventually reach the Supreme Court. Once confirmed by the Supreme Court, a ruling is considered definitive.[39]

The charges brought are those specified in the existing Argentine criminal code, as in the Juntas Trial. More recently, charges have been brought for rape and sexual abuse, but the investigation of these has proved challenging (Balardini, Oberlin, and Sobredo 2011). The role of HROs is akin to that of private prosecutors, representing victims or victims' relatives before the courts. In Argentina's criminal procedural code, a private prosecutor or plaintiff has almost the same powers as the public prosecutor. At the beginning of the current phase of trials, this leeway given to private case-bringers was crucial, as the scope of action of the public prosecutor was very limited relative to that of the judge. A major reform of the role of the Public Prosecutor's Office (Procuración General de la Nación) changed this, as we will see below.

Challenges in the third phase of trials

Even though the international and national contexts in this phase clearly favoured criminal prosecution, trials still faced initial obstacles. First, as there was no real oversight from the Supreme Court, each judge had a wide margin of discretion. This allowed judges opposed to the trials to indulge in delaying tactics.[40] In 2006 and 2007, only four trials were conducted, with a total of 17 defendants convicted. Second, the lack of judicial or political guidelines for conducting the investigations meant they were treated as a string of uncoordinated, unrelated criminal cases. Each claim involving an individual victim was considered a separate case, and common patterns were overlooked, so the trials did not accurately reflect the systematic character of the crimes. This process was inefficient, wasted judicial resources, and placed burdens on survivors, who often had to testify on numerous occasions (CELS 2012).

Threats and acts of violence against those involved in court cases were also a problem. Attempts at intimidation peaked in 2006 when Jorge Julio López, a witness and former victim of forced disappearance, disappeared again shortly after testifying. The connivance of the Buenos Aires Police Force, against whom he had testified, was widely suspected. Others suffered threats or violence from unidentified people who claimed to be opponents of the trials. Fortunately this did not seem to dissuade most witnesses, and even though López never reappeared, nothing similar has happened since then.

Measures to improve trials

Towards the end of Néstor Kirchner's administration, HROs proposed measures to improve the criminal justice process. These included establishing special units within the Public Prosecutor's Office and the executive branch (CELS 2007). In 2007, the Public Prosecutor's Office established the Prosecutorial Unit for Crimes against Humanity (Procuraduría de Crímenes contra la Humanidad), which develops legal strategies to coordinate trials nationwide.[41] This unit is a key state actor and a valuable ally of the HROs. The Truth and Justice Programme was also created in 2007, reporting directly to the executive branch, in order to implement a nationwide witness protection programme and carry out risk assessments of each trial. However, the risk assessments had not been fully implemented as of 2014. A special unit of the Supreme Court was also set up to improve the transparency of the process by communicating outcomes of trials. Finally, in 2009, the Supreme Court created an inter-branch commission, comprising representatives of the executive, the legislature, and the Public Prosecutor's Office, in an effort to strengthen links between state bodies working on the trials. However, in the opinion of the former coordinator of the Prosecutorial Unit, it did not manage to produce a clear, positive impact on the trials.[42]

Congress, for its part, expressed strong symbolic commitment to the trials with a 2010 declaration describing them as 'state policy' that should and would persist independent of political alternation (*Página*/12 2010). Finally, in February 2012, the Court of Cassation established a set of practical rules to accelerate trials, prevent unnecessary delays, and regulate the production of evidence, particularly the treatment of witnesses.[43] This was influenced by a set of guidelines for witness treatment produced by CELS, working with survivors, in 2011. The guidelines, distributed to all judicial operators involved in the trials and also to other countries including Chile and Uruguay, are an example of appropriate state-HRO collaboration and also of regional accountability networking.

Opponents of criminal accountability

Although pro-military views find little echo in public opinion, a group of retired officers and wives still demonstrate regularly against trials. Private defence lawyers' associations have also organised debates questioning trials' policy (Waisberg 2014). However, opponents of accountability raised their profile dramatically in 2014. Economic elites are now attempting to exercise a veto, having become increasingly implicated as investigations reach beyond direct perpetrators to questions of incitement, facilitation, and secondary participation. These groups have publicly attacked trials, questioning their respect for due process. They have also accused the Public Prosecutor's Office of appointing prosecutors who lack independence, having previously represented victims in a private capacity or through HROs (Romero 2014; *La Nación* 2014). Probably as a result, judges are dismissing charges against these defendants, refusing to take into account the evidence collected in emblematic cases (Dandan 2015a; *La Nación* 2015).

Current status of trials

In this new stage of criminal accountability, trials have grown in scope as well as number. Figure 3.1 shows marked differences between the three phases of criminal justice in terms of the numbers of suspects convicted or acquitted in each phase.

Although the comparability of phase 1 is limited by its short duration, the contrast between phases 2 and 3, which cover a similar span of years, is evident. The effect of amnesty, which was in force during phase 2, is clear: the few convictions

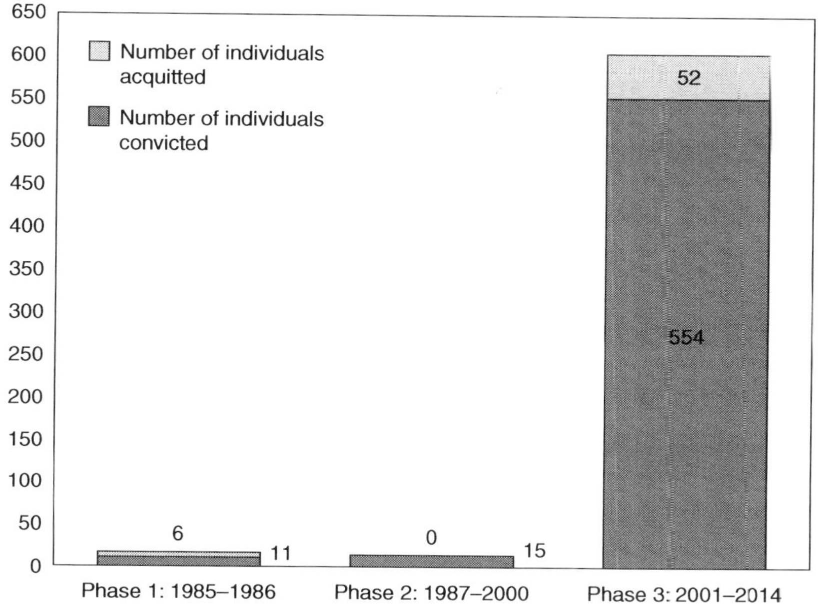

Figure 3.1 Outcomes of trials in three phases of criminal justice in Argentina, 1985–2014
Source: Procuraduría de Crímenes contra la Humanidad 2015.

were based on the loophole regarding child abduction. The outcomes of phase 3, on the other hand, reflect the annulment of amnesty, more than a decade of trials, and the fact that, especially since 2010, it has been common to see convictions of up to 30 defendants in a single trial.

During phase 3, a total of 134 trials were completed, with 554 defendants convicted and 52 acquitted. Most of these trials involved a minimum of ten victims and/or five defendants; many are large and complex 'mega-cases' with hundreds of victims. To quantify the criminal justice dimension of accountability correctly, we need to consider the numbers of victims and defendants involved in these mega-cases rather than only counting the number of trials. We should also consider the details of each trial: the rank and seniority of its defendants, the type and seriousness of charges brought, and the proportionality of sentences to the gravity of the crimes. Across the 134 trials that produced verdicts by the end of 2014, the charges brought most frequently were unlawful deprivation of liberty (i.e. kidnapping or forced disappearance, 31 percent of all charges), torture (28 percent), and murder (20 percent). The proportion of defendants convicted of 'crimes against sexual integrity' increased between 2013 and 2014, reaching two percent. The length of sentences imposed on the convicted is an important factor in people's perception of whether or not justice has been achieved. Sentences imposed by Argentine judges are relatively high compared to sentences for similar serious crimes committed in other Latin American countries. At the end of 2014, almost half of convicted defendants had been sentenced to life imprisonment (45 percent), while 38 percent had been given prison sentences of between 16 and 25 years.[44]

Only 21 of the 134 judgments were fully confirmed by the Supreme Court for all the defendants involved.[45] There is a persistent delay – on average, two years and six months – between the initial verdict in a case and the last stage of appeal. The fact that many judgments are not completely finalised has had a direct negative impact on other dimensions of accountability. Several notorious perpetrators have stood for elected public office, since Argentine law does not permit the enforced annulment of a candidacy until any criminal conviction that would otherwise bar the candidate from standing is final. This limits effective lustration of state institutions, even today (Morales 2011). Lack of confirmation of sentences can also keep them from being carried out: many courts delay the decision on where a convict will serve his or her sentence until the verdict is finalised.[46]

As of December 2014, there were 15 trials under way. They included the Operation Condor case, which is investigating former high-ranking Argentine military officers and one Uruguayan officer for coordinated crimes committed by the dictatorships of Argentina, Chile, Brazil, Bolivia, Uruguay, and Paraguay against victims from those countries. This trial, the most comprehensive of its type, began in March 2013 and was expected to end around September 2015. Meanwhile, at least 1,200 defendants are currently awaiting trial, 955 of whom have never been sentenced before. Sources close to the trials agree that successful judging of the remaining cases will require a paradigm shift in how trials are organised. Mega-cases have raised the number of defendants judged in each trial, but they usually require a considerable amount of time, two to three years, to reach a verdict.[47] The above-mentioned cassation rules have not resolved this problem completely. Some of the major delays have been overcome, but problems persist with judicial staffing, and it has proved difficult to conduct a steady number of hearings every month. Meanwhile, over 200 defendants have died without reaching trial (Procuraduría de Crímenes contra la Humanidad 2015).

Conclusions

Argentina's path towards accountability has been far from linear. Different government administrations in the 1980s, 1990s, and early 2000s moved back and forth on the issue. In 2003, the pace accelerated, with eventual convergence between state will and civil society demands. The constant factor in this otherwise uneven trajectory has been the pro-accountability struggle of HROs and other civil society actors.

Despite the persistence of a small group opposing accountability, the Argentine state has acknowledged the responsibility of its armed forces and their civilian allies for atrocity crimes and has adopted 'state terrorism' as the applicable terminology. This has superseded previous official use of the 'two devils' theory, which held state and guerrilla forces to be equally responsible for dictatorship-era violence.

There is general support across the society for transitional justice, and broad repudiation of the last dictatorship and its crimes. In one graphic example, former dictator Jorge Rafael Videla died in prison in 2013, largely reviled or ignored by the mass media and social discourse in general. This decisive shift in attitude is the result of a combination of factors, including strong HROs; executive support for accountability; a critical mass of judges and prosecutors willing to act; sensitivity to international human rights law and to regional developments, including those spearheaded by the inter-American system; and effective memory policies. This full package of transitional justice mechanisms and strategies has achieved a relatively high level of overall accountability today, though with variations and limitations, as described above.

Although each mechanism has had important results, and together they have produced a trend towards accountability, synergies between mechanisms have rarely been fully explored in the policy-making process. Symbolic reparation policies, for instance, do not often take into account the narratives produced by trials. Truth policies, including official archives or victim databases, do not cross-reference truth commission records with economic reparations or judicial files.

Criminal justice has become the most visible mechanism over the past decade, with many of the institutional reforms and innovations related to transitional justice carried out in this field. Prosecutions have been consolidated and extended over time, with strong support from society and with good results in producing truth revelations, solid convictions, and proportionate sentencing.[48] Given that the struggle to initiate trials is over, any remaining questions now revolve around the quality and wider significance of the trials being held in Argentina today, including their utility in providing access to justice for victims. Difficulties include, first, defining who should be counted as a victim, and second, devising a meaningful way of assessing the added value that measures such as financial reparations have offered to victims. Another issue is whether the state is concerned with the quality of trials, beyond their mere existence. Finally, it remains to be seen whether trials either have or can have positive effects beyond their contribution to victims' rights, such as by effecting changes in institutional culture that might assist guarantees of non-repetition.

On a broader institutional level, significant reforms are still pending, particularly at the level of the judiciary. In 2013, Cristina Fernández's government presented several bills whose stated intent was to democratise judicial procedures and introduce election of judges. However, the Supreme Court and other relevant actors are resisting the reforms as initially proposed, so their introduction and eventual impact on trials and other TJMs remain uncertain.[49] The reform debate is also about efficiency: delays in human rights cases are a serious problem, as the advanced age of many participants could lead to so-called biological

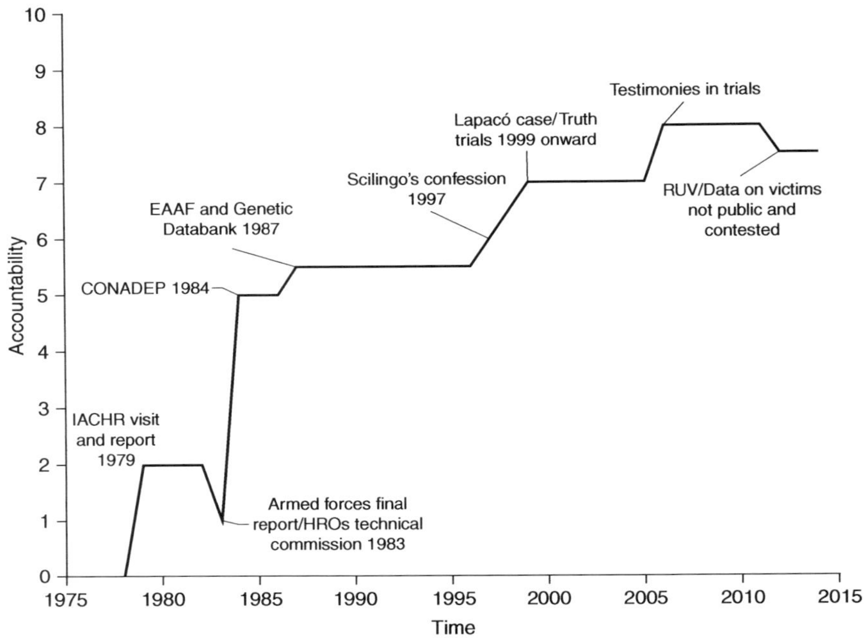

Figure 3.2 Argentina: the truth dimension of accountability, 1983–2014
Source: Authors' construction, 2015.

impunity for these perpetrators. Reform of other institutions is still needed. Despite some significant restructuring, there are ongoing challenges regarding the depth and completeness of institutional reform in the armed forces and in the security and intelligence services. Consequences include the persistence of repressive and violent practices, as well as incidents of illegal espionage against civil society activists.[50]

Trials are also increasingly exposing the role of economic and financial elites, including corporate actors, in supporting the dictatorship and in directly instigating or profiting from its human rights crimes. Between 2012 and 2014, several criminal cases were opened against some of these elites, as well as against former and serving justice personnel for prevarication and neglect of duty during the dictatorship. As of late 2015, however, there had been little progress in the quest for criminal liability for these actors.[51]

Survivors and victims' relatives have been the main protagonists of the transitional justice process: opposing the dictatorship, combating repression, denouncing crimes nationally and abroad, fighting impunity, and ensuring reflection on past atrocities and ways of promoting non-repetition. Another important role they have played is as witnesses, which has been crucial in the production of evidence.

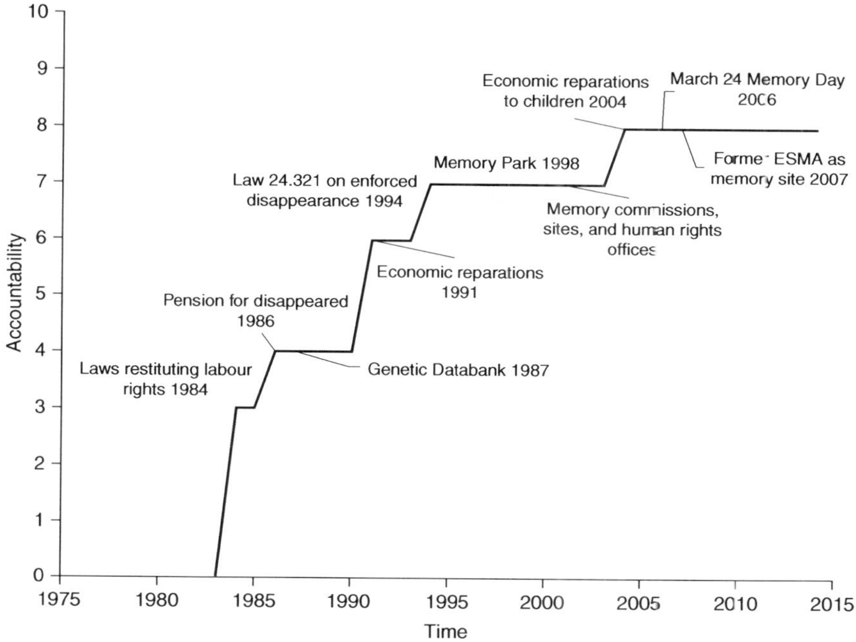

Figure 3.3 Argentina: the reparations dimension of accountability, 1983–2014
Source: Authors' construction, 2015.

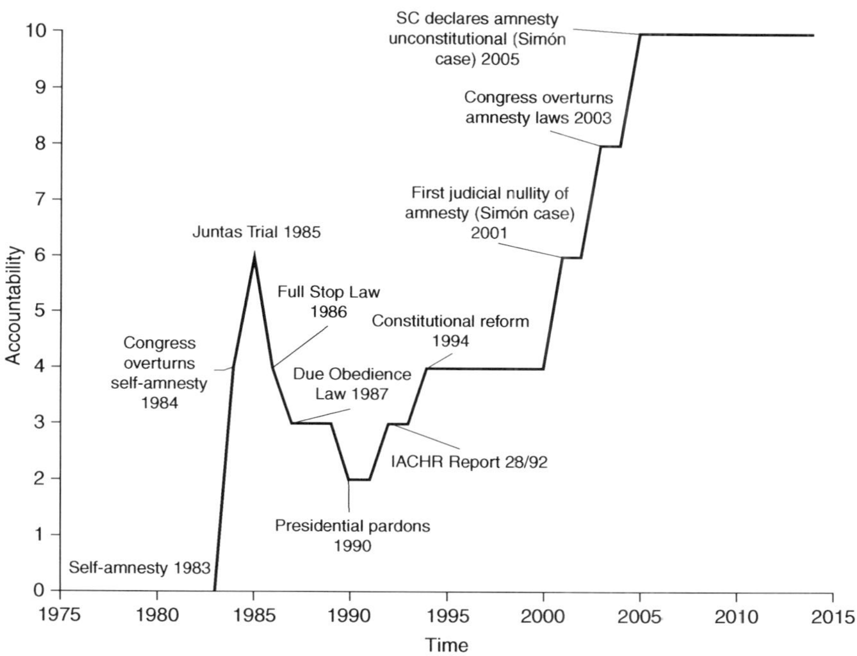

Figure 3.4 Argentina: the overcoming amnesty dimension of accountability, 1983–2014
Source: Authors' construction, 2015.

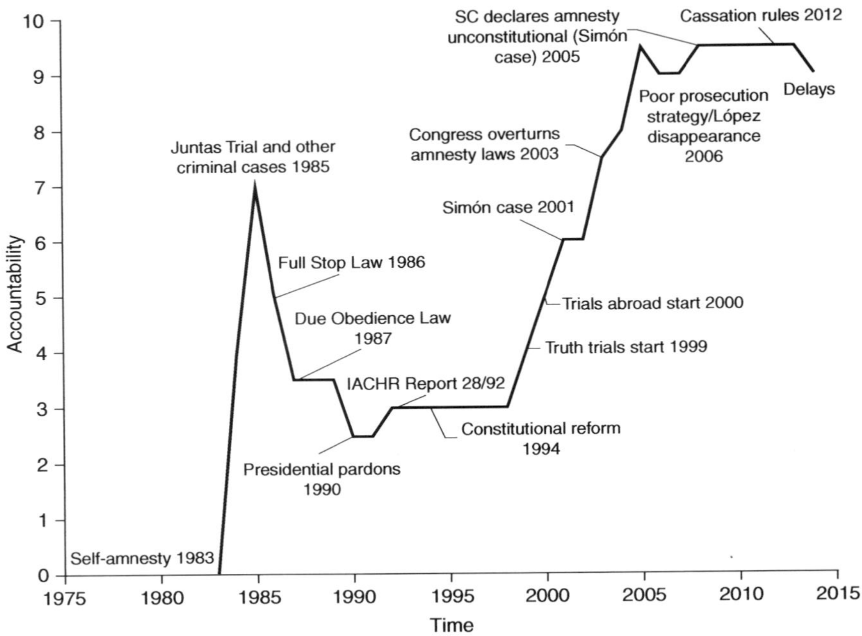

Figure 3.5 Argentina: the trials dimension of accountability, 1983–2014
Source: Authors' construction, 2015.

Testimonies are often the main or sole source of evidence in a case, given the frequent destruction or concealment of contemporary documentary evidence. In numerous cases, the witnesses are themselves victims, and this dual role adds complexity to the work of eliciting their testimonies, requiring sensitivity and technical expertise. Judicial operators are often not prepared for this task; many survivors have complained of mistreatment in the process of giving testimony. It is also important to point out the lack of a gender-sensitive approach in transitional justice mechanisms in Argentina. This was not recognised as an issue until, with the flowering of the third justice phase, a clear trend towards gendered speech emerged in victims' testimonies. However, judicial operators have failed to ensure that gender-related crimes are correctly investigated.

Although the case of Argentina demonstrates how difficult it is to set transitional justice mechanisms into motion, it also shows how the efforts of different actors can coalesce and lead to the consolidation of pro-accountability strategies. Though challenges undoubtedly remain, much government policy has successfully affirmed victims' and society's rights to memory, truth, justice, and reparations.

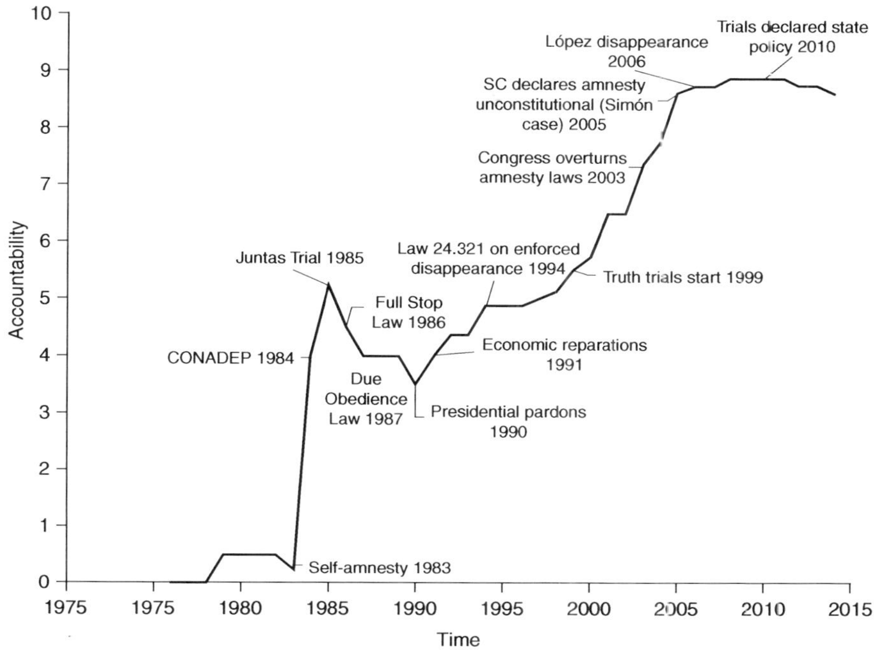

Figure 3.6 Argentina: overall trend towards accountability, 1983–2014
Source: Authors' construction, 2015.

Notes

* This chapter was written while the author was research coordinator of the Centre for Legal and Social Studies (Centro de Estudios Legales y Sociales, CELS) in Buenos Aires. The author thanks CELS assistant researchers Mariel Alonso and Andrea Rocha. Thanks also to Peter Winn and Catalina Smulovitz for comments on the chapter.

1 Argentina underwent a series of coups d'état between 1930 and 1976, which strengthened the political power of the armed forces as well as alliances between the military, elite economic actors, and the Catholic Church hierarchy. These alliances gave the armed forces sufficient autonomy to undertake political action (Calveiro 2006).

2 This is the figure given by the 1984 truth commission. A more current running total is kept by a government agency operating under the auspices of the state-run National Memory Archive. The figure, which had reached close to 12,000 victims by the end of 2014, is not, however, in the public domain (see the section below on truth, subsection on Unified Register of Victims).

3 The iconic relatives' association Abuelas de Plaza de Mayo (Grandmothers of Plaza de Mayo) continues to search for these kidnapped children. By December 2014, 116 of an estimated 400 grandchildren had been found. They included the grandson of the organisation's president, whose identification in October 2014 made international headlines.

4 'Peronist' and 'Peronism' refer to political leaders, parties, or tendencies that claim descent from the ideas and actions of charismatic leader Juan Domingo Perón (1895–1974), a former general who served three terms as Argentine president. Peronist ideas defy easy characterisation on a left-right spectrum, but many contemporary Argentine political movements, including that of current President Cristina Fernández de Kirchner, declare allegiance to Peronism. For recent discussions of the phenomenon, see Karush and Chamosa (2010) and Sidicaro (2010). For a classic critical study, see Halperín Donghi (1994).

5 This was first instance judge Gabriel Cavallo's ruling, in 2001.

6 Examples are the Argentine League for the Rights of Mankind (Liga Argentina por los Derechos del Hombre, LADH); the Ecumenical Movement for Human Rights (Movimiento Ecuménico por los Derechos Humanos, MEDH); the Peace and Justice Service (Servicio Paz y Justicia, SERPAJ); and the Permanent Assembly for Human Rights (Asamblea Permanente por los Derechos Humanos, APDH).

7 In September 1979, the IACHR made an *in loco* visit to Argentina. The visitors heard direct testimony from thousands of people, including relatives of the disappeared. The resulting report, published in 1980, denounced a range of systematic violations.

8 Formed by APDH, MEDH, CELS, Familiares, and Abuelas, the Technical Commission classified disappearances by demographic and occupational variables, identified perpetrator names and ranks, and located clandestine detention centres in order to hand the data to the legislature (Balardini 2015).

9 Presidential Decree 187/83, 15 December 1983, my translation.

10 Snow also had a hand in training professionals in Chile and other countries around the region, while the EAAF has worked in all the other countries in this study. See www.eaaf.org.

11 Law 23.511 of 10 July 1987.

12 Scilingo was later jailed in Spain after agreeing to travel and testify before judge Baltasar Garzón in a universal jurisdiction case. He was sentenced in 2005 to 640 years' imprisonment.

13 Civil society organisations often campaign around a figure of 30,000 disappearances, a long-established number based on projections made from dictatorship records. State agencies do not wish to contest this figure, and as a result no official, updated figure has been made public. Jorge Condomí, RUV staff member, interview by author, 27 January 2013. All author interviews for this chapter were conducted in Buenos Aires.

14 Law 23.059 of 22 March 1984; Law 23.062 of 23 May 1984; Law 23.053 of 22 February 1984; Law 23.117 of 30 September 1984; Law 23.238 of 10 September 1985; Law 23.523 of 28 October 1988.

15 Law 24.043 of 27 November 1991; Law 24.411 of 3 January 1995.

16 Law 24.321 of 8 June 1994.

17 Law 22.924 of 24 September 1983.

18 Law 23.040 of 22 December 1983.

19 See details on the Argentine justice system in the trials section of this chapter.

20 Law 23.521 of 4 June 1987.

21 Decree 1002/89 of 10 October 1989. Junta members or other senior figures already convicted were freed, along with 43 high-ranking officials then under investigation. A pardon was needed because, as commanders, they were not covered by the Due Obedience Law.

22 Author interviews with Gastón Chillier, executive director of CELS, 20 April 2012; Carolina Varsky, then litigation director of CELS, currently coordinator of the Prosecutorial Unit for Crimes against Humanity of the Public Prosecutor's Office, 16 March 2012; and Valeria Barbuto, executive director of the non-governmental organisation Memoria Abierta, 3 March 2012.

23 The regional context included the detention of former Chilean dictator Augusto Pinochet in London in 1998, which influenced the subsequent detention of former junta members Videla and Emilio Massera for child abduction in Argentina, and extradition requests from European countries seeking to prosecute former Argentine military officers. See the section on trials as well as Roht-Arriaza (2005).
24 The Ministry of Defence reformed training of the armed forces in 2011. Candidates can now attend national universities alongside civilians, studying curricula that include international human rights and humanitarian law.
25 See discussions of foreign trials and the inter-American system in the trials section.
26 Claudia was traced alive in 1999 and her original identity restored in 2000, thanks to Abuelas.
27 Carolina Varsky interview, 16 March 2012.
28 Decree 579/2003 of 8 August 2003.
29 Law 25.779 of 2 September 2003.
30 Enrique Arancibia Clavel was a former Chilean secret police agent, resident in Argentina, who had been convicted in Argentina in 2000 for the 1974 car bomb murder of Chilean general Carlos Prats and his wife, an Operation Condor crime. Arancibia was being sought by Chilean authorities carrying out a domestic investigation of the same episode. The Argentine appeal court had initially denied the request, declaring that the statute of limitations applied.
31 Although precedent, even Supreme Court precedent, is not theoretically binding in the Argentine system, no court has subsequently opted to dissent from the line taken in the Simón verdict.
32 Presidential Decrees 157 and 158, 13 December 1983.
33 Prosecutorial Unit data provided to the author.
34 'Mignone, Emilio F., s/ recurso extraordinario presentación en causa 761 E.S.M.A.'; 'Lapacó, Carmén Aguilar de, s/ recurso extraordinario presentación en causa 450'. Both documents were filed before the FCA and are retained in the CELS archive.
35 On 7 October 1998 the IACHR received a petition presented by Carmen Aguilar de Lapacó against Argentina.
36 For instance, in March 1990, the Supreme Court of France convicted former Argentine navy captain Alfredo Astiz *in absentia* for the disappearance of two French nuns in Argentina. Italy, Germany, and Sweden also opened several trials for crimes committed in Argentina against their nationals. In November 1999, Spanish judge Baltasar Garzón ordered the prosecution of 98 members of the Argentine military for dictatorship-era crimes, requesting the extradition of 48 of them.
37 It was argued that the requested individuals had already been tried for the same crimes, even though previous investigations had been aborted due to amnesty or had culminated in pardons.
38 The first case from this reopened phase to reach the trial stage, in 2006, was the Simón case, which had produced the breakthrough against impunity.
39 When the procedure is fully written, once the judge arrives at a conviction or an acquittal, the verdict can be revised in the second instance by the corresponding FCA, not the Court of Cassation, which only acts regarding oral procedures.
40 Pablo Llonto, human rights lawyer, interview by author, 12 July 2012; Ana Oberlin, former human rights lawyer and current adviser to the Human Rights Secretariat of the Ministry of Justice, interview by author, 5 October 2012.
41 When the unit was established in 2007, it was known as the Prosecutorial Unit for Coordinating and Monitoring Cases of Human Rights Violations Committed under State Terrorism. The name changed in 2013.
42 Pablo Parenti, former coordinator of the Prosecutorial Unit for Crimes against Humanity of the Public Prosecutor's Office, interview by author, 23 November 2012.

43 Resolution 1/12 of the Court of Cassation, March 2012.
44 This statistic, like the ones relating to charges, considers all charges and penalties imposed on each defendant, most of whom have been convicted on multiple counts and/or in more than one case.
45 Appeals are complicated by the fact that each individual convicted in a single case can appeal separately to the Supreme Court.
46 Carolina Varsky interview, 16 March 2012.
47 Pablo Parenti interview, 23 November 2012; Carolina Varsky interview, 16 March 2012.
48 There are no national opinion polls specifically dedicated to human rights policy. However, in 2011, the Universidad de Buenos Aires included the subject in its regular election-time opinion poll. After the 2011 presidential elections, 80 per cent of those surveyed declared themselves in favour of the trials. See De Angelis (2011).
49 For debates on institutional reform of the judiciary, see Lantos (2013).
50 On the relationship between lack of security forces reform and present-day violent practices or espionage, see CELS annual reports from 2006 to 2012. In March 2015, Congress passed a law to dismantle and replace the State Secretariat of Intelligence, a change whose full implications have yet to emerge. The action was not, however, part of a systematic reform initiative. Rather, it was a reaction to a destabilisation context involving the death of public prosecutor Alberto Nisman, who was in charge of investigating the infamous 1994 bombing of a Jewish community centre in Buenos Aires and who had close links with members of the Intelligence Secretariat who were opponents of the government. This complex tangle of events is beyond the scope of this chapter; case documents are available on the Supreme Court's official news site (Centro de Información Judicial 2015). The Nisman affair brought the murky role of the unreformed security services into the spotlight, finally prompting the government to pass a law to dissolve the Secretariat.
51 Landmark criminal cases concerning civilian participation in crimes against humanity have included prosecutions of Ledesma company president Carlos Blaquier, former directors of Ford Motor Argentina, and the former head of the Argentine Securities and Exchange Commission. Many of these cases, however, were dismissed by the courts in early 2015.

References

Abuelas de Plaza de Mayo. 2008. *Las Abuelas y la genética: El aporte de la ciencia en la búsqueda de los chicos desaparecidos*. Buenos Aires: Abuelas de Plaza de Mayo.

Acuña, Carlos, and Catalina Smulovitz. 1991 *¿Ni olvido ni perdón? Derechos humanos y tensiones cívico-militares en la transición argentina*. Buenos Aires: Centro de Estudios de Estado y Sociedad.

Balardini, Lorena. 2015. 'Estrategias de producción de información de las organizaciones de derechos humanos en Argentina: Los usos de la sistematización y la estadística en la búsqueda de verdad y justicia.' Master's thesis, Universidad de Buenos Aires.

Balardini, Lorena, Ana Oberlin, and Laura Sobredo. 2011. 'Gender Violence and Sexual Abuse in Clandestine Detention Centers: A Contribution to Understanding the Experience of Argentina.' In *Making Justice: Further Discussions on the Prosecution of Crimes against Humanity in Argentina*, 106–41. Buenos Aires: Center for Legal and Social Studies; New York: International Center for Transitional Justice.

Brysk, Alison. 1994. *The Politics of Human Rights in Argentina: Protest, Change and Democratization*. Stanford, CA: Stanford University Press.

Calveiro, Pilar. 2006. *Poder y desaparición: Los campos de concentración en Argentina*. Buenos Aires: Colihue.

CELS (Centro de Estudios Legales y Sociales). 2005. *Derechos humanos en Argentina: Informe 2005*. Buenos Aires: Siglo XXI.

——2006. *Derechos humanos y control civil sobre las Fuerzas Armadas*. Buenos Aires: CELS.

——2007. *Action Lines to Strengthen the Process of Seeking Truth and Justice* Buenos Aires: CELS.

——2012. *Derechos humanos en Argentina: Informe 2012*. Buenos Aires: Siglo XXI.

CELS, et al. 1988. *Culpables para la sociedad, impunes por la ley*. Buenos Aires: CELS.

Centro de Información Judicial. 2015. 'El juez Rafecas desestimó la denuncia presentada por el fiscal Nisman.' Agencia de Noticias del Poder Judicial Corte Suprema de Justicia de la Nación, 26 February.

CONADEP. 1984. *Nunca Más: Informe de la Comisión Nacional sobre la Desaparición de Personas*. Buenos Aires: EUDEBA. Republished in English as *Nunca Más: The Report of the Argentine National Commission on the Disappeared*. New York: Farrar, Straus, Giroux, 1986.

Crenzel, Emilio. 2012. *Memory of the Argentina Disappearances: The Political History of Nunca Más*. New York: Routledge.

Dandan, Alejandra. 2015a. 'Una falta de mérito que es absolución encubierta.' *Página/12*, 17 March.

——2015b. 'Para tener futuro hay que saber qué nos pasó.' *Página/12*, 20 May.

De Angelis, Carlos F. 2011. 'Una agenda que cruza la frontera del voto.' *Página/12*, 25 October.

Gorini, Ulises. 2008. *La otra lucha: Historia de las Madres de Plaza de Mayo (1983–1986)*, vol. 2. Buenos Aires: Editorial Norma.

Guembe, María José. 2006. 'Economic Reparations for Grave Human Rights Violations: The Argentinean Experience.' In *The Handbook of Reparations*, edited by Pablo de Greiff, 21–54. Oxford: Oxford University Press.

Halperín Donghi, Tulio. 1994. *La larga agonía de la Argentina peronista*. Buenos Aires: Ariel.

Hayner, Priscilla B. 2011. *Unspeakable Truths: Transitional Justice and the Challenge of Truth Commissions*. 2nd ed. New York: Routledge.

IACHR (Inter-American Commission on Human Rights). 1992. *Argentina: Cases 10.147, 10.181, 10.240, 10.262, 10.309 and 10.311*. Report 28/92, 2 October. Washington, DC: OAS.

——2000. *Carmen Aguilar de Lapacó, Argentina: Case 12.059*. Report 21/00, 29 February. Washington, DC: OAS.

Junta Militar. 1983. *Documento final de la Junta Militar sobre la guerra contra la subversión y el terrorismo*. Buenos Aires: La Junta.

Karush, Matthew B., and Oscar Chamosa. 2010. *The New Cultural History of Peronism: Power and Identity in Mid-Twentieth-Century Argentina*. Durham, NC: Duke University Press.

La Nación. 2005. 'Para el Ejército, es un paso necesario.' 15 June

——2013. 'El CELS ratificó la impugnación contra César Milani por su presunta vinculación con la dictadura.' 18 December.

——2014. 'Juicios teñidos de graves sospechas.' 3 March.

——2015. 'Dictaron la falta de mérito en una causa contra Vicente Massot.' 10 March.

Lantos, Nicolás. 2013. 'La Justicia, los buitres y la AMIA'. *Página/12*, 2 March.

Mignone, Emilio. 1986. *Iglesia y dictadura*. Buenos Aires: Colihue.

Mignone, Emilio, and Augusto Conte. 1981. 'El caso argentino: Desapariciones forzadas como instrumento básico y generalizado de una política.' Presented at the conference 'La política de desapariciones forzadas de personas', Paris, 31 January–1 February.

Morales, Diego R. 2011. 'Restricting Access to Public Office for Perpetrators of Crimes against Humanity: The Argentine Experience.' In *Making Justice: Further Discussions on the*

Prosecution of Crimes against Humanity in Argentina, 50–68. Buenos Aires: Center for Legal and Social Studies; New York: International Center for Transitional Justice.

Nino, Carlos S. 1991. 'The Duty to Punish Past Abuses of Human Rights Put into Context: The Case of Argentina.' *Yale Law Journal* 100(8): 2619–40.

——1998. *Juicio al mal absoluto*. Buenos Aires: Ariel.

Página/12. 2003. 'Hasta Alfonsín acepta la nulidad.' 7 June.

——2010. 'Diputados declaró "política de Estado" a los juicios por los crímenes de lesa humanidad.' 12 May.

Procuraduría de Crímenes contra la Humanidad. 2015. *Informe sobre el estado de las causas por delitos de lesa humanidad en todo el país: Los números del 2014*. Buenos Aires: Ministerio Público Fiscal, Procuración General de la Nación.

Roht-Arriaza, Naomi. 2005. *The Pinochet Effect: Transnational Justice in the Age of Human Rights*. Philadelphia: University of Pennsylvania Press.

Romero, Luis Alberto. 2014. 'Derechos humanos, de la justicia a la venganza.' *La Nación*, 24 March.

Schurman, Diego. 2005. '"Este fallo nos devuelve la fe en la Justicia", dijo Kirchner.' *Página/12*, 15 June.

Sidicaro, Ricardo. 2010. *Los tres peronismos: Estado y poder económico*. Buenos Aires: Siglo XXI.

Smulovitz, Catalina. 2012. '"The Past Is Never Dead": Accountability and Justice for Past Human Rights Violations in Argentina.' In *After Oppression: Transitional Justice in Latin America and Eastern Europe*, edited by Vesselin Popovski and Mónica Serrano, 64–85. Tokyo: United Nations University Press.

Verbitsky, Horacio. 2004. *El Vuelo*. Buenos Aires: Editorial Sudamericana.

Waisberg, Pablo. 2014. 'Abogados de represores de Latinoamérica se reúnen en Buenos Aires.' *Infojus Noticias*, 14 August.

Chapter 4

Uruguay

Halfway towards accountability

Francesca Lessa and Elin Skaar[*]

'If you were to place Uruguay on a scale from 0 to 10, where 0 is total impunity for past human rights violations and 10 is full accountability, where would you locate your country?' This is one of the questions we asked about 30 interviewees in Montevideo during our fieldwork in March 2012. We interviewed people from different sectors of society: legal professionals (judges, lawyers, prosecutors), academics (historians, political scientists, psychologists), activists from human rights and civil society organisations, trade union representatives, politicians, and journalists, among others.[1] Most people we talked to, irrespective of their background and their views on the question of how to respond to past human rights violations, awarded Uruguay a 6 on the 10-point imaginary impunity–accountability scale. In other words, Uruguay was generally perceived to be a bit more than halfway down the road to full accountability for past abuses.[2]

Since 2013, several events in Uruguay point to a slowing or partial reversal of this progress, especially in the area of criminal justice. Parallel to these negative developments, however, there has been progress in the areas of truth-finding and reparations. This suggests to us that that the country still deserves a 6 overall on the accountability scale. Whatever rating is applied, Uruguay's almost three-decades-long trajectory from impunity to some accountability has been far from smooth but rather has been characterised by alternating periods of progress and setbacks.

Transitional justice measures in Uruguay came in response to repression carried out during the period of civil-military rule (1973–85), which coincided with military governments in the rest of the Southern Cone and Brazil. Unlike Argentina, which had long periods of alternating civilian and military governments, Uruguay had largely been a stable democracy before that period. Apart from dictatorial intervals in the 1930s and 1940s, the country had a distinctive experience with liberal and participatory democracy, a rising and educated middle class, and growing financial markets. By the late 1960s, however, Uruguay was caught in a downward spiral of social and political polarisation, ideological tensions, and the erosion of civil liberties. Torture was increasingly used as a counter-insurgency technique in the fight against the urban guerrilla movement known as the Tupamaros. The deepening economic and political crisis led to the installation of a brutal dictatorial regime, including both civilian and military components, in June 1973.

While in other countries of the region the military took over by force, in Uruguay it was gradually invited into politics from the late 1960s onward. Accelerating this process, President Juan María Bordaberry of the right-wing Colorado Party placed the judiciary under military control in April 1972. He then carried out an *autogolpe* (self-coup), handing over the executive branch to the military's National Security Council in February 1973. In June of that year, Bordaberry finally dissolved Parliament and suspended the constitution. By the late 1970s, Uruguay had shattered its image of being the 'Switzerland of Latin America' and earned a new title: the 'torture chamber of Latin America', reflecting the state's widespread use of illegal detention, imprisonment, and torture (Pearce 1980). Most victims were activists on the political left, including politicians, students, trade unionists, teachers, and journalists. The country's small size and population enabled the regime's repressive apparatus to deeply infiltrate both public and private life (Gillespie 1991). The result was an oppressive culture of fear and *insilio* (internal exile) that instilled passivity and compliance, nearly paralysing the society (Perelli 1992).

The human cost of repression in Uruguay, with a population of approximately 2.8 million at the time, was large. Between 300,000 and 500,000 Uruguayans fled the country. More than 60,000 people were arrested and detained, of whom 5,000–6,000 were held as long-term political prisoners (Lessa and Fried 2011). In the 1970s, Uruguay was reported to have the highest percentage of political detainees per capita in the world (Sondrol 1992). However, compared to other countries examined in this volume, Uruguay had a relatively small absolute number of people who were murdered or forcibly disappeared. Data released from the Human Rights Secretariat in December 2014 confirmed the occurrence of 123 politically motivated assassinations and 192 cases of forced disappearance (*La República* 2014).[3] A feature particular to Uruguay is that the majority of cases of forced disappearance occurred outside the country's borders, especially in Argentina, within the framework of the transnational coordination of repression under Operation Condor.[4]

In the early 1980s, a pacted transition brought about a return to democracy. The military stepped out of the government after democratic elections in late 1984, following the plan set earlier that year in negotiations between military commanders and political leaders at Montevideo's Club Naval. However, with the right-wing Colorado government winning the elections, strong links to the military were preserved; accountability for past wrongs was not the principal subject for discussion at the time of transition in 1985. Impunity for past atrocities prevailed for almost two decades after the end of civil-military rule.

Nevertheless, Uruguay in recent years has begun to come to terms with its legacy of human rights violations and to initiate some transitional justice measures. Most importantly, the validity of Uruguay's enduring amnesty law has been repeatedly challenged. Uruguay has also had several attempts at both official and unofficial truth-finding, and the government has set in motion measures to pay reparations to victims. When evaluating Uruguay's trajectory in dealing with the past, it is worth noting that transitional justice developments between 1985 and 2004 occurred in a context of state-sponsored legal impunity, which fundamentally restricted the scope of judicial action. For almost 20 years, a human rights official told us, 'the Uruguayan state adopted a closed up policy of impunity without any fissures, which was absolutely counter-productive for the country'.[5] While there were tiny steps towards criminal accountability, impunity remained basically unaffected until 2004.[6]

The slow and irregular move towards accountability has obviously not taken place in a vacuum. As in many other countries in the region, civil society has been the main driving force in demanding truth and justice for past human rights violations. Activists inside Uruguay and exiles abroad have used the language of human rights to articulate their demands and denounce atrocities perpetrated both nationally and internationally (Markarian 2005). A particularity of the Uruguayan case is the strong link between the human rights movement, the main labour union PIT-CNT (Plenario Intersindical de Trabajadores – Convención Nacional de Trabajadores) and certain politicians, principally in the Frente Amplio (Broad Front).[7] In fact, unlike in Argentina, Chile, and Guatemala, where relatives and victims have been at the forefront of mobilisations for accountability, a distinctive feature in Uruguay is the heterogeneity of the groups struggling for justice (Burt, Fried Amilivia, and Lessa 2013).

Receptiveness, on the part of the executive and judges, to these demands has grown over time from almost nil to considerable. In this chapter we highlight some of the factors that have contributed to this shift, as well as some of the obstacles that persist. We argue that important political changes at the national level explain the start of the shift towards more accountability at the turn of the millennium and that this process has been complemented, and at times accelerated, by regional and international developments.

Amnesties: two decades of impunity for human rights violations

Unlike in Argentina, Brazil, and Chile, where the dictatorial regimes implemented self-amnesty laws before transition, no such legislation existed in Uruguay. Accounts of the political negotiations that produced the Pacto del Club Naval affirm that no formal guarantees of impunity were agreed between the commanders of the armed forces and representatives of the three political parties participating in the talks: the Colorado Party, the Frente Amplio, and the Unión Cívica.[8] Therefore, immediately upon transition, victims and their relatives presented claims to the courts regarding human rights violations. Judges began investigating the allegations of atrocities. In response, the right-wing Colorado government of President Julio María Sanguinetti downplayed the gravity of the human rights violations perpetrated in Uruguay, arguing that it was necessary to turn the page on the past and look to the future to achieve peace.

Throughout the 1980s, the government emphasised the need to consolidate democracy through 'peaceful change' (*cambio en paz*). It's 1985 National Pacification Project included Law 15.737, known informally as the National Pacification Law. This provided for the release of all political prisoners, except those who had committed 'blood crimes' and whose sentences would be reviewed by the courts (Barahona de Brito 1997). Since Art 5 of Law 15.737 explicitly excluded from the amnesty's remit human rights crimes committed by military or police officials, initially there seemed to be no intention to pardon human rights violations. However, as denunciations of atrocities increased in the courts, and judges started summoning alleged perpetrators, the military began to express discontent. The Colorado government responded swiftly to resolve the question by political means (Skaar 2007).

The Expiry Law and state-sanctioned impunity

Political parties were deeply split over how to handle the human rights issue. After much political wrangling, Parliament in December 1986 enacted Law 15.848, the Ley de Caducidad de la Pretensión Punitiva del Estado. Known in English as the 'Expiry Law' or simply the 'amnesty law', it was designed to terminate nearly all judicial proceedings involving the security forces. Article 1 suspended the state's punitive capacity regarding crimes committed prior to 1 March 1985 by military and police officials in fulfilment of their functions or while following orders. A few exceptions were made: judicial proceedings at the indictment stage (Art 2), although there were none, and crimes committed for economic gain (Art 2). The law also entrusted the executive with the task of conducting investigations into cases of disappeared adults and minors (Art 4).

Significantly, Art 3 obliged the courts to transmit all allegations of past violations to the executive, which had the exclusive responsibility to decide on a case-by-case basis whether or not the Expiry Law was applicable. Article 3, in particular, undermined the separation of powers and judicial independence, as it divested the judiciary of its functions and transferred them to the executive, thus ensuring governmental control over any progress in criminal accountability.

Between 1986 and 2004, all governments applied the Expiry Law to prevent human rights cases from being examined by the courts.[9] As a result, impunity prevailed in Uruguay for the first two decades of democratic life after the transition (Roniger 2011).

Challenges to the Expiry Law

The Expiry Law has been the subject of repeated civil society, political, and legal challenges, both nationally and internationally. Shortly after its adoption in 1986, the law was cemented by two important events. First, in a 3–2 decision in 1988, the Supreme Court of Justice (SC) deemed the law constitutional, effectively endorsing the government's official policy of impunity.[10] Second, in 1986, human rights activists had initiated a referendum with the aim of overturning the Expiry Law; that referendum, held in April 1989, resulted instead in 55 per cent of Uruguayans voting to retain it (Roniger 1997). This democratic seal of approval seemingly rendered the government immune to international criticism of the amnesty. Critical reports by the Inter-American Commission on Human Rights in 1992 and by the United Nations (UN) Human Rights Committee in 1993, 1994, and 1998, as well as several reports by Amnesty International, were pointedly ignored by the government.

Nonetheless, after almost two decades of state-endorsed impunity, a new and broad democratic mobilisation emerged to challenge the amnesty law. Between 2007 and 2009, the main trade union PIT-CNT, the student federation, human rights non-governmental organisations (NGOs), cultural and public figures, and some Frente Amplio legislators launched a campaign to hold a second public vote on whether the Expiry Law should be annulled. The plebiscite, held on 25 October 2009 in conjunction with national elections, ultimately failed, as less than 50 per cent voted in favour of eliminating the law (Lessa 2014).

As pointed out by several of our informants, including both human rights activists and legal professionals, the failure of the campaign may largely be attributed to internal disagreements within the Frente Amplio on how to deal with the past. Although this left-wing coalition had traditionally been an ally of the human rights cause and had promoted transitional justice after it was voted into power in 2004, the Frente only very timidly endorsed the plebiscite (Lessa 2013c). The coalition, as well as its presidential candidate at the time, José Mujica, focused on winning the presidential and parliamentary elections and did not actively support the plebiscite. This was likely a result of the fact that the coalition remained deeply divided internally over how to deal with the Expiry Law. While several of the Frente's constituent parties like the Partido por la Victoria del Pueblo, Nuevo Espacio, and the Communist Party strongly campaigned for the plebiscite, other factions of the coalition prioritised the continuity of government (Lessa and Fried 2011).

After the failed plebiscite, politically heated discussions continued over what to do with the amnesty law. The Frente Amplio government headed by President Mujica (2010–15) initially sought a so-called interpretative law that would clarify the Expiry Law. After months of political wrangling between the Chamber of Deputies and the Senate, the interpretative bill collapsed in Parliament.

Parallel to these civil society and political efforts, the amnesty law was being challenged in Uruguayan courts. In 2000, a first instance civilian court of Montevideo ordered investigation into the detained-disappearance of Elena Quinteros Almeida, a Uruguayan teacher who disappeared in 1976. Though the aim was to establish the facts and not to criminally prosecute the defendant, the judge in the case challenged the power that the Expiry Law gave to the president to order investigations or criminal prosecution (Skaar 2011). In 2002, a first instance criminal court in Montevideo formally charged the former minister of foreign affairs, Juan Carlos Blanco, with the unlawful kidnapping and disappearance of Quinteros. This was the first time a judge accepted going ahead with prosecution in a case of human rights violations stemming from the dictatorship period. To get around the Expiry Law, the lawyers in the case argued that Blanco was a civilian and was therefore not covered by the law, which grants impunity only to military and police. Moving away from its own 1988 decision, the Supreme Court in 2009 and 2010 handed down three landmark rulings declaring Arts 1, 3, and 4 of the Expiry Law in violation of the constitution and several human rights treaties, marking a positive leap on the accountability scale.[11]

The Expiry Law was also strongly criticised by the Inter-American Court of Human Rights. In a February 2011 ruling in the emblematic Gelman case, the Court declared the Expiry Law to be in violation of Uruguay's international human rights obligations. The Court condemned Uruguay for the disappearance of María Claudia Gelman and the illegal alteration of the identity of her infant daughter Macarena.[12] According to informants interviewed in Montevideo in the legal sector, academia, and human rights NGOs, the Gelman ruling worked as an effective catalyst in bringing about the eventual derogation of the amnesty law. International pressure mounted on Uruguay to comply with the Court's ruling. Although Uruguayan judges were previously not indifferent to regional legal developments in human rights, they had reacted much more slowly than their counterparts in Chile and Argentina (Skaar 2011). After Gelman, a heightened sensitivity to international precedents signalled a new trend in Uruguay.

Eventually, a second legislative challenge to the Expiry Law was successful, and Parliament derogated the law on 27 October 2011. Law 18.831 re-established the state's punitive capacity regarding crimes of state terrorism committed before 1 March 1985 and declared them to be crimes against humanity. Amnesty has thus formally come to an end, but achieving justice for dictatorship crimes remains an uphill struggle. Indeed, as detailed below, there has been a backlash in favour of impunity since then. Only a handful of trials have been completed over the past three years and just one new prosecution has been initiated since 2011, despite many fresh allegations of atrocities presented to the courts.

Trials: advancing criminal accountability through the courts

Criminal accountability for past human rights violations in Uruguay has taken place in a civil law-based inquisitorial judicial system that, unlike most other judicial systems in Latin America, has remained virtually unreformed since the dictatorship (Skaar 2011). The judiciary is well institutionalised and quite professional, giving it among the highest scores in Latin America on the rule of law index (World Justice Project 2014). Yet it is deeply hierarchical and conservative in nature. Supreme Court judges wield substantial power over lower court judges with respect to appointments and disciplinary measures, making judicial independence a tricky issue. The structure and nature of the court system no doubt partly helps to explain why justice for past wrongs is being delayed (Skaar 2011).

Criminal prosecutions for dictatorship crimes in Uruguay may be divided into three phases, closely related to the status of the amnesty law. Immediately after transition, numerous cases of human rights violations (HRV) were brought to court, only to stall when the adoption of the Expiry Law in 1986 led to their closure. There followed a period of almost no activity in this area (1986–2002).[13] The third phase of criminal trials for dictatorship crimes – the main focus of our analysis – began in 2002 and has been characterised by a few, rather spectacular, verdicts.

Exploiting loopholes in the Expiry Law

The first breach in the logic of impunity and the Expiry Law occurred in 2002 in the Elena Quinteros case. Elena's mother, with the support of lawyer Pablo Chargoñia, succeeded in having the previously archived criminal case into her daughter's fate reopened, based on the innovative legal argument that the Expiry Law did not apply to civilians. As a result, in October 2002, Judge Eduardo Cavalli charged the dictatorship's former foreign minister, Juan Carlos Blanco – a civilian – with Elena's unlawful imprisonment. Coming 17 years after the transition, Blanco's trial and preventive detention was the first to take place in post-dictatorship Uruguay; as such, it constituted an historic achievement in the struggle against impunity. The case set the tone for how potential loopholes in the amnesty could be exploited while the law was still in force.[14]

Progress in criminal accountability was directly related to whether executives applied the Expiry Law to permit or prevent criminal investigations of alleged atrocities. After 20 years of conservative rule, the first Frente Amplio government, headed by President Tabaré Vázquez (2005–10), allowed some judicial investigations to move forward in a series of specific crimes. These included economic crimes, crimes committed by civilian or military/police officials of the dictatorship, crimes committed abroad, and the illegal appropriation of children, all of which the president considered to fall outside the amnesty law's remit. This resulted in the opening of judicial proceedings in approximately 25 cases, encompassing about 60 victims in total. Subsequently, President José Mujica, also of the Frente Amplio (2010–15), followed the trend set by his predecessor.[15]

Since 2005, civilians, police and military officers, and even two former heads of state (Juan María Bordaberry and Gregorio Álvarez) have been indicted, prosecuted, and sentenced for crimes committed both within Uruguay and – more often – outside its borders, principally in Argentina. We highlight a few emblematic cases. The first charges ever brought in Uruguay against military and police officials took place in 2006, when a criminal court judge in Montevideo prosecuted six military officers and two policemen for 28 disappearances of Uruguayans in Buenos Aires in 1976 (SERPAJ 2006). In 2009, in the first judgment to be handed down regarding past crimes, the defendants received sentences ranging from 20 to 25 years' imprisonment for aggravated homicide (SERPAJ 2010). This judgment was upheld by the Supreme Court in 2011.

In another landmark case, Uruguay in 2010 became one of the first countries in Latin America (indeed the world) to hold a former head of state accountable for past human rights violations. A Montevideo court sentenced former dictator Bordaberry to 30 years' imprisonment for orchestrating two political murders and nine disappearances and for leading the 1973 coup d'état (de León Orpi 2011). The same year, former foreign minister Blanco was sentenced to 20 years for the aggravated homicide of Elena Quinteros, a sentence confirmed by the Court of Appeals in 2012 (Pernas 2012). In 2011, Bordaberry and Blanco also received 30-year prison terms for the aggravated homicides of two prominent politicians kidnapped and murdered in Buenos Aires in 1976 (*La República* 2011a).[16] In 2011, the Supreme Court confirmed the 25-year sentence of former dictator Gregorio Álvarez (1981–85) for 37 aggravated murders (Palermo 2011).

In 2010, Judge Mariana Mota applied the legal term 'disappearance' in the case of two Uruguayan citizens who disappeared in Paraguay in 1977. The Montevideo Court of Appeals confirmed Mota's sentence in 2011, thus accepting the application of the crime of forced disappearance for the first time in Uruguayan legal history (Rodríguez 2011). Finally, judicial proceedings began in 2010 against one active and one retired general for the murder of literature professor and communist militant Nibia Sabalsagaray in 1974. General Miguel Dalmao was prosecuted and sentenced to 28 years in prison in 2013 for Sabalsagaray's death (*La República* 2013), the first active duty military officer ever to receive such a sentence.

As this brief overview shows, trials have taken place in relation to active duty and retired police and military officials as well as civilians, including two former dictators and the dictatorship's foreign minister. They have concerned crimes that occurred both in Uruguay and outside the country, particularly in Argentina and Paraguay. The vast majority of trials have been for murder or aggravated murder; in only one case has the crime of disappearance been accepted. As will be discussed below, however, there has been much resistance in Uruguayan courts against applying international law on torture and disappearance (Guianze 2011).

While progress in these emblematic cases is clearly welcome, lawyer Chargoñia warns that this selective approach also constitutes 'a form of impunity'. He contends that it runs the risk of 'overshadowing other individuals and their responsibility', given that the machinery of state terrorism, of systematic torture and illegal transfer of prisoners went well beyond these symbolic cases and relied on an extensive number of people and resources.[17]

Recent legal developments

In late 2011, alongside efforts to derogate the Expiry Law in Parliament, human rights activists worked to present new allegations of past crimes to the courts. This wave of denunciations occurred because they feared that, after 1 November 2011, a statute of limitations could be invoked to shelve criminal investigations into dictatorship crimes. Thus, in September 2011, 50 former political prisoners filed accusations of torture, while another 30 did so for similar abuses at the clandestine detention centre known as 300 Carlos. In October 2011, the student federation, together with the NGO Iguales y Punto and lawyer Federico Álvarez Petraglia, helped present 170 new denunciations of torture, illegal detention, and kidnapping (*Subrayado* 2011). Female former prisoners also presented denunciations of torture, particularly sexual violence (Contreras and Touriño 2011). While torture and prolonged imprisonment were the principal characteristics of the repression, the focus of trials up to that point had been on disappearances and assassinations.[18] These important denunciations turned the spotlight back on torture, paving the way for prosecutions for this crime.

However, the picture a few years later looks quite bleak. As of December 2014, there were 256 criminal cases making their way through the judicial system. Yet only six prosecutions (2 per cent) had gone though all stages of appeal and had received a final ruling by the Supreme Court. Just eight cases (3 per cent) had reached the indictment phase, while the majority (164 cases, 63 per cent) were still at the pre-indictment stage. Between 1985 and 2014, 33 individuals were tried for dictatorship crimes, 19 of whom ended up spending time in prison. Since the overturning of the Expiry Law in 2011, only one new trial into past crimes has been initiated – in March 2012 – while many of the torture allegations presented to the courts are still in the pre-indictment stage (Chargoñia 2014, 30, 37). Between the end of 2011 and the end of 2014, only six trials advanced in the courts: two resulted in proceedings being shelved and two absolved four defendants. There were two condemnatory verdicts for Colonel Tranquilino Machado and General Dalmao in separate criminal investigations regarding the murders of Ramón Peré and Nibia Sabalsagaray. Uruguay thus presents a stark contrast with Argentina, where, during the same period, 58 trials were concluded.

In addition to the extremely slow pace of criminal proceedings, the stance of the Supreme Court on the question of whether the dictatorship's crimes constitute crimes against humanity has also shifted the balance back towards impunity. In a February 2013 judgment, and in several subsequent judgments that year, the Supreme Court, invoking the principle of non-retroactivity of criminal law, declared that Arts 2 and 3 of Law 18.831 – the law derogating the amnesty law – were unconstitutional. The Court further argued that dictatorship crimes should be subject to a statute of limitations. This conservative jurisprudence has been criticised both nationally and internationally. The Inter-American Court unequivocally rejected the Supreme Court's argument regarding the statute of limitations, saying that it constituted an obstacle to full compliance with the 2011 verdict in the Gelman case (Lessa and Le Goff 2013). Some prosecutors and judges have distanced themselves from this jurisprudence and vowed to continue investigating. Yet, as human rights activists have highlighted, 'the stance of the SCJ [Supreme Court of Justice] on statutory limitations and the unconstitutionality of Law 18.831 allow defendants' lawyers to generate delays upon delays by presenting unconstitutionality appeals and prescription claims', with the goal of delaying the justice process indefinitely (Lessa and Le Goff 2014).

Drivers of change and remaining obstacles to criminal accountability

Victims and survivors, supported by human rights NGOs and a handful of human rights lawyers, have pushed for justice through the Uruguayan courts since the time of transition, but their efforts have been increasingly successful only in recent years. There has been a sharp upturn in independent action by judges and prosecutors willing to hear human rights cases since the turn of the millennium. This helps to explain this positive development in criminal accountability, as shown in Figure 4.2.

Although the number of judges (Alberto Reyes, Estela Jubette, Mariana Mota), prosecutors (Mirtha Guianze, Ana María Tellechea), and lawyers (Pablo Chargoñia, Walter De León, Álvarez Petraglia, and Pilar Elhordoy) making progress on these cases is still relatively small, they have been essential in bringing about some accountability. If the judicial apparatus had not been receptive to claims for truth or justice consistently voiced by the victims and relatives, either these cases would not have been heard (as has been a dominant trend in many countries) or they would have stalled due to lack of evidence (Skaar 2013). Yet the inconsistent stance of the Supreme Court on the Expiry Law – first declaring the law unconstitutional in a unanimous decision in the Sabalsagaray case in 2009, and then ruling in 2013 on the partial unconstitutionality of the Expiry Law's derogation – no doubt sends mixed messages to lower court judges. The ambivalence of the Supreme Court on how to deal with the past is probably due, at least in part, to internal divisions over how to apply national versus international law to the human rights cases stemming from the dictatorship.

There are numerous political and legal obstacles to full criminal accountability. First, the Frente Amplio government, despite taking unprecedented steps since 2005, has nonetheless failed to adopt clear-cut policies favouring accountability.[19] Indeed, the government continues to give mixed and tentative signals, as illustrated by its failure to fully endorse the 2009 plebiscite on the Expiry Law and by the debacle of the proposed interpretative law in 2010 and 2011.

Second, the executive has not collaborated sufficiently with the judiciary in providing access to archives and other types of documentation; in some instances, it has actively blocked the provision of information. Scholar Gerardo Caetano laments the condition of state archives and argues that the state must proactively search for those files that relate directly to political repression, not only for use by scholars and historians, but also, and most importantly, to support ongoing judicial investigations.[20]

Third, judicial investigations have been slow and inefficient. The almost 200 denunciations presented in October 2011 preceding the derogation of the Expiry Law have largely languished in the judicial system. Judges report that they struggle with the lack of information needed to make progress on difficult human rights cases. Military personnel have systematically refused to tell the truth about what happened when they have been called by judges to testify, although they have provided some general information about certain incidents. According to one of the high-profile judges handling human rights cases, Judge Mariana Mota, 'the vertical hierarchical structure of the military is very strong and very much respected'.[21] Rather than rely on military confessions, then, judges have to depend largely on other sources. The secretariat set up in the wake of the Peace Commission (discussed in the next section) is supposed to supply the courts with such information, but although there is willingness to do so, no formal structure is in place to ensure the necessary flow of information.[22]

Furthermore, even though a new unit was set up in 2013 within the Ministry of Interior to support the investigation of state terror crimes, many judges were unaware of its existence, since the Supreme Court failed to transmit this information to them. Victims themselves and their relatives commonly play a fundamental role in cases of past crimes, presenting denunciations to the courts and submitting relevant proof and documentation (Chargoñia 2011). The lack of witness protection is also considered to be a problem.[23] The inquisitorial system is still used in Uruguay, so investigative judges are in charge of obtaining all relevant documentation in the case; these same judges later pass judgment, a procedure described as 'absurd' by a first instance judge. There is no system of technical assistance provided to the investigative judges by the prosecutors, as is done in Argentina. There are also no specialised courts to deal with human rights cases, as there are in Chile and Guatemala.[24]

Fourth, there is resistance within the judiciary to dealing with human rights cases. The Uruguayan judiciary has been described as conservative, cautious, 'resistant to change, and very orthodox in its interpretation of the laws' (Brinks 2008, 199). A point frequently brought to our attention was the lack of training in human rights issues and international law, as well as the lack of exchanges with judges and prosecutors in other countries, even neighbouring ones (Guianze 2011).[25] Although there have been some improvements in recent years, judges, especially older ones, persist in disregarding international treaties and international human rights law in their judgments.[26] Judges reluctant to deal with human rights cases tend to keep on applying national law rather than invoking international human rights law in their judgments. The designation of enforced disappearances as 'continuous crimes' (*delitos permanentes*), adopted in Argentina and Chile, has yet to be assimilated in Uruguayan jurisprudence (Guianze 2011).

The main point of contention is application of the term 'homicide' (a common crime) rather than 'disappearance' (an internationally defined crime). Homicide is subject to statutes of limitations: it has a limitation of 20 years, though this was increased for dictatorship crimes, in light of their gravity, to 26 years and eight months. Disappearance is considered a continuous crime and is, therefore, exempt from statutes of limitations. This has a direct bearing on determining which cases can be investigated by courts and which cannot. Indeed, most Uruguayan judges have characterised past violations as common crimes, following national legislation, rather than as crimes against humanity. Although international law has the same legal standing as national law, Uruguay has been very slow to incorporate the norms of international law into its jurisprudence.

Truth-finding: multiple, complementary attempts

Like criminal accountability, truth-finding in Uruguay has been a lengthy process, stretching over four decades. While only one truth-finding attempt fits the formal definition of truth commissions used in this volume, we offer below a more inclusive overview of both informal and formal truth-finding efforts since transition.

Parliamentary and civil society inquiries into past human rights violations

Unlike the official truth commissions set up by the executive branch of the state in Argentina in 1983 and Chile in 1990, the first attempt at truth-telling in Uruguay was sponsored by opposition parties in Parliament. In the mid-1980s, the Frente Amplio and the Blanco party set up three investigative commissions to clarify some cases of disappearances and political murders.[27] These commissions gathered important information and testimonies, but due to their limited resources and powers, they failed to find conclusive proof of an institutional decision-making process leading to violations. Neither the military nor the government ever responded to their final reports; these were never officially announced or acknowledged and it remains very difficult to gain access to them. President Sanguinetti dismissed the commissions' findings, publicly stating that the investigations did not clarify the authorship of the crimes or produce credible conclusions (Barahona de Brito 1997). In 1990, the Senate established yet another investigative commission to determine whether former Senator Juan Carlos Blanco of the Colorado Party bore any responsibility for the 1976 disappearance of Elena Quinteros, but it found no grounds to initiate a lawsuit.

The most significant attempt to shed light on the past was carried out by the Uruguayan branch of the regional human rights organisation SERPAJ (Servicio Paz y Justicia/Peace and Justice Service). In March 1989, the group released its report, *Nunca Más*, documenting atrocities committed in Uruguay between 1972 and 1985 and analysing the impact of state terrorism on the society (SERPAJ 1989). The SERPAJ report was, for two decades, the only publicly available document to provide a comprehensive overview of the repression. Despite the lack of government support and military cooperation combined with limited human and financial resources, the SERPAJ investigation was stronger than the parliamentary inquiries (Hayner 2001). It uncovered important information on abuses that would be used in court cases and as background material for a government-sponsored truth commission ten years later. The information gathered by the parliamentary commissions and SERPAJ became particularly instrumental in later years, when subsequent administrations promoted further truth-seeking inquiries into dictatorship crimes.

Civil court cases seeking truth

Truth-finding has also taken place through court procedures and the search for disappeared children. With the amnesty law still in place, a handful of lower court judges in the 1990s instigated trials with the aim of aiding the search for the disappeared rather than bringing criminal action against those responsible. Pushing these cases in a context of state-induced impunity, however, came at a high cost for the careers of these bold judges, who suffered undue pressure from their superiors or were transferred to other courts and forced to drop their cases (Skaar 2011).

These first signs of internal pressure within the judicial hierarchy eventually evolved into a pattern of sanction against judges willing to investigate past atrocities. The most recent manifestation was the transfer of Judge Mariana Mota from a Montevideo-based criminal first instance court to a civil court in early 2013. Mota, the judge who prosecuted the former dictator Bordaberry, had over 50 cases of dictatorship crimes on her docket when she was transferred by the Supreme Court.

The Comisión para la Paz

Truth was further sought through more formal institutional measures. In 2000, President Jorge Batlle (2000–5) of the Colorado Party established the Comisión para la Paz (Peace Commission) to gather information on enforced disappearances that occurred between 1973 and 1985 (Allier 2005). Composed of political and religious figures, the Commission worked for two years. Its final report confirmed the disappearance of 26 Uruguayans in Uruguay and over 130 in the region, mainly in Argentina but also in Paraguay and Chile (Comisión para la Paz 2003). The report showed that disappeared citizens in Uruguay had been detained in official or unofficial actions and submitted to physical abuse in clandestine detention, and that many had died as a result of torture.

In its report, the Commission recommended the creation of a follow-up secretariat (Secretaria de Seguimiento de la Comisión para la Paz), which was duly established. It also called for the creation of the legal status of 'absent due to enforced disappearance' and for the extension of Uruguayan legal norms to cover crimes such as torture and disappearance. Other recommendations stipulated dissemination of the report's content and inclusion of study of the dictatorship in educational curricula and teacher training.

The Peace Commission was the first official initiative through which the state acknowledged certain crimes of the repression, 15 years after transition. Despite its many shortcomings, it signalled, together with the Gelman case, a political opening that 'allowed for progress and a switch in the mentality'.[28] It contributed to public discussion of previously silenced issues such as disappearances, torture, and the kidnapping of children. The Commission was, however, fiercely criticised by human rights and victims' groups, who rejected its final report. Relatives of the disappeared faulted the Commission for giving them only a certificate testifying that their loved one had effectively disappeared at a certain time and place, while providing no other information. Other criticisms related to the Commission's exclusive focus on disappearances and its failure to include crimes like torture and prolonged imprisonment, which had been hallmarks of the repression (SERPAJ 2007). The Commission hardly resembled other well-known international truth-seeking bodies, as it was granted very limited powers and resources, had to rely only on voluntary testimonies, and was denied access to archives.

Although the human rights community pinned high hopes on the Commission when it was established, the controversies provoked by its report had perhaps a negative overall effect on accountability. It was widely perceived as yet another attempt by the executive to close the books on the past. Nevertheless, it is generally agreed that the Commission represented a breach with the former state policy of total impunity. The report acknowledged, for the first time, the existence of state terrorism, providing space for truth – however incomplete – to emerge. Also, several of the report's recommendations would have a positive influence on accountability later on, including a call for reparations to victims of abuse.

Further advances

Parallel to the workings of the Peace Commission, high-profile individual searches by the families of two disappeared children resulted in the location of Macarena Gelman in 2000 and of another missing child, Simón Riquelo, in 2002. The crimes starkly illustrated the collaboration between the Argentine and Uruguayan regimes within the framework Operation Condor. Macarena – born to Argentine parents – was appropriated by the family of a police chief in Uruguay, while Simón – born to Uruguayan parents in exile in Argentina – was raised by the family of a policeman in Buenos Aires.

Yet another form of truth-finding took place under the Frente Amplio government of President Vázquez, who ordered excavations to take place at military sites to look for remains of the disappeared. The first successful discovery of this kind in Uruguay came in 2005 and resulted in the identification of a member of the Uruguayan Communist Party who had disappeared in 1978. Also in 2005, the remains of Fernando Miranda, kidnapped in 1975, were found at the headquarters of the 13th Infantry Battalion (*Clarín* 2005; *La República* 2006). These discoveries had an extraordinary impact on Uruguayan society, featuring on all television channels and in front-page newspaper headlines. The location of remains of the disappeared effectively demonstrated beyond doubt the perpetration of atrocities by the state, as well as its subsequent cover-up.

In June 2005, the executive for the first time instructed the armed forces to carry out investigations into the fate of disappeared detainees. The military submitted a report in which it made unprecedented admissions, acknowledging illegal detentions, the practice of torture, the use of clandestine flights to transfer political prisoners from Buenos Aires to Montevideo, clandestine burials, and the cremation of human remains (Fuerzas Armadas de Uruguay 2007). In 2007, the executive also released, in Spanish, *Historical Investigation on Disappeared-Detainees*, compiled by researchers from the Universidad de la República, who gathered documents and archival information. In 2008, the same team of historians published *Historical Investigation on the Dictatorship and State Terrorism in Uruguay (1973–1985)* (Presidencia de la República 2007, 2008).

Discoveries continued under the next government. In February 2011, President Mujica ordered excavations to resume in the search for the remains of María Claudia Gelman and for a clandestine cemetery known as Arlington (*La República* 2011b). In October 2011, human remains were again discovered on military land, in this case the 14th Battalion of Toledo. They were later identified as those of Julio Castro, a 68-year-old teacher and journalist executed in 1977 (Cavallo and Pérez 2011). A few months later, in March 2012, on the same site where Julio Castro had been buried, searchers found the remains of trade unionist Ricardo Blanco, who disappeared in 1978 (*El País* 2012). The discovery of additional bodies profoundly affected the public and coincided with important events, including the derogation of the amnesty and a public acknowledgement of state responsibility in the Gelman case, discussed further below.

Material and symbolic reparations

Reparations in Uruguay have principally taken place in the wake of the Peace Commission's work, and upon its recommendations. In the 1980s, no reparations were paid to victims of human rights abuses; initial provisions mainly targeted returning exiles and employees unfairly dismissed during the dictatorship, as specified in the government's 1985 National Pacification Project (Barahona de Brito 1997). However, according to scholar Louise Mallinder, the 1985 National Pacification Law (Law 15.737) 'can be viewed as a form of reparations' in that it released political prisoners from prison and provided some form of restitution in an effort to 'undo some of the harm that had been inflicted during military rule'. Furthermore, she notes, the 1985 law also created the National Repatriation Commission 'to facilitate and support the return of all exiles to Uruguay'. Article 25 of the law 'stated that public officials who had been dismissed by the military *junta* because of their political beliefs could be reinstated in their former posts, or where this was not possible, they or their relatives could be awarded a pension' (Mallinder 2009, 1, 34, 35). Only since 2005, though, has the government taken important steps in providing reparations to victims of physical abuse and to their families.[20] All reparations are granted by law and relate to individual victims and claimants, with no instances of collective reparations.

Following recommendations by the Peace Commission, the Law on Forced Disappearances (Law 17.894) of September 2005 created the legal category of 'absent due to enforced disappearance' for citizens who disappeared inside and outside Uruguay. In October 2006, the Law on Pension Rights (Law 18.033) granted special reparatory pension rights to individuals who either for political or trade union reasons had been unable to work between February 1973 and 1985.[30] A special commission was established in the Ministry of Labour and Social Security to process applications by claimants and distribute benefits. In September 2009, what is known as the Reparations Law (Law 18.596) finally recognised the systematic practices of repression, torture, disappearances, and homicide by the state. A special commission was set up in the Ministry of Education and Culture to pay reparations to victims, including political prisoners, minors born in detention or disappeared, exiles, and torture victims.

It is too soon to tell how extensive or comprehensive these various reparations programmes will turn out to be, but progress so far is promising. Between 2010 and August 2014, over 1,100 applications were submitted to the Ministry of Education Special Commission, which awarded 506 symbolic reparations to victims of state terror and health benefits to 269 people, while 74 applications were dismissed. Economic reparations were also granted to 364 people. These included compensation to 84 children born in captivity and kept away from their parents for more than six months; 196 families of the disappeared; 80 people who had suffered gross torture; and four children who had been disappeared for more than a month (Zecca 2014).

These efforts, however, still fall short in some respects. Although the recent legislation aims to compensate all victims of state terrorism, the Uruguayan association of former political prisoners, Crysol, has highlighted delays in offering medical and psychological support. Crysol representatives, as well as the UN special rapporteur on the promotion of truth, justice, reparation, and guarantees of non-recurrence, particularly emphasised that the law fails to meet international standards on reparations, as it does not encompass all categories of possible victims and forces recipients to choose between reparations and pension provisions. Article 22 is particularly criticised for requiring those who enjoy the benefits of the law to give up their right to bring cases against Uruguay, both domestically and internationally (Fassanello 2010).

In addition to monetary reparations and compensation policies, there have also been instances of symbolic reparations, two of which stand out. First, the Cultural Centre and Museum of Memory (MUME) was inaugurated in December 2007 with support from the Montevideo municipal government (*intendencia*) and the national government through the Ministry of Education. Its creation was endorsed by several social and human rights organisations, including the relatives of the disappeared, SERPAJ, Crysol, and the Social Rehabilitation Service (SERSOC). The MUME is dedicated to the recuperation of the memory of state terrorism and of the efforts of the Uruguayan people in their struggle against the dictatorship (Lessa 2010). Thousands of people have visited MUME, where exhibitions, theatre, *murga* musical theatre, literature readings, and cinema workshops are regularly held to make people feel an active part of the museum.

Second, on 21 March 2012, a public act of acknowledgement of international responsibility and recovery of memory, ordered by the Inter-American Court in the Gelman ruling, took place, despite initial resistance by President Mujica and political controversy surrounding the event. A memorial plaque was unveiled to honour María Claudia Gelman and all the victims imprisoned in the former clandestine detention centre known as Centro de Altos Estudios Nacionales (SERPAJ 2012). President Mujica acknowledged Uruguay's responsibility for María Claudia Gelman's disappearance in an official speech in Parliament, attended by members of the legislature, executive, and judiciary, as well as the military high command, with Macarena and her grandfather Juan Gelman also present (*La República* 2012). Although the speech was a landmark in terms of establishing officially the state's responsibility for the atrocities committed, it was brief and perfunctory. President Mujica had already stated publicly that he would not 'go one millimetre more' than what was required by the regional court. Historian Aldo Marchesi highlights this attitude of 'always doing less than what could be done', and points out that the state could have 'taken advantage of this opportunity to recognise the violations against the Gelmans as well as acknowledge the crimes committed against all Uruguayans'.[31]

Conclusions

In an interview in 2012, public prosecutor Mirtha Guianze asserted that Uruguay was characterised by 'impunidad de hecho y de derecho' (factual and legal impunity).[32] This rather pessimistic view captures the difficulties and challenges faced in coming to terms with the atrocities of the past. The legal obstacle to criminal prosecution, the Expiry Law, was for decades reinforced by other sources of impunity, such as the lack of political will to investigate, the resistance of the judiciary, and the limited resources provided by the state to support any examination of the past.

Yet as the analysis in this chapter has shown, there has been a definite movement in the direction of more accountability over the past 15 years. It started tentatively in 2000, when the Batlle government came to power, although impunity still featured centrally in the political arena. The curve towards accountability became noticeably steeper after the Frente Amplio government took office in 2005, suggesting that one of the principal explanations for the general shift from impunity towards accountability in Uruguay is political will.[33] The Frente Amplio government, although internally split, signalled to civil society that there was room for public deliberation of these issues, and it signalled to the judiciary that addressing human rights violations could be done without causing institutional instability.

The major expressions of increased accountability for past human rights violations in Uruguay are the following:

- the various truth-telling initiatives – most notably the SERPAJ report and the Peace Commission report, which provided an overview of the systematic character of the repression, but also the location of remains of the disappeared, discoveries that had great symbolic value;
- a few trials, which have documented the violence and repression in specific court cases and ensured criminal accountability;
- the imprisonment of high-level military officials and civilian leaders, showing that even top leadership has to stand to account for the wrongs they have committed;
- the reparation programmes, which have made the state accountable to the victims for past wrongs and are expected to have a restorative effect on victims;
- the public acknowledgement by President Mujica of the dictatorship's involvement in systematic repression, accepting the state's responsibility for the violations and implying that the state can or should be held accountable for them; and
- most importantly, the derogation of the Expiry Law, so that it no longer provides a legal framework that hinders criminal accountability for past human rights violations.

It is important to recognise that accountability goes beyond the sum of various individual transitional justice mechanisms. The culture of fear that dominated Uruguayan society for so long is arguably no longer present. The fact that the military no longer constitutes a threat to democracy makes the political context very different from that of 1985, allowing more space in which to choose a pro-human rights stance. With the overturning of the Expiry Law, the legal framework appears more conducive to accountability now than at any time in the past three decades. Additional factors include several laws in place regarding reparations and Supreme Court rulings that favour accountability. Overall, there is increased sensitivity to human rights and to international norms of human rights protection and Uruguay has signed several key international conventions.[34]

The picture is not all rosy, though. A series of events over the past five years have raised serious questions about the depth of the Frente's commitment to accountability. They include the failed plebiscite in 2009, the debacle of the interpretative law in 2011 and, most recently, the reluctance demonstrated by President Mujica in his public acknowledgement of the Gelman case.

It should thus come as no surprise that there remain many obstacles to full accountability for past human rights violations. As pointed out by UN special rapporteur Pablo de Greiff, 'Uruguay still has an important chapter of its past that it has not adequately resolved. To really advance towards the future and continue on the path of development requires compliance with the rights to truth, justice, reparation, and guarantees of non-repetition. This is the responsibility of the three branches of power that make up the State' (UNGA 2014, 3, our translation).

More specifically, obstacles include:

- lack of political will and absence of clear-cut policies favouring accountability;
- lack of collaboration from the executive in providing access to archives and allocating sufficient judicial resources, especially human rights training for judges and prosecutors;
- slow and inefficient judicial investigations;
- a judiciary that is resistant, conservative, and reactive in human rights matters, especially within the Supreme Court;
- the explicit sanctioning of judges and prosecutors who take on human rights cases; and
- practical limitations to more criminal accountability related to the lack of material evidence, the lack of witnesses, and the enduring threat of the statute of limitations.

Many Uruguayans feel that there is room for still more accountability, given the extent of needs and demands that have not been satisfactorily addressed by the state. A large number think that the type of repression that was most common under the dictatorship, namely illegal imprisonment and torture, has not received sufficient attention, either in terms of detailed official documentation or in the

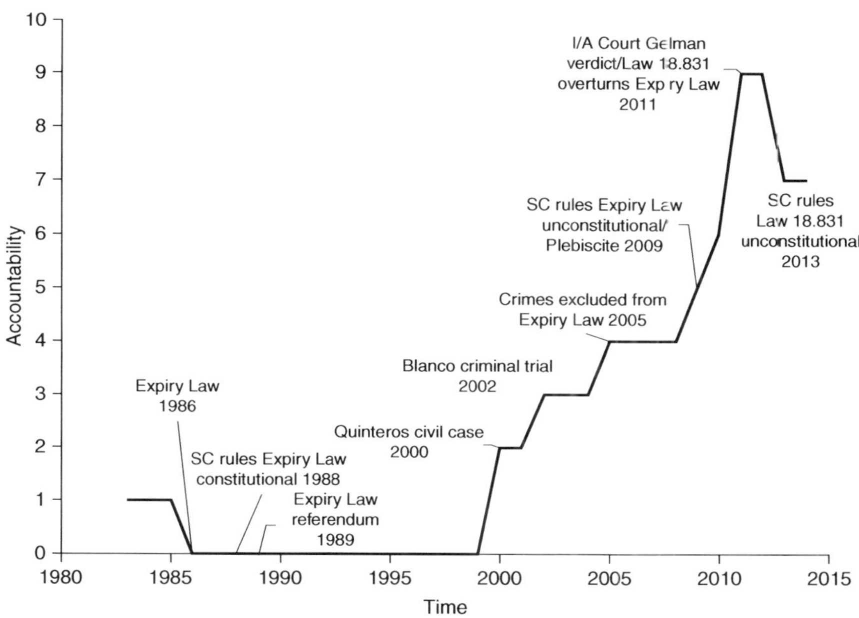

Figure 4.1 Uruguay: the overcoming amnesty dimension of accountability, 1983–2014
Source: Authors' construction, 2015.

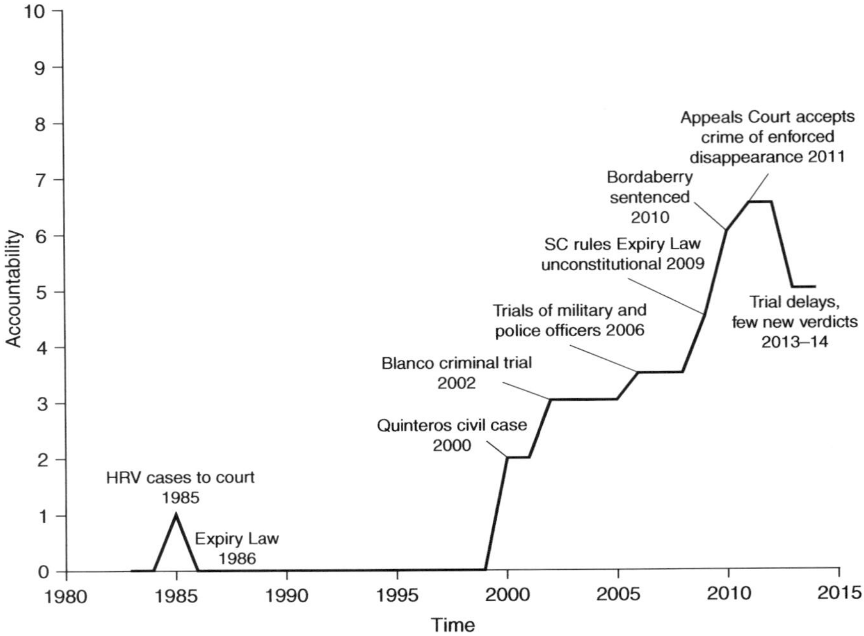

Figure 4.2 Uruguay: the trials dimension of accountability, 1983–2014
Source: Authors' construction, 2015.

field of reparations. There is discontent with the scope of reparations and the pace at which they are being paid. In sum, accountability remains partial and tentative, and many of the actors who benefited from impunity continue to obstruct justice and truth.

On balance, however, we can say that Uruguay's progress along the scale from impunity towards accountability has been significant, especially during the past decade, a period that has seen the most positive developments. With the institutional and legal limitations at least partly removed, the quest for greater accountability in Uruguay now turns mainly on the political and judicial will to push for it. A recent report by the International Commission of Jurists underscored the difficulties, especially the obstruction by the Ministry of Defence and the recent jurisprudence of the Supreme Court that hindered progress during the Mujica administration. The jurists called on the new government of President Vázquez, inaugurated on 1 March 2015, to overcome the paralysis in human rights investigations and give a fresh impetus to the search for the disappeared (ICJ 2015). The current government in Uruguay thus has an historic opportunity to deliver truth, justice, and reparations to victims of human rights atrocities and their families, as well as to the rest of society.

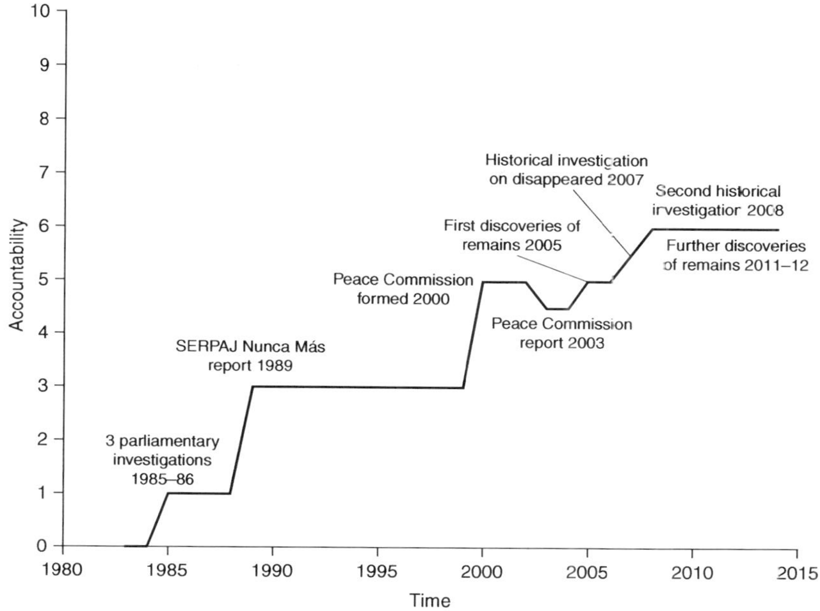

Figure 4.3 Uruguay: the truth dimension of accountability, 1983–2014
Source: Authors' construction, 2015.

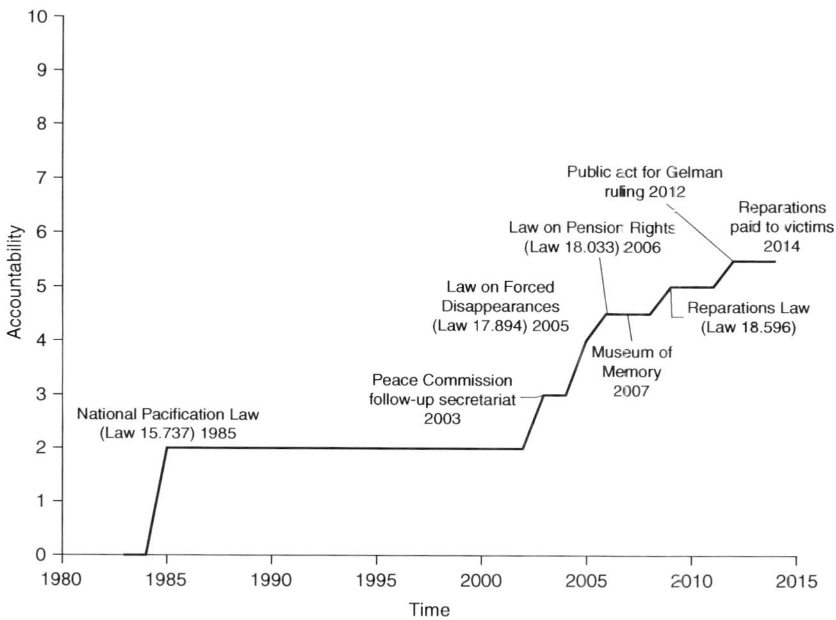

Figure 4.4 Uruguay: the reparations dimension of accountability, 1983–2014
Source: Authors' construction, 2015.

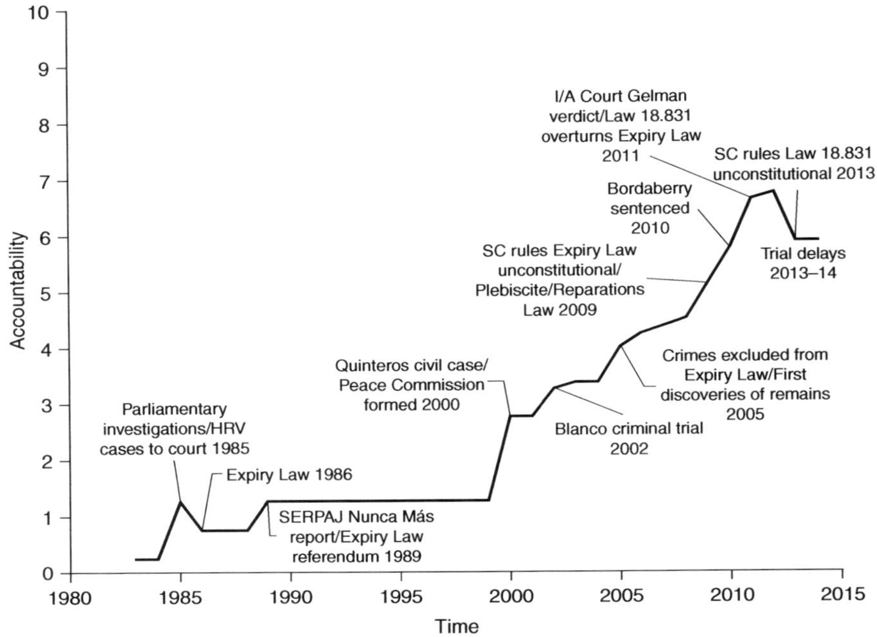

Figure 4.5 Uruguay: overall trend towards accountability, 1983–2014
Source: Authors' construction, 2015.

Notes

* The authors thank Gabriela Fried and Luis Roniger for helpful comments on earlier drafts, and Soledad Pache and Catalina Vallejo for transcribing the interviews conducted in Montevideo in 2012 and translating them from Spanish to English.

1 Each informant was given a set of core questions, followed up with additional questions according to the person's area of expertise. Our analysis in this chapter also draws on interviews conducted in Montevideo by Francesca Lessa in 2007, 2008, 2009, and 2010, and by Elin Skaar in 2002 and 2003.
2 For the definitions of impunity and accountability used in this volume, see Chapter 2.
3 In 2013, the Peace Commission's follow-up secretariat was renamed the Human Rights Secretariat for the Recent Past. It is part of the President's Office.
4 For details on Operation Condor, see Chapter 1.
5 Javier Miranda, national human rights secretary, Ministry of Education and Culture, interview by authors, 15 March 2012. All author interviews for this chapter were conducted in Montevideo.
6 Raúl Olivera, Human Rights Secretariat of the PIT-CNT labour union, interview by authors, 14 March 2012.
7 Frente Amplio was founded as a coalition of more than a dozen fractured leftist parties and movements in 1971.

8 The other major political party, the Partido Nacional, known as the Blancos, did not participate in the Club Naval talks (Barahona de Brito 1997).

9 Colorado President Sanguinetti (1985–90 and 1995–2000) archived 49 cases of disappearance, while Colorado President Batlle (2000–5) shelved the noted case of the disappearance of María Claudia Gelman in 2003. Regarding cases of murder, Sanguinetti closed down ten cases, using the Expiry Law as a pretext, while Colorado President Luis Alberto Lacalle (1990–95) halted four cases in 1990, Vice President Enrique Tarigo one case in 1987, and President Vázquez one case in 2005. Moreover, potential investigations into 34 other cases of human rights violations were also stopped by applying the law (Rodríguez 2011).

10 Supreme Court of Justice, Judgment 184, 'Denuncia – inconstitucionalidad de la Ley 15.848, Arts. 1, 2, 3 y 4', 2 May 1988.

11 These rulings came in the Sabalsagaray case (2009), Amaral García Hernández case (2010), and Organización de los Derechos Humanos case (2010).

12 Inter-American Court of Human Rights (I/A Court HR), *Case of Gelman v Uruguay*, Merits and Reparations, Judgment of 24 February 2011. Macarena Gelman was born in late 1976 during her mother's clandestine detention in Montevideo after her illegal transfer from Buenos Aires (Demasi and Yaffé 2005). Argentine poet Juan Gelman, Macarena's grandfather, looked for his grandchild for over 20 years. After a successful international campaign in 1999 supported by numerous intellectuals and Nobel laureates, in February 2000, President Jorge Batlle announced that Macarena had been located in Montevideo, and Juan Gelman was finally reunited with her.

13 There was an interim period in the late 1990s and early 2000s when some judges pushed for the rights to truth rather than justice through the courts. We discuss this in the section on truth.

14 For more details on the Quinteros case, see Skaar (2011, 157–59, 163–66).

15 Alberto Breccia, secretary of the executive, interview by authors, 16 March 2012.

16 Bordaberry died while under house arrest on 17 July 2011.

17 Pablo Chargoñia, lawyer, interview by authors, 12 March 2012.

18 Members of SERPAJ, interview by authors, 21 March 2012.

19 Federico Álvarez Petraglia, human rights lawyer, interview by authors, 12 March 2012.

20 Gerardo Caetano, academic at Universidad de la República, interview by authors, 21 March 2012; Constanza Moreira, senator representing Frente Amplio, interview by authors, 20 March 2012.

21 Mariana Mota, criminal court judge, interview by authors, 22 March 2012.

22 Ibid.

23 Mirtha Guianze, criminal public prosecutor, interview by authors, 12 March 2012.

24 Summary evidence from interviews with judges and prosecutors conducted in Montevideo in March 2012.

25 This point was noted by many of our informants, both judges and prosecutors.

26 One informant attributed this to 'laziness and ignorance'. Javier Miranda interview, 15 March 2012.

27 For details, see Lessa (2013a, 2013b).

28 Javier Miranda interview, 15 March 2012.

29 In June 1991, the government paid over US$2 million to terminate judicial proceedings in civil trials for damages suffered by victims of illegal detention and disappearances that had been presented in the early 1990s by the Uruguayan Institute of Legal and Social Studies (Instituto de Estudios Legales y Sociales del Uruguay) (Allier 2010).

30 The law also covered political prisoners and persons forced to live clandestinely or leave the country.

31 Aldo Marchesi, history professor at Universidad de la República, interview by authors, 14 March 2012.

32 Mirtha Guianze interview, 12 March 2012.
33 This point of view was supported by many of our informants, including Miranda.
34 Convention on the Non-Applicability of Statutory Limitations to War Crimes and Crimes Against Humanity, accession 21 September 2001; Law 18.026, implementing the Rome Statute of the International Criminal Court, ratified 28 June 2002, approved by Parliament, and entered into force in 2006. For a list of all international conventions ratified by Uruguay, see https://www1.umn.edu/humanrts/research/ratification-uruguay.html.

References

Allier, Eugenia. 2006. 'The Peace Commission: A Consensus on the Recent Past in Uruguay?' *European Review of Latin American and Caribbean Studies*, 81 (October): 87–96.

——2010. *Batallas por la memoria: Los usos políticos del pasado reciente en Uruguay*. Montevideo: Trilce.

Barahona de Brito, Alexandra. 1997. *Human Rights and Democratization in Latin America: Uruguay and Chile*. Oxford: Oxford University Press.

Brinks, Daniel M. 2008. *The Judicial Response to Police Killings in Latin America: Inequality and the Rule of Law*. New York: Cambridge University Press.

Burt, Jo-Marie, Gabriela Fried Amilivia, and Francesca Lessa. 2013. 'Civil Society and the Resurgent Struggle against Impunity in Uruguay (1986–2012).' *International Journal of Transitional Justice* 7(2): 306–27.

Cavallo, Mauricio, and Mauricio Pérez. 2011. 'Torturado, ejecutado y desaparecido: El maestro Julio Castro sacudió ayer al Uruguay.' *La República*, 2 December.

Chargoñia, Pablo. 2011. 'Avances, retrocesos y desafíos en la lucha judicial contra la impunidad.' In *Luchas contra la impunidad: Uruguay 1985–2011*, edited by Gabriela Fried and Francesca Lessa, 163–74. Montevideo: Trilce.

——2014. 'Después de la sentencia Gelman: Nuevos debates y desafíos en la lucha contra la impunidad de graves violaciones a los derechos humanos en el pasado reciente.' In *Derechos humanos en el Uruguay: Informe 2013–2014*, 27–42. Montevideo: Servicio Paz y Justicia.

Clarín. 2005. 'Hallan restos de un desaparecido en Uruguay.' 29 November.

Comisión para la Paz. 2003. *Informe final de la Comisión para la Paz*. Montevideo: Presidencia de la República.

Contreras, Mariana, and Rosario Touriño. 2011. 'Escrito en el cuerpo: Tortura y violencia sexual en dictadura: la otra gran batalla política.' *Brecha* (Montevideo), 4 November.

de León Orpi, Walter. 2011. 'Juan María Bordaberry: El dictador latinoamericano condenado por delitos de lesa humanidad.' In *Luchas contra la impunidad: Uruguay 1985–2011*, edited by Gabriela Fried and Francesca Lessa, 175–87. Montevideo: Trilce.

Demasi, Carlos, and Jaime Yaffé, eds. 2005. *Vivos los llevaron … Historia de la lucha de Madres y Familiares de Uruguayos Detenidos Desaparecidos (1976–2005)*. Montevideo: Trilce.

El País. 2012. 'Restos óseos son de Ricardo Blanco.' 17 April.

Fassanello, Daniela. 2010. 'Crysol exige al Estado que cumpla con la Ley de Reparación Integral.' *La República*, 19 September.

Fuerzas Armadas de Uruguay. 2007. 'Informes de las Fuerzas Armadas al Presidente de la República Oriental del Uruguay, Dr. Tabaré Vázquez.' In *Investigación histórica sobre detenidos desaparecidos*, vol. 4, sec. 3. Montevideo: Presidencia de la República.

Gillespie, Charles Guy. 1991. *Negotiating Democracy: Politicians and Generals in Uruguay*. Cambridge: Cambridge University Press.

Guianze, Mirtha. 2011. 'La Ley de Caducidad, las luchas por la justicia y la jurisdicción universal de los derechos humanos en el Uruguay.' In *Luchas contra la impunidad: Uruguay 1985–2011*, edited by Gabriela Fried and Francesca Lessa, 189–202. Montevideo: Trilce.

Hayner, Priscilla B. 2001. *Unspeakable Truths: Confronting State Terror and Atrocity*. New York: Routledge.

ICJ (International Commission of Jurists). 2015. *Uruguay: La lucha por verdad y justicia en la encrucijada – nuevo informe*. Geneva: ICJ.

La República. 2006. 'Confirmaron ayer en "un 99,96%" la identidad de Fernando Miranda.' 2 March.

——2011a. 'Juez no alcanzó a notificar a Bordaberry fallo condenatorio.' 23 July.

——2011b. 'Retoman excavaciones en busca del cementerio clandestino "Arlington".' 3 February.

——2012. 'Juan Gelman asistirá al acto de hoy.' 21 March.

——2013. 'Justicia condena con 28 años de prisión a general Miguel Dalmao por dar muerte a Nibia Sabalsagaray.' 9 May.

——2014. 'Secretaría de DD.HH presentó nómina de diez nuevos casos de personas desaparecidas o secuestradas en dictadura.' 19 December.

Lessa, Francesca. 2010. 'The Missing Memory of Transitional Justice: How Argentina and Uruguay Confronted Past Evils, 1983–2009.' PhD diss., London School of Economics.

——2013a. 'Investigative Commission on the Kidnapping and Assassination of Former National Representatives Zelmar Michelini and Héctor Gutiérrez-Ruiz.' In *Encyclopedia of Transitional Justice*, edited by Lavinia Stan and Nadya Nedelsky, vol. 3, 255–60. New York: Cambridge University Press.

——2013b. 'Investigative Commission Requested by Senator Juan Carlos Blanco Regarding His Conduct in the Ministry of External Relations in the Case of Elena Quinteros.' In *Encyclopedia of Transitional Justice*, edited by Lavinia Stan and Nadya Nedelsky, vol. 3, 260–64. New York: Cambridge University Press.

——2013c. *Memory and Transitional Justice in Argentina and Uruguay: Against Impunity*. New York: Palgrave Macmillan.

——2014. *¿Justicia o impunidad? Cuentas pendientes en el Uruguay post-dictadura*. Montevideo: Penguin Random House.

Lessa, Francesca, and Gabriela Fried. 2011. 'Las múltiples máscaras de la impunidad: La Ley de Caducidad, desde el Sí Rosado hasta los desarrollos recientes.' In *Luchas contra la impunidad: Uruguay 1985–2011*, edited by Gabriela Fried and Francesca Lessa, 31–44. Montevideo: Trilce.

Lessa, Francesca, and Pierre-Louis Le Goff. 2013. '"Breaking the Wall of Impunity" in Uruguay.' Al Jazeera, 6 May.

——2014. 'Elusive Justice in Uruguay.' Al Jazeera, 13 February.

Mallinder, Louise. 2009. *Uruguay's Evolving Experience of Amnesty and Civil Society's Response*. Working Paper 4 from Beyond Legalism: Amnesties, Transition and Conflict Transformation, project of the Institute of Criminology and Criminal Justice, Queen's University Belfast.

Markarian, Vania. 2005. *Left in Transformation: Uruguayan Exiles and the Latin American Human Rights Networks, 1967–1984*. New York: Routledge.

Palermo, Pablo Galain. 2011. 'La justicia de transición en Uruguay: Un conflicto sin resolución.' *Revista de Derecho Penal y Criminología* 3(6): 221–70.

Pearce, Jenny. 1980. *Uruguay: Generals Rule*. London: Latin America Bureau.

Perelli, Carina. 1992. 'Youth, Politics, and Dictatorship in Uruguay.' In *Fear at the Edge: State Terror and Resistance in Latin America*, edited by Juan E. Corradi, Patricia Weiss Fagen, and Manuel Antonio Garretón, 212–32. Berkeley: University of California Press.

Pernas, Walter. 2012. 'Ojos y oídos vendados.' *Brecha*, 23 February.

Presidencia de la República. 2007. *Investigación histórica sobre detenidos desaparecidos: Publicación mayo 2007 en cumplimiento del artículo 4° de la ley no. 15.848*. 5 vols. Edited by José Pedro Barrán, Gerardo Caetano, and Alvaro Rico. Montevideo: Presidencia de la República.

——2008. *Investigación histórica sobre la dictadura y el terrorismo de Estado en Uruguay (1973–1985)*. 3 vols. Edited by José Pedro Barrán, Gerardo Caetano, and Alvaro Rico. Montevideo: Presidencia de la República.

Rodríguez, Lourdes. 2011. 'Tribunal de Apelaciones aceptó la figura de desaparición forzada en el caso Calcagno.' *La Diaria*, 29 July.

Roniger, Luis. 1997. 'Human Rights Violations and the Reshaping of Collective Identities in Argentina, Chile and Uruguay.' *Social Identities* 3(2): 221–46.

——2011. 'Transitional Justice and Protracted Accountability in Re-democratised Uruguay, 1985–2011.' *Journal of Latin American Studies* 43(4): 693–724.

SERPAJ (Servicio Paz y Justicia de Uruguay). 1989. *Nunca más Uruguay: Informe sobre las violaciones a los derechos humanos 1972–1985*. Montevideo: SERPAJ. Republished in English as *Uruguay Nunca Más: Human Rights Violations, 1972–1985*. Philadelphia: Temple University Press, 1992.

——2006. *Derechos humanos en el Uruguay: Informe 2006*. Montevideo: SERPAJ.

——2007. *Informe anual de SERPAJ 2007*. Montevideo: SERPAJ.

——2010. *Derechos humanos en el Uruguay: Informe 2010*. Montevideo: SERPAJ.

——2012. *Derechos humanos en el Uruguay: Informe 2012*. Montevideo: SERPAJ.

Skaar, Elin. 2007. 'Legal Development and Human Rights in Uruguay: 1985–2002.' *Human Rights Review* 8(2): 52–70.

——2011. *Judicial Independence and Human Rights in Latin America: Violations, Politics, and Prosecution*. New York: Palgrave Macmillan.

——2013. 'Wavering Courts: From Impunity to Accountability in Uruguay.' *Journal of Latin American Studies* 45(3): 483–512.

Sondrol, Paul C. 1992. '1984 Revisited? A Re-examination of Uruguay's Military Dictatorship.' *Bulletin of Latin America Research* 11(2): 187–203.

Subrayado. 2011. 'Denuncias masivas de delitos de la dictadura: 170 nuevos casos.' 29 October.

UNGA (United Nations General Assembly). 2014. *Informe del Relator Especial sobre la promoción de la verdad, la justicia, la reparación y las garantías de no repetición, Pablo de Greiff*. Human Rights Council, 27th session. A/HRC/27/56/Add.2. New York: United Nations.

World Justice Project. 2014. *WJP Rule of Law Index 2014*. Washington, DC: World Justice Project.

Zecca, Emiliano. 2014. 'Mapa de las reparaciones a las víctimas del terrorismo de Estado.' Portal 180.com, 11 December.

Chapter 5

Brazil

The tortuous path to truth and justice

*Glenda Mezarobba**

Brazil's National Truth Commission, inaugurated in May 2012 by Brazil's first female president, Dilma Rousseff, published its final report in December 2014. The Commission addressed a concentrated period of state violence during two decades of authoritarian military rule, from 1964 to 1985, although its mandate included human rights violations committed over the course of four decades (1946 to 1988). While other, more limited commissions had initiated Brazil's truth-seeking process in the mid-1990s, the full-scale National Truth Commission was not launched until nearly a quarter-century after the end of the dictatorship – a notably late start compared to truth commissions in other countries of the region.

Among the countries considered in this book, Brazil is the largest in both territory and population: around 202 million in 2015, making it the world's fifth most populous country. In comparison to the rest of the region, Brazil suffered a relatively low number of fatalities linked to dictatorship-era repression. The National Truth Commission certified 434 deaths or disappearances for the entire dictatorship period, just slightly more than in each of the much less populous countries of Uruguay and Paraguay. However, like those two countries, Brazil suffered a very high incidence of non-fatal torture. This raises the question of why Brazil, chronologically the third country in the region to reinstall democratic rule, nevertheless did not feel the need to launch an official truth commission until so recently. The answer, in part, is that Brazil never adopted a holistic transitional justice policy, such as those in other countries, that seemed to see truth as a first step. Instead, initial official transitional justice initiatives, when they came, focused almost entirely on compensatory or reparatory measures. On the whole, Brazil's transitional justice process to date can be characterised as reparations-driven.

Moreover, if we attempt to draw up a general balance sheet across the areas of truth, justice, and reparations, 30 years after the end of the dictatorship, it is clear that Brazil has yet to systematically address the human rights violations committed during military rule. The advances in reparations already noted were largely begun a decade after transition, under the social democratic government of Fernando Henrique Cardoso (1995–2003). There was also progress in the field of truth under the centre-left Labour governments of Luiz Inácio Lula da Silva

(2003–11) and Dilma Rousseff (2011–). The amnesty law of 1979 nonetheless remains largely unchallenged across the political spectrum, although it has come under specifically legal pressure in recent years.

This chapter analyses Brazil's process towards accountability for past human rights violations, highlighting the constraints imposed by the amnesty law and the delays in the search for truth. The chapter starts with some brief historical background on the authoritarian regime and the transition to democracy. Subsequent sections address amnesty, prosecutions, reparations, and the recently concluded Truth Commission before reaching general conclusions about the Brazilian path towards accountability.

Authoritarian rule and the transition to democracy

Following the 1964 coup d'état that deposed democratically elected President João Goulart, the Brazilian military became part of the Operation Condor network that operated across the Southern Cone (see Chapter 1). Following the precepts of the Cold War national security doctrine, the Brazilian military government used brutal violence to eliminate what it perceived to be internal left-wing subversion. Individuals and organisations on the left were singled out as targets; those deemed enemies of the state were persecuted and tortured; and some were forcibly disappeared. The main political parties were abolished soon after the coup. Student unions were suspended, and the principal labour unions, including the main trade union structure, Comando Geral dos Trabalhadores, were shut down, with hundreds more placed under government administration. In the first few months of authoritarian rule, approximately 10,000 civil servants were removed from their posts, and more than 40,000 people were placed under police investigation (Arns 1985, 61). The first decree issued by the military government after the coup, Institutional Act 1 of 1964, suspended political rights. Over the course of 21 years of dictatorship, an estimated 50,000 people were detained by the military government at one time or another (Gorender 1987, 235).

Two general features distinguished Brazilian authoritarian rule from some of the other authoritarian regimes established in Latin America during the same period. First, Brazil did not have one single dictator. Instead, there were five different presidents and one three-person military junta, during the period of authoritarian rule. The presidents were selected by an electoral college and ratified by the National Congress, giving an appearance of normality and of a civilian–military regime. The second feature was that during military rule the country's regular institutional framework was more or less maintained, although with many adjustments. The National Congress continued to function, although it was suspended a few times. This gave the regime some degree of legality and perhaps even a spurious legitimacy among certain sectors of society. Political participation was restricted, but the fact that elections were held for the National Congress allowed space for a limited form of political expression that was not possible in other Latin American countries under military rule.

In December 1968, the dictatorship switched to a harder line, closing the National Congress in what became known as the 'coup within the coup'. Over the next ten years, during which time the right to *habeas corpus* was widely flouted, the torture of political prisoners became widespread. By 1974, it was known that at least 20 people previously under arrest by the repressive apparatus had disappeared (Arns 1985, 22). Other forms of persecution included loss of political party or union membership or, in the case of students, expulsion or exclusion from state and private secondary schools, colleges, and universities. Secret files were kept on many perceived regime opponents, of all classes and social backgrounds. Those who were the objects of such surveillance found themselves facing a range of difficulties in daily life, especially in the job market (Dallari n.d.). One estimate suggests that by the end of the 1970s, more than half a million people had suffered some form of politically motivated violation, ranging from imprisonment and torture to forcible disappearance, exile, removal from office, or arbitrary prosecution (UEE 1979).

The military government counted heavily on the support of the military justice system to stay in power. Military criminal, procedural, and organisational codes were deployed and/or modified to serve alongside a newly introduced National Security Law from 1969, as a legal basis for the irregularities and abuses practised by the military government. This battery of legal instruments regularised and gave new formal powers to the so-called security agencies, empowering them to arrest any person, redefining crimes against national security, and expanding the jurisdiction of the military justice system to include common crimes such as bank robberies (D'Araujo, Soares, and Castro 1994, 19). Capital punishment was reintroduced in 1969. It was never formally invoked, however: the regime resorted instead to summary execution or secret torture sessions as a method of killing opponents (Fausto 2000, 481).

Elite-controlled political transition

Political transition to democracy in Brazil was a gradual process.[1] It started after the military-appointed president, General Ernesto Geisel, assumed power in 1974 with a promise to initiate a policy of *distensão*, or easing of tension. The next president, General João Figueiredo, introduced an *abertura*, a more definite political opening geared towards redemocratisation. This lasted until 1985. Both periods allowed a certain degree of political liberalisation: political persecution gradually decreased, and political parties created by, and acceptable to, the regime began to operate. The Brazilian dictatorship ended without direct presidential elections. Tancredo Neves, the civilian successor to the last general in power, was chosen indirectly by an electoral college, but he died unexpectedly before taking office. His vice president-elect José Sarney, a former ally of the military, took over as president.

Brazil's slow and negotiated transition to democracy has been described as an agreement between elites. Some former exiles and victims of political persecution were gradually allowed to reclaim a place at the table alongside their more conservative peers, on condition that they abandoned any radical projects or plans. The military gradually withdrew from politics in exchange for civilian politicians' tacit acceptance that military intervention had been necessary. According to Sabadell and Mavilla, 'to shut the door on this period, there was to be a "reciprocal pardon", without any investigation into the violations, or even a humanitarian effort to provide the victims and their families with documentation so they could learn the truth about the events or recover the bodies of the people who died or disappeared' (2003, 108–9, my translation).

It was in this context of conservative, elite-controlled transition, beginning in 1974, that an amnesty law was passed in 1979. Compared to amnesties in neighbouring countries, the law enjoyed possibly unique levels of popular support. It did not come under challenge either during or after the transition, as the idea of amnesty or an amnesty law was understood at the time quite differently in Brazil than in the rest of the region. In Brazil, the law was enacted largely as a result of public pressure, a measure intended to benefit regime opponents and others who were being persecuted. Its initial aim was to facilitate the transition to democratic rule by allowing opponents of the regime to be released from prison and/or to fully re-enter national political and social life. The law was not, in other words, the brainchild of the regime, nor was it initially conceived as a way to benefit regime agents who had committed human rights violations. Lawyers, survivors, and victims' relatives pushed for it as a method to secure democratic freedom for the opposition. In practice, however, the military actively appropriated the amnesty law to preclude criminal prosecution of its own members, even for core atrocity crimes.

Amnesty

Amnesty has a long tradition in Brazilian history as a legal and political instrument. Immediately after the 1964 coup, intellectuals and public figures demanded amnesty for political prisoners and other citizens who had been stripped of their political rights by the military regime. Over the next decade, as the regime detained and imprisoned ever-larger numbers of people, the demand for amnesty to benefit political prisoners spread to broad sectors of the society. This became an important political issue, one that tested the limits of the regime.

In February 1978, the Brazilian Committee for Amnesty (Comitê Brasileiro pela Anistia, CBA), a civil society grouping, was founded to coordinate the push for amnesty. The CBA demanded the immediate pardon and release of all political prisoners and the politically persecuted. It also demanded the cessation of torture, the reinstatement or return to the country of those removed from office or exiled, the investigation of disappearance cases, and the revocation of the National Security Law. These demands, although couched in the language of amnesty, pointedly did not include amnesty for those who had committed human rights violations. In other words, the popular call for amnesty did not imply support for granting impunity to public officials, regime agents, or dictators (CBA 1978). This version of the pro-amnesty movement gradually spread across the country and gained wide-ranging support, both within Brazil and abroad.[2]

In response to this increasingly vocal and popular demand, the National Congress passed the amnesty law (Law 6.683) in August 1979. The law granted amnesty to 'all of those who, in the period between 2 September 1961 and 15 August 1979, committed political crimes' (or 'related' crimes). The law, which makes no mention of torture, was phrased in an elliptical manner and did not provide a definition of political crimes. Those who were found guilty of what the dictatorship considered to be violent crimes (termed 'blood crimes') were excluded from amnesty. This provision, targeted at left-wing opponents of the regime, ruled out amnesty for 'terrorism', robbery, kidnapping, and assault. The amnesty did allow for the immediate release of political prisoners not convicted of the excluded crimes mentioned above. By October 1980, the last political prisoner – as defined by the regime – was set free. The law also provided for the reinstatement of some people previously dismissed or expelled from their jobs and for the return of exiles. Some years later, after transition, the democratic 1988 constitution appeared to reaffirm the amnesty law's validity: Art 3 of the Transitional Constitutional Measures Act (Ato das Disposições Constitucionais Transitórias) repeated the terms of the original law. Indeed, it established categories of survivors whose rights to promotion, pensions, and employment had been abrogated by the dictatorship for exclusively political reasons.

At the time of its enactment in 1979, the amnesty law represented an attempt to re-establish relations between the military and regime opponents, even those who had been removed from office, banished, imprisoned, or exiled. The law invoked notions of pacification and harmonisation of differences. It was seen, even by some regime opponents, as a way to overcome an impasse, thereby contributing to a future transition to democratic rule (Mezarobba 2006, 146–47). In practice, however, the legislation soon acquired implications far removed from those advocated by social movements and human rights defenders, who had not contemplated extending amnesty to the agents of repression. In effect, the regime was able to use support for the idea of amnesty for its own purposes.

In hindsight, then, it seems evident that the Brazilian state's habitual approach to dealing with the dictatorship legacy took shape as early as 1979, with the approval of the amnesty – a law that prioritised oblivion and the negation of truth. Since then, accountability for past crimes in Brazil has continued to be strongly influenced by this logic constructed during the dictatorship. Thus, the concept of amnesty is still widely perceived as valid. The main obstacle to accountability has been the specific manner in which the amnesty law has been interpreted since it came into force: as a guarantee of impunity for state agents who committed grave human rights violations. The next section discusses the implications of this for advances in – or rather, stagnation of – attempted trials and prosecutions for crimes of the past.

Trials

Brazil's legal system is grounded in the civil law tradition. The country's federal political structure means it effectively has a dual system, with legal codes and legislation enacted primarily at the federal (central, national) level, but also by states and municipalities. The Federal Supreme Court (Supremo Tribunal Federal, STF) is the highest national court, responsible for safeguarding the constitution and functioning as a court of review. There is also a Superior Court of Justice (Superior Tribunal de Justiça), created by the 1988 constitution and charged with standardising the interpretation of federal laws and defending the rule of law.

The Public Prosecutor's Office (Ministério Público da União) is an autonomous body, working at both the federal and state levels. It is popularly known as 'the people's defender'. The office is responsible for bringing criminal cases to trial, but its responsibilities also include requesting the judge to acquit a defendant if the public prosecutor becomes convinced of his or her innocence. Although prosecutors are empowered by law to directly conduct criminal investigations, they do so only in major cases, usually involving alleged wrongdoing by police or public officials. They are also in charge of supervising police work and police investigations. In addition to their duties in criminal cases, Brazilian prosecutors are authorised by the constitution to take action against private individuals, commercial enterprises, or federal, state, or municipal authorities where such action is merited to protect minorities, the environment, or the population in general.

Lack of criminal accountability in domestic courts

When it first emerged in 1978, the civil society amnesty movement called for members of the Brazilian security forces to be held criminally responsible for atrocity crimes. Since the end of the dictatorship, however, this demand has gradually disappeared, even from the discourse of many victims' relatives. Very few criminal cases testing the limits of the amnesty appear to have been brought before the judiciary since the law was passed almost four decades ago. This limited history of attempts to pursue criminal justice is partly explained, I would argue, by the lack of faith that survivors and victims' families have in the legal system. However, it also reflects the military regime's success in persuading society to forget about human rights crimes and accept impunity for the perpetrators (Mezarobba 2008). Another, more specifically technical, factor is that serious crimes such as torture and homicide, those that are potentially at issue here, are considered 'crimes of public initiative'. This means that it is up to the Public Prosecutor's Office to initiate such cases and, until very recently, prosecutors failed to act upon or even acknowledge this duty. Private individuals, including victims and relatives, have very limited powers to challenge or attempt to rectify such inaction. Even if they do, their claims must be channelled through the Public Prosecutor's Office itself, which is free to decide whether or not their complaints have merit.

Despite this official inaction, the Brazilian state has been held legally responsible on a number of occasions for the imprisonment, torture, death, or disappearance of victims of political persecution. The first known successful case was in 1973, when eight military and two police officers were sentenced by a military court for torturing 14 soldiers, four of whom died as a result. The military justice system's investigation was initiated at the request of the army minister (Melo 1997, 8). In 1978, in the case of journalist Vladimir Herzog, who was murdered in 1975 while imprisoned in São Paulo, a judge found the state guilty of illegal arrest, of not ensuring the victim's physical and moral integrity, and of torture, requiring the prosecutor to investigate the criminal responsibilities of those involved. This set a precedent, and similar court rulings followed. Some recognised the civil liability of the state, but none assigned criminal responsibility to its agents.

The first reported application of the amnesty law to preclude punishment of alleged perpetrators of human rights violations was in the Superior Military Court (Superior Tribunal Militar, STM) in April 1980. A request was made for the prosecution and punishment of three individuals who, it was alleged, had four years earlier tortured and blinded a political prisoner, Milton Coelho de Carvalho. Although the violence against Carvalho was a matter of record and was recognised as proven in the original military court verdict and in the STM's own verdict, the military judge denied the claim. Hence, with the sole exception of the 1973 case mentioned above, no state agent, either civilian or military, has ever been punished for past crimes.

A very recent trend towards recognising, and attempting to address the criminal responsibility of agents of the military dictatorship period, therefore, represents a significant, although as yet incipient, change to this long history of denial and omission. It seems to reflect a growing awareness on the part of the Public Prosecutor's Office of its responsibilities towards the victims and their families, based on knowledge acquired mainly since the turn of the twenty-first century. The years 2008 and 2009 saw the first initiatives by the Federal Prosecution Service (Ministério Público Federal) to actively investigate the criminal responsibility of former public agents involved in gross human rights violations during the dictatorship. In this period, federal prosecutors initiated several criminal investigations to shed more light on past cases of abduction, disappearance, and murder or summary execution. Data from the end of 2013 indicated that, to that point, the Federal Prosecution Service had initiated almost 200 individual criminal investigations and filed six sets of criminal and/or civil charges involving 11 former agents of the dictatorship. Two of the attempts to file charges were rejected, while four remain under consideration in 2015.

The major domestic legal challenge to date against the general principle of amnesty – unrelated to a particular case – also occurred in 2008. A 'private' group of members of the legal profession, rather than public prosecutors per se, was responsible: the Brazilian Bar Association brought a legal challenge before the

Federal Supreme Court, arguing that continued amnesty for state agents who had committed gross human rights violations during the dictatorship violated 'fundamental constitutional precepts'. In its 2010 response, however, the STF highlighted the bilateral nature of the amnesty and claimed that it was a political settlement, outside the purview of the judicial branch to review.[3]

Turning to the inter-American system

In Brazil, as elsewhere in the region, the lack of response from domestic courts has led some victims to seek redress in the inter-American system. For instance, in 1982, several families filed a liability case in court against the Brazilian state, seeking to clarify the circumstances surrounding the deaths of members of the Araguaia guerrilla movement and the whereabouts of their remains. The Guerrilha do Araguaia was an armed offshoot of the Communist Party of Brazil, formed to resist the military regime. At the beginning of 1972 the group had approximately 70 fighters. The same year, army expeditions were sent to the Araguaia region to wipe out the group. By the end of 1974 their mission was complete: the group had been annihilated, and reports indicate that the bodies of the guerrilla fighters were subsequently exhumed and incinerated or thrown into rivers as part of an official cover-up.

After exhausting all available domestic remedies without achieving a satisfactory outcome in their case, the families appealed in 2001 to the Inter-American Commission on Human Rights (IACHR). The Commission referred the case to the Inter-American Court of Human Rights. In December 2010, the Court concluded that the provisions of the Brazilian amnesty law are not compatible with the American Convention on Human Rights and lack legal effect, thus rendering the law invalid as an obstacle to investigation of the facts and identification and punishment of those responsible. The judgment declared Brazil responsible for the forced disappearance of 62 people between 1972 and 1974, and ordered the state to carry out a criminal investigation of the facts and reveal the truth about the crimes.[4] The Court's October 2014 follow-up report on compliance with the judgment found that although certain aspects, including indemnification and official acknowledgement, had been implemented, the amnesty law was still being allowed to impede investigation and prosecution. The Court also criticised unnecessary delays and difficulties in the still-unsuccessful search for remains.[5] By the end of 2015, no significant new developments had been reported despite the ongoing efforts of a 'Transitional Justice Working Group', set up by state prosecutors immediately after the Inter-American Court sentence specifically to press for compliance with it.

Non-applicability of amnesty to 'continuous crimes'

Thus, arguments against the validity of the amnesty law, or against its applicability to internationally defined atrocity crimes, including torture, have been advanced but have not yet had substantial effect. Recently, however, there are signs of possible movement in regard to arguments based on existing domestic law about so-called 'continuous' or 'ongoing' crimes – that is, crimes that began during, but persisted after, the period covered by the amnesty law. This mainly applies to forced disappearances in which the victim's remains have never been found.

In October 2012, the federal justice system received a complaint from the Federal Prosecution Office of São Paulo against three men (a former colonel, a retired civil police commissioner, and a serving police commissioner) for the 1971 kidnapping of Edgar de Aquino Duarte. Duarte, a former naval fusilier expelled from the armed forces soon after the 1964 coup, was later detained and illegally held prisoner for three years before disappearing in 1973. The complaint utilised the 'continuous crime' rationale: according to a decision by the Ninth Federal Criminal Court of São Paulo, the amnesty law does not apply to the case because the kidnapping is still going on today, and will only end when the victim is released, if he is alive, or when his mortal remains are found.

Following the same line of reasoning, in 2012 prosecutor Otávio Bravo of the military justice system reopened 39 cases of disappearance. Although witness statements indicate that some of the victims were killed under torture, their bodies were never found. This allows for the legal reasoning that the crime of kidnapping is continuing today. Bravo supported this initiative based on three points: the decision in the Araguaia case; the fact that Brazil had recently (in 2010) ratified the International Convention for the Protection of All Persons from Enforced Disappearance; and the decisions of the Federal Supreme Court in two hearings, in 2009 and 2011, regarding the extradition from Brazil of individuals who allegedly participated in dictatorship crimes in Argentina. In Brazilian jurisprudence, the state can only extradite a person if the crime of which he or she is accused is not subject to a statute of limitations that, under Brazilian law, has already expired. In the process, the Federal Supreme Court accepted the precept that enforced disappearance is equivalent to kidnapping. This is considered a continuous crime in Brazil and thus is not subject to a statute of limitations (Virissimo 2012).

Reparations

Whereas little progress has been made to date with respect to criminal justice for past violations, there have been significant efforts in the field of reparations to victims and survivors of repression. Reparations, both economic and symbolic, have been made through both administrative and judicial routes. Administrative reparations programmes were initially targeted mainly at the relatives of victims who were killed or forcibly disappeared, but they were later expanded to include survivors of political persecution. Overall, reparations have been the principal transitional justice measure used by the Brazilian state, as well as the earliest to be pursued in any systematic fashion. The activities of the Special Commission on the Dead and Disappeared for Political Reasons and the Amnesty Commission, discussed below, also expanded the symbolic dimension of reparations through an unexpected truth-telling effect and a deliberate focus on the cultivation of historical memory initiatives. In this way we see signs of a 'domino effect' in which reparations activities, including acknowledgement of responsibility and official apologies, have arguably been part of the groundswell leading to the present growth of truth and justice demands.

During the period of military rule, economic awards for damages were paid to victims, survivors, or their relatives, as ordered by court decisions. Although such cases cannot be considered part of transitional justice processes per se, they set a precedent for recognising the civil liability of the state. A case initiated by torture survivor Walter Alberto Pecoits reached a judgment in 1971, giving him the right to compensation for costs and loss of earnings until his full recovery, as well as to 'a pension that satisfactorily compensates his inability to work'.[6] In 1978, in the Vladimir Herzog case, the Court ordered the Brazilian state to pay damages to the victim's widow and children for the pecuniary loss and for pain and suffering resulting from his death under torture, even though a Military Police inquiry had confirmed the official story of a suicide and the State Attorney's Office accepted this conclusion. Since then, the Brazilian state has been held liable several times for the imprisonment, torture, death, or disappearance of politically persecuted persons (see Mezarobba 2012). Again, all such legal decisions have recognised only the state's civil liability.

Law of the Disappeared

In the Brazilian case, accountability for past crimes, broadly understood, began to move forward after the transition to democracy, with the gradual loss of power of the military and the incorporation of human rights policies into the national agenda. During the first term of Fernando Henrique Cardoso, in 1995, the Law of the Disappeared (Law 9.140) was enacted by the National Congress. The demand for accountability was long-standing, and the law was the outcome of continuous pressure exerted by relatives of the dead and disappeared and by human rights non-governmental organisations. With the passage of the law, the Brazilian state officially recognised, for the first time, its responsibility for the gravest human rights violations that had taken place during the military regime.

The Law of the Disappeared reaffirmed the conciliatory intent – and, by implication, the legitimacy – of the amnesty. However, it also stressed the pursuit of justice and the continuity of the state's responsibilities.[7] Victims' relatives welcomed the government's initiative to deal with the issue of the disappeared, but they expressed some reservations. One was that the law exempted the state from its obligation to identify and ascribe responsibility to those who were directly involved in the practice of torture or in deaths and disappearances. Another was that the burden of proof in each political persecution case fell on the relatives themselves. Relatives also questioned the fact that only families could request recognition of the state's responsibility, making the issue appear to be a series of private grievances rather than a matter of public duty. Several amendments were proposed to the draft law, but none of them were accepted.

The Law of the Disappeared was thus approved in its original form. Under the law, the Brazilian government immediately recognised as dead a total of 136 people who had been recorded as forcibly disappeared for political reasons, and whose names were listed in the law's Appendix I. It was the first time that the state, without a judicial ruling, admitted objective responsibility for the illicit actions of its security agents involved in crimes such as kidnapping, arrest, torture, forced disappearance, and murder. Under the law, family members of the dead and disappeared gained the right to receive compensation from the state, based on a sliding scale. A nominal amount, equivalent at that time to US$3,000, was multiplied by the number of remaining years the disappeared person could have been expected to live. Appendix II of the law contained a table for calculating these payments.

After pressure from victims' relatives, the Law of the Disappeared was modified by two subsequent laws. In 2002, Law 10.536 extended the period for cases to be included by nine more years, that is, up until the new constitution was promulgated in October 1988. In 2004, Law 10.875 allowed the inclusion of victims who were killed in clashes with the police in public demonstrations. It also included those who had committed suicide as a result of political persecution, which included imminent jailing or psychological damage inflicted through 'acts of torture carried out by government agents'.

The Law of the Disappeared can be considered principally a reparations measure, although it had important acknowledgement functions with respect to state responsibility and the status of the disappeared. The law also established a significant truth-telling forum, the Special Commission on the Dead and Disappeared for Political Reasons.

Acknowledging survivors

Although the amnesty law provided a limited right to reinstatement of military personnel and civil servants dismissed for their opposition to the regime, it did not adequately address the multiple kinds of persecution inflicted on such persons. In an example of survivor mobilisation, organised groups of politically persecuted individuals in several states of the country persuaded the government to send to the National Congress a bill providing, among other things, economic reparations for those who had been impeded from practising their professions by the dictatorship. Like the Law of the Disappeared, this initiative was not a response to wide societal demand but resulted from the actions of survivors themselves, with the support of deputies and senators. Law 10.559, which came into force in 2002, met nearly all of their demands.

Law 10.559 recognised five rights held by survivors of political persecution who had subsequently been granted amnesty: the right to a declaration of the condition of *being* politically amnestied; the right to financial reparation; the right to include in the length of service (e.g. for the purpose of calculating a pension) the period during which a person was suspended or blacklisted; the right to finish any programme of study that had been interrupted or to receive accreditation for qualifications obtained overseas during exile; and the right to reinstatement for civil servants, other public employees, and people who had been summarily dismissed, without due process, under emergency legislation. Most importantly, the law spelled out the various types of political persecution measures used by the military regime that should, henceforth, be recognised as a basis for awarding the status of 'politically amnestied person', with its associated entitlements. These victims became known as *anistiados* (amnestied, i.e. people who have already received amnesty) and *anistiáveis* (amnestiable, i.e. people still seeking amnesty).

The financial reparation provided under the law to those eligible is by nature indemnificatory.[8] It can be carried out in either of two ways: as a single payment, set at 30 times the monthly minimum wage for each year of persecution, to those people who, while qualifying, are unable to prove their past employment; or as a permanent and regular monthly payment to those who can prove their employment relationship.[9] The law also stipulates that all politically persecuted persons have a right to receive backdated payments for up to five years before the date on which they first applied for amnesty. However, since the approval of Law 11.354 in 2006, any applicant seeking to exercise this right has to draft a 'declaration of compliance' expressing agreement with the value, manner, and conditions of payment. The applicant must also retract any lawsuits he or she has filed against the state, and agree to refrain from bringing any later legal challenge over the amount received.

Law 10.559 focuses exclusively on reparations for loss of earnings and does not contemplate non-material damages, such as psychological and moral harm. The courts continue to be the only route for pursuit of these latter demands.

Activating survivor reparations: the Amnesty Commission

In August 2001, even before Law 10.559 was finally approved, the Amnesty Commission (Comissão de Anistia) was formed. Operating under the Ministry of Justice, the Commission receives and processes applications for recognition of *anistiado* status. Relatives can apply in cases where the original survivor has died. Along with copies of personal documents, the applications must contain information on the politically persecuted person's professional life. Where it is not possible to include the documentary evidence required, the applicant can request that the Commission take steps to obtain it. All applications must spell out which rights or entitlements are being claimed, and on what grounds (i.e. the circumstances under which the affected person was victimised). The two-dozen official commissioners are not remunerated for their work. By law, the Commission must always include one representative nominated by the Ministry of Defence and another nominated by survivors' groups. The Commission generally acts with more flexibility than the judicial branch, making broad and non-restrictive interpretations of the claims received.

In the period 2001–10, the Amnesty Commission received 68,517 applications and adjudicated 57,628; of these, it granted 38,025 and denied the rest. Among the requests granted, 13,571 included some sort of financial reparation (Comissão de Anistia 2010). The formal awarding of the status of 'politically amnestied person' is announced in the official public gazette, *Diário Oficial da União*, just as it was during the dictatorship.

In addition to their economic effect, the reparation functions of the Amnesty Commission have led to some measure of truth-telling, providing another example of how the various dimensions of transitional justice are interrelated. In order to assess requests for amnesty, commissioners must gather a significant amount of information, including witness statements and documents, some of which originated from authoritarian-era repressive agencies. Since 2008, the Commission has also organised 'amnesty caravans' as part of an outreach programme to recover, debate, and reflect on the country's recent history. Each caravan includes cultural seminars, public hearings, and the adjudication of applications for amnesty. As of June 2014, 86 such caravans had been organised around the country.

The Brazilian state, then, has made some progress in meeting its obligation to offer reparations in both economic and symbolic terms. Throughout 2014, the year of the 50th anniversary of the coup, multiple official and unofficial events such as debates, exhibitions, and launches of books and films about the dictatorship took place around the country and abroad.

Truth-finding

Despite the absence of criminal accountability for human rights violations, there have been significant efforts to establish the facts regarding these violations. Truth-finding in Brazil has unfolded in two main phases. In the first phase, beginning immediately after the transition to democratic rule, efforts by social movements, civil society groups, and churches predominated. In the second phase, formal, state-sponsored efforts were added to the continuing efforts of non-state entities. The second phase included a full truth commission, which was proposed under the presidency of Lula da Silva and carried out under the first presidency of Dilma Rousseff.

Early attempts at truth-finding: civil society groups and churches take the lead

During the last part of the dictatorship, with the state unwilling to investigate human rights violations committed by its agents, an unofficial truth investigation was mounted under the auspices of the Catholic Archdiocese of São Paulo and the World Council of Churches, without the government's knowledge or support.[10] From 1979 on, files from the military justice system were secretly copied and smuggled out of the country by defence lawyers. In 1985, just months after the return to civilian rule, the results of the investigation were published as a book titled *Brasil: Nunca mais* (*Brazil: Never Again*). Based on a substantial body of evidence, collected during proceedings of the Superior Military Court and through recordings of denunciations of torture made by prisoners appearing before military courts, the report revealed how the system of repression had operated (Arns 1985). It included a list of 125 victims of politically motivated disappearance. *Brasil: Nunca mais* quickly became a bestseller in Brazil and was for many years the only authoritative, although not government-supported, narrative of human rights violations. Soon after its publication, a list of 444 military torturers was made public by the press, but neither the report nor this list of names generated any specific demand for an end to impunity. In spite of the efforts made, particularly by the relatives of the dead and disappeared, the situation remained unchanged for several years.

The Special Commission on the Dead and Disappeared for Political Reasons

The state-run Special Commission on the Dead and Disappeared for Political Reasons (Comissão Especial sobre Mortos e Desaparecidos Políticos, CEMDP) was created in 1996 by the Law of the Disappeared to formally recognise those murdered by the dictatorship. Its members were appointed by the president and included representatives from victims' families, the armed forces, the Federal Prosecution Service, the Foreign Ministry, the Human Rights Commission of the Chamber of Deputies, and civil society organisations. The CEMDP's mandate was to officially acknowledge individual cases of disappearance that were not listed in Appendix I of the Law of the Disappeared, locate their bodies, and assess requests for compensation under Art 10 of the law. Families of disappeared persons not previously acknowledged had 120 days from the date the law entered into force to submit applications, although additional evidence could be added subsequently. The CEMDP examined denunciations of politically motivated deaths and deaths by unnatural causes occurring in police facilities or 'similar facilities' between 2 September 1961 and 15 August 1979.[11] Importantly, the CEMDP interpreted 'similar facilities' as a juridical-political (rather than physical) concept, arguing that the state's responsibility must be recognised in each case where a non-natural death happened to a victim in state custody, irrespective of the location where he or she was held.

The CEMDP concentrated initially on obtaining death certificates for victims at civil registry offices. The 1996 legislation, like similar legislation passed elsewhere in the region, created a new category: death certificates could now make special reference to the Law of the Disappeared, given that the usual means of certifying an officially recognised cause of death were not available. Previously, the amnesty law had only allowed for a 'declaration of absence' in regard to disappeared persons. This amounted to a certificate of presumption of death, for the purposes of dissolving marriages and resolving inheritance issues, but the new certificates were regarded as a more permanent, or more acceptable, solution.

In the first phase of its work, the CEMDP analysed 339 possible cases of death or politically motivated disappearance in addition to the 136 the state had already recognised in Appendix I of the 1995 law. It concluded this stage in 2006, with 118 cases dismissed on the grounds that they lacked merit. The CEMDP did not investigate or try those responsible; it only analysed the circumstances surrounding the deaths, attempting to determine whether the victims had been killed by state agents and, if so, how this happened. In 2006, the CEMDP began collecting blood samples from victims' relatives to set up a DNA databank. This was done in an attempt to improve scientific accuracy in the identification of skeletons and any other mortal remains that might be uncovered in future. To date, the CEMDP continues to gather information on the possible location of clandestine graves in cities and rural areas where militants are likely to be buried, especially in the region of the Araguaia River.

The CEMDP's contribution to truth did not go unnoticed. In 2007, the Special Human Rights Department of the Brazilian Presidency (Secretaria Especial dos Direitos Humanos) published *Direito à memória e à verdade* (*Right to Memory and Truth*), which summarises the work of the CEMDP and presents the stories of fatal victims of the dictatorship. This book is the first official document of the Brazilian state that attributes to members of the security forces crimes such as torture, rape, dismemberment, decapitation, concealment of corpses, and the murder of opponents who were already in jail and, therefore, defenceless. These accounts also disproved earlier official propaganda stating that victims had committed suicide or had been killed while attempting to escape or during armed confrontation with the police. The book refers explicitly to 'state terror', stating that the victims 'died in struggle, as opponents of a regime that came about through violation of the democratic constitutional order' (Secretaria Especial dos Direitos Humanos 2007, 30, my translation). It is quite critical of past interpretations of the amnesty law that exclude investigation of such cases.

The CEMDP was set up as an agency of the Brazilian state, not of a particular government administration. Compared to the Amnesty Commission, which is also an official body, it has operated more independently of the government. Its results have both been accepted by successive governments and entered into the official record. It has had some impact on public opinion. Relatives received reparations if their loved one's case was acknowledged. Nonetheless, together with human rights groups, relatives' groups continued to campaign for an official truth commission that would also address crimes against survivors

Late truth: a state-sponsored truth commission

During President Lula da Silva's administration, a working group was created to draft a law that would establish an official, government-sponsored truth commission.[12] The commitment of then minister of human rights Paulo Vannuchi, a survivor of the dictatorship who had also worked on the church-sponsored Nunca Mais project, was crucial in creating the working group, drafting the bill, and pushing for its passage. With strong support from sectors of civil society and from human rights groups, the Brazilian Truth Commission Law (Law 12.528) was approved unanimously at the end of Lula's last term, in November 2011. On 16 May 2012, President Rousseff launched the National Truth Commission (Comissão Nacional da Verdade, CNV) in a ceremony attended by her four civilian predecessors in the presidency.

The CNV's overriding objectives, according to Law 12.528, were to 'realise the right to historical memory and truth, and promote national reconciliation'.[13] In her speech, President Rousseff, herself a former political prisoner and a victim of torture, called upon all Brazilians to understand and acknowledge the country's full history:

> Ignoring history does not pacify; on the contrary, it keeps sorrow and rancour latent. Disinformation does not help to appease – it only enables intolerance to flourish. Shadows and lies cannot promote peace. Brazil deserves the truth. The new generations deserve the truth and, more than anything, those who lost friends and relatives, and who continue suffering as if they were dying again and again, every single day, deserve the factual truth.
>
> (Rousseff 2012; my translation)

The CNV's mandate included clarifying cases of torture, forced disappearances, and concealment of corpses, even if the crimes were committed outside Brazil; identifying the perpetrators, where possible; revealing the structures, locations, institutions, circumstances, and social consequences of grave human rights violations; and forwarding to the relevant public bodies (such as the prosecutors' office or judiciary) all information that could be helpful in locating the mortal remains of victims. Although the law covered crimes carried out between 1946 and 1988, a period bookended by the adoption of two democratic constitutions, the CNV's members decided to focus their efforts on the dictatorship years, from 1964 to 1985. Totally independent of the government, the Truth Commission was empowered to name perpetrators, compel testimony, and subpoena officials, including military officials. Its mandate also included recommending public policy reforms.

The CNV was composed of seven members, appointed by the president for a period of two years. Its members were required to be persons identified with the defence of democracy and constitutional institutions, and with respect for human rights. Beginning in May 2012, the CNV's staff was organised into 13 working groups, each studying a distinct theme such as gender violence, the treatment of indigenous groups, or actions against the Araguaia guerrillas. Over the course of its work, the CNV was linked with 217 collaborators, including researchers, consultants, volunteers, and administrative personnel. The Commission conducted or supported 80 public hearings and audiences in the federal district and in 14 of the 26 states of the country. The creation of the CNV made explicit a latent demand for truth, and about 100 other truth commissions were set up around the country.

The CNV signed collaboration agreements with 43 of these state or institutional commissions. Despite this wide reach, occasional criticisms were raised about lack of transparency and participatory mechanisms in the operations of the CNV.

Its mandating law enabled the CNV to coordinate its work with other public agencies, especially with the National Archives, the CEMDP, and the Amnesty Commission. Official sources of information were also consulted. Although the files of the armed forces from the dictatorship era had been mostly destroyed, the Truth Commission did not have to start from scratch. Some significant official archives have been located and opened since 1989. Millions of previously secret documents from the National Information Service (Serviço Nacional de Informações) and the Foreign Ministry and Federal Police, for example, were sent to the National Archives, where the CNV was able to access them. The CNV worked principally by examining existing accounts and documents rather than by holding oral public hearings to gather new evidence. Only 1,116 new testimonies were collected by CNV up to October 2014 (CNV 2014, vol. 1, 55). This was controversial among survivors, who had hoped for a more accessible public forum.

The CNV's mandate, initially set to expire in May 2014, was extended by President Rousseff until December of that year at the request of survivors and relatives. The Truth Commission's final report, released on 10 December 2014, disclosed the names of 377 perpetrators of atrocities, including the five dictatorship-era presidents plus the three members of the military junta that ruled the country between 31 August and 30 October 1969. Although the CNV did not have the legal authority to put defendants on trial, and had no prosecutorial power, its final report argued that the amnesty law should not apply to the named individuals because of the grave nature of the crimes they committed. In other words, it supported the argument that crimes against humanity cannot be subject to statutes of limitations or amnesty. The final report explicitly recommended that the relevant public bodies determine the legal responsibility – criminal, civil, and administrative – of the public officials involved in gross human rights violations that occurred during the period investigated.

Conclusions

Like other countries in Latin America, Brazil has experienced both advances and setbacks in its movement towards accountability for past human rights violations. Overshadowing all progress, however, is the fact that compliance with the state's obligation to prosecute atrocity crimes, including torture, is still pending. As of 2015, not a single perpetrator has been imprisoned for crimes committed during the dictatorship, except for the 1973 case mentioned earlier in this chapter. This situation continues despite the Inter-American Court ruling of November 2010, which stated that the provisions of the Brazilian amnesty law that prevent the investigation and punishment of serious human rights violations are not compatible with the American Convention, have no legal effect, and should not impede investigation of the facts. At the beginning of 2015, however, after reviewing the

National Truth Commission's report, the Federal Prosecution Service announced that it would start new criminal cases against state agents involved in dictatorship crimes. In early 2015, for the first time, several criminal claims were pending before the judiciary, despite the obstacles presented by the amnesty law.

Reparations, by contrast, are a dimension of accountability that has been relatively well addressed under the 1995 Law of the Disappeared and subsequent legislation. The expansion of beneficiaries in 2002 and 2004 was well received by relatives of the victims. The CEMDP has made significant efforts to promote accountability through truth-telling, in particular by expanding the state's responsibility for deaths of persons in custody through an emphasis on the concept of 'similar facilities'. But the CEMDP did not manage to achieve its goal of determining the whereabouts of victims. The Amnesty Commission has also advanced social acknowledgement and truth-telling, as well as symbolic and material reparations. However, Brazil still has a long way to go in recognising and fulfilling the rights to reparation of those once held to be enemies of the state.

For example, the 2002 law expanding reparations to survivors only applies to those who qualify for, and are prepared to go through the procedure of applying for, the status of *anistiado* (amnestied person). The fact that this term continues in common use can be seen as perpetuating the euphemistic language of transition or even the perverse logic of the dictatorship. According to the evidence available, Brazil is the only country in our sample that has managed to construct a logic by which victims, rather than perpetrators, must actively apply for amnesty. Furthermore, the rights of some categories of people affected by grave human rights violations, such as torture, are overlooked, and it may be no coincidence that the word 'victim' did not even appear in official discourse until 2011 (when it occurred in the law that created the National Truth Commission).

Indeed, 30 years after the end of the dictatorship, transitional justice has unfolded essentially on the terms envisaged by the military, in line with the negotiated, gradual path of the transition itself. It is no exaggeration to speak of a logic of amnesia constructed by the dictatorship. How else can one explain why the current reparations legislation allows much greater monetary compensation to the politically persecuted, who are able to demonstrate loss of income, than to the families of the dictatorship's fatal victims? How else are we to understand the fact that the National Security Law, dating from the military regime, remains in force? This logic of amnesia is only very slowly dissipating.

Apart from relatively small groups of relatives or survivors, Brazilian civil society has been largely absent from the accountability debate since 1979. It has only recently started to become involved, especially through truth and memory initiatives. In terms of prospects for the future, half of today's Brazilian population is under 30 and has no living memory of, or stake in, the dictatorship. They struggle to survive in a society marked by high rates of violence, where access to justice is still precarious. Supported by the findings and recommendations of the National Truth Commission, the process of accountability for past crimes could gain a new impetus, enabling Brazil to begin deconstructing the logic of forgetfulness. The

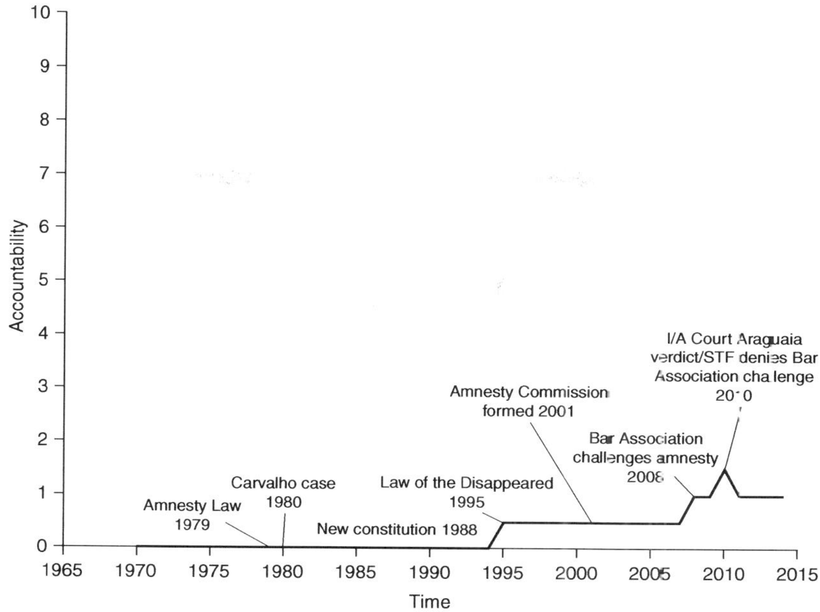

Figure 5.1 Brazil: the overcoming amnesty dimension of accountability, 1979–2014
Source: Authors' construction, 2015.

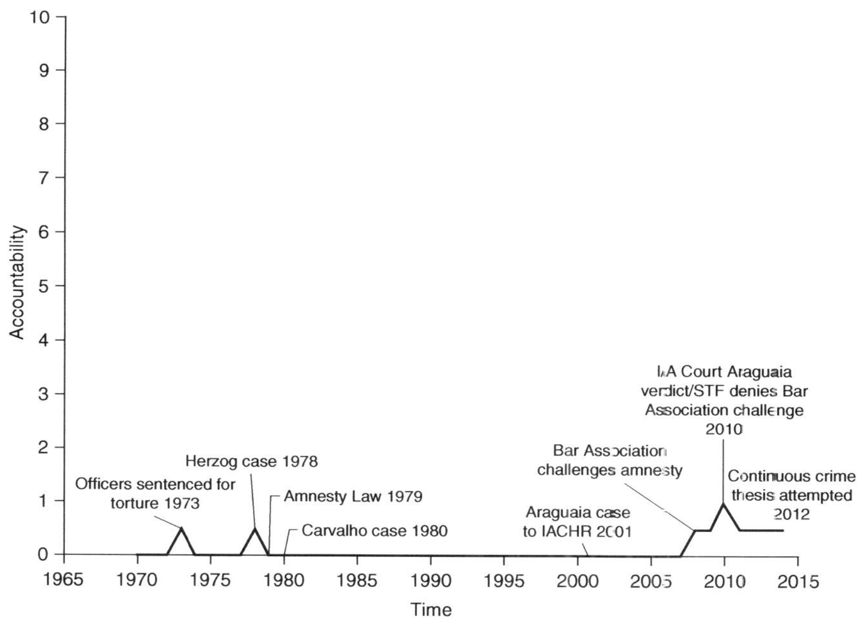

Figure 5.2 Brazil: the trials dimension of accountability, 1979–2014
Source: Authors' construction, 2015.

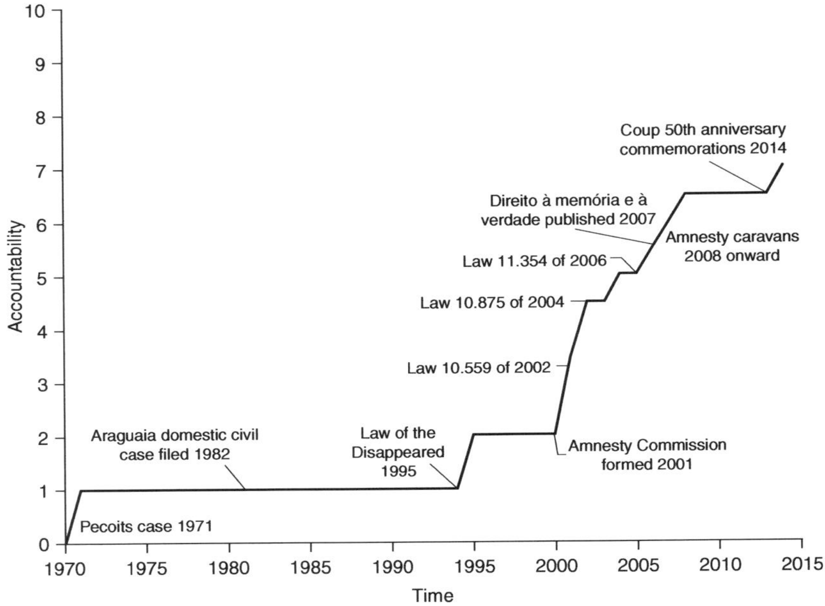

Figure 5.3 Brazil: the reparations dimension of accountability, 1979–2014
Source: Authors' construction, 2015.

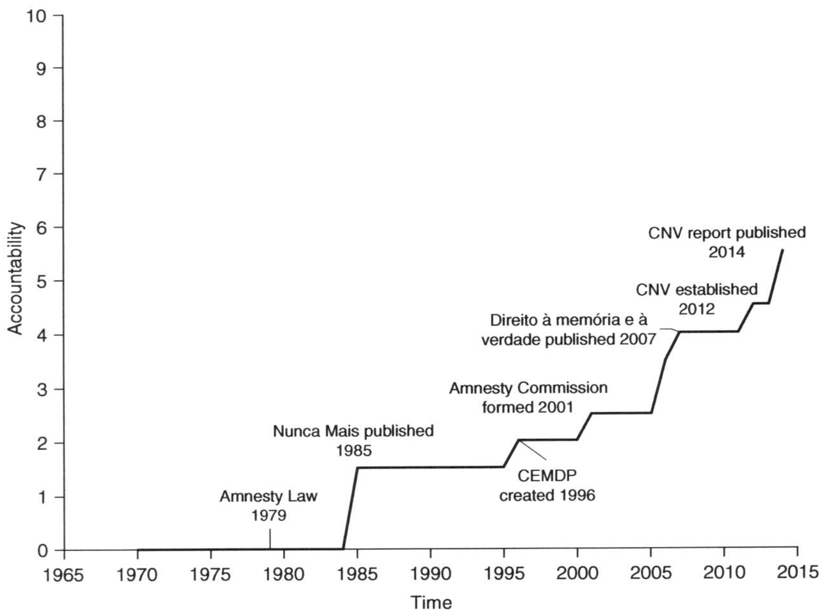

Figure 5.4 Brazil: the truth dimension of accountability, 1979–2014
Source: Authors' construction, 2015.

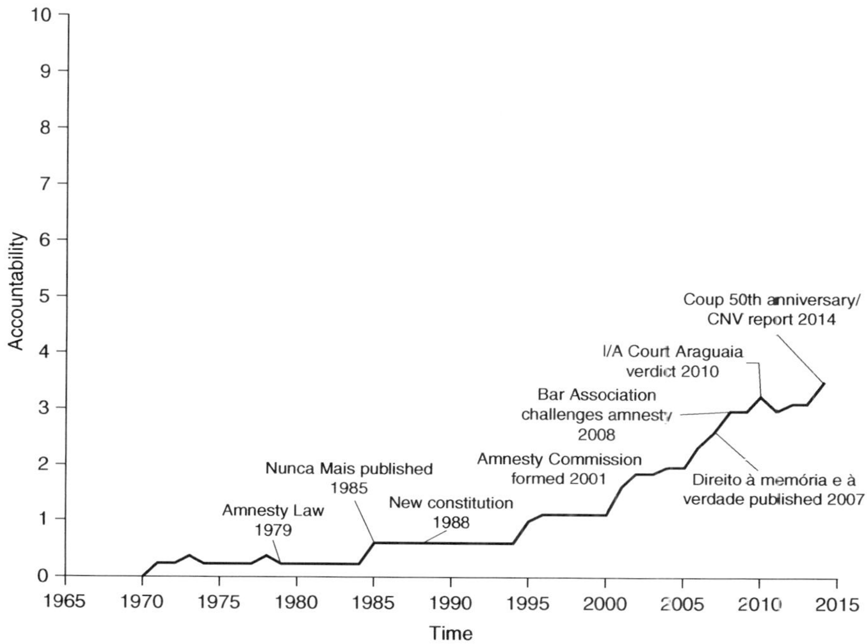

Figure 5.5 Brazil: overall trend towards accountability, 1979–2014
Source: Authors' construction, 2015.

challenge is to make clear, for a mainstream population concerned with political corruption and 'ordinary' violence, the connection between the past and the present in order to construct a better future.

Notes

* The author thanks Professor Roberto Marcondes Cesar Jr. for all his help.

1 See Stepan (1986), Sallum (1996), and Soares, D'Araujo, and Castro (1995) for more detailed accounts.

2 One of the many Brazilian entities that supported the pro-amnesty movement was the National Conference of Brazilian Bishops (Conferência Nacional dos Bispos do Brasil). The CBA office in Paris, for its part, sent an open letter to the Brazilian government protesting the dictatorship's crimes and demanding general and unrestricted amnesty. Simone de Beauvoir, Julio Cortázar, Gabriel García Márquez, Jean-Luc Godard, François Jacob, Alfred Kastler, Alain Resnais, and Jean-Paul Sartre were among the 5,000 intellectuals and artists who signed the letter (Greco 2003, 266).

3 Supremo Tribunal Federal, verdict in Argüição de Descumprimento de Preceito Fundamental (ADPF) no. 153, April 2010. The ADPF recourse is an extraordinary measure designed to allow the STF to rule on major constitutionality issues arising from introduction of the 1988 constitution.

4 Inter-American Court of Human Rights (I/A Court HR), *Case of Gomes Lund et al. ('Guerrilha do Araguaia') v Brazil*, Judgment of 24 November 2010.
5 I/A Court HR, *Case of Gomes Lund et al. ('Guerrilha do Araguaia') v Brazil*, Monitoring Compliance with Judgment, 17 October 2014.
6 In August 1964, Pecoits, a surgeon, former mayor, and impeached deputy, was detained for interrogation, during which he was assaulted and blinded in his left eye. Ordered by the judiciary to pay damages, the state appealed but ended up losing after the decision was ratified by the Federal Supreme Court. Note by rapporteur Judge Oswaldo Trigueiro, Tribunal de Justiça, Recurso Extraordinário, Apelação 214–70 (Curitiba, 14 November 1979); Supremo Tribunal Federal, Recurso extraordinário 71.729, Paraná (Brasília, 8 June 1971).
7 That is, new rulers inherit from their predecessors active responsibility or liability for the commission of a past violation, at least until such time as the new rulers act to recognise the illegality of that violation. At that point, of course, they acquire distinct responsibilities, such as that of investigation and prosecution of the violation (see Robertson 2000).
8 Claims for compensation cannot be made by all survivors. According to Law 10.559, only individuals prevented for exclusively political reasons from conducting economic activities can make these applications.
9 In the second option, the value of this payment – essentially a lifelong monthly pension – generally corresponds to the remuneration that the victim could expect to receive if he or she were employed. It is established based on evidence presented by the applicant, information from official bodies, and market research, taking into account the survivor's profile. In any case, the value of the monthly payments cannot be below the national minimum wage nor above the ceiling set by the constitution for remuneration of civil servants.
10 An international fellowship of Protestant churches with headquarters in Geneva, the World Council of Churches was key in supporting human rights work in other Latin American countries, including Chile.
11 Law 10.559 covered the same time period as the amnesty law. The legislature considered that the Brazilian constitutional order had already been broken on 2 September 1961, when a military intervention tried to interrupt the tenure of Vice President João Goulart after the resignation of President Jânio Quadros (January–August 1961).
12 The author advised on preparation of the draft bill that established the National Truth Commission. In this capacity she led part of the dialogue with the Ministry of Defence and the armed forces and coordinated research on gender violence and sexual violence during the military dictatorship.
13 My translation. The text of the law is available in Portuguese on the Brazilian presidency website, www.planalto.gov.br/ccivil_03/_Ato2011-2014/2011/Lei/L12528.htm.

References

Arns, Dom Paulo Evaristo. 1985. *Brasil: Nunca mais*. Petrópolis, Brazil: Vozes.

CBA (Comitê Brasileiro pela Anistia). 1978. *Carta de princípios e programa mínimo de ação*. São Paulo: Arquivo da Fundação Perseu Abramo.

CNV (Comissão Nacional da Verdade). 2014. *Relatório da Comissão Nacional da Verdade*. 3 vols. Brasília: CNV. http://www.cnv.gov.br/.

Comissão de Anistia. 2010. *Relatório anual da Comissão de Anistia 2010*. Brasília: Ministério da Justiça.

Dallari, Dalmo de Abreu. n.d. *Anistia e restauração de direitos*. São Paulo: Comitê Brasileiro pela Anistia.

D'Araujo, Maria Celina, Gláucio A. D. Soares, and Celso Castro. 1994. *Os anos de chumbo: A memória militar sobre a repressão*. Rio de Janeiro: Relume Dumará.

Fausto, Boris. 2000. *História do Brasil*. São Paulo: Universidade de São Paulo.

Gorender, Jacob. 1987. *Combate nas trevas*. São Paulo: Ática.

Greco, Heloisa. 2003. 'Dimensões fundacionais da luta pela anistia.' PhD diss., Universidade Federal de Minas Gerais.

Melo, Murilo Fiuza de. 1997. 'Ditadura condenou torturadores.' *Jornal do Brasil*, 25 May.

Mezarobba, Glenda. 2006. *Um acerto de contas com o futuro – A anistia e suas consequências: Um estudo do caso brasileiro*. São Paulo: Humanitas/FAPESP.

——2008. 'O preço do esquecimento: as reparações pagas às vítimas do regime militar – uma comparação entre Brasil, Argentina e Chile.' PhD diss., Universidade de São Paulo.

——2012. 'Brazil.' In *Encyclopedia of Transitional Justice*, edited by Lavinia Stan and Nadya Nedelsky, vol. 2, 67–73. Cambridge: Cambridge University Press.

Robertson, Geoffrey. 2000. *Crimes Against Humanity: The Struggle for Global Justice*. New York: New Press.

Rousseff, Dilma. 2012. 'Discurso da Presidenta da República, Dilma Rousseff, na cerimônia de instalação da Comissão da Verdade.' Speech delivered at Palácio do Planalto, Brasília, 16 May.

Sabadell, Ana Lucia, and Olga Espinoza Mavilla, eds. 2003. *Elaboração jurídico-penal do passado após mudança do sistema político em diversos países: Relatório Brasil*. São Paulo: Instituto Brasileiro de Ciências Criminais/IBCCRIM.

Sallum, Brasilio Jr. 1996. *Labirintos: Dos generais à Nova República*. São Paulo: Hucitec.

Secretaria Especial dos Direitos Humanos. 2007. *Direito à memória e à verdade: Comissão Especial sobre Mortos e Desaparecidos Políticos*. Brasília: Secretaria Especial dos Direitos Humanos.

Soares, Gláucio Ary Dillon, Maria Celina D'Araujo, and Celso Castro. 1995. *A volta aos quartéis: A memória militar sobre a abertura*. Rio de Janeiro: Relume Dumará.

Stepan, Alfred. 1986. *Os militares: Da abertura à Nova República*. Rio de Janeiro: Paz e Terra.

UEE (União Estadual dos Estudantes). 1979. *Caderno da anistia*. São Paulo: Arquivo da Fundação Perseu Abramo.

Virissimo, Vivian. 2012. 'Promotor militar explica tese jurídica que abre brecha na Lei da Anistia.' *Sul 21*, 1 April.

Chapter 6

Chile

Incremental truth, late justice

*Cath Collins with Boris Hau**

Chile is one of the classic cases of post-authoritarian transition. The excessive caution of its early transitional justice trajectory gradually gave way to what some now consider to be a success story of incrementalism. The formal justice dimension of the 1990 transitional settlement was notably truncated, but substantial changes occurred after 1998. Although right-wing political figures and the armed forces initially opposed these changes vigorously, their veto power diminished substantially over the first decade of transition. Generational replacement and attitudinal change also had an effect, and by 2014 the political right showed signs of at least considering a definitive break with its authoritarian past.

Today Chile arguably ranks second only to Argentina at the regional forefront of domestic accountability for past crimes. In terms of the present-day context in which transitional justice operates, Chile is the only country of our nine country sample, and indeed the only country in South America, that is a member of the club of free-market developed economies, having been admitted in 2010 to the Organisation for Economic Co-operation and Development. The country's macroeconomic indicators[1] certainly place it ahead of much of the rest of South America, although inequality remains a cause for concern and an occasional source of social unrest. Such relative prosperity, however, means that remaining transitional justice challenges, particularly in reparations, must be considered a product of lack of political will rather than fiscal incapacity. The social mobilisation of recent years has also begun to explicitly question an economic model and constitution that are increasingly seen as authoritarian-era legacies ripe for change.

The Pinochet regime

Until 1973, Chile was one of the more economically and politically developed and stable countries of the region, with a constitutionalist tradition and an almost complete lack of military intervention in politics. The armed forces nevertheless seized power on 11 September 1973, overthrowing an elected socialist government. The ensuing right-wing military regime headed by General Augusto Pinochet would remain in power for 17 years. Pinochet came to represent the archetypal Latin

American dictator, and his authoritarian regime was both transformational and brutal. Dictatorship-era violence was carried out almost exclusively by the state. Political opposition was decimated through classic police state tactics: forced disappearance, extrajudicial execution, and torture. Between September 1973 and December 1989, at least 3,216 people were killed or forcibly disappeared, and 38,254 more survived political imprisonment and torture.[2] Most victims were male, under 30 years old, of left-wing political affiliation or active in trade unions and other forms of social organising or civil resistance.

Most regime-perpetrated fatal violence was concentrated in the five-year period immediately following the coup. Clandestine torture and extermination centres were set up across the country, and a shadowy political police force systematically targeted members of left-wing parties and groups, all by then operating underground. Other manifestations of repression included politically motivated blacklisting and forced or self-imposed exile. Up to 200,000 people left the country between 1973 and 1990, many never to return (Collins 2010b; Lira and Loveman 2005). The legislature was suspended, and emergency powers, almost continuously renewed, restricted civil and political rights for the duration of the regime. The regime also implemented a radical neo-liberal economic restructuring, enshrined in a 1980 authoritarian constitution that in some important respects survives to the present day (C. Huneeus 2007; Barros 2002).

Formal democratisation and the return of elected government occurred in 1990, after presidential and legislative elections were held in 1989 according to the timetable set by the military regime. These led to the election of a centrist Christian Democrat president at the head of a centre-left coalition, the Concertación, which treated human rights violations as a major campaign issue. Serious political violence and violations largely ceased at the point of transition. Early truth and reparations measures were carried out, but in the justice sphere, a pre-existing amnesty law was preserved. There was minimal change to existing legal and normative frameworks, with no purges of the security forces or public administration. The balance of power in the Senate was held by elected or designated right-wing representatives sympathetic to the Pinochet regime.

Relatives and survivors who expected vigorous transitional justice action saw their hopes go largely unmet under four consecutive Concertación presidencies (Patricio Aylwin, 1990–94; Eduardo Frei Ruiz-Tagle, 1994–2000; Ricardo Lagos, 2000–6; and Michelle Bachelet, 2006–10). Chile did, however, ratify a series of human rights instruments over the period, after acceding to the inter-American human rights system in August 1990.[3] It also carried out a major judicial reform package beginning in 1996, creating space within which transitional justice efforts would later take root. The Chilean judiciary's receptivity to international law is tempered by a certain sense of self-sufficient exceptionalism, but has been demonstrably advanced through cases for past crimes (A. Huneeus 2010; Collins 2013b).

In 2010, the right-wing Alianza coalition won presidential elections, ushering in a four-year interregnum under President Sebastián Piñera. Michelle Bachelet was, however, returned for a second presidential term beginning in 2014, leading a modified version of the Concertación coalition. The 2013 election campaign coincided with significant anniversaries, including the 40th anniversary of the military coup and the 15th anniversary of Pinochet's 1998 arrest in the United Kingdom. The atmosphere surrounding these events demonstrated that the country still grapples with questions of historical memory connected to its transitional justice trajectory (Collins, Hite, and Joignant 2013).

Current transitional justice dynamics play out within a framework of ostensibly solid, rights-compliant structures that, nonetheless, have hidden drawbacks. Chile has a National Human Rights Institute, inaugurated in 2010, but no official rights ombudsman. The national courts are open to privately initiated criminal or civil claims for dictatorship-era crimes brought by relatives or survivors. A smaller, but growing, number of cases have been brought *ex officio* since 2011. But a 1978 amnesty decree law remains technically in place, although it is currently set aside for episodes classified as continuous crimes, war crimes, and crimes against humanity.

Truth recovery: truth without judicial consequences

Truth recovery in Chile initially consisted of unofficial rather than official measures, with human rights defenders amassing an unparalleled repository of documentation about repression as it happened. Exceptionally, for the region and perhaps the world, official activities added to the mix after transition have included two official truth commissions. One focused on deaths and disappearances, the other on survivors. Notably, the later commission tried to divest truth of judicial consequences: equally notable civil society activism has begun to challenge this state of affairs.

Chile's first official truth commission, the National Commission on Truth and Reconciliation (Comisión Nacional de Verdad y Reconciliación, CNVR), is known as the Rettig Commission after its chairman, Raúl Rettig. It was convened in 1990 to study grave human rights violations and acts of politically motivated state and non-state violence committed between September 1973 and 10 March 1990. Its initial report, issued in 1991, named 2,298 individual victims of death and forced disappearance, but it did not name survivors of torture, although it acknowledged widespread use of the practice. The report attributed 88.1 per cent of deaths or disappearances to 'state agents or persons acting in their service'; 7.3 per cent to agents of 'unknown' affiliation; and the remaining 4.6 per cent to non-state (including left-wing) actors (CNVR 2007). A successor body, the National Corporation for Reparations and Reconciliation (Corporación Nacional de Reparación y Reconciliación, CNRR), was to complete an assessment of still-pending individual cases, locate the disappeared, and administer reparations to relatives of those named. In 1996 the CNRR added almost 900 names, giving a cumulative total of 3,195 recognised victims of death and disappearance at that time. The final fate and whereabouts of 1,183 of the 3,195 remained unknown (CNRR 1996).[4]

This first phase of truth recovery was connected to reparations and, in theory, to justice: Rettig and CNRR archives were placed at the disposition of the judicial branch. This action brought no prosecution and punishment, as both were precluded by amnesty, but it did attempt to turn the courts into an auxiliary truth mechanism. President Aylwin invited the courts to apply an interpretation of amnesty long argued by human rights defenders, according to which its correct point of application would be after full investigation. This initiative did not prosper, since most judges simply ignored this request. Nonetheless, the Rettig Commission, unlike subsequent measures, left open a connecting door between truth and justice.

A second official initiative in truth recovery was the Mesa de Diálogo (roundtable dialogue), set up in August 1999 and culminating in 2001 (Government of Chile 2001). The Mesa was not a truth commission but a negotiating exercise carried out between the government and the armed forces, with the participation of some human rights lawyers and the Catholic Church, to resolve the problem of the remaining disappeared. The Mesa was built around the belief that only continued protection from judicial consequences would encourage informants to tell what they knew. It also perpetuated the myth that the security forces were not institutionally to blame and held no institutional information about the disappeared. Accordingly, armed forces representatives participating in the Mesa did not directly volunteer information. Instead, a six-month phase of data-gathering was opened during which churches, the armed forces, and the police were to pass on information about the disappeared offered by individuals under cover of secrecy and anonymity.

The outcome was a list, published in January 2001, naming only a few dozen victims and claiming that most had been 'thrown into the sea'. Some of the information provided was later disproved in the course of unrelated judicial investigations, while evidence also emerged of censorship to remove references to family members of serving officers. Associations of victims' relatives felt vindicated in having refused to take part in the Mesa.

The third official initiative was Chile's second truth commission, the National Commission on Political Imprisonment and Torture (Comisión Nacional sobre Prisión Política y Tortura), announced by President Lagos in 2003. Known as the Valech Commission after its chairman, it was the centrepiece of a broader human rights policy called No Hay Mañana sin Ayer (No Tomorrow Without Yesterday) (Government of Chile 2003). The Valech Commission operated between 2004 and 2005 and received testimony in Chile and abroad, from or on behalf of people who had survived detention or torture by state agents during the dictatorship.

The Commission's final report, published in 2004, and annex, published in 2005, catalogued horrific practices, including the torture of children and the sexual assault of pregnant women (CNPPT 2005). The immediate media impact was perhaps even greater than that of the Rettig Commission in its day. Reparations were updated and extended to the almost 30,000 individuals named. The experience also galvanised some survivors to form autonomous associations, which later pressed for more action. Formal justice implications, however, were deliberately ruled out: all Valech testimony and supporting documentation was subject to a strict 50-year embargo, also applicable to judges. Legal custody of the archives was given to the (then-pending) National Human Rights Institute, and they were eventually placed in a sealed vault in the Museum of Memory and Human Rights, inaugurated in 2010. This sealing off of judicial consequences, justified as necessary to protect survivors' privacy, provoked sharp criticism from some, who were angered at being offered 'more truth' instead of full justice. The measure later came under legal challenge, as explained below.

As with Rettig, the time-limited dynamic and narrow remit of Valech unleashed demands that could not be fully satisfied. Accordingly, and for reasons explored in more depth below, a second iteration of both was carried out in 2011. The awkwardly titled Presidential Advisory Commission for the Classification of Detained-Disappeared Persons, Victims of Political Execution and Victims of Political Imprisonment and Torture became popularly known as Valech II. It was not a full truth commission but a reopening of the Rettig and Valech lists. Cases previously considered 'not proven' could be resubmitted if new information had emerged; cases not submitted previously could also be presented. Valech II, which lasted for 18 months, began under President Bachelet but concluded under the right-wing presidency of Piñera. This undoubtedly contributed to the muted official reception when its lists, published in August 2011, added 9,795 people to the Valech survivors' list and 30 people to the rolls of the dead and disappeared (Comisión Asesora Presidencial 2011).

Certain aspects of Valech II gave rise to bitter complaints among survivors, including the much lower rate of acceptance of cases submitted when compared to Valech I. The attempt to make it the definitive round of classification was also challenged by survivors, demonstrating new levels of awareness of, and familiarity with, the vocabulary of rights and entitlement rather than benefits or concessions.[5] Its status as a truth-producing authority for wider society was questionable, since it only published lists of names plus statistical appendices. Nonetheless, in classifying two ex-agents as torture survivors, Valech II opened up an uncomfortable debate, already under way in other countries, by demonstrating that victim and perpetrator were not mutually exclusive categories. This led to questioning of the automatic link between inclusion on the list and access to reparations, showing that the principle of entitlement based on victimisation alone – rather than on moral approbation or personal or group affinity – had still not entirely prevailed among survivors' associations.

A broad and deep stratum of civil society initiatives underlies, motivates, and shapes official measures in all dimensions of Chile's transitional justice trajectory. Official truth-telling was brought about by, and still coexists with, a continuous outpouring of rich, conflicting unofficial accounts of repression and its present-day consequences. These include narratives, testimonies given in and out of court, films, artistic expressions, exile accounts, archives of churches and non-governmental organisations (NGOs), oral histories, academic and independent research, and investigative journalism. They feature heroic, self-serving, and self-exculpatory accounts and confessions ranging from the tragic to the defiant and grotesque. Clustered around significant dates and events such as anniversaries, deaths, exhumations, and judicial revelations, these declarations of unofficial truths are intimately connected to the institutional milestones and official measures related in the earlier part of this chapter. A war of words, facts, and interpretations continues to be fought in Chile over issues as apparently straightforward as whether this was or was not a dictatorship and whether its atrocities were or were not crimes. The sources and versions multiplied further in late 2013, around the 40th anniversary of the 1973 coup. The debate has widened in scope to incorporate questions about collusion and moral responsibility on the part of civilian politicians, business leaders, and media magnates who benefited from the regime (Winn et al. 2014; Observatorio DDHH 2013b; Collins, Hite, and Joignant 2013).

In this context, official truth-telling, while substantial, is still deficient in certain aspects. The Rettig Commission produced relatively little new information about individual cases.[6] There was an absence of justice follow-up, as we have seen, and Aylwin proved reluctant to press the matter of openly dismissive and defiant responses by the armed forces and the judicial branch to the final published report (Collins and Fuentes 2012). Nonetheless, the report represented a first official acknowledgement of human rights violations, particularly significant in a setting where official lies and propaganda had previously been the order of the day. The fact that the commissioners unanimously endorsed the report's findings was also important, since four of the nine were known supporters of the military regime. Valech and Valech II expanded formal truth-telling to take account of individual survivors. They nonetheless represented a step backward from Rettig in at least two ways. The truth they produced was neither complete nor publicly accessible, and it was deliberately insulated from justice, through legislated secrecy, just as the courts had finally begun to respond to justice demands.

Chile's official truth initiatives have rarely been in synch with other signals sent by official action and inaction, and they have not led to clear, consistent official repudiation of the authoritarian government and its crimes. When Pinochet died in 2006, he was denied a state funeral but granted full military honours at a ceremony attended by the defence minister. Not until 2010 did the country boast a state-funded museum that told the story of the period.

Official truth-telling has also been sporadic, with each iteration dissolved as soon as its immediate mandate is completed. Victim lists have not been consolidated over time, and trial outcomes that contradict or complement past accounts have not been incorporated. Truth recovery, in sum, has been more reactive than proactive. Actions have been taken in response to competing pressures, with grassroots groups advocating for more truth, countered by military and right-wing actors' preference for self-justification or silence. Truth measures also sometimes appear to be offered as a substitute for more decisive justice action.

Reparations measures: addressing irreparable harm

This section focuses on policy measures clearly demarcated as reparations. It is, therefore, limited, as noted in Chapter 1, to measures with a preponderant state component. This definition necessarily leaves aside vital developments in Chile's memory landscape in the same period, other than those whose official sponsorship was so substantial that they can be classed as symbolic reparations.[7] Civil claims in the courts are included in the discussion insofar as they intersect with the economic dimension of reparations.

Administrative reparations programmes were perhaps the most substantial and complete of the Concertación's early transitional justice initiatives. Specific economic and symbolic entitlements were offered, incrementally, to relatives of the disappeared (mostly after Rettig, from 1991); returning exiles (between 1990 and 1994); almost all categories of directly and indirectly affected victims, including human rights defenders (specialist mental health support and access to the public health system, from 1991 on); blacklisted workers (pension credits and/or top-ups, from 1993); some former political prisoners (expunging of spurious criminal records, in 2004 and 2007); and acknowledged survivors (from 2004).[8] Economic reparations through the judicial rather than administrative route also emerged as a possibility after 1998.

By 2004, the full menu of economic measures deployed included pensions and lump-sum payments, regularisation of social security contributions, access to regular and specialised health services, customs concessions for returnees, housing subsidies, partial or full scholarships for secondary or tertiary education, and the restoration of confiscated assets – although not all measures were offered either from the beginning, or to all categories of affected persons.

The symbolic or moral components and counterparts of these economic measures included exemption from compulsory military service for children and grandchildren of direct victims, the restoration of voting and candidature rights to former political prisoners, and the identification and return of remains to family members. Memorialisation also became increasingly important and visible over time, although private initiative has remained more significant than public impetus in this area. Only one early project – a wall of names of the dead and disappeared, inaugurated in the capital's General Cemetery in 1994 – was fully state-funded, although the state human rights programme later began to offer logistical and financial support to private (civil society) initiatives.

Official measures orientated towards society as a whole – guarantees of non-repetition – clustered in two main periods. Over several years beginning in 1990, Chile ratified a series of human rights treaties, as noted above. Much later, in 2009, it ratified the Rome Statute of the International Criminal Court. That same year, initiatives first announced in 2003, including the National Human Rights Institute and the Museum of Memory and Human Rights, were finally set in motion. The long delays were largely due to right-wing opposition. Further changes to reparations measures in recent years have been limited to tinkering with amounts, extending entitlement to new categories of people (such as survivors, after Valech), and, periodically, reacting to some minor scandal by announcing a clampdown on supposedly 'false' victims.[9] Civil claims, more prevalent after 2000, also began to be treated by the courts as an independent channel of access to reparations, which, it was argued, must be provided alongside administrative programmes.

The passage of time has made clear that reparations were designed without thought to life-cycle issues or the possibility of multiple victimisations. They seem to reflect the supposition that cash transfers would allow people to meet their needs through the market. These weaknesses could face criticism based on emerging international standards regarding adequacy and sufficiency in reparations. Indeed, Chile's second adverse Inter-American Court of Human Rights verdict for dictatorship-era crimes came in a case alleging inadequacy of reparations (the García Lucero case).[10]

Negative interactions between measures have emerged over time, as have gaps in information and access. Negative interactions include insistence by state legal representatives that civil claims be forfeited where administrative reparations have previously been received, or the requirement that survivors who were subject to more than one form of victimisation that now carries a pension entitlement (e.g. individuals who were blacklisted for political reasons but also imprisoned and subjected to torture) receive only one of those entitlements. Only some pension entitlements, moreover, can be inherited by dependants after the person's death. Gaps include the fact that, in keeping with Chile's e-government drive, outcomes of Valech II were published exclusively on a web page, an outlet particularly ill-suited to the age and socio-economic profile of the most vulnerable users of reparations. The job of helping people gain access to entitlements, within often arbitrary application deadlines, has fallen principally to civil society: reparations services have been piecemeal and geographically scattered, with no single point of access. The Human Rights Programme, which provides social work assistance to relatives, is not open to survivors. Some offices in charge of reparations are now defunct, leaving the responsibility to the state benefits office, Instituto de Previsión Social, which has no specialised knowledge in this area.

Chile's administrative reparations programme nonetheless scores relatively highly in both absolute and comparative terms for its gradual expansion of reach and its fit between proposals and delivery. The Program of Reparations and Comprehensive Health Care (Programa de Reparación y Atención Integral en Salud, PRAIS) is often cited internationally as an example of best practice. Nonetheless, PRAIS's virtues mainly lie in service beyond the call of duty by its dedicated staff, many themselves survivors or relatives (Lira and Loveman 2005). Nor should PRAIS in its entirety be considered reparations: strictly speaking, other than specialist counselling, it only offers access to the lowest tier of the – generally poor – public health system for direct and indirect victims, relatives, survivors, human rights defenders, and their family groups. Delivery of basic health care according to need is an economic and social rights entitlement, rather than the redressing of specific harm as part of an acknowledgement process. Official language surrounding reparations still uses a vocabulary of 'benefits' rather than 'entitlements', weakening the consistent message of recognition and apology that Correa (2012) insists should be one yardstick of appropriate reparations.

Self-amnesty: the war of attrition against impunity

Chile's amnesty law, Decree Law 2.191, was introduced by the regime in 1978 and is still in force. The law as enacted was strikingly broad, referring to all 'criminal acts' (*hechos delictuosos*) committed between 11 September 1973 and 10 March 1978.[11] It attempted to dissolve criminal responsibility for crimes committed in the first five years of the dictatorship, the period that had the highest incidence of serious violations.

The law was applied routinely and vigorously by military and regular courts both before and immediately after transition, as we will see below. This broad application has only gradually been limited since 1998, by interpretive (judicial) means. As of mid-2015 there have been no legislative changes to, or revocations of, the amnesty law. Before 2004, the only prosecutions that could take place were those that exploited specific exceptions, loopholes, and temporal exclusions, focusing, for example, on the smaller but still significant number of repressive crimes that took place after the 1978 decree. Since 2004, however, court rulings have made significant inroads into the law, reducing its applicability to crimes committed within its four-and-a-half-year temporal range.

Higher courts gradually came to accept an argument put forward by human rights defenders since the law's inception: that war crimes and crimes against humanity cannot be amnestied. This logic was reinforced by the Inter-American Court of Human Rights ruling in the Almonacid case in 2006, which described the decree law as an illegitimate 'self-amnesty', designed, above all, to dissolve the responsibility of state agents for state harms constitutive of internationally prohibited human rights violations; as such, the law was deemed incompatible with Chile's international obligations.[12] Today, dictatorship-era terror crimes can be successfully prosecuted where any or all of the following circumstances apply: the crime is specifically excluded from the text of the decree law; the crime was committed after 10 March 1978; the crime is a forced disappearance (treated as kidnapping, i.e. as a continuous crime); or the crime constitutes a war crime or crime against humanity. If a bill currently before the legislature in 2015 becomes law,[13] these interpretations, which are currently a stable majority preference in Chile's higher courts, should become obligatory. If such a law is not enacted, the fact that the amnesty statute remains in place will leave this shift at least theoretically susceptible to reversal if judicial opinion changes.

Between 1973 and 1990, the Chilean courts' deference to and complicity with the regime, including rejection of almost 10,000 *habeas corpus* writs over the period, made it unthinkable that they would hold the security forces to account even before amnesty offered a pretext for inaction. Military courts routinely claimed jurisdiction over incidents connected with security operations, only to pre-emptively apply amnesty. At transition in 1990, hundreds of cases had been permanently closed or temporarily suspended. The challenge for human rights lawyers over the subsequent decade was twofold: to get the files into the ordinary (non-military) court system and to prod that system into action. The process began haltingly in the early to mid-1990s, with lower courts acting in isolated cases. However, it was often impeded by Supreme Court reaffirmations of amnesty and/or by reassertion of military jurisdiction. It was not until after 1998 that the principles of civilian jurisdiction and of non-amnestiability of the gravest crimes began to make noticeable inroads into impunity.

The changes in interpretation of amnesty since 1990 can be divided into four phases, distinguished by shifts that emerged or became consolidated in each period. In the first phase, crimes excluded from amnesty in the text of the legislation were finally successfully prosecuted, leading to guilty verdicts against two former political police chiefs in the Orlando Letelier assassination case in 1993, confirmed in 1995. Next, crimes committed in the 1980s, beyond the temporal reach of amnesty, were investigated, as they could and should have been during the dictatorship itself. This strategy proved the most likely to produce proportionate sentences, with a handful of life terms handed down.

In a third phase, courts began to accept a thesis previously argued by human rights lawyers (though often, and mistakenly, attributed to Pinochet case judge Juan Guzmán). In the case of a person who disappeared before 1978 but remained missing after that date, the post-1978 'portion' of the disappearance could still be prosecuted under the charge of kidnapping. Kidnapping, the closest charge in the domestic criminal code to forcible disappearance, begins when a person is forcibly deprived of his or her liberty and does not cease until the person is returned or their whereabouts become known. Since 1990, lawyers and courts have proposed a variety of interpretations of these cases: that for the still-disappeared, this cessation never happened; that it happened at transition in 1990; that it happened in 1991, with the Rettig report; or that the applicability of kidnapping charges had ceased if it was demonstrated that the victim had been freed (or, more likely, killed) in the interim. In all except the last case, those responsible could be held to have 'still been committing' kidnap at some time after the March 1978 date on which amnesty protection lapsed. The high-water mark of this phase came in the 2004 Sandoval case, the first in which the Supreme Court upheld the 'continuous crime' thesis as the main basis for conviction.[14] Finally, since 2004, crimes constituting war crimes or crimes against humanity are considered non-amnestiable, removing them from reach of the decree even if they were committed before March 1978.

These four phases were not a tidy, inexorable ratcheting up towards further accountability, nor do they represent consistent planning or strategy on the part of one identifiable key actor or set of actors. Only the fourth phase, moreover, rests explicitly on principles of international, rather than solely domestic, law. Each phase contained internal setbacks, and none is irreversible. In July 2013, for example, the Supreme Court suddenly refused to recognise kidnapping as a continuous crime. The refusal did not lead to amnesty in that instance, but only because the case was still recognised as a crime against humanity.

Majorities on the five-person criminal bench of the Supreme Court accepting pro-accountability arguments have been slim and changeable. Principles that appear to be established can suffer rollbacks. In 2014 and 2015, for example, a series of cases classified by the Rettig Commission as political executions were dismissed because a judge concluded they were not crimes against humanity. On the whole, however, amnesty and statutes of limitations are no longer being applied in the automatic fashion that previously underwrote impunity.

The amnesty decree law's contribution to accountability is clearly a negative one, as was intended. Interpretive narrowing since the late 1990s, while significant, has only addressed war crimes and crimes against humanity and has not ruled on the law's legitimacy or constitutionality. Calls for repeal or annulment are often resisted using the argument that there is no need to alter a statute that is not being applied in practice.[15] The 2006 Almonacid verdict accordingly found little echo with political authorities, who made an initial promise of compliance but then delayed a full eight years before sponsoring a bill that 'interprets' the criminal code in such a way as to bring the amnesty law in line with international obligations. The making of a promise, followed by a long hiatus during which it is not fulfilled, has been characteristic of the amnesty debate, as has been the ambiguous language of 'interpretation' and 'compatibility' rather than repeal or annulment.

The text of the draft bill, as submitted in late 2014, explicitly states that it would not modify or do away with the existing amnesty law but merely clarify its scope and limits – limits that would have been observed from the start had the law been correctly applied. This approach, known as an 'interpretive law', modifies the criminal code rather than the amnesty law itself. The justification is to avoid accusations of retroactive changes to law, an always controversial practice – though, like so much else considered unthinkable in Chilean transitional justice, carried out in neighbouring Argentina. The bill also offers a face-saving device to right-wing legislators, who would not be asked to directly vote down the existing law. However, as the new bill also explicitly rules out full or partial statutes of limitations for criminal and civil claims, it remains doubtful what proportion of the political right could be persuaded to lend parliamentary support. The prospect of the draft ever becoming law receded even further in July 2015, when its executive sponsorship was withdrawn without explanation. With the fate of the bill uncertain, judicial interpretation, rather than executive or legislative action, continues to provide the principal impetus for overcoming the impunity-producing effects of amnesty.

Judicial accountability for past crimes: justice for all?

It is important to note that crimes associated with dictatorship-era human rights violations in Chile are initially handled under the investigative magistrate system, which was phased out in the mid-1990s for other kinds of cases. In this written system, based on the accumulation of documentary proofs in a case file rather than a series of adversarial, court-based hearings, a single judge investigates, brings charges, and delivers an initial verdict. This can then be appealed to the criminal bench of the district appeal court; the case may also be reviewed by the five-person criminal bench of the Supreme Court. Individuals directly affected by crimes can trigger an investigation by submitting a complaint (*querella*) to one of about 30 specialised human rights case magistrates, depending on the region of the country where the crime occurred. In recent years, judges have also allowed relatives' associations and the state Human Rights Programme to initiate such cases (Collins 2010a). Criminal investigations initiated by private complaint can occur with or without associated claims for civil damages (see below). Those initiated *ex officio*, or by the state Human Rights Programme, cannot contain a civil claim against the state.

Criminal prosecution of dictatorship-era crimes received a major new impetus in 1998. This was driven, like almost all previous transitional justice changes, by campaigning and legal activism on the part of a small, ageing, but persistent band of relatives, human rights groups, and lawyers.[16] Although occasional newsworthy moments, including the 1998 Pinochet arrest, riveted national attention, there was no mass movement clamouring for accountability. Nor did the government or the judiciary spontaneously decide to pursue different policies. What happened was rather a small but significant shift in receptivity by judicial actors to privately sponsored legal actions. In early 1998, criminal complaints against Pinochet himself were admitted for the first time. Their number swelled to a flood by the end of the year after Pinochet's unexpected detention in the United Kingdom on torture charges levelled from Spain (Brett 2009; Roht-Arriaza 2005). Once Pinochet returned home in 2000, sporting a triumphalist demeanour that gave the lie to his supposedly faded mental faculties, a reformed Supreme Court showed less tolerance for the former dictator's misdeeds.[17] In March 2000, Pinochet was stripped of parliamentary immunity for the first time. In December that year he was charged with 15 counts of kidnap and 55 counts of murder in a case known as the 'Caravan of Death'.

Legal claims had not previously focused on Pinochet. Dusty case files in NGO offices and court archives, supplemented in the 1990s by testimony from returning exiles, instead covered a multitude of other sins and sinners. The paltry information about disappearances provided to the Mesa de Diálogo had the unintended consequence of reviving, rather than pre-empting, judicial activity. In June 2001, nine senior judges were designated to work exclusively, and 51 preferentially, on human rights cases. These included cases for individuals mentioned in the Mesa information, but crucially they also included all outstanding similar cases from around the country. The judicial designations were renewed and expanded in 2002 and 2004. Beginning in 2010, a Supreme Court judge was assigned as coordinator for human rights cases, a role taken on in 2014 by the Court president himself.

Juridical obstacles previously treated as insurmountable were overcome through creative interpretation and strategic litigation. Cases were recovered from military courts, which eventually ceased to contest jurisdiction. The governmental Human Rights Programme began to proactively assist relatives with legal cases around disappearances and, later, executions. In 2000, the first verdicts were delivered in these reopened cases. Case numbers also continued to grow, as relatives' groups adopted a goal that every recognised victim of death or disappearance should have his or her case investigated in this new phase of credible, if still highly imperfect, justice.

As of 1 December 2015, just over 1,048 criminal investigations remained open, with around 150 more completed since 1998. No more than 150 of these open cases were for torture that the victim survived: the vast majority were for deaths and disappearances; most had been initiated by relatives rather than state authorities. The five recurring criminal charges successfully brought were kidnapping, homicide, criminal conspiracy, ill treatment (torture), and illegal burial of remains. One hundred and sixty-three individuals were either serving or had served prison sentences for their part in those crimes, while 181 more former agents had been definitively convicted but given non-custodial sentences. Around 1,029 living former military or security service employees were under formal investigation or subject to convictions with appeals still pending. Many were charged with multiple offences.[18]

In 1998, the principal socio-political obstacles to formal accountability through the courts were apathy, excessive caution, and apprehension about political consequences. The three main legal obstacles were statutes of limitations (also referred to as 'prescription'), double jeopardy (*cosa juzgada*), and the amnesty decree law. From 2002 onward, the Supreme Court began to use national, and then international, law precepts to set aside these obstacles. In this they followed the lead of case litigators: human rights case lawyers, usually poorly paid or not paid at all, who took up or continued cases after 1998. Defendants also had lawyers and legal strategy, but their previously untouchable status was under serious threat, and their invocations of amnesty were increasingly rejected. The double jeopardy argument, contending that former agents had already been 'tried' via perfunctory military court procedures, was finally demolished by the Supreme Court in 2010. A major remaining obstacle is the protracted time frame of the resulting investigations. Less than 15 per cent of cases opened or reopened since 1998 had reached a conclusion by mid-2015 (Observatory case data), and many survivors, relatives, and perpetrators have not lived to see the outcomes.

Relatives, survivors, and lawyers have, however, found or won over allies in state institutions. The Human Rights Programme and the state forensic service (Servicio Médico Legal, SML) are good examples. Led since 2006 by an experienced pathologist who is also a survivor, the SML invested heavily in cultivating the confidence of relatives and survivors without compromising due process, educating judges in the correct use of scientific evidence, and training local medical examiners in international protocols for the collection of evidence in torture cases.

Cases for past crimes offered opportunities to familiarise new young technicians and senior judges alike with international and regional human rights standards. Judicial branch learning is still limited, however, by the fact that such cases are predominantly seen by the small cohort of designated judges, who vary widely in their own predispositions or levels of acceptance of human rights principles. Human rights case judges, moreover, are not held in universal esteem among their colleagues, some of whom reportedly treat them with a mixture of suspicion and disdain.[19]

The outsider status that comes with being agents of accountability in a largely indifferent system has also affected the specialised human rights brigade of the detective police (Policía de Investigaciones, PDI). Initially part of a wider Internal Affairs Unit, the brigade was formed in the early 1990s by a far-sighted official. It accumulated information and testimony from an eclectic group of former agents and returned exiles while – and often because – the amnesty law blocked prosecutions. The success of investigative magistrates in recent cases owes much to the detectives who work alongside them. Cultivating informants and low-level ex-collaborators allowed detectives to track down auxiliary personnel, such as the mechanics who had serviced airplanes from which political prisoners were thrown alive into the sea. Likewise, mismatches between credible testimony about disposal sites and the absence of remains at those places led detectives to discover military cover-up operations to rebury remains just before the 1990 transition. This rendered a group of younger officers, some still serving, susceptible to threat of prosecution since their crimes, though minor, had happened more than a decade after the protection offered by amnesty had expired. Younger agents' knowledge was, therefore, valuable but potentially self-incriminating. Detectives accordingly applied a mix of handling techniques and basic human psychology. They exploited historical grudges held by the uniformed police (Carabineros) against the military and played lower ranks of all forces off against officers, who were resented because they were better protected by the armed forces once prosecutions began.[20]

Policing successes, however, were uneven and fragile. Cooperation with relatives' associations improved measurably in the first few years after 1998, when cases made demonstrable progress. The associations, however, resented subsequent slowdowns. They were also suspicious of the PDI's need to cultivate relationships with agents, as information gaps narrowed to facts that only perpetrators might know. The brigade also became a victim of its own success. When cases began to threaten serving military officers, direct and indirect pressure was brought to bear, with experienced brigade commanders reassigned or sidelined. The turnover of investigative magistrates also undermined some carefully constructed police strategies. For example, when (now deceased) judge Víctor Montiglio took over one case, he immediately charged almost all the former agents named in the file. Some had previously been treated as informants rather than suspects, and some had been given explicit guarantees to that effect. Word spread among other potential informants, and this disincentive became one of several factors that reduced the truth-producing potential of trials after 2007.

Proportionality of sentencing: 'half prescription', prison conditions, and early release

Each minor breakthrough in creating accountability through the criminal process in Chile has been met by subsequent retrenchment. When judicial disinclination to prosecute started to be overcome, amnesty and institutional silence were the next lines of defence. Next, a mixture of intimidation and political pressure was used to impede investigation, protect higher and serving officials, and keep information hidden. Currently, when conviction and sentencing cannot be avoided completely, lenient sentencing, luxurious prison conditions, and early release have been used to cushion the blow. The most substantial criminal sentences of the new period came between 2004 and mid-2007, after which there was a steep decline in their severity. This came from revival of a formula called 'half prescription', allowing sentences to be reduced significantly in cases where over half the allotted statute of limitations period for the crime had elapsed. This action contradicts the courts' acceptance that prescription, per se, cannot apply. The option seems to have no justification other than as a compromise to resolve divergent judicial views about the acceptability of conviction.[21] Since 2007, only around 35 per cent of final sentences have included time in prison.[22] This leniency seems clearly disproportionate to the gravity of the offences.

Lenient sentences have fuelled informal justice initiatives, including street-based denunciations of former agents at their homes and workplaces, carried out since the mid-2000s by flash mobs summoned through social networking. This activity, known as *funa*, has equivalents around the region. Its existence demonstrates that popular or community-level justice can be more confrontational and denunciatory than the reconciliation-based models that restorative justice theories often espouse. *Funa* also highlights the inevitable selectivity of formal prosecutions, as it tends instead to target civilian collaborators and others considered morally, even if not legally, culpable.

Prison conditions and benefits are another bone of contention. In 2012 and 2013, an apparently routine practice of granting early release to convicted perpetrators came to light. Relatives' associations pressed sympathetic parliamentarians to table motions demanding the outlawing of such benefits, along with other privileges including the payment of full military pensions to perpetrators and their detention in relatively luxurious special facilities. Although currently serving military officers have learned to maintain some critical distance from the legacy of the regime, many retain instinctive sympathies for their elderly former comrades. Unexpectedly, however, the right-wing Piñera government closed one of the special facilities in 2013, triggering the suicide of an inmate. The aftermath saw an apparent parting of the ways between the military and the civilian political right, at least over the issue of prisoner treatment.

Judicial treatment of civil claims

Civil claims were initially viewed with ambivalence by relatives and survivors, but since 2010, they have become more common. The state's response reveals clearly the contradictory attitudes that still prevail in official circles, whether between the judicial branch and other state actors or within the judicial branch itself. Civil claimants for damages can sue the individual perpetrator and/or the state. In either case, at appeals level, the case may be heard by one of two specialised benches in the relevant district appellate court. The distribution depends on whether the claim is made as part of a criminal case, in which case it goes to the criminal bench, or as a separate, stand-alone civil claim, in which case it goes to the constitutional bench. Constitutional benches have regularly dismissed stand-alone civil claims, invoking prescription. This view is supported by the Consejo de Defensa del Estado, a statutory agency representing government legal interests that has supported criminal prosecution but opposed civil liability. In this way, the state has stepped back in exclusively civil cases from the acknowledgement of state responsibility that the truth commissions supposedly provided.

Where civil and criminal aspects of a case have been seen together, criminal benches have given varied responses. Some have refused to rule on the civil part of a claim, asserting that it is beyond their purview. Others have awarded substantial damages. Still others have drawn an apparently artificial distinction between prescription for criminal actions – ruled out in cases of crimes against humanity – and prescription of the civil liability aspect of the same case, which has been accepted.

These inconsistent judicial criteria produce an appearance of juridical insecurity, generally frowned upon by legal professionals, whatever their views about the matter at hand. An attempt to have a full sitting of the Supreme Court resolve the matter in early 2013 did not succeed. The full sitting of the Court found that prescription could be applied to civil (not criminal) liability, although it made a small concession regarding calculation of the date of admissibility of actions.[23] Precedent is not, however, binding in the Chilean judicial system, and although pronouncements of the full Court are by convention afforded a certain weight, on this occasion the Court's position was simply ignored by the next criminal bench verdict on the issue. The bench duly awarded damages, adding for good measure that judicial and administrative reparations should not be considered mutually exclusive and that damages could therefore be sought even where pensions had previously been paid. In early 2015, discrepancies were finally resolved in a pro-accountability manner: a little-noticed administrative declaration by the Supreme Court channelled all types of civil claims to the criminal bench.

In Chile's notably legalistic culture, court pronouncements are widely looked to even if or when the justice system as a whole is not particularly well respected.[24] In the specific area of past crimes, although perpetrators have attempted to discredit judicial verdicts as motivated by personal animosity or judicial radicalism, these accusations are not taken seriously by anyone familiar with the Chilean courts. Accordingly, this criticism has not led to widespread public discounting of verdicts. Revisionism, outright denial, and claims that convicted perpetrators are 'political prisoners' jailed for 'serving the country' have been largely confined to a small fringe group, one with which the mainstream right does not want to be publicly associated. In an opinion poll carried out by the Universidad Diego Portales in 2009, the majority of respondents said that trials for dictatorship-era crimes ought to continue (59 per cent) and believed that Pinochet and his civilian collaborators had been fully cognisant of the regime's crimes (75 per cent) (UDP 2009).

Extensive time-series work by Carlos Huneeus suggests a similar, though far from dramatic, evolution towards a critical view of the regime and its crimes.[25] The causal effect, if any, of trials on social repudiation is hard to disentangle, however, and the public profile of trials undoubtedly diminished after Pinochet's death in late 2006. The written nature of the process, with no oral sessions in court, eliminated courtroom drama. Chile's trials never evoked the same level of public interest as trials in Argentina, where crowds lined the Plaza de Mayo in Buenos Aires to await a verdict in the ESMA case in 2011.[26] The high point of public catharsis in Chile was probably the second jailing of ex-general Manuel Contreras, former chief of the 1973–77 iteration of the political police, in 2005. Contreras was hauled ignominiously to Santiago's central court in handcuffs to be notified of a guilty verdict in the Sandoval case after he had failed to attend court, coolly choosing instead to give a television interview from his home. Various relatives and survivors cite those images as the event that finally convinced them domestic justice was possible, seven years after the first complaints of the new phase and the Pinochet case in Spain.

Incidents such as the discovery of remains, or scandals over early release, do still make national news. The quest for national and international visibility has partly motivated recent cases for well-known victims such as Víctor Jara, Salvador Allende, and Pablo Neruda. Although cases broadened somewhat in 2014 to investigate some civilians, including well-known right-wing politicians, it remains unlikely that major new revelations will emerge from ongoing judicial processes. The return of Bachelet in 2014 for a second presidential term was expected by some to lead to a revival of truth and memory initiatives. However, her second administration was quickly overtaken by other preoccupations, including cross-party corruption scandals and calls for a new constitution. The first confrontation over past accountability, a 2015 hunger strike by former political prisoners demanding improved reparations, met with a muted and distant official response. Political will, or at least political prioritisation of accountability, has remained notably lower than in Argentina.

Conclusions

Chile began its return to democracy with an almost unbroken legacy of impunity for extensive human rights violations. Its highly controlled transition, with

Pinochet remaining at the head of the army, made it unlikely that these issues would be comprehensively addressed, at least initially. The negative example of neighbouring Argentina, where trials sparked military unrest, persuaded Chile's centre-left government to renounce the search for criminal justice. Instead, it pursued a low-key transitional justice process focused on truth and reparations, which did not encroach unduly on entrenched military and right-wing interests. Persevering human rights defenders and relatives continued to press for more truth, justice, and unambiguous acknowledgement of past terror practices, but they were undermined by growing social invisibility. In a context of relatively high levels of 'stateness' and institutional solidity, other issues occupied the public policy agenda. Transitional justice questions only occasionally, and uncomfortably, intruded into the self-ascribed success story of the Chilean transition.

The year 1998, however, proved to be a critical juncture. Judicial reforms left the still-conservative judiciary slightly more open to private claim-bringing. The fallout from Pinochet's arrest and 500-day detention in London, meanwhile, exceeded the capacity of the government and military to contain a groundswell of justice demands and memory activism.

New truth-telling initiatives were controversial in attempting to seal off justice channels, and the expansion of reparations was regarded as relatively ungenerous. Formal justice is, therefore, the dimension of Chile's transitional justice package that has seen most change since 1998, even though it still falls short of the ideal-type construct of accountability as active state fulfilment of international obligations to investigate, prosecute, and punish. The prevalent discourse in and around the courts and related institutions today is one of professionalism and neutrality, portraying accountability actions as 'merely' a matter of justice institutions fulfilling their duties. Although undoubtedly correct, this position offers little to explain the previous abdication of duty, given the high levels of formal and *de facto* continuity between past and present justice institutions and the persistence of the same legislative framework, including the self-amnesty law. The changes can be partly explained by the decline of former veto players, who have been sidelined or quietly disowned by the political right and by a military establishment that is being forced to come to terms with reduced levels of political influence.

Chile's transitional justice trajectory, then, has been painstaking. Different agencies and individuals took the initiative at different times, but were rarely accompanied or supported by consistent state commitment. This fact has operated to both the disadvantage and the advantage of those pressing for more accountability activity. Although such actors have been denied sustained access to state resources or political support, they have been able to take quiet advantage of islands of cooperation or empathy within the state, including, lately, within the judicial branch. This has enabled the construction of small but solid bulwarks of truth, justice, and reparations activity. Their very isolation and apparent insignificance can make these enclaves easy to overlook but also difficult to extinguish: even during the right-wing presidency of 2010–14, supporters of accountability were able to prevent major backsliding.

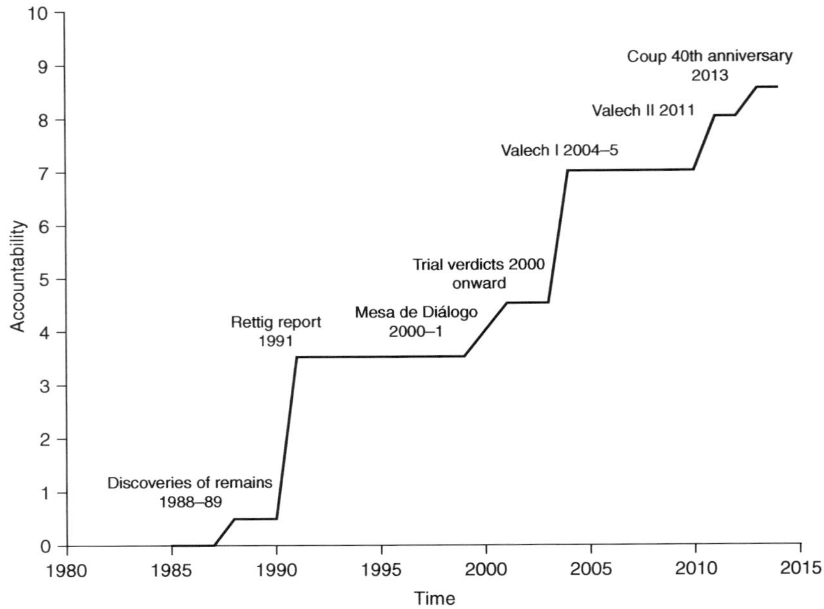

Figure 6.1 Chile: the truth dimension of accountability, 1990–2014
Source: Authors' construction, 2015.

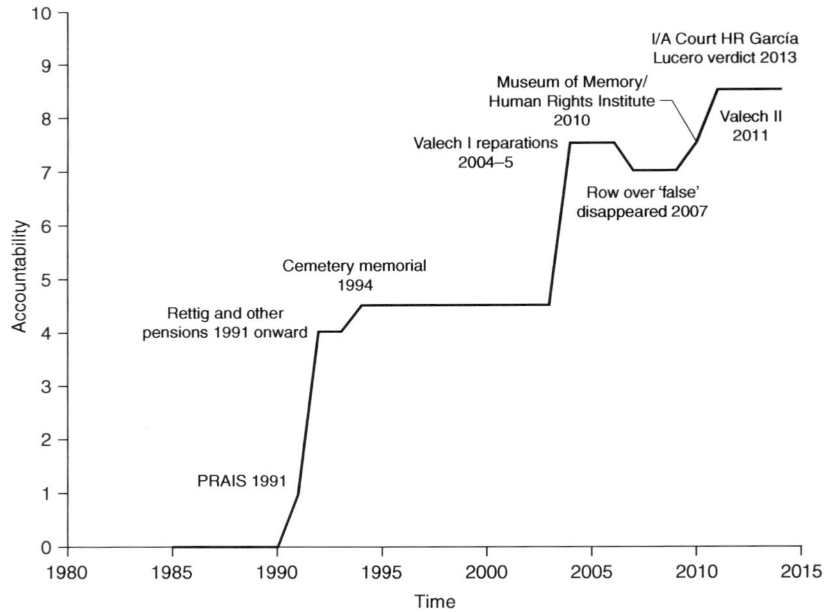

Figure 6.2 Chile: the reparations dimension of accountability, 1990–2014
Source: Authors' construction, 2015.

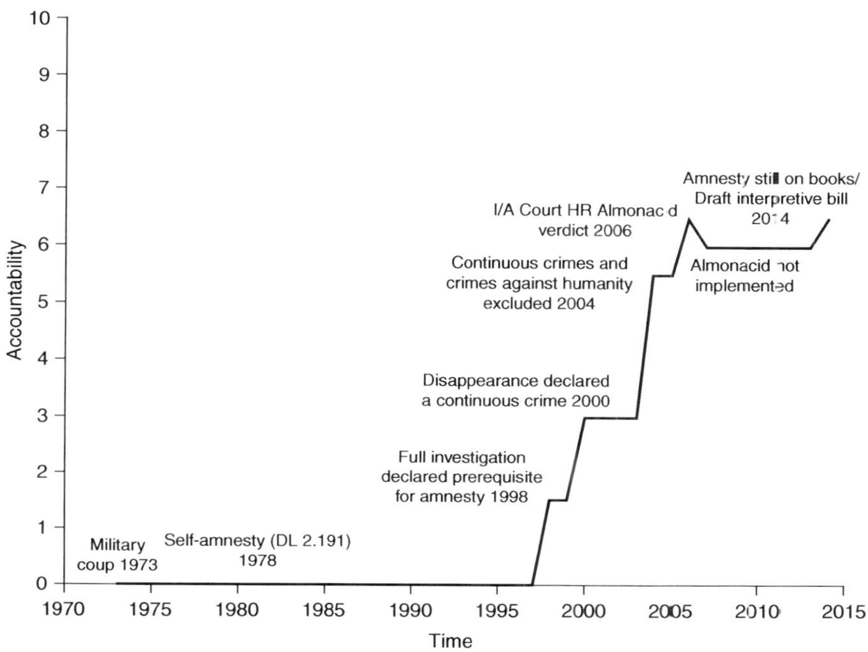

Figure 6.3 Chile: the overcoming amnesty dimension of accountability, 1990–2014
Source: Authors' construction, 2015.

Rather than enthusiastically deploying transitional justice politics as a way to make a mark, as has happened to some extent in Argentina under the Kirchner and Fernández presidencies, Chilean presidents have played a cautious back-seat role, reacting, balancing, and calculating rather than innovating. Continuing the comparison with Argentina, we might conclude that Chile, even allowing for its less propitious transitional conditions, learned the art of excessive circumspection and self-limitation early and was less able than its neighbour to shake off the habit of deference to past authoritarians and their present-day supporters. As a result, justice and memory initiatives, in particular, have been constructed in the sphere of low rather than high politics. Their protagonists, relatively few in number, have nonetheless managed to make common cause with institutions such as the judicial branch in ways that reinforce the latter's view of itself as a disinterested guardian of unchanging values.

Thus, the sum of Chile's transitional justice balance sheet remains positive but contradictory. There have been substantial recent inroads into explicit impunity for past crimes and the beginnings, even more recently, of social questioning of broader legacies such as a neo-liberal economic model and an undemocratic

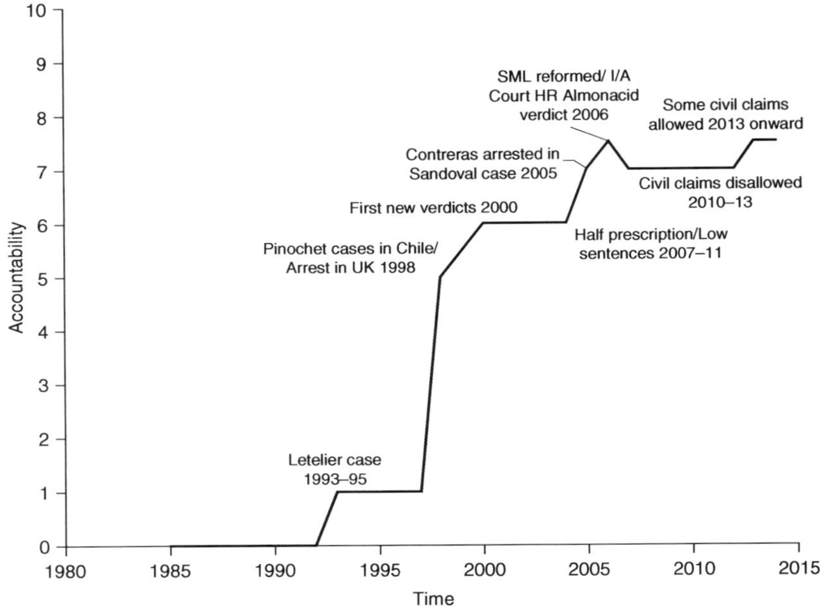

Figure 6.4 Chile: the trials dimension of accountability, 1990–2014
Source: Authors' construction, 2015.

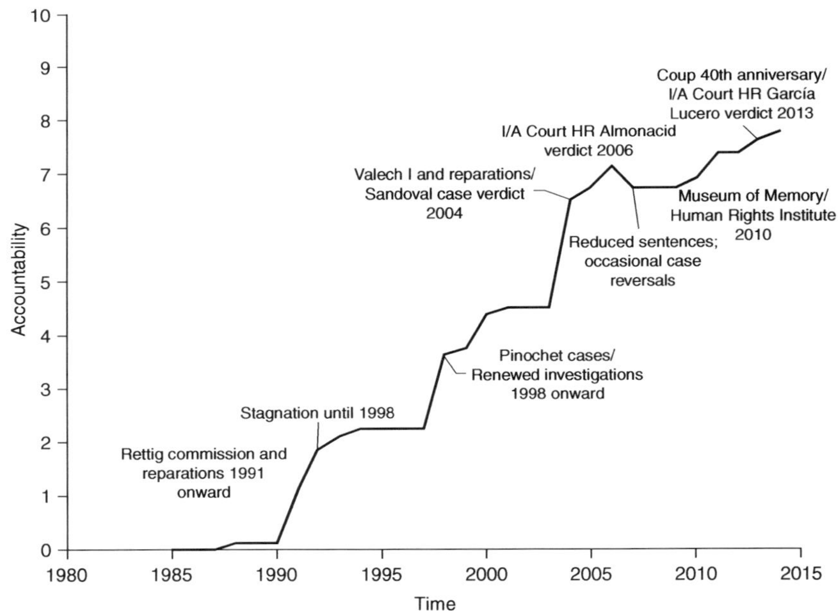

Figure 6.5 Chile: overall trend towards accountability, 1990–2014
Source: Authors' construction, 2015.

constitution. The past nonetheless continues to weigh heavily, and on balance unfavourably, on the quality of public human rights discourse and the promotion of further accountability advances.

Notes

* The authors thank the current and former team members of the Transitional Justice Observatory (Observatorio de Justicia Transicional, formerly Observatorio de Derechos Humanos) at the Universidad Diego Portales in Santiago, Chile, 2008–15: Juan Pablo Delgado, Karinna Fernández, Florencia González, Jennifer Herbst, Rodrigo Hernández, Alice Pfeiffer, Antonio Poveda, Tábata Santelices, María Ignacia Terra, and Paulina Zamorano. Many issues analysed here have also been addressed in the Observatory's publications, bulletins, and annual reports of various years. All are available in the Observatorio section of the university's Centro de Derechos Humanos website, www.derechoshumanos.udp.cl.

1 See Inter-American Development Bank figures at http://data.iadb.org/.

2 Victim numbers changed with each successive truth commission report, and with the 2007 discovery of minor errors (see below), but cumulative figures are not available in any official source. The most accurate summary to date is by the Transitional Justice Observatory (Observatorio DDHH 2013a).

3 Chile signed the American Convention on Human Rights in 1969 but ratified it only in 1990. The United Nations Convention against Torture, which the regime signed in 1987, would become germane to legal wrangling over the fate of Pinochet a decade later. For other accessions and ratifications made in the immediate aftermath of transition, see Loveman and Lira (2000, 495). Chile signed the Rome Statute of the International Criminal Court in 1998 but did not ratify it until 2009. The country was one of the original 2007 signatories of the International Convention for the Protection of All Persons from Enforced Disappearance, which entered into force in 2010.

4 Numbers of those still disappeared have declined over time as remains have been found.

5 It was argued, correctly but for the first time, that since the condition of victimisation did not lapse, the recognition of it by the state should not be subject to deadlines imposed for administrative convenience.

6 Since military personnel would not testify and no regime archives were handed over, Rettig relied heavily on information already placed in the public domain by human rights organisations.

7 Significant changes in the media, artistic, cultural, and even physical landscape, including a flowering of recovered memory sites, commemorative events, televisual production, and other actions, are discussed by, among others, Wilde (1999, 2013), Stern (2004, 2006, 2010), Hite (2013), Hite and Collins (2009), and Lazzara (2006).

8 For details of measures, see Collins (2013a, 147–48, table 7.2) as well as Spanish-language publications by the Transitional Justice Observatory at www.derechoshumanos.udp.cl/.

9 Investigations prompted by the 2007 reappearance, alive and well, of a man classed by Rettig as disappeared finally revealed no more than a dozen total cases of error.

10 Inter-American Court of Human Rights (I/A Court HR), *Case of García Lucero et al. v Chile*, Preliminary Objection, Merits, and Reparations, Judgment of 28 August 2013. The case produced a relatively conservative pronouncement from the Court on the central topic of reparations, but the verdict declared in passing that states' duties to prosecute require *ex officio* action rather than simple toleration of private action. See Observatorio DDHH (2013b, 2014).

11 Art 3, however, excludes a range of 'minor' crimes ranging from homicides within the family to armed robbery and drunk driving.

12 *Almonacid Arellano v Chile*, Judgment of 26 September 2006.
13 A draft bill was finally introduced by the presidency in December 2014 to codify these interpretations without annulling or derogating the amnesty law, as explained below in the section on amnesty.
14 See an account of this and other key cases in Observatorio Justicia Transicional (2014).
15 Those calling for repeal included the UN Human Rights Council, following Chile's second Universal Periodic Review in 2014. See Observatorio Justicia Transicional (2014).
16 Among the most notable organisations were the Agrupación de Familiares de Detenidos Desaparecidos (AFDD); the Agrupación de Familiares de Ejecutados Políticos (AFEP); the Corporación de Promoción y Defensa de los Derechos del Pueblo (CODEPU); and the Fundación de Ayuda Social de las Iglesias Cristianas (FASIC). Many of their lawyers had previously worked in the renowned legal department of the Catholic Church's Vicaría de la Solidaridad.
17 Supreme Court reforms after 1996 included specialisation into criminal and civil benches, the introduction of non-career judges, and the retirement of its oldest (and most reliably pro-Pinochet) members.
18 Figures in this paragraph are drawn from publications of the Human Rights Programme of Chile's Ministry of the Interior, 18 December 2014, supplemented by Observatory records.
19 This observation is drawn from regular interviews and conversations with both serving and retired case judges, as well as a case actors' meeting convened by the Transitional Justice Observatory in late 2012.
20 One experienced case detective claimed that 'one of the biggest strategic errors of the armed forces was not to protect the lower ranks and civilian employees. [...] I would say to them, "Are you going to stand for that?" and sometimes they'd talk.' Author interview with former brigade detective, identity withheld, 2013.
21 One defence lawyer was categorical: 'We found a formula that suited everyone – convictions, money [damages], and low sentences.' Mauricio Unda, defence lawyer for former agents accused of human rights violations, interview by author, Santiago, 13 August 2013.
22 Authors' calculation based on Observatory database records as of mid-2015.
23 This apparently obscure point in fact rescued some claims from lapsing. It was based on the logic that since prescription is designed to ensure timely action by a claim bringer (in this case, the private party who suffered harm), it is important to determine at what stage that party was free to start an action and could, therefore, reasonably have been expected to do so. The Court decided that publication of the first Rettig report marked a relevant milestone, signalling state responsibility at a time when democratic opening made it, at least theoretically, possible to access the courts.
24 Sergio Muñoz, Supreme Court president, interview by author, Santiago, 6 January 2015.
25 This information, published at regular intervals since 1996, is available on the website of the Centro de Estudios de la Realidad Contemporánea (http://www.cerc.cl/). See also Huneeus and Ibarra (2013).
26 The case concerned the detention centre at the Escuela de Mecánica de la Armada (ESMA) in the Argentine capital; see Chapter 3.

References

Barros, Robert. 2002. *Constitutionalism and Dictatorship: Pinochet, the Junta, and the 1980 Constitution*. Cambridge: Cambridge University Press.

Brett, Sebastian. 2009. *The Pinochet Effect: Ten Years On from London 1998*. Report of a conference held at Universidad Diego Portales, Santiago, 8–10 October 2008. www.derechoshumanos.udp.cl.

CNPPT (Comisión Nacional sobre Prisión Política y Tortura). 2005. *Informe de la Comisión Nacional sobre prisión política y tortura*. Santiago: Reedición Ministerio del Interior. Original edition 2004.

CNRR (Corporación Nacional de Reparación y Reconciliación). 1996. *Informe sobre calificación de víctimas de violaciones de derechos humanos y de la violencia política*. Santiago: CNRR.

CNVR (Comisión Nacional de Verdad y Reconciliación). 2007. *Informe de la Comisión Nacional de Verdad y Reconciliación*. Santiago: CNVR. First published 1991.

Collins, Cath. 2010a. 'Human Rights Trials in Chile During and After the "Pinochet Years."' *International Journal of Transitional Justice* 4(1): 67–86

——2010b. *Post-Transitional Justice: Human Rights Trials in Chile and El Salvador*. University Park: Pennsylvania State University Press.

——2013a. 'Human Rights Policy under the Concertación.' In *Democratic Chile: The Politics and Policies of a Historic Coalition, 1990–2010*, edited by Kirsten Sehnbruch and Peter Siavelis, 143–72. Boulder, CO: Lynne Rienner.

——2013b. 'The Politics of Prosecutions.' In *The Politics of Memory in Chile: From Pinochet to Bachelet*, edited by Cath Collins, Katherine Hite, and Alfredo Joignant, 61–90. Boulder, CO: Lynne Rienner.

Collins, Cath, and Claudio Fuentes. 2012. 'National Commission on Truth and Reconciliation, the Rettig Commission.' In *Encyclopedia of Transitional Justice*, edited by Lavinia Stan and Nadya Nedelsky, vol. 2, 295–300. Cambridge: Cambridge University Press.

Collins, Cath, Katherine Hite, and Alfredo Joignant, eds. 2013. *The Politics of Memory in Chile: From Pinochet to Bachelet*. Boulder, CO: Lynne Rienner.

Comisión Asesora Presidencial para la Calificación de Detenidos Desaparecidos, Ejecutados Políticos y Víctimas de Prisión Política y Tortura. 2011. *Informe de la Comisión Presidencial Asesora para la Calificación de Detenidos Desaparecidos, Ejecutados Políticos y Víctimas de Prisión Política y Tortura*. Santiago: Comisión Asesora.

Correa, Cristián. 2012. 'Reparation Programs for Mass Violations of Human Rights: Lessons from Experiences in Argentina, Chile and Peru.' In *Transitional Justice: Handbook for Latin America*, edited by Félix Reátegui, 409–42. São Paulo: ICTJ/Brazilian Ministry of Justice.

Government of Chile. 2001. *Declaración de la Mesa de Dialogo sobre Derechos Humanos*. Santiago: Government of Chile. http://www.ddhh.gov.cl/filesapp/Declaracion_Acuerdo_Final.pdf.

——2003. *No hay mañana sin ayer: Propuesta del Presidente Ricardo Lagos en materia de derechos humanos*. Santiago: Government of Chile. http://www.ddhh.gov.cl/filesapp/propuesta_DDHH.pdf.

Hite, Katherine. 2013. *Politics and the Art of Commemoration: Memorials to Struggle in Latin America and Spain*. Abingdon, UK: Routledge.

Hite, Katherine, and Cath Collins. 2009. 'Memorial Fragments, Monumental Silences and Reawakenings in 21st-Century Chile.' *Millennium Journal of International Studies* 38(2): 379–400.

Huneeus, Alejandra. 2010. 'Judging from a Guilty Conscience: The Chilean Judiciary's Human Rights Turn.' *Law and Social Inquiry* 35(1): 99–135.

Huneeus, Carlos. 2007. *The Pinochet Regime*. Boulder, CO: Lynne Rienner.

Huneeus, Carlos, and Sebastián Ibarra. 2013. 'The Memory of the Pinochet Regime in Public Opinion.' In *The Politics of Memory in Chile: From Pinochet to Bachelet*, edited by Cath Collins, Katherine Hite, and Alfredo Joignant, 197–238. Boulder, CO: Lynne Rienner.

Lazzara, Michael. 2006. *Chile in Transition: The Poetics and Politics of Memory*. Gainesville: University Press of Florida.

Lira, Elizabeth, and Brian Loveman. 2005. *Políticas de reparación: Chile 1990–2004*. Santiago: LOM.

Loveman, Brian, and Elizabeth Lira. 2000. *Las ardientes cenizas del olvido: Vía chilena de reconciliación política 1932–1994*. Santiago: LOM.

Observatorio DDHH (Observatorio de Derechos Humanos) http://www.derechoshumanos.udp.cl/. 2013a. *Totals of Victims and Survivors of Massive HRVs Committed during the 1973–1990 Dictatorship Officially Recognised by the Chilean State*. Santiago: Centro de Derechos Humanos, Universidad Diego Portales. http://www.derechoshumanos.udp.cl/.

——2013b. *Truth, Justice and Memory for Dictatorship-Era Violations – 40 Years after the Military Coup*. Transitional Justice Institute Research Paper 14-05. Newtownabbey, Northern Ireland: Ulster University. Originally published in Spanish in *Informe anual sobre derechos humanos 2013*, 21–68. Santiago: Centro de Derechos Humanos, Universidad Diego Portales.http://www.derechoshumanos.udp.cl/.

——2014. *Jurisprudential Milestones in Human Rights Cases: Chile 1990–2013*. Santiago: Centro de Derechos Humanos, Universidad Diego Portales. http://www.derechoshumanos.udp.cl/.

Observatorio Justicia Transicional. 2014. '¿Una nueva medida de lo posible? Verdad, justicia, memoria y reparaciones posdictadura.' In *Informe anual sobre derechos humanos 2014*, 21–62. Santiago: Centro de Derechos Humanos, Universidad Diego Portales. http://www.derechoshumanos.udp.cl/.

Roht-Arriaza, Naomi. 2005. *The Pinochet Effect: Transnational Justice in the Age of Human Rights*. Philadelphia: University of Pennsylvania Press.

Stern, Steve J. 2004. *Remembering Pinochet's Chile: On the Eve of London 1998*. Durham, NC: Duke University Press.

——2006. *Battling for Hearts and Minds: Memory Struggles in Pinochet's Chile, 1973–1988*. Durham, NC: Duke University Press.

——2010. *Reckoning with Pinochet: The Memory Question in Democratic Chile, 1989–2006*. Durham, NC: Duke University Press.

UDP (Universidad Diego Portales). 2009. *Perceptions of Human Rights in the National Public Opinion Survey of the Universidad Diego Portales, Santiago, Chile*. Santiago: ICSO-UDP.

Wilde, Alexander. 1999. 'Irruptions of Memory: Expressive Politics in Chile's Transition to Democracy.' *Journal of Latin American Studies* 31(2): 473–500.

——2013. 'A Season of Memory: Human Rights in Chile's Long Transition.' In *The Politics of Memory in Chile: From Pinochet to Bachelet*, edited by Cath Collins, Katherine Hite, and Alfredo Joignant, 31–60. Boulder, CO: Lynne Rienner.

Winn, Peter, Steve J. Stern, Federico Lorenz, and Aldo Marchesi. 2014. *No hay mañana sin ayer: Batallas por la memoria en el Cono Sur*. Santiago: LOM.

Chapter 7

Paraguay

Accountability in the shadow of Stroessner

*Cath Collins**

Paraguay has had a limited, but significant, transitional justice experience since emerging in 1989 from one of the longest one-person dictatorships in Latin America and the world. The country's protracted process of coming to terms with the Alfredo Stroessner era (1954–89) became internationally visible only in 2008, when an official truth commission (TC) published its final report. Latin America's fifth-smallest country, sparsely populated Paraguay, is one of the region's least-known cases of transitional justice, just as it is rarely given the attention it deserves in other aspects of comparative politics. However, the country's transitional justice history is richer than is often appreciated.

With no formal amnesty law in place – something that can be attributed to the unexpected timing of the regime's downfall – some early trials were held. Other measures have included a truth commission, reparations, and memory initiatives. The shadow of Stroessner and the Colorado Party machine looms over a country still beset by endemic corruption, a weak or captured state, and slow – though recently improving – macroeconomic performance.[1] The 2012 impeachment and removal of progressive centre-left president Fernando Lugo attracted short-lived international attention, but the holding of elections in 2013 largely placated external concern. The return to power of the Colorado Party, one that Stroessner virtually came to embody, suggests that important political legacy issues remain unresolved.[2]

The Stroessner regime

The particularities of the country's political history make Paraguay difficult to classify and its transition hard to date precisely. General Stroessner's 35-year regime, both unipersonalist and corporatist, has been characterised variously as 'republican despotism' (Delich 1981), 'neo-sultanistic patrimonialism' (Riquelme 1994, 239–40, 243), and the 'omnivorous state' (Arditi 1992, 15). Whatever the label applied, it is clear that the regime was distinct in many ways from those of its South American neighbours. Paraguay's less industrialised nature and the much earlier beginning of military rule meant that its authoritarian project, at least in the early years, was anti-peasant and despotic rather than neo-liberal and late industrial. Although United States (US) aid was fundamental in propping up the regime,[3] the US-originated National Security Doctrine adopted by the regime in the 1980s was merely a new expression of a fervent home-grown anti-communism reaching back at least as far as the 1930s.

Rather than modernising or industrialising, the regime dedicated itself to personal enrichment, patronage, and a web of clientelistic relations that reinforced Stroessner's position as father of the nation. Some grandiose infrastructure projects were completed, but the binational Itaipú Dam hydroelectric project – Stroessner's major economic legacy – became a cash cow and source of political capital rather than an engine of national development.[4] When the dam's construction and related subsidies came to an end in 1981, economic growth stalled. What remained was largely cotton and soya cultivation along with smuggling and counterfeiting, for which Stroessner's Paraguay became well known (Fassi 2010; Telesca 2011). The unregulated informal economy became at least as important as the official one, while Stroessner harboured unsavoury associates including Nicaraguan ex-dictator Anastasio Somoza, international drug barons, and even Nazi doctor Josef Mengele.

In the sphere of internal politics, a permanent state of emergency suspended *habeas corpus*, and the entire police service became a personal army. Thousands of informants (known as *pyragüés*) were recruited. In contrast to the clandestine practices of other Southern Cone regimes, in Paraguay the transformation of police cells, barracks, and prisons into torture centres for political opponents and other undesirables was no secret. Since torture was exemplary terror, its existence had to be made known. From 1968 onward, Pastor Coronel, the feared and sadistic head of the Investigative Police, operated openly in offices close to the civic centre of the capital, Asunción. Dreadful stories told about what went on there reached the proportion of tragic myth without ever exceeding the awful reality. Abuses were carefully documented in internal records by the regime itself; ledgers discovered in 1992 in the so-called Terror Archive (see below) included albums with harrowing photos of long-term political prisoners, gaunt and haunted-looking, of all ages and both sexes.

Particularly egregious violence was inflicted on indigenous communities, on Church and peasant league members, and on anyone whose pretensions to small-scale land title interfered with Stroessner's drive to hand out tracts of agribusiness land to cronies under the pretext of land reform. These transfers came to be known as *tierras mal habidas* – lands acquired in bad faith. This practice was documented in detail by the 2008 Truth and Justice Commission (Comisión de Verdad y Justicia, CVJ), which found that it contributed to a mass population exodus over the course of Stroessner's 35-year rule.

The Commission concluded that exile affected at least one in every 360 adults (CVJ 2008, Conclusiones y Recomendaciones, 25).[5] Naming names, it listed 9,923 individuals who had suffered disappearance, execution, torture, detention, and/or exile. It further estimated that these practices affected over 20,000 victims, or one in 64 of Paraguay's adult population,[6] although only 425 are classified as victims of disappearance or political executions (CVJ 2008, Conclusiones y Recomendaciones, 25–31). Around a third of the disappearances of Paraguayan citizens took place in Brazil or Argentina because of population displacement and Paraguay's central role in Operation Condor. This coordinated military repression strategy, operating across the Southern Cone and Brazil from at least 1975, carried out cross-border kidnappings, rendition, and assassination of political opponents (see Chapter 1).

Transition, after a fashion

In his fourth decade of uninterrupted rule, Stroessner was finally toppled from power – not by regime disintegration or a popular uprising, but because elements of his own party and military command structure turned against him. The events of 1989 resemble a palace coup more than a formal political transition. They were spearheaded by Andrés Rodríguez, an army general and close relative of Stroessner by marriage. After a brief power struggle within the party, Rodríguez took power on 2 October 1989. Stroessner was allowed to leave for Brazil, while his interior minister Sabino Montanaro fled to Honduras.[7] Other officials of the ousted *militante* faction remained in the country but without access to power.

Although there was much pro-democracy and anti-corruption rhetoric, Rodríguez was, for the most part, an unlikely reformer. There were important institutional changes, particularly the adoption of the 1992 constitution (still in force), which severed the umbilical cord between the military and the Colorado Party, declared allegiance to representative democracy, and outlawed torture, forced disappearance, and 'politically motivated murder' (Title II, Art 5). Pastor Coronel, the embodiment of these practices, was put on trial. But these advances were accompanied by considerable continuity (Lambert and Nickson 2012). The pursuit of a handful of Stroessner's cronies, known as *stronistas*, for corruption was abandoned after they agreed to return a portion of the millions they had embezzled. Stroessner himself, although never allowed to return, remained honorary president of the Colorado Party. The feared National Technical Directorate of the national police (Dirección Nacional de Asuntos Técnicos, DNAT) was only dissolved four years later, in 1993, by another Colorado president, Juan Carlos Wasmosy (1993–98). Although some reparations were then approved, and a truth commission was subsequently established (see below), Paraguay's highly unequal, almost feudal pattern of land tenure and power relations remained essentially unchanged.

Views as to when Paraguay's democratic transition really began, or indeed whether it has happened at all, accordingly differ (Abente Brun 2011). Mauricio Schvartzman famously portrayed 1989 as a 'pretransition'. He was, moreover, sceptical that Paraguay's radically asymmetrical social structure would permit the brief flowering of popular participation, later described by Rivarola (2009), to translate into a genuine civil society capable of sustaining real democracy (Schvartzman 1989). The new constitution in 1992 certainly marked a limited political opening. However, the shift from military to party dominance required little more than a change of emphasis for Colorado elites. Formal political alternation, and the first successful handover from one uninterrupted elected presidency to another, did not take place until 2008. In the interim, successive Colorado presidents fell in and out of favour with one another and with the military. Their feuds were bitter and sometimes deadly.[8] In 2008, although the Colorado Party kept its electoral majority, a loose alliance of left-wing and social movement parties including the Liberal Party took a respectable 31 of 80 seats in the lower house, and 17 of 45 Senate places. In presidential elections that same year, the Supreme Court was prevailed upon to allow would-be coup leader and former fugitive Lino Oviedo to return from abroad and run for office, taking advantage of a presidential pardon. The move suited the Colorados, as they believed he would split the opposition vote. Oviedo's candidacy instead split the Colorado vote, allowing centre-left former bishop Fernando Lugo a slender but undeniable 10 per cent margin of victory.

The Lugo presidency of 2008, which ended in 2012, awoke high and perhaps unrealisable expectations among those who sought a definitive political opening and long-postponed advances for the country's poor. Although he was forced to govern with an unwieldy coalition of social movement, centre, and right elements, Lugo made a real effort to live up to the 'new left' identity he sought to embrace.[9] Opponents seized on sexual peccadilloes and unfulfilled promises to block reform. Congress was, in any case, still controlled by the Colorado Party. Challenges to the cronyism that pervaded the state bureaucracy provoked fierce resistance. Flagship social policy measures had to be implemented by presidential decree instead of by the more sustainable path of legislation with cross-party support. The same was true of most transitional justice measures passed during Lugo's term, including follow-up to the truth commission report, published in mid-2008 almost simultaneously with his accession.

Although transitional justice issues were by no means central to national politics under Lugo, they played a cameo role in his eventual downfall. In May 2010, a group of peasant farmers occupied state land, in the district of Curuguaty, also claimed by a former Colorado senator in what was clearly an instance of the *tierras mal habidas* practice denounced by the truth commission. An ensuing police operation, in June 2012, resulted in 17 deaths. Colorados took advantage of the incident to launch an impeachment-style challenge to Lugo's presidency. Although constitutionally mandated mechanisms were used, Lugo was, in effect, railroaded out of office in what is often referred to in the country as a 'constitutional coup'. Paraguay was suspended from the Mercosur regional trading bloc by fellow members Argentina, Brazil, and Uruguay, and calls were made in the Organization of American States for its suspension under the democracy clause. However, the promise of scheduled elections proved enough to dampen external protest. Lugo was replaced first by his own vice president, Federico Franco, and then, in 2013, by a new Colorado Party leader, multi-millionaire sports magnate Horacio Cartes.

The Terror Archive

The 1992 discovery of dictatorship-era police documents in Asunción played a significant role in subsequent memory initiatives, reparations dynamics, and judicial processes, in Paraguay and in other countries of the region. The resulting archive has become at one and the same time a truth, justice, symbolic reparation, and memory initiative (Boccia Paz, Palau Aguilar, and Salerno 2007). In December 1992, activist lawyer Martín Almada and investigative magistrate José Agustín Fernández came across a room stacked high with apparently abandoned documents from the now-disbanded Investigative Police, detailing thousands of cases of detention and surveillance. The two were searching, under judicial warrant, for information requested by returned exile Almada, under 1992 constitutional *habeas data* provisions, about his own illegal detention and his wife's disappearance in the 1970s. The documents were removed to court buildings, while Fernández and a more senior judge continued searching police buildings in the capital, placing more official paperwork under judicial seal.

Those involved in the seizure, recovery, and painstaking deciphering of the sources now believe that the collection had been selectively censored to remove incriminating evidence regarding individuals who remained in high office. Some even suspect that the whole 'discovery' may have been manufactured, to direct attention towards police crimes and away from Colorado or military officials. This view is bolstered by the account of a former police officer who claims that he, not Almada, first alerted authorities to the existence of the document trove, and that the documents had, moreover, been deliberately deposited, only days before the judicial search, in the station where they were found.[10] Whatever their provenance, the sources provided a wealth of revelations about Paraguay's domestic state terror policies and about Operation Condor. Efforts to preserve the collection, popularly known as the Terror Archive, turned into an unprecedented collaboration between reformist elements of the post-1990 government, civil society organisations, and outside donors.[11] Judicial reform money from the US Agency for International Development funded microfilming and cataloguing. Most documents were opened to public access almost immediately, a move that may have led to some inappropriate release of information but whose symbolic benefit was felt to outweigh the dangers.[12] Later collaborations brought in the National Security Archive, a US-based non-governmental organisation (NGO) (Osorio and Enamoneta 2007). Specialising in the declassification of US official documentation, the organisation now regularly facilitates data exchanges between activists, lawyers, and judicial authorities across jurisdictions in accountability cases throughout the Americas (see, for example, Chapter 9 on Guatemala).

Subsequent developments with the Terror Archive have been far from smooth. In 1997, then President Wasmosy issued an administrative decree transferring official custody of state documentation to what was termed the General Archive of the Nation. The transfer would have included the contents of the

Terror Archive, at the time under judicial administration. Judicial employee Rosa Palau, in charge of the Archive, relayed to the then Supreme Court president her suspicions that the decree was a ruse to spirit the documents away. The Supreme Court declared that the Terror Archive content would not be released because it contained evidence of ongoing criminal investigations. Nonetheless, active judicial and state prosecutorial use of the Archive has been lacking, and Palau describes the function of its present staff as 'custodianship' rather than proactive judicial use of its contents.[13] The Archive is more often used for reparatory than for judicial purposes: individuals can file *habeas data* petitions directly through the Archive, submitting the documents recovered to reparations entities (see below).

The tussle between Almada and state authorities regarding access to and ownership of documents also continues. Despite lacking any official authority, Almada has subsequently made it his business to track down, and appropriate, other dictatorship-era document collections. Copies of these are periodically 'donated' to the Court, or the Archive, in particular whenever his authority or remit are questioned by state institutions or by survivors who believe they may be mentioned in the documents.[14] Such tension between various actors and branches of the state over ownership, use, and preservation of key documentary evidence is a recurrent theme in the region. Another recurring feature is an enhanced willingness of national authorities to tolerate transitional justice initiatives when these provide demonstrable international prestige. A visit to Paraguay by members of the Inter-American Court of Human Rights spurred efforts to rehouse the Terror Archive, as its dank and rundown condition was deemed an embarrassment.[15] The Archive is now part of a specially created Museum of Justice installation in the main court buildings in Asunción. The accompanying exhibit depicts Paraguay's pre- and post-conquest judicial history, from a rights-based perspective, in Spanish and in the more widely spoken Guaraní language.

The Terror Archive's collections are open to students, researchers, judicial staff, and the general public. Among the first to show interest were individuals wishing to consult their own and others' personal files. The extensive use of secret informants by the regime has thrown up ethical challenges similar to those faced by the ex-Stasi archive in Berlin. Rosa Palau explains: 'The only documents taken off public access almost immediately were the lists of informants. Lots of people are mentioned without corroboration, and we can't know for sure whether a person who informed did so under duress … [Nowadays] if you want to see someone else's personal file, we ask for a *habeas data* petition or their written permission.'[16] A photo album labelled 'homosexuals' was also kept away from public access, testament, perhaps, to continuing discrimination.[17] Requests from judges, prosecutors, or truth commission researchers for documents have come from Paraguay, Uruguay, and Brazil, but principally from Argentina, reflecting higher accountability activity in Argentina as well as the centrality of Paraguay in Operation Condor.

Trials: the search for criminal justice for Stroessner-era crimes

One example of transnational accountability triggered by a document from the Terror Archive is the case of rendition, to Argentina from Paraguay, of two Uruguayan activists and three Argentine detainees. Victims' relatives brought a case in Paraguay, and resulting indictments in 1994 included agents from each of the three countries involved. Operation Condor cases in Argentina and elsewhere have also included victims of Paraguayan nationality, and there have been recent efforts to use universal jurisdiction principles to lodge Paraguay cases in Argentine courts. A handful of criminal cases taking place in Paraguay itself show that although formal accountability has been patchy, it has not been entirely absent (Aseretto 2011).

Given high levels of Colorado continuity, the fact that any regime agents at all were prosecuted may seem surprising, and the fact that the regime's most feared agent of terror was tried as early as 1992 appears counterintuitive. However, score-settling within Colorado ranks played its part. Over the course of its 100-year-plus history, the party became a widely based, all-embracing social institution as well as an elite vehicle. As in the case of the Partido Revolucionario Institucional in Mexico, ideology mattered less than the perpetuation of the state and party machine. Accordingly, any and all means, including judicial denunciation of rivals from within the same party, were used to resolve internal disputes while preserving overall party dominance.

Pastor Coronel, possessor of potentially compromising information as well as a personal militia, was imprisoned almost immediately after the 1989 coup. Independent civil society, although fragmented and beleaguered, included a small number of educated urban activists capable of sustaining an accountability agenda. The vulnerable and porous judicial system could occasionally be played to advantage. At the top, the Supreme Court was significantly – though, as it turned out, temporarily – improved by a period of genuine reform around the time of the drafting of the new constitution. Thus, in 1992, a criminal complaint or *querella*, originally brought in 1989 by the widow of prominent anti-regime activist Mario Schaerer Prono, assassinated in 1976, produced a guilty verdict against Coronel and three more perpetrators. The verdict would not be confirmed until 1996, nor enforced until 1999, but a first step had been taken.[18] More would follow.

Pastor Coronel and former police chief Lucilo Benítez were also convicted, in 1995, of the attempted murder of survivor Alberto Alegre Portillo, and together with others, of the murder and torture of Amílcar Oviedo, victim of disappearance.[19] A torture case brought by Agrarian League survivors produced similar verdicts in 2000. A subsequent case over emblematic, long-time political prisoner Napoleón Ortigoza was ongoing in mid-2015, as was an Operation Condor case brought by Martín Almada in the 1990s using Terror Archive documents.[20] A 1989 case concerning the disappearance of Miguel Angel Soler produced a first judgment in 1997, confirmed by the Supreme Court in July 2007. Another case brought in 1989 by survivor Julián Cubas took 14 years to reach an initial verdict, by which time Coronel was dead and the other perpetrators were deemed to have served sufficient time on remand to be eligible for immediate release.

These early cases tended to be against the same group of defendants, on behalf of high-profile victims with relatively well-educated and affluent relatives. Poor rural victims, by far the majority, were and remain underrepresented. In addition, cases have largely focused on disappearances or homicides, despite the fact that in Paraguay, as in Uruguay and Brazil, most repression took the form of illegal detention and torture. Triggers for judicial activity have included the 1989 coup and return of exiles, the 2008 truth commission report, the 2009 return of former minister Montanaro, and the finding of remains through exhumations (see below). As mentioned above, much activity stimulated by the Terror Archive discovery is not criminal investigation but civil action aimed at truth recovery or compensation. Such actions typically began with *habeas data* requests, submitted by individuals or relatives directly to the Archive or via the human rights Ombudsman's Office that began operating in 2001.

Relatives in three of the cases discussed above also resorted to the inter-American human rights system. Paraguay became a party to the American Convention on Human Rights in 1989 and recognised the jurisdiction of the Inter-American Court of Human Rights four years later, in March 1993. Soon afterwards, in December 1995, the Condor-related case of Agustín Goiburú was submitted to the Inter-American Commission on Human Rights (IACHR). Similar submissions were made in June 1996 on behalf of the Ramírez Villalba brothers and Carlos Mancuello. The Commission accumulated the cases in 2004 and referred them to the Inter-American Court in 2005. The final ruling, of 22 September 2006, found against Paraguay. It ordered the expediting of national investigations, the location and return of remains, a public act of apology, a monument to the four victims, and reparations to their families. It also ordered the improvement of national criminal code definitions of the crimes of torture and forced disappearance, along with human rights training for the national police.[21]

The decision applauded interim developments in Paraguay, including the then-ongoing truth commission, the development of the Terror Archive, and the naming of a public square in honour of victims of disappearance.[22] However, it condemned the slowness of national cases, noting that the Goiburú case had been under way for at least 17 years. The Court also questioned an extradition request that the state claimed to have made to Brazil for Stroessner in 2001, noting that no evidence of the request had been supplied, and it rejected the argument that the lack of a bilateral extradition treaty prevented Paraguay from making a similar request to Honduras for Montanaro. Within two years of the decision, initial verdicts were delivered in the Goiburú case and the Mancuello case had been concluded by the Supreme Court.

Drivers of, and obstacles to, criminal prosecution

Most of the cases mentioned above were privately instigated and represented by lawyers from a Paraguayan NGO linked to the Catholic Church, the Churches'

Committee for Emergency Assistance (Comité de Iglesias para Ayudas de Emergencia, CIPAE). The nature of the Catholic Church in Latin America, as an internationally networked and socially influential organisation with unparalleled grassroots presence, allowed it to provide a base for non-state social mobilisation. In Paraguay, as in Central America, the Church's role in popular education and social justice-orientated rural organising during the 1950s and 1960s made it an early target of direct repression. The role of individual leaders at the apex of the Catholic hierarchy was key in Paraguay, as it had been in El Salvador under Archbishop Oscar Romero. Although traditional Catholic anti-communism and conservatism persisted,[23] the Catholic Church in Paraguay came to generally oppose regime actions. Paraguay's history of immigration from Northern Europe has also given Protestant churches a small but significant social presence. Among them, the Mennonite church broadly supported the regime, but pastors and lay leaders of other Protestant churches joined forces with the Catholic Church to make CIPAE an ecumenical enterprise.

Organisations similar to CIPAE emerged across Latin America under authoritarian rule, and they often networked with each other across countries. CIPAE, for instance, exchanged experiences with the Social Aid Foundation of Christian Churches (Fundación de Ayuda Social de las Iglesias Cristianas, FASIC) in Chile. Both had strong funding from, and solidarity links with, the World Council of Churches. This support was, perhaps, particularly necessary in Paraguay given its relatively low level of domestic development and the virtual stifling of civil society autonomy by Stroessner and the Colorado Party. Paraguay also had national chapters of region-wide Latin American human rights defence movements of lay Christian origin. These included the Peace and Justice Service (Servicio Paz y Justicia, SERPAJ) which patiently accumulated information, provided emergency relief, and carried out valiant justice interventions.[24] Such organisations usually operated from a liberationist and/or grassroots identity during authoritarianism and political violence, with strong lay leadership and a horizontal structure. After transition, however, many acquired a more pronounced institutional or clerical emphasis. The Catholic Church as a whole in the region returned to conservative social doctrine, stepping back from justice engagements in favour of a more restricted focus on truth initiatives. Thus, while Paraguay, like Chile, saw Catholic bishops presiding over official truth initiatives, in both countries pro-justice organisations staffed by lay people were wound down or closed altogether by the Catholic hierarchy.[25]

Interviewed in 2009 and 2012 for this study, CIPAE legal staff enumerated 25 new cases brought between 2009 and 2011, mostly for disappearances. They highlighted obstacles to mobilisation, including the success of the Colorado Party, during and after the Stroessner era, in 'freezing the social structure' into a 'feudal mentality'.[26] CIPAE did not identify the judicial branch as the principal problem, given that no amnesty law exists and international prohibitions on statutes of limitations for crimes against humanity have been respected. Criticisms instead focus on relative prosecutorial inaction: 'The cases that have been completed are the ones where we did all the investigative work ourselves.'[27] The official follow-up body to the truth commission, the Truth, Justice and Reparations Directorate (Dirección General de Verdad, Justicia y Reparación), was also criticised: 'They could have pushed more, to point out that the state hasn't done enough … The state should be opening cases *ex officio*.'[28] The perceived inadequacy of the public prosecutor's response was linked to the continuation of authoritarianism, or at least of Colorado patronage.[29] Interviews in 2015 echoed this criticism, pointing out that initiatives in non-judicial dimensions of transitional justice are more easily tolerated because they are less politically threatening to current elites.[30]

As in other countries in this study, judicial reform also marked a turning point for criminal accountability in Paraguay. Reforms took effect in 2001, and cases are assigned to the old or the new system according to when the first complaint was received. Following this criterion, criminal complaints or *habeas data* petitions made after 2001 go to the police or state prosecutor. Those that were presented directly to an investigative magistrate, as was the previous practice, continue under that system. Only victims or relatives can bring a formal complaint (*querella*), which implies the right to be a full party to any subsequent investigation and case. The Ministerio Público, or Public Prosecutor's Office, now oversees state prosecutorial activity in such cases. In 2010, it was also assigned formal responsibility for the justice dimension of truth commission follow-up.[31]

The Truth, Justice and Reparations Directorate is supposed to coordinate with the Ministerio Público around prosecutions. Contact began even before the truth commission report was published, and a human rights section was formally set up within the Ministerio Público in 2007. However, according to the Directorate, the number and quality of prosecutors assigned has always been inadequate.[32] Another obstacle has been deficiencies in the existing criminal code definition of torture (Art 309). This requires proof of ongoing physical consequences attributable directly to torture, a rigid and medically inappropriate standard. Justice system reforms have also brought additional problems regarding the applicability of changes to pre-reform crimes. As the old inquisitorial system was phased out, perpetrators sought to invoke the legal principle that post hoc changes in law should only be applied where favourable to defendants. They argued that, in Paraguay as elsewhere, internationally prohibited atrocity crimes such as torture were not punishable under existing domestic law at the time they were committed. The Paraguayan Prosecutor's Office has, however, generally taken the view, increasingly adopted elsewhere in Latin America, that existing *jus cogens* prohibitions of torture rendered it a crime during the 1970s and 1980s irrespective of whether domestic law explicitly prohibited it.[33] The rather lax attitude of the same office to ongoing cases and the possibility of bringing new ones had not, however, changed noticeably, according to sources consulted in mid-2015.

A lack of case information, exacerbated by the rural isolation of many of the regions where atrocities occurred, is yet another obstacle to criminal accountability. This problem places Paraguay closer to its Peruvian and Central American counterparts than to its Southern Cone neighbours. The resulting practical difficulties were illustrated by input from the official forensic unit, the National Team for Investigation, Search, and Full Identification (Equipo Nacional para la Investigación, Búsqueda e Identificación Plena, ENABI), to a meeting of the Truth, Justice and Reparations Directorate attended by the author in April 2012. ENABI reported that only about a third of the 117 disappearance case files that the unit had studied in depth contained even basic information: 'in some, we only have a name'.[34] Unit head Rogelio Goiburú also discussed previously undocumented deaths caused by military landowners in the border region with Brazil. Taking illegal possession of the lands through Stroessner's *tierras mal habidas* practice, officers allegedly eliminated remaining indigenous populations and forced locals to provide slave labour. The same meeting discussed the feasibility of using the upcoming inauguration of an official memory site in the area as a chance to 'slip away' and inspect a rumoured secret burial site. This illustrates the lengths to which sympathetic state employees often go in improvising creative ways to bypass official stonewalling.

ENABI also reported that while the military continues to oppose excavations on military installations, the present-day police force has proved more cooperative.[35] Exhumation and identification efforts, which began in 2006, saw some progress by mid-2015, with the remains of 34 victims of dictatorship-era forced disappearance believed to have been recovered, although definitive identification remained pending. Pressure from human rights organisations, with external lobbying support, achieved the signing in 2014 of an official agreement between the government and the independent Argentine forensic anthropology agency – long involved on an informal basis in excavations in Paraguay – for DNA identification and technical assistance.[36] ENABI, however complained, in 2015, that only half of the originally promised resources had actually materialised. In its new incarnation within the Ministry of Justice, ENABI's office employed only a single paid state employee, one volunteer, and three young staff members paid for by Diakonia, an NGO. The office's stated intention to use final identifications to push for the opening or reinvigoration of criminal cases means it is already pressing the Ministerio Público to coordinate lists of names and collect new information on the disappeared.[37]

In summary, although results of exhumations occasionally make headlines, public discussion about criminal accountability seems relatively muted in Paraguay compared to other countries in the region. The non-governmental umbrella organisation CODEHUPY (Human Rights Coordinating Committee of Paraguay/Coordinadora de Derechos Humanos del Paraguay) stated in its 2014 annual report that most cases are stalled (CODEHUPY 2014). In part, this may reflect the relatively small number of cases that exist, focused moreover on crimes perpetrated by now-obsolete police institutions and a wing of the Colorado Party that is no longer ascendant. There is also a more generalised sense of pervasive impunity, linked to the long and broad colonisation of society by a still-dominant Colorado Party with a strong social base. Rural isolation and absolute poverty remain high; expectations for democratic change are low.[38] All these factors militate against the repudiation of past crimes.

In addition, at the risk of perpetuating stereotypes, the impact of formal justice in Paraguay may also be lower than in other Southern Cone countries, given the generally low esteem in which state institutions as a whole are held. Since it is generally expected that state functionaries will be arbitrary, self-serving or at best politically subservient, even enlightened behaviour by individuals risks being seen as a badge of personal merit rather than a sign of institutional improvement or a reason for renewed faith in justice. Nonetheless, the judiciary can provide openings for reform-minded professionals who want to escape the Colorado stranglehold on public life and see the rule of law affirmed – especially, perhaps, at lower levels, where party patronage in appointments is less evident than at Supreme Court level. The readiness of a few officials within the justice system, albeit usually lower-level officials, to take action has led to some genuine advances in transitional justice. Civil claim-making through the Ministerio Público, and *habeas data* processing through the Archive or the Ombudsman's Office, have assisted truth and reparations even where criminal accountability has remained elusive or the processes themselves have been flawed (see below).

Truth-telling: Paraguay's Truth and Justice Commission

The substantial contribution of the Terror Archive to truth-telling in Paraguay has been outlined above. Members of Archive staff have also been key in parallel initiatives, with many apparently official transitional justice measures owing much in practice to mixed state-civil society protagonism. This blurring of the boundaries between public and private is perhaps accentuated by the personalistic nature of Paraguayan politics and public life. The Truth and Justice Commission and follow-up Directorate share this characteristic: unusually for the region, many commissioners and staffers are also survivors or relatives of prominent victims. This may account for the notably denunciatory tone of the Commission's report, but it also exposed the Commission to accusations of excessive subjectivity. Personalism has also proved damaging to the credibility of the follow-up Directorate, particularly with repeated accusations of high-handedness or even malfeasance, which by 2015 became difficult to ignore.

The Terror Archive and truth commission were separated by over a decade, and one was not a consequence of the other. They are, however, indirectly connected through the work of the Historical Memory Group (Mesa Memoria), formed in 2002. Rosa Palau traces the Mesa's origins to the intervention of French sociologist Alain Touraine.[39] Touraine's visit to Paraguay as part of a UNESCO delegation in 2000 led him to propose a return visit during which civil society and academics would discuss ways forward for truth and memory work. The 2002 gathering identified three priorities: a truth commission, a 'year of historical memory' to generate awareness, and a museum of memory. A follow-up group then developed a blueprint for a truth commission, drawing on experience from around the region.[40] The legislature narrowly approved the project in 2003, with only a single-vote majority in the Senate. Sufficient Colorado support was secured by extending the time frame of investigation from the originally proposed end point (1989 or 1992) to 2003. This diluted the exclusive focus on Stroessner-era crimes, muddying the waters as to which faction of the Colorados should bear most responsibility.[41]

The Truth and Justice Commission ('Anive haguã oiko' in Guaraní) began its work in October 2004 and reported in August 2008. Created by Law 2225 of 2003, it continued for four years, although it was expected to have an 18-month duration. Its mandate and powers were relatively broad: although non-judicial, the body could compel witnesses to attend, recommend reparations, and pass on any information of evidentiary value to the judicial branch (Law 2225, Arts 1, 5, 2d, 2e). Its composition, entirely national, was relatively unusual: one representative each from the judicial branch and legislature, three from the civil society human rights organisations that had campaigned for it, and four 'proposed by the Commissions of Victims of the Stroessner dictatorship' (Law 2225, Art 7). Although these last two categories may seem to overlap, the vagaries of Paraguayan politics meant that self-described 'victims' groups' included Colorados of the non-*stronista* tendency, keen to have their chance to steer deliberations. The nine commissioners selected Bishop Mario Medina from among their number as chair.

The Commission suffered from underfunding and indifference. Once its work exceeded the original time frame, its staff simply ceased to be paid for a time.[42] Nonetheless, it carried out hearings and interviews with just over 2,000 people in Paraguay, Argentina, Brazil, and Spain between 2005 and 2008. A mental health team was set up to support witnesses and provide documentation that might help them claim to reparations in future. Hearings were supplemented with analysis of case files of approximately 10,000 individuals, obtained from human rights organisations and official bodies including the Foreign Ministry and – unusually – the armed forces. Names of alleged perpetrators were, again unusually, published in the hard-hitting final report. Paraguay's Truth and Justice Commission is also one of the few official truth commissions in Latin America – Guatemala's is the other notable example – that clearly attributed shared responsibility to outside powers. It accused the United States and, to a lesser extent, Brazil of having propped up the regime and knowingly collaborated in its repressive activities.

The report also analysed the economic backdrop to the *stronista* regime and dedicated an entire volume to the issue of *tierras mal habidas* (CVJ 2008, vol. 4). This volume constitutes a courageous denunciation of the country's still-powerful quasi-feudal landed elites. In its conclusions, the report declared null and void the existing titles to around two-thirds of the land distributed between 1954 and 2003 (7.8 million hectares of a total of 12.2 million) (CVJ 2008, Conclusiones y Recomendaciones, 58, paras. 194–95). The Commission also refuted the claim that transition has been genuinely achieved: 'Many institutions, particularly those related to justice, law, security, and citizen protection, have been given a democratic makeover but retain many of the characteristics of a totalitarian system' (CVJ 2008, Conclusiones y Recomendaciones, 22, para. 59, my translation).

The report closed with an extensive list of recommendations and proposed reparations, including public apologies and memorialisation, economic reparations, purging of the security forces, criminal prosecution, and vetting of future political candidates. Victims of sexual violence and indigenous communities, it suggested, should receive specific attention and apologies. It also recommended that a national human rights secretariat should be established and given a more proactive role than the existing Ombudsman's Office (see below). This recommendation was not followed to the letter, but the Commission itself was transformed in 2009, as mentioned above, into the Truth, Justice and Reparations Directorate, operating under the auspices of the Ombudsman's Office and charged with overseeing follow-up to the Commission's own report. Registers of recognised victims are kept by the Directorate, and newly reported cases can, in theory, be added. Commission files can supposedly be viewed by accredited researchers, although victim testimony about sexual violence or involving minors is anonymised. Some national researchers report apparently arbitrary decisions by Directorate staff as to which material can and cannot be consulted.[43]

As with many such reports, the expansive 'wish list' of recommendations contrasts with the very limited follow-up on the ground. The Commission itself – now the Directorate – reports only minimal results. At a regional consultation in Buenos Aires in January 2013, former truth commissioner and current Directorate head, Yudith Rolón, estimated no more than 10 per cent compliance with the recommendations[44] (see also DGVJYR 2009, 2011). Many of these modest advances, moreover, came through presidential decree rather than legislation, creating the risk that they could become unenforceable under new presidencies of the post-2012 era.[45] Carmen Coronel, head of the human rights umbrella network CODEHUPY, perhaps foresaw this precariousness when she suggested, in early 2012, that while the Commission's work had been valuable and well executed, there had been a failure to capitalise on it with appropriate follow-up.[46]

Language and communication difficulties have been one impediment, with Paraguay the only Southern Cone country where an indigenous language, Guaraní, is more widely spoken than Spanish. Although testimony could be given to the Commission in either language, the full report was in Spanish; only unofficial or executive summaries exist in Guaraní. Formal literacy and access to print and electronic media are also low, with community radio still a principal source of information. The civil society organisations in the Mesa Memoria nonetheless took some action. In 2011, anticipating the country's bicentenary celebrations, they published manuals for teachers and serialised versions of Commission findings in national and local newspapers (CODEHUPY et al. 2011). In 2014, the Mesa spearheaded similar popular education initiatives around the 60th anniversary of the Stroessner coup. It successfully resisted occasional forays into revisionism, including attempts to repatriate Stroessner's remains with official honours, or name Stroessner's grandson as Paraguay's ambassador to the United Nations (UN).

Nostalgia for the authoritarian past, and occasional expressions of the continuity of that past, have been one obstacle to future-facing human rights compliance.

Another has been a persistent tendency, also common in Central America, for the popular press and the political right, now in government, to blame human rights groups for present-day criminality, implying that rights discourse gives aid and comfort to 'common criminals'. In one example, in June 2014, Paraguay's interior minister likened the country's human rights organisations to Colombia's FARC guerrilla movement after one self-styled human rights group in Paraguay offered to act as go-between with a small left-wing armed group suspected of a kidnapping (CODEHUPY 2014, 664). The involvement of human rights organisations in calling for due process guarantees in the Curuguaty massacre case has led to similar outbursts.

Reparations

Although reparations have been a part of the post-authoritarian transition in Paraguay, they have suffered from some critical weaknesses, notably questionable administration and political manipulation of the Ombudsman's Office. This office, the Defensoría del Pueblo, was first defined in the 1992 constitution, but did not come into existence until 2001, when its first director was appointed. Manuel Páez, a former bureaucrat under the Stroessner regime, had no background in human rights. Despite a petition to Parliament by human rights organisations calling for his removal, he was appointed for a second term in 2004. His mandate definitively expired in 2008, but he was still in his post seven years later, despite repeated expressions of disquiet by, among others, the UN Human Rights Committee and the UN Committee on Enforced Disappearances (see official reports published in 2013 and 2014 respectively).

The fate of the Ombudsman's Office is particularly central to transitional justice, since despite its theoretically broad remit, its main areas of activity in practice have been consumer rights and administration of reparations for dictatorship-era crimes. In regard to the latter it has been criticised as unduly bureaucratic and accused of demanding bribes and awarding reparations to people who are not genuine victims (CODEHUPY 2014, 677).[47] The ongoing scandal over the failure to oust Páez, and mounting criticism of the style and probity of current Directorate head Yudith Rolón, have coalesced around reparations issues. The issue came to a head in early 2015, when human rights groups finally forced a process of candidatures and public hearings for the new ombudsman. Rolón, who chose to apply for the post, was roundly attacked at a public hearing by a group of victims who accused her of taking illegal 'commissions' for processing reparations applications. The appointment issue had still not been resolved by the time of the parliamentary recess at the end of 2015, by which time Rolón had been formally named as a suspect in a criminal investigation for fraud. In 2013, the ENABI forensic team chose to distance itself from the Directorate altogether, successfully petitioning the Justice Ministry to incorporate the team into the new Vice Ministry of Justice and Human Rights.[48] The Ministry subsequently came up with a new name, Directorate of Reparations and Historical Memory, which is misleading as regards both the specific purpose of the team and its stated determination to press for justice actions to be taken in response to its eventual findings.

Material reparations

Administrative economic reparations were introduced by Law 838 of 1996, which stated that the Ombudsman's Office would oversee payments. Political opposition, however, stalled implementation for a further five years, until 2001. Even once the office was up and running, the absence of a central register of victims made it difficult to prove entitlement. The onus was on survivors to take the initiative, using *habeas data* petitions to obtain documents needed to qualify for sliding-scale monetary reparations.[49] This unwieldy procedure presents high access barriers and entry costs for less formally educated victims, who are the majority. Although a victims' register was later produced by the truth commission, in practice Terror Archive documentation on prison admissions and releases is given more weight for purposes of establishing entitlement to reparations. This is generally reasonable given the non-clandestine, formally registered, nature of most detentions, although it neglects violations carried out in unofficial settings.

The existence of regional branches of the Ombudsman's Office in each administrative district has somewhat reduced the need for relatives and survivors to travel to the capital to present applications. These can also, in theory, be submitted to any court building nationwide. It is the job of the Ombudsman's Office to finally determine what, if anything, a person is entitled to receive. A 2011 modification of the reparation laws attempted to streamline the process and reverse the burden of proof, placing the onus on state institutions rather than on individual rights holders to seek out necessary official documents. Delivery mechanisms nonetheless still seem cumbersome, and they are certainly not confidential. Press inserts appearing in the main national daily newspapers in April 2012 summoned survivors and relatives in batches, according to ID number, to an administrative building in central Asunción. They were strictly instructed to attend only on the specified dates and to bring official identity documents or forfeit payment, another practical entry barrier.

Law 838/96 still serves as the principal basis for official reparations, as modified to some extent by later laws.[50] The 1996 law allows payments to survivors or victims' relatives for forced disappearance, extrajudicial execution, extrajudicial detention, detention on political charges for over a year, and torture 'with manifest and serious physical and psychological consequences' (Art 2) committed by state agents between 1954 and 1989. Each person can submit a claim in only one category. The most significant modifications to the law include vacillation about final application deadlines, which were first extended, then abolished, then reintroduced before being abolished once again by Law 4838 of 2011. This law recognised that since the condition of having been a victim was a permanent one, the right to claim accompanying entitlements should not be time-limited. By contrast, the 2008 modification of the law (Law 3603/08) was, in general, more restrictive. It added a requirement of two eyewitnesses to the usual kinds of civil case proof previously specified, reduced the amount paid to those who had been imprisoned for less than a year, and reinstated a final cut-off date for applications (later revoked). It did, however, expand the categories of direct relatives who could apply. As mentioned above, the 2011 modification concentrates on process rather than content, removing deadlines for application and setting peremptory duties and deadlines for the relevant authorities, rather than the applicant, to obtain necessary official documentation and communicate a final decision.

Symbolic reparations

After the 1989 coup, several places named for former President Stroessner were renamed: for example, the city Puerto Presidente Stroessner became Ciudad del Este. Such initiatives, however, cannot really be termed symbolic reparations, since the renaming was done by the general's enemies within the Colorado Party as a repudiation of his rule (*destronización*) rather than as a statement about human rights. With the 1992 constitution, however, came a brief flowering of 'rights talk'. This period saw certain symbolic initiatives, such as the renaming of a city centre square in honour of victims and human rights defenders.[51]

Perhaps the most significant space to be reclaimed was the headquarters of DNAT, popularly known as La Técnica. Previously a notorious detention and torture site in the city centre, it was inaugurated as the Museo de las Memorias (Museum of Memories) in 2006. Again the drive and commitment of particular individuals was key. The building was recovered at the insistence of survivor Martín Almada, and the museum is the project of a foundation honouring Almada's first wife Celestina Pérez, a victim of *stronista* terror. The state continues to own the building, and until 2013 it seconded Ministry of Education and Culture staff to work on museum outreach programmes. The foundation nonetheless presides over the museum with a somewhat proprietorial air. It has been known to complain about the state preference for housing documents found in the building, or in subsequent searches of other sites, in the official Terror Archive.

Displays in the museum explain the major features of regime terror, its relation to Operation Condor, and its effects on indigenous and other excluded communities. The museography is nonetheless a curious mixture of authentic and reconstructed scenarios and artefacts. An apparently faithful recreation of Pastor Coronel's office obscures the fact that he presided over a different, separate branch of the police and indeed operated from a separate building. A portrait of Stroessner looms over the mock-up, and the anteroom features a collection of torture implements purchased for purposes of display. A cell block at the back of the complex has been preserved, showing a life-size human figure, prostrate and swathed in filthy bandages, chained to a rusty bathtub. The effect of the installation – the result of a promise made to an early school visitor group that they could design a contribution to the permanent collection – is disturbing. By 2014, the museum was reporting around 3,000 visitors a year (CODEHUPY 2014), although it was reportedly somewhat in decline by mid-2015.

Museum director María Stella Cáceres and educator Gabriela Rolandi, interviewed in 2012, said that general public awareness of dictatorship-era historical memory in Paraguay had been low until 2003, then climbed around 2004 with the inauguration of the truth commission. It levelled off again until 2010, when the impending bicentenary of the Republic in 2011 again galvanised human rights groups. Determined to make sure the dictatorship period was featured, these groups wanted human rights defenders included among the pantheon of national heroes to be officially celebrated during the year. The Mesa Memoria organised a National Memory Week in 2012 and contributed to the reclaiming of three other former detention centres in 2011 and 2012 (CEPAG 2012; Mesa Memoria Histórica 2011). The first of these sites, Pastor Coronel's investigations headquarters, was opened in April 2011. Tours were offered by a former prisoner hired by the Truth, Justice and Reparations Directorate as a guide. The site is gloomy, damp, and oppressive and is visibly falling into disrepair thanks to leaking roofs and pervasive water damage.[52] According to CODEHUPY (2014), it was under permanent threat of repossession by the national police, as the site is still part of a police complex. In December 2011, the Ministry of Education and Culture organised an homage to victims at Emboscada, Stroessner's largest concentration camp for political prisoners, housed in a former prison complex in the country's Cordillera district. Renovations included explicit commemoration, in the form of a plaque, but demolished original features of the site.

In April 2012, the Abraham Cué memory site was inaugurated in a police barracks in the rural district of Misiones. The police chief who spoke at the event gave a resounding and apparently heartfelt acknowledgement of past police responsibility for 'events that shame us'. Human rights organisation representatives present agreed that this reflected a genuine desire on the part of a younger generation of police officers to disassociate themselves from the past, although denunciations of torture and even of extrajudicial killings in rural areas continue to this day.[53] The last word at the ceremony was skilfully appropriated by an elderly man, who approached the podium pleading to be allowed to read a poem in honour of the victims. After delivering the poem in Spanish, the speaker switched to Guaraní and launched a blistering political critique of virtually all the authorities present. A plaque was unveiled and the visitors from the capital clambered back into their vehicles. While it is hard to gauge what effect such activities have beyond the immediate circles of activists who propose them and the authorities who approve, fund, and organise them, they certainly make an impression on the casual visitor.

In an interview, however, María Stella Cáceres of the Museo de las Memorias declared herself unconvinced about official commitment to symbolic reparations. The inter-ministerial commission set up in 2010 to create a network of 'sites of conscience', she said, was 'a typical example of the state trying to appropriate something without really understanding it.'[54] While the development of yet another mixed state-civil society body could be viewed positively as signalling a desire to respond to citizen initiatives, civil society members were included only in a consultative capacity.[55] Furthermore, this, like all such initiatives, was susceptible to rollback by the state after 2012.

Contacts consulted in 2015 tended to agree that the Cartes administration had not launched the kind of all-out assault on memory or transitional justice initiatives that some had feared. However, the vulnerability of state memory policy to changes of administration makes it generally strategic to push for, yet not depend fully on, state responsiveness. A cautionary tale is provided by the short-lived story of human rights programming on Paraguay's first nationwide public TV channel, which began broadcasting in late 2011. The channel's first director had a background in human rights. He promoted a series entitled '35', consisting of direct testimony of the 35-year-long Stroessner period. Aired repeatedly due to the channel's early dearth of material to fill schedules, the series allowed direct testimonies in Guaraní to reach a significant proportion of the population. Immediately after the constitutional coup of 2012, however, the new presidency intervened to change the management of the channel. The director was dismissed, and Alfredo Boccia, Terror Archive researcher and well-known columnist and journalist, resigned to protest the purge. Boccia, interviewed in April 2012, before these events, discussed how early human rights defence and memory initiatives such as the Jesuit-run magazine *Acción* had been complemented by new ones aimed at a younger, educated urban audience through the virtual museum project MEVES.[56] Boccia also pointed out that site recovery is moving memory interventions towards the previously neglected interior of the country, where many of the relevant sites are located. Although sceptical about justice prospects, given a Supreme Court whose nominations are subject to party-political machinations (*cuoteo*), Boccia was, however, positive about the truth commission's achievements and the impact of the Terror Archive and recent television testimonies.

In summary, some of the material aspects of reparations policy have been addressed, albeit within serious constraints of resources and state capacity. But symbolic reparations have not been sufficient to indicate willingness on the part of traditional elites to recognise the Colorado Party's direct responsibility for Stroessner-era crimes. Nor have these actors indicated a commitment to exercise power in a more transparent way that reflects democratic values. Instead, concerns over trafficking, corruption, and ordinary criminality have been used to justify resort to *la mano dura* – the iron fist – including hard-line security rhetoric and a resort to military forces for internal policing (CODEHUPY 2014).

Conclusions

In one sense it is surprising how much has been achieved in Paraguay in the areas of truth, reparations, and even justice, given the long and all-consuming nature of the oppressive regime as well as the incompleteness of subsequent political change. The fact that transitional justice mechanisms managed to gain a foothold owes a great deal to voluntarism and the leadership of persistent individuals. It

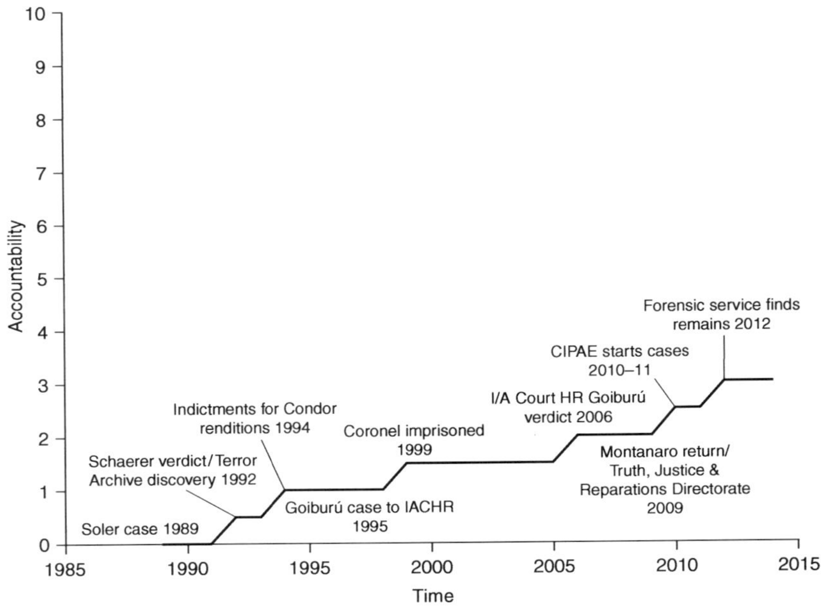

Figure 7.1 Paraguay: the trials dimension of accountability, 1989–2014
Source: Authors' construction, 2015.

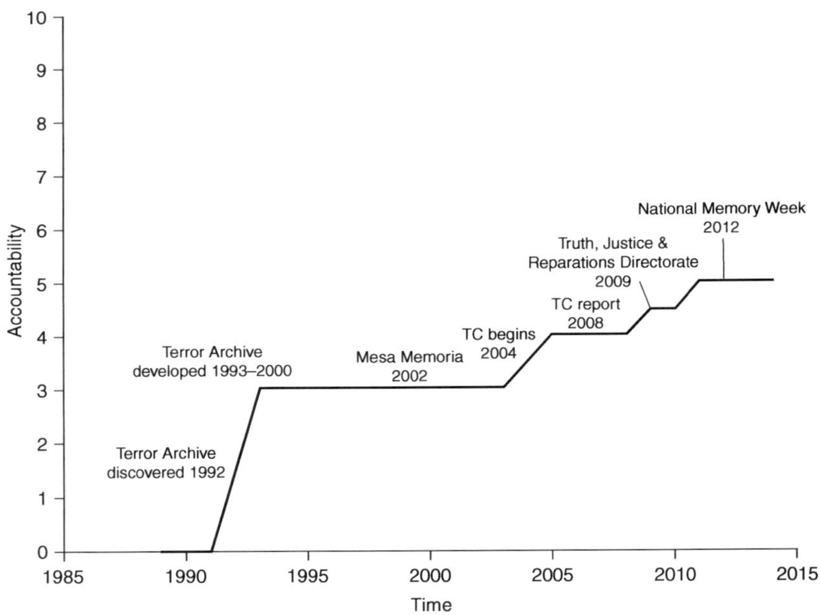

Figure 7.2 Paraguay: the truth dimension of accountability, 1989–2014
Source: Authors' construction, 2015.

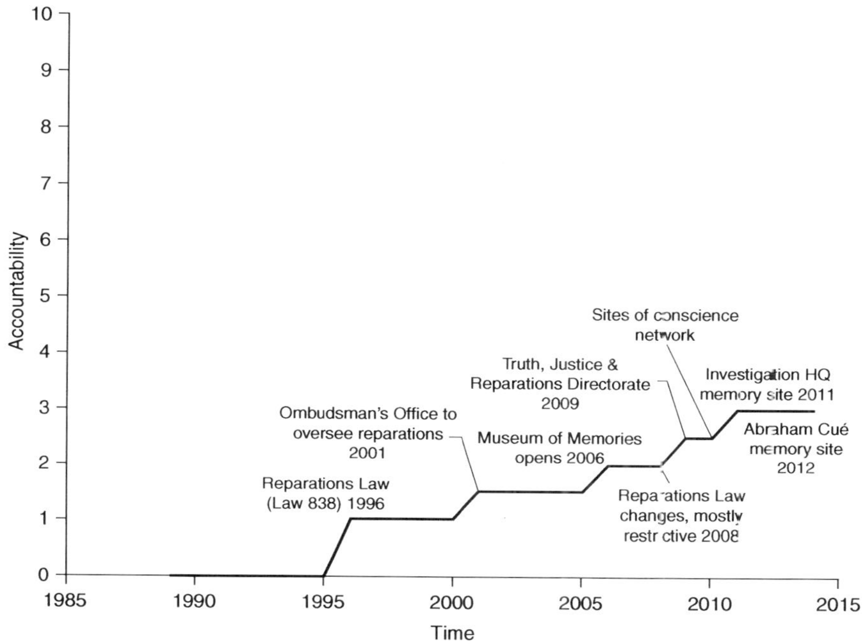

Figure 7.3 Paraguay: the reparations dimension of accountability, 1989–2014
Source: Authors' construction, 2015.

is due, as well, to the opening provided by internal rivalries within the Colorado Party after Stroessner, as politicians have occasionally found transitional justice concerns a useful stick with which to beat their political enemies. Just as the regime became personalised under Stroessner, early judicial accountability has been perhaps unduly limited to those regime figures presenting the most obvious targets, guilty as they undoubtedly were. The truth commission was more courageous than others in denouncing broad civilian culpability and responsibility. However, fundamental questions, such as the inter-penetration of the military with the Colorado Party, and of both with persistent feudal power structures, have still not been addressed by the state or wider society.

One brief window of opportunity was opened by the 1992 constitution-making process, another by the social mobilisation that culminated in the 2008 Lugo presidency. Both periods were utilised by a relatively small group of capable and well-organised activists to score modest successes in human rights discourse and practice. Ultimately, however, the combined weight of *Coloradismo* and undemocratic political practice more broadly proved a formidable obstacle to change and innovation, including in transitional justice. The unhappy fate of the Ombudsman's Office is a case in point, as are the increasingly vocal concerns

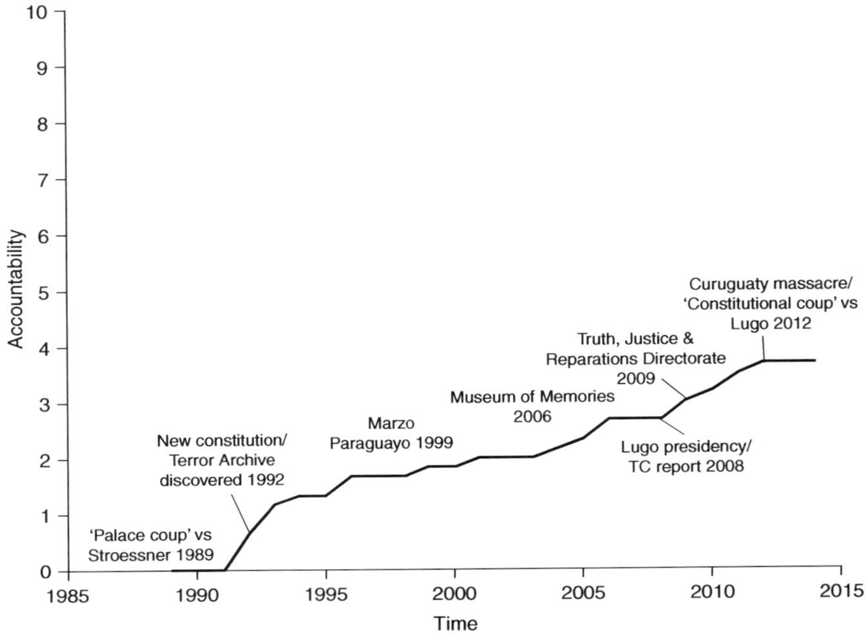

Figure 7.4 **Paraguay: overall trend towards accountability, 1989–2014**
Source: Authors' construction, 2015.

about the operations of the Truth, Justice and Reparations Directorate. In this sense, Paraguay's experience highlights the limited and reversible nature of changes won through activist-led efforts to exploit limited shifts in national politics. When democratic space is particularly fragile, and the justice system generally regarded as compromised, accountability gains from transitional justice mechanisms are also vulnerable to being weakened or reversed.

Notes

* The author thanks Boris Hau and Pelao Carvallo, who provided research and bibliographic assistance for this chapter.

1 Inter-American Development Bank data for 2014 (available online at http://data.iadb.org/) give Paraguay a nominal gross domestic product per capita of US$4,536, placing it in the World Bank's lower-middle-income category.

2 The Colorado Party was not a personal vehicle but a powerful corporatist entity: it long preceded Stroessner and has outlived him. Founded in 1887, it ruled until 1904, and then again from 1947 until Lugo's accession in 2008. After Lugo's removal and a 14-month interim presidency, a Colorado president, Horacio Cartes, was sworn in once again in August 2013.

3 Paraguay was perhaps the third-largest recipient of US Alliance for Progress money in the 1960s (Nickson 2011, 288), despite having a population of only around 2 million.

4 Membership in the Colorado Party was a prerequisite for army personnel and all public servants. Contracts and sinecures were handed out based on party loyalty and did not require anything so taxing as actual work. When Itaipú was audited under the Lugo presidency, it emerged that many party members on the official payroll had never reported for work. Some had continued to draw salaries after their death.

5 The final report of the Truth and Justice Commission was published in nine volumes. The last volume presents the Commission's conclusions and recommendations.

6 The population jumped to 4.5 million shortly after Stroessner's removal, mainly due to mass return from exile (Pereira 2011). By 2014 it stood at around 6.5 million.

7 Stroessner died in Brazil in 2006. The return in 2009 of Montanaro, elderly and infirm, sparked some demands for accountability, including for the enforcement of an outstanding arrest warrant. Montanaro sought refuge in a military hospital and died in 2011.

8 Examples abound. Lino Oviedo, a military commander-in-chief under President Wasmosy, launched an unsuccessful rebellion when he faced dismissal. He was later involved in El Marzo Paraguayo, a notorious incident on 26 March 1999 in which seven people were shot and more than 100 wounded by unknown snipers at a street protest. Oviedo, widely rumoured to have been behind the crime, fled to Argentina and then Brazil, where he continued to seek a return to Paraguayan politics.

9 On the left turn in Latin American politics in the late 1990s, see Levitsky and Roberts (2011).

10 Dr Alfredo Boccia, psychiatrist, columnist, and author on memory, interview by author, 25 April 2012; Rosa Palau, director, Museo de la Justicia y Centro de Documentación y Archivo para la Defensa de los Derechos Humanos (the Terror Archive), interviews by author, 17 September 2009, 25 April 2012, and 21 August 2015. Palau still oversees the Terror Archive. Additional sources include documents and press cuttings by and concerning ex-police *comisario* Ismael Aguilera from the Terror Archive collection, copies on file with author. All author interviews for this chapter were conducted in Asunción.

11 Civil society organisations included the non-governmental Centro de Documentación y Estudios (CDE) and the ecumenical Comité de Iglesias para Ayudas de Emergencia (CIPAE), formed in 1976.

12 Rosa Palau interview, 17 September 2009.

13 Rosa Palau interview, 21 August 2015.

14 For example, a folder entitled 'Investigación de Rescate Histórico Documental' (DH008/2012), presented to the Supreme Court in 2013 without the prior knowledge of the Archive, contained authenticated photocopies of documents apparently obtained from the Paraguayan Navy Archive. Cover image and notes on file with author.

15 Rosa Palau interview, 25 April 2012.

16 Ibid.

17 The 'social cleansing' aspect of Stroessner-era repression remains underreported. The unsolved murder of radio announcer Bernardo Aranda in 1959 unleashed a homophobic witch hunt, with 108 allegedly gay men arrested. Their names were made public, with many suffering decades of abuse and ostracism as a result. The case was not considered by the truth commission, attracting criticism from gay rights activists (Ramos 2012).

18 Sentencia Definitiva 25, First Criminal Court, 1992. Montanaro and Stroessner, originally on the list of the accused, were left out of the verdict because Paraguay does not allow trial *in absentia*. On the original crime, see Marecos (2011). The 25-year sentences were confirmed and enforced by the Supreme Court on 7 May 1999, in the aftermath of El Marzo Paraguayo. Coronel died in prison in 2000.

19 The Portillo case's first instance ruling, of 6 April 1995, was finally confirmed by the Supreme Court in July 1999 with eight-year sentences. In the Oviedo case, torture was prosecuted as *lesiones* (injuries), a lesser charge with lower penalties.
20 The absence of a central case record makes it difficult to track all relevant investigations. This list is illustrative, not exhaustive.
21 Inter-American Court of Human Rights (I/A Court HR), *Case of Goiburú and Others v Paraguay*, Judgment of 22 September 2006, sec. XIII, para. 192, sub-paras. 1–16.
22 Ibid., paras. 169, 170, and 174.
23 At least one Catholic bishop appears on lists of official informers discovered in the Terror Archive.
24 Founded in Argentina, SERPAJ also operates in Brazil, Uruguay, Paraguay, El Salvador, Colombia, and Chile.
25 In 2014, Paraguayan Bishop Mario Medina, former truth commission president, retired, accentuating a conservative turn in Catholic Church politics.
26 Edgar Vázquez, lawyer and collaborator with the CIPAE legal team, interview by author, 18 September 2009.
27 Rodolfo Aseretto, lawyer and director of CIPAE legal team, interview by author, 26 April 2012.
28 Ibid.
29 Edgar Vázquez interview, 18 September 2009.
30 Rosa Palau interview, 21 August 2015; Rogelio Goiburú, head of the state team for location and identification of the disappeared, interview by author, 20 August 2015.
31 Notably, Paraguay's truth commission is one of few in Latin America to have explicitly included justice alongside truth in its name and mandate.
32 Interview by author with personnel of the Truth, Justice and Reparations Directorate and ENABI (Equipo Nacional para la Investigación, Búsqueda e Identificación Plena), 26 April 2012.
33 Note from the assistant public prosecutor for human rights to all public prosecutors, issued in response to a challenge made in the Eusebio Torres case, ref. Nota F.A. DD.HH no. 8, dated 16 October 2007, on file with author.
34 Federico Tatter, then staff member of ENABI, remarks to the Truth, Justice and Reparations Directorate steering committee meeting, 26 April 2012.
35 Rogelio Goiburú, head of ENABI, remarks to Truth, Justice and Reparations Directorate steering committee meeting, 26 April 2012.
36 The Equipo Argentino de Antropología Forense (EAAF) is a non-governmental forensic team, established in 1984, which assists the investigation of human rights violations in Argentina and worldwide.
37 The author met with the ENABI team in its new headquarters on 20 August 2015.
38 In region-wide Latinobarómetro surveys (http://www.latinobarometro.org/lat.jsp), Paraguay regularly shows continued adhesion to authoritarian values. Respondents express disapproval not only of the quality and performance of existing democratic arrangements and practice in the country, but also, to some degree, of the very idea of democracy as the best or 'least bad' governing arrangement. For more on the quality or deficiencies of present-day Paraguayan democracy, see Abente Brun (2012).
39 A weighty intellectual figure in Latin America and parts of Europe, Touraine, one-time president of the Association for Research and Study of Archives in Latin America, regularly crops up in the backstory of truth and memory initiatives in the region. He exemplifies the long-standing transregional dimension of Latin American human rights defence and transitional justice initiatives concerning Latin America.
40 Experts consulted included Javier Ciurlizza, from Peru, and Carlos Beristain, a Spanish national with long experience in Guatemala, Colombia, and El Salvador (see Chapter 8).
41 Some pushback against this stratagem can be seen in the truth commission's final report. Although the preamble cites the official time frame of 1954–2003, by p. 2, the

report prefers to talk of 'violations committed [...] basically during the Stroessner dictatorship (1954–89)' (CVJ 2008, Conclusiones y Recomendaciones, 2.

42 Staff of the Truth, Justice and Reparations Directorate, interviews by author, 17 September 2009.

43 Interviews by author in Asunción, identities withheld at interviewees' request, August 2015.

44 Yudith Rolón, executive secretary, Truth, Justice and Reparations Directorate, interviews by author, 17 September 2009 and 26 April 2012.

45 These decrees include, among others, Decree 2736 of 2004, which convoked the truth commission; Decree 1875 of 2009, declaring its report 'of national interest'; Decree 7101 of 2011, setting up the ENABI forensic team; and Decree 3138 of 2009, declaring the reparations programme a national priority. The 2010 creation of an inter-ministerial committee for memory sites was also carried out by decree.

46 Carmen Coronel, coordinator, Coordinadora de Derechos Humanos del Paraguay (CODEHUPY), interview by author, 27 April 2012.

47 The operations described here are those of the Ombudsman's Office (Defensoría). The truth commission follow-up Directorate is administratively dependent on the Ombudsman's Office but is operationally separate.

48 See Decree 10.970 of 3 May 2013.

49 Under Law 838/96, Art 5, payments were highest for disappearance or execution, then torture, then illegal imprisonment. Law 3603 of 2008 modified the 1996 law in certain details but preserved the relative distribution of payments.

50 In reverse chronological order, by year: Laws 4381 and 4838 of 2011, Law 3603 of 2008, Law 3075 of 2006, Law 2494 of 2004, and Law 1935 of 2002.

51 Much later, after El Marzo Paraguayo, a similar initiative saw the square where the sniper killings had taken place renamed Democracy Square.

52 The author made field visits to the investigations headquarters memory site on 25 April 2012 and 21 August 2015, and interviewed Melanio Enciso, guide and survivor, during the first visit.

53 National human rights organisations submitted a civil society-produced report to the Inter-American Commission on Human Rights in October 2014, denouncing extra-judicial killings of peasant leaders committed between 1989 and 2013 (CODEHUPY 2014, 655).

54 María Stella Cáceres, director, Museo de las Memorias, interview by author, 24 April 2012. The Red de Sitios Históricos y de Conciencia del Paraguay was established in 2010 by Decree 5619.

55 Decree 5619/2010, Art 2, specifies that the network is made up of representatives of the Supreme Court; Ministries of the Interior, Exterior, Justice, Labour, Education and Culture, and Defence; the Ombudsman's Office; the Itaipú and Yacretá dam projects and, lastly, civil society groups in a consultative capacity (*en carácter consultivo*).

56 Museo Virtual de la Memoria y Verdad sobre el Stronismo (Virtual Museum of Truth and Memory about Stronismo), www.meves.org.py.

References

Abente Brun, Diego. 2011. 'Después de la Dictadura.' In *Historia del Paraguay*, edited by Ignacio Telesca, 295–313. Asunción: Taurus.

——2012. 'Estatalidad y calidad de la democracia en Paraguay.' *América Latina Hoy* 60 (April): 43–66.

Arditi, Benjamín. 1992. 'El Estado omnívoro: Poder y orden político bajo el stronismo.' In *Adiós a Stroessner: La reconstrucción de la política en el Paraguay*, 15–70. Asunción: RP Ediciones.

Aseretto, Rodolfo, ed. 2011. *Fallos judiciales sobre casos de violaciones a los derechos humanos*. Asunción: Comité de Iglesias para Ayudas de Emergencia.

Boccia Paz, Alfredo, Rosa Palau Aguilar, and Osvaldo Salerno. 2007. *Paraguay: Los archivos del terror*. Asunción: Corte Suprema de Justicia/Centro de Documentación y Archivos para la Defensa de los Derechos Humanos.

CEPAG (Centro de Estudios Paraguayos Antonio Guasch). 2012. 'Memoria activa vs impunidad.' Special issue, *Acción: Revista de reflexión y diálogo de los Jesuitas del Paraguay*, no. 322 (March).

CODEHUPY (Coordinadora de Derechos Humanos del Paraguay). 2014. *Situación de los derechos humanos: Paraguay 2014*. Asunción: CODEHUPY.

CODEHUPY, Diakonia, Comité de Iglesias para Ayudas de Emergencia, Fundación Celestina Pérez de Almada, and Servicio Paz y Justicia Paraguay. 2011. *Dictaduras ¡Nunca más! Resumen del Informe de la Comisión de Verdad y Justicia – Paraguay*. Asunción: CODEHUPY.

CVJ (Comisión de Verdad y Justicia). 2008. *Informe final de la Comisión de Verdad y Justicia, Paraguay*. 9 vols. Asunción: CVJ.

Delich, Francisco. 1981. 'Estructura agraria y hegemonía en el despotismo republicano paraguayo.' *Estudio Rurales Latinoamericanos* 4(3): 239–55.

DGVJYR (Dirección General de Verdad, Justicia y Reparación). 2009. *Informe de gestión 2009*. Asunción: Defensoría del Pueblo, DGVJYR.

——2011. *Informe de gestión 2010–2011*. Asunción: Defensoría del Pueblo, DGVJYR.

Fassi, Mariana. 2010. *Paraguay en su laberinto*. Buenos Aires: Capital Intelectual.

Lambert, Peter, and Andrew Nickson. 2012. 'A Transition in Search of Democracy.' In *The Paraguay Reader: History, Culture, Politics*, edited by Peter Lambert and Andrew Nickson, 321–23. Durham, NC: Duke University Press.

Levitsky, Steven, and Kenneth M. Roberts, eds. 2011. *The Resurgence of the Latin American Left*. Baltimore: Johns Hopkins University Press.

Marecos, Adriana. 2011. *Tortura y muerte: El caso Schaerer Prono*. Asunción: Corte Suprema de Justicia/Centro de Documentación y Archivos para la Defensa de los Derechos Humanos.

Mesa Memoria Histórica. 2011. *Memorias/Hoy* 1(1). http://mesamemoriahistorica.org.py/publicacion/.

Nickson, Andrew. 2011. 'El régimen de Stroessner (1954–1989).' In *Historia del Paraguay*, edited by Ignacio Telesca, 265–94. Asunción: Taurus.

Osorio, Carlos, and Mariana Enamoneta, eds. 2007. *Rendition in the Southern Cone: Operation Condor Documents Revealed from Paraguayan 'Archive of Terror'*. Electronic Briefing Book 239, Part II (English version). Washington, DC: National Security Archive.

Pereira, Raquel. 2011. 'El exilio: Elemento de consolidación de la dictadura del General Alfredo Stroessner.' In *Migrantes: Perspectivas (críticas) en torno a los procesos migratorios del Paraguay*, edited by Gerardo Halpern, 316–32. Asunción: Apé Paraguay.

Ramos, Anselmo. 2012. '"A Hundred and Eight and a Burned Body": The Story Not Told by the Truth and Justice Commission.' In *The Paraguay Reader: History, Culture, Politics*, edited by Peter Lambert and Andrew Nickson, 305–8. Durham, NC: Duke University Press.

Riquelme, Marcial. 1994. 'Towards a Weberian Characterization of the Stroessner Regime in Paraguay (1954–89).' In *The Paraguay Reader: History, Culture, Politics*, edited by Peter Lambert and Andrew Nickson, 239–44. Durham, NC: Duke University Press.

Rivarola, Milda. 2009. *Transición, desde las memorias*. Asunción: Decidamos/Diakonia.

Schvartzman, Mauricio. 1989. *Mito y duelo: El discurso de la 'pre-transición a la democracia en el Paraguay*. Asunción: BASE-IS.

Telesca, Ignacio, ed. 2011. *Historia del Paraguay*. Asunción: Taurus.

UN Committee on Enforced Disappearances. 2014. *Concluding Observations on the Report Submitted by Paraguay under Article 29, Paragraph 1, of the Convention at its 102nd and 103rd Meetings (CED/C/SR.102 and 103), held on 16 and 17 September 2014*. CED/C/PRY/CO/1, 20 October. New York: United Nations.

UN Human Rights Committee. 2013. *Concluding Observations on the Third Periodic Report of Paraguay, Adopted at the 107th Session (11–28 March 2013)*. CCPR/C/PRY/CO/3, 29 April. New York: United Nations.

Chapter 8

El Salvador

The difficult fight against impunity

*Elena Martínez Barahona and Martha Liliana Gutiérrez Salazar**

This chapter analyses the trajectory from impunity towards accountability in El Salvador from the end of the civil war in 1992 through 2014. The violence dates back much further, however, and it is useful to begin with a brief account of the country's long history of conflict and ideological polarisation. Hume (2014, 385) describes El Salvador as 'a country in which politics, violence and economics have been entwined since independence from Spain in 1821'. In the century following independence, this tiny Central American state used repression and terror to ensure the continued political and economic hegemony of a small but powerful elite (Dunkerley 1982).[1] This group consisted mainly of landowners who controlled plantation-style production of coffee, then the country's principal export.[2] Following a military coup in 1931, an attempted communist-led popular uprising in 1932 was brutally put down by government troops, who massacred up to 30,000 peasants.[3] The military then consolidated its hold on power, retaining control of the machinery of state in exchange for serving the interests of the economic elite (Stanley 1996, 7).

El Salvador was thus a highly militarised state long before the counter-insurgency war against left-wing insurgents began. Violent military intervention in politics was common, with the army often deployed in favour of private elite interests. By the end of the 1970s, the armed forces were launching attacks against sections of the civilian population and against several groups of armed guerrillas.[4] These groups merged in 1980 into the Farabundo Martí National Liberation Front (Frente Farabundo Martí para la Liberación Nacional, FMLN).[5] The FMLN sought to overturn a semi-feudal political and economic structure dominated by a few wealthy families. Its social change agenda was shared by a range of popular and pro-poor organisations that emerged in the 1960s across many parts of the region, inspired by the Cuban revolution but also by Catholic liberation theology. The military met this alleged subversive threat with extreme and widespread repression, using forced disappearances, killings, rapes, massacres, and internal displacement to combat the guerrillas and undermine peasant support for them.

Large numbers of Salvadorans died during the conflict, which affected the country's few urban centres as well as the countryside. According to Seligson and McElhinny (1996, 224), over 75,000 people were killed in a country then numbering approximately 5 million inhabitants.[6] Government forces, and paramilitary death squads affiliated with them, were heavily supported and financed by US training, weapons, and aid in the context of Cold War anti-communism. They appeared ready to kill anyone they suspected of sympathy for the guerrillas, with *campesinos* (peasant farmers) among the most frequent victims. According to El Salvador's official United Nations-sponsored truth commission, more than 85 per cent of the serious acts of violence were carried out by state agents or those acting under their direction (Wood 2003, 8). In contrast to the semi-clandestine tactics employed by Southern Cone police states, extreme violence in Central America often occurred in public, or its results were deliberately displayed in public.

Over the course of the 1980s, critical voices within the United States increasingly questioned continued US military aid to the Salvadoran government. A series of events fuelled rising grassroots opposition among US citizens to their government's involvement in the conflict. These included the assassination in 1980 of Archbishop Oscar Romero, an outspoken defender of the poor, and the murder by Salvadoran state agents of four US churchwomen and two US agrarian reform experts in 1980–81. A continuous influx of Salvadoran refugees into the United States, some of whom were sheltered by US churches, highlighted the appalling human rights record of the Salvadoran regime.

Centre-right civilian president José Napoleón Duarte (1984–89) came under pressure to improve human rights performance and effect judicial reform. Duarte was, however, replaced in June 1989 by President Alfredo Cristiani of the hard-line, right-wing Nationalist Republican Alliance (Alianza Republicana Nacionalista, ARENA). A negotiated solution to the armed conflict was made possible not by ideological softening on the far right, but by the abrupt end of the Cold War – which led to declining US interest in sustaining the conflict – and by the inability of the army to militarily defeat the FMLN. Thus, formal peace in El Salvador, signed under the Cristiani presidency, emerged from a strategic stalemate (Karl 1992, 149).[7]

El Salvador's early peace arrangements favoured impunity, meaning that the prospect of accountability was deferred to a remote horizon. The truth commission set up as part of the peace agreement initially provided important but incomplete truth, followed immediately by a broad amnesty law. This law, adopted by the Salvadoran Congress in the wake of the accords, effectively guaranteed impunity both to state-aligned forces and to the guerrillas, which is essential to understanding the FMLN's continued reluctance to act against amnesty. The subsequent two decades of ARENA-dominated government saw official policy inclined towards denial of atrocity crimes, other than those committed by the left.[8] Non-governmental organisations (NGOs) representing relatives and victims began, in 2000, to press for exhumations in the search for the missing. They also lobbied the Supreme Court (SC) to rule on the amnesty law. In the face of implacable opposition from the Public Prosecutor's Office (Fiscalía), however, no change was seen until after the executive handover of

2009. The narrow victory that year of the FMLN's Mauricio Funes led to advances in symbolic recognition of victims, although impunity largely continued to prevail in the justice sphere.[9]

The peace process and initial steps towards accountability

When analysing the transitional justice process in El Salvador, it is important to consider it as part of a larger picture of reconstruction after armed conflict. As in other Central American cases, the high-intensity conflict made a peace agreement an urgent priority from a humanitarian and human rights perspective. As we will see below, however, the deference to human rights and international humanitarian law did not outlive the signing of the final peace accord, since shortly afterward the former combatants, by then transformed into political parties, agreed on an amnesty law whose breadth clearly contravened those same standards.

Peace negotiations mediated by the United Nations (UN), with support from a group of Central American states, began in early 1990. The first two sessions, in Geneva and Caracas in April and May, established a framework agenda for the negotiations. A July 1990 agreement in San José emphasised combatants' obligations to respect human rights law and international humanitarian law. The establishment of a UN-supported truth commission was stipulated in Mexico City in April 1991; both sides agreed that the recommendations of the commission would be treated as binding. In September of that year, agreements were reached in New York for an oversight commission, the National Commission for the Consolidation of Peace (COPAZ); for military reform and an ad hoc commission to review the human rights records of some commanders in the armed forces; for a new civilian police force to include ex-FMLN members; and for agrarian reform. Finally, on 16 January 1992, the Chapultepec Accords were signed by the Salvadoran government and the FMLN in Mexico City. The accords laid out how the FMLN was to be admitted into civilian political life and mandated military and paramilitary demobilisation, judicial and electoral reform, and some economic changes.[10]

The United Nations Observer Mission in El Salvador (ONUSAL) was established to monitor human rights and the implementation of the agreements. ONUSAL operated from July 1991 to April 1995. The scaled-down United Nations Mission in El Salvador (MINUSAL) then remained in the country to verify implementation of outstanding points of the agreements. ONUSAL and MINUSAL reflected the international community's commitment to remain involved in the peace process, as well as post-Cold War optimism about the role of the UN in a multilateral world. UN involvement in El Salvador became emblematic of this new activism and has been generally regarded as a success. However, like many other peace processes, the process in El Salvador has been criticised for its failure to address truth, justice, and reparations for victims and survivors (Popkin 2000; Lazo Fuentes and Rey Tristán 2011).

Truth-finding

The Commission on the Truth for El Salvador (Comisión de la Verdad para El Salvador, CVES) was mandated to investigate 'serious acts of violence' committed between 1980 and 1991 (UN 1993, 11).[11] Appointed by the UN secretary-general, the truth commission was composed exclusively of foreign nationals as commissioners and staff (Buergenthal 1996, 13). The Mexico City peace accords of April 1991 clearly stated that 'the commission shall not function in the manner of a judicial body'. However, the text made no mention of the option of a substantive amnesty.

The CVES operated for eight months, from July 1992 to March 1993. Receiving 22,000 complaints about all kinds of violations, the commission was overwhelmed and chose to focus its report on only 33 'paradigmatic' cases, supposedly representative of the overall patterns of violence. The report, published in March 1993 under the title *From Madness to Hope: The 12-Year War in El Salvador*, concluded that the armed forces and state-linked paramilitaries were responsible for 85 per cent of fatal violations (UN 1993). The unprecedented naming of over 40 individual military perpetrators – and of others, including the Supreme Court president, FMLN commanders, and some politicians found directly or indirectly at fault – made an essential contribution to later reform. The CVES justified its naming of names, in the face of strong behind-the-scenes government pressure to desist, by arguing that the justice system would prove itself incapable of accountability and that naming was therefore the only effective sanction that many perpetrators would undergo. It made clear that, based on previous performance, the judiciary, especially the Supreme Court, was a major contributor to impunity.

The report's long list of concrete and detailed recommendations included dismissal of 'officers of the Salvadorian armed forces who are personally implicated in the perpetration or cover-up of serious acts of violence, or who did not fulfil their professional obligation to initiate or cooperate in the investigation and punishment of such acts' (UN 1993, 176). It also called for the removal of public servants and judicial personnel who covered up serious acts of violence; banning from future public office of known perpetrators for at least ten years; institutional reforms; armed forces and security service reform, including reduction of military strength, the civilianisation of domestic policing, and the creation of a new police force; justice system changes, including the replacement of the entire Supreme Court and the introduction of statutory human rights bodies; and material and moral compensation to the victims of violence (UN 1993, 176–86). The report also emphasised the need to set up an entity to monitor compliance.

Achievements and limitations of the truth commission

The government, the judiciary, and the armed forces immediately and strenuously rejected the CVES report, and President Cristiani criticised it for not contributing to 'national reconciliation'. The armed forces issued a statement on 23

March 1993 denouncing the report as 'illegal, unethical, partial and disrespectful' and defended the military's record in 'preserving our democratic and republican system' (quoted in IACHR 1994, chap. II, part 2). The FMLN was not satisfied either, as some of its own commanders were denounced for serious infractions of international humanitarian law. Opponents predictably seized on the commission's international composition, something to which they had consented in advance, in an effort to discredit the results. However, the UN and, eventually, the United States pressed the government to formally accept the report (Sieder 2001).

The fact that the final report focused on a selection of paradigmatic cases could be interpreted as silencing or rendering invisible a large number of victims, a danger the report itself acknowledged (UN 1993, 13). The implications included reduction of the scope of accountability: despite the importance of the truth commission's work and its report, many crimes went unpunished and indeed have not even been officially recognised.

Although the mandate stated that the commission's recommendations were legally binding, implementation depended on the balance of power between the armed forces and the two other signatories to the peace accords, ARENA and the FMLN. Since none of the signatories had any real interest in carrying out the entire reform package, no governmental implementation unit was ever established. ONUSAL did, however, push for progress, leading to, among other things, the 1995 ratification of the Optional Protocol to the International Covenant on Civil and Political Rights and acceptance of the jurisdiction of the Inter-American Court of Human Rights in the same year. A new Criminal Procedure Code was adopted in 1996,[12] and judicial appointments and judicial review processes were also overhauled (Popkin 2002). Implementation otherwise has been patchy. The Human Rights Ombudsman's Office (Procuraduría para la Defensa de los Derechos Humanos) was established and has spoken out in national debates on war-era atrocities and other issues, but it has struggled in the face of political manipulation and attempts to sideline it. Exhumations carried out since 2001 have led to the identification and recovery of some of the tens of thousands of victims who remained missing at the time of the peace agreements.

The Ad Hoc Commission

The New York session of the peace negotiations provided for the creation of an Ad Hoc Commission, responsible for vetting the armed forces. The Commission's five members included three Salvadoran lawyers with 'recognized independence of judgment and unimpeachable democratic credentials', selected, after consultation, by the UN secretary-general (as provided in the Chapultepec Peace Accords, chap. I). The two remaining members were to be appointed by the country's president, a provision that significantly lowered initial expectations about the seriousness of the endeavour. Given only three months to evaluate officers' past conduct and human rights record, the Commission handed over its final, confidential, report to national authorities and the UN in September 1992. The report recommended the disbanding of notorious units such as the Atlacatl Battalion as well as a series of individual transfers and dismissals.

These recommendations were ignored until the CVES report, published six months later, underlined the issue of notorious perpetrators still holding senior military rank. Concerted UN and US economic pressure was then applied to achieve the eventual removal of some of those on the list. By July 1993, ONUSAL reported general compliance with the Ad Hoc Commission, although all the removed officers kept full military honours and pension rights, and many retained an influential role in national and political life. Orders banning these individuals from holding future elected office were also successfully challenged later in the courts, on the grounds that non-judicial processes such as the Ad Hoc Commission or CVES did not have the power to suspend the political rights of individuals.

The Ad Hoc Commission was designed as a vetting mechanism rather than a truth-telling exercise, as evidenced by its confidentiality. However, the list of names it provided was reinforced by the later public findings of the CVES. Taken together, the two commissions served a significant truth-telling and institutional reform function.

Amnesty

Although the peace agreements contained some measures intended to end the endemic impunity that had characterised El Salvador for decades, other provisions hindered accountability, particularly in formal criminal justice. Just after the signing of the Chapultepec agreement, the legislature approved an initial amnesty law (Decree 147 of 1992) known as the National Reconciliation Law. Article 6 stated that this amnesty would not extend to anyone later identified by the truth commission as a perpetrator of 'serious acts of violence' (*graves hechos de violencia*). However, a year later, and only five days after receipt of the CVES report, Congress passed the new General amnesty law for the Consolidation of Peace (Decree 486 of 1993). This much broader law derogated the exception in Art 6 of the previous law and provided for the extinction of both criminal and civil liability, effectively offering a guarantee of total impunity.

The 1993 law was approved thanks to 47 votes from the three right-wing parties that together held a majority in the legislature – ARENA and two others. There were 13 abstentions by Christian Democrats and nine opposing votes from the Democratic Convergence (Convergencia Democrática), a moderate left-wing grouping then serving as the political arm of the FMLN. The FMLN itself had not yet competed in elections as a recognised party, but it was notable, nonetheless, that its leaders did not come out clearly against the amnesty law. Some leaders of the FMLN now claim that they only supported the narrower, CVES-compliant 1992 law that was designed to allow them to return to the country and take part in pre-accord negotiations (Valencia Caravantes and Peña 2014). Rubén Zamora, who stood as presidential candidate for the FMLN in 1994, suggested recently that the 1993 General amnesty law went much further than peace negotiators had anticipated in allowing for impunity (Zamora 2012). It was the only Latin American amnesty of the period that explicitly attempted to rule out civil action as well as criminal investigation (Collins 2010, 47).

Challenging and defending the amnesty law

The 1993 amnesty law imposes a clear obstacle to trials, as was its intent. It has also been used by the courts and the Public Prosecutor's Office to pre-empt investigations. It was condemned by the Inter-American Commission on Human Rights as early as 1994 and domestic challenges to the law's constitutionality reached the courts in 1993, 1997, and 1998. In response to the direct challenges on constitutional grounds, the Constitutional Chamber of the Supreme Court in September 2000 upheld the constitutionality of the law, although in a slightly qualified decision that opened the door to some judicial action for accountability.[13] The ruling left individual judges theoretically empowered to order investigation of a limited range of serious crimes or crimes by state employees committed during the presidential term in which the amnesty was issued. That term began on 1 June 1989, long after many of the country's most notorious massacre episodes. This limited discretion was not sufficient to allow for accountability, however: judges continued to find ways to abandon investigation even of self-evidently grave crimes that had clearly occurred within the relevant temporal range. An example is the first judicial resolution to be emitted after the 'loophole' ruling in a case to which the exception should clearly have applied. It conceded that the Supreme Court ruling suggested the inapplicability of amnesty, but it promptly closed the case by invoking statutes of limitations.[14]

The amnesty law remains broad and comprehensive, and no additional court decision since 2000 has limited its scope. In other words, there has not been the kind of gradual recognition of pre-existing exceptions under international law, providing that crimes against humanity cannot be amnestied, that has taken place in other countries discussed in this volume. Legislative modification or annulment has not even been considered. In September 2013, the Supreme Court admitted a new lawsuit seeking the judicial annulment of amnesty, filed on 20 March 2013 by private actors including Benjamín Cuéllar of the Human Rights Institute of the Jesuit University in San Salvador (Instituto de Derechos Humanos de la Universidad Centroamericana, IDHUCA). The case had not been decided as of July 2015.

One case that was kept alive despite the amnesty barrier was that of the Jesuit massacre. On 16 November 1989, six Jesuit priests, including university rector Ignacio Ellacuría, together with their housekeeper and her teenage daughter, were slaughtered by soldiers on the campus of the Universidad Centroamericana, the Jesuit University in San Salvador. The assassinations were carried out under cover of an FMLN assault on the capital, and attempts were made to frame the guerrillas for the crime. The case was pursued by lawyers at IDHUCA, where most of the victims had worked. An early show trial in 1991, designed to placate international opinion, prosecuted some footsoldiers, but they were hastily granted amnesty. IDHUCA continued to press the issues of command responsibility and the involvement of high-level political figures, allegations supported by the truth commission's account of the incident. In 1999, IDHUCA applied to have the Jesuit case reopened in order to investigate the intellectual authors of the crime. This petition was formally postponed until after the Supreme Court ruling of September 2000 in the amnesty constitutionality case mentioned above. At that point, the judge in the Jesuit case ruled that, although she might have been willing to disallow amnesty under the terms of the new ruling, the Jesuit case was closed due to the expiry of the statute of limitations.

Although the verdict in the Jesuit case might have been a technical victory against the broad scope of the amnesty law, the case itself did not advance further in El Salvador, and the precedent was not accepted by judges or prosecutors. Instead, the case was later pursued in Spain, based on European citizenship linkages of the victims – a route not available to relatives of the many Salvadoran victims of rural massacres, who died, as they had lived, in anonymity. It is no accident that the cases that have moved forward in regard to El Salvador are those with some special claim to international notoriety. Salvadoran authorities, made nervous by third-country cases, by Inter-American Commission and Inter-American Court rulings, and by the weakening or overturning of similar amnesty laws elsewhere around the region, attempted to shore up the amnesty before the Inter-American Commission in 2007. They requested a special hearing at which FMLN peace negotiator Salvador Samayoa stood alongside his ARENA colleagues, then in government, to defend continuing broad amnesty as the cornerstone of the country's peace, 15 years after the signing of the final peace accords.

In 2012, the inter-American system, ruling in the El Mozote massacre case, delivered its clearest condemnation yet of the Salvadoran amnesty law and one of its strongest statements in general about states' duties to prosecute and punish.[15] However, as of mid-2015, this effort to remedy the exceptionally broad scope of the Salvadoran amnesty had not produced any formal change. According to press reports, in March 2015 the Salvadoran government agreed, during the Universal Periodic Review by the United Nations Human Rights Council, to amend the amnesty law. However, as the 1993 General amnesty law was enacted by the Congress, such a change would require action by the legislative or the judicial branch, upon request from the government. By mid-2015, no such action had yet been taken.

Justice seeking

In addition to questions about the desirability of formal legal accountability for past violations in El Salvador, on which there is still no political consensus, there is also the practical issue of feasibility. In thinking about this, it is worth bearing in mind that the search for justice has taken place against the backdrop of a society still characterised, as throughout its post-independence history, by elite privilege and extreme, almost feudal, inequality – the very conditions that inspired guerrilla action. Moreover, the country's courts are still weak, despite the extensive judicial reforms detailed below.

Judicial reform

Attempts to reform the judicial and criminal justice system during and after the war were extensive, yet in many ways so ineffectual, that they represent a distinctive dimension of the Salvadoran accountability trajectory. Much of the non-military US aid given to El Salvador during the war was ploughed into the judicial system. CVES recommendations further emphasised the need to revise the criminal justice process. The system in place at the time, designed on the inquisitorial model, regularly failed to meet basic standards of expediency and transparency, tending to be confession-based rather than evidence-based. Investigative proceedings were mostly written, but also often secret, giving no real possibility of external oversight or defence challenges. The fact that the same judge who investigated also brought charges and delivered an initial verdict, while common in such systems, was seen as particularly problematic in a setting where individual judges were regularly subjected to pressure or outright threats. Indeed, a significant number of judicial personnel were assassinated during the war.

However, as we will see, the prosecutor-driven model that replaced this system in 1996 also allows for considerable individual discretion. High levels of individual control over outcomes can work for or against accountability, depending on the predisposition of the judge or prosecutor. The 1996 reform introduced an adversarial, public prosecutor-driven system in which the Public Prosecutor's Office took over the conduct of criminal investigations, prosecution, and the bringing of charges, leaving judges to conduct trial proceedings. The impact on accountability prospects remains unclear, as everything now depends on the criteria that the public prosecutor, rather than specific judges, chooses to apply. Criminal code reform also reduced the already short statute of limitations periods, which proved a significant obstacle for later attempts at accountability.[16]

The Public Prosecutor's Office is not, in itself, any more or less predisposed to autonomy and independence than the judicial branch although, in practice, the appointment of its chief prosecutor – like the appointments of Supreme Court judges – is subject to executive and legislative ratification. In post-war El Salvador this has generally meant a chief prosecutor (*fiscal general*) acceptable to the ARENA party and/or to the FMLN, the latter not necessarily more reliably anti-amnesty than the former. The Public Prosecutor's Office, like the judicial branch before it, depends on auxiliary justice system actors to carry out investigations; while these have undergone structural change, this can mask behavioural continuity. A new civilian police force, the Policía Nacional Civil, is, like its militarised predecessors, limited in technical and forensic capacity. It also continues to include individuals implicated in the war-era crimes it might be asked to investigate. The official Human Rights Ombudsman's Office, which is also part of the post-peace accords and post-reform landscape, has made strong and well-founded critiques of lack of accountability in the Jesuit, Archbishop Romero, and El Mozote cases. However, it does not have formal powers to compel other state organisms to act on its findings.

Judicial reform since the peace accords, then, has not yet led to significant changes in accountability outcomes. A shift in institutional responsiveness to legally framed claims, key in other country settings studied in this book, has not been observable in either the courts or the Public Prosecutor's Office. There has been no move to set up specialised units to expedite prosecution of human rights-related cases, as in other countries. Isolated cases have moved forward in domestic or international venues, but they have done so in response to private, rather than state, initiatives.

Trials and civil claims in domestic courts

During the war, virtually the only atrocity cases that reached the domestic courts were those for crimes committed by the guerrillas. Various FMLN members were tried and convicted, insofar as the generally ramshackle justice system allowed, but state and paramilitary violence was only punished where exceptional circumstances – usually meaning pressure from the United States – demanded (Collins 2010).

The post-war period has seen domestic case activity, which is summarised in this section (a review of international case activity follows in the next sections). As part of the research project Against Impunity: Transitional Justice in Central America, funded by the Spanish Agency for International Development Cooperation, the present authors built a database of all war-related cases that could be traced in the national criminal justice system as of early 2012. This information was supplemented and updated in July 2015 from media sources and reports from local NGOs. Although the results are necessarily incomplete, given a lack of reliable official information, we are confident that this represents the best available overview of current case activity.[17] Sources include one governmental agency – the Human Rights Ombudsman's Office – plus six key NGOs.[18] As of mid-2015, this database included 68 cases initiated between 1980 and 2013.

These data, while limited, show a predictably restricted court caseload during the war, followed by a steady rise in complaints after publication of the CVES report. Half the cases (34 of 68) were still at the preliminary investigation (evidence collection) stage in July 2015. The courts had issued two acquittals and six convictions. A further 26 criminal investigations had been archived, that is, shelved by military courts, the Public Prosecutor's Office, or civilian trial courts. Archived cases included the Jesuit case, for which the statute of limitations was invoked in 2000. Of the 68 cases, 32 were for extrajudicial executions, 24 for forced disappearance, seven for torture, two for terrorism, one for sexual assault, one for kidnapping, and one for attempted murder. All related to crimes committed by state agents or by paramilitaries linked to the state.

In 43 cases, NGOs participated in bringing the case to the courts. The cases for forced disappearance resulted from a litigation strategy by Asociación Pro-Búsqueda, a Jesuit-founded NGO that searches for children separated from their parents during the war.[19] The cases for torture were mainly brought after 2010, when survivors, backed by IDHUCA, began to organise in dialogue with international actors and demand justice.[20] IDHUCA and Pro-Búsqueda are the organisations most active in accompanying relatives or survivors in making justice demands. The human rights promotion group Centro Madeleine Lagadec is also doing significant legal work, as did the Catholic human rights office Tutela Legal before it closed.

A separate dimension of judicial activity deals with the administrative task of exhuming and identifying bodies from mass graves for the purpose of certifying death. This process, particularly supported by the Centro Madeleine Lagadec, allows relatives to move forward with resolving inheritance issues or forming new relationships. Local magistrates can and have ordered exhumations for this purpose. The results could be considered an advance in truth-telling, but official exhumations do not follow the protocols that would be necessary for later criminal proceedings. By contrast, exhumations carried out under private initiative are more likely to have an evidence-collection goal appropriate for criminal justice. These include excavations at the mass grave site of El Mozote, carried out at regular intervals since 1992 at Tutela Legal's behest, by an Argentine-based forensic team.[21]

Some small steps have been taken to create more space for domestic criminal accountability. In 2009 and 2010, the Constitutional Chamber of the Supreme Court handed down *habeas corpus* rulings ordering the Public Prosecutor's Office to expedite investigation into the wartime disappearance of three children.[22] In 2010, the same chamber diluted the monopoly of the Public Prosecutor's Office on prosecutorial discretion, which has allowed it, as we have seen, to act as a very efficient gatekeeper against war-era cases. The Court urged criminal procedure reform to restore to victims of any crime the option of exercising criminal action should the Public Prosecutor's Office fail to do so through negligence or disinclination.[23] The legislature subsequently passed Decree 1010 of 2012, modifying Art 17 of the Criminal Procedure Code in the general direction recommended by the Court. However, no substantial progress on such cases has yet resulted.

Role of the inter-American human rights system

The failures of the political and justice system to prosecute, combined with the very broad scope of amnesty, have led some pro-accountability actors to seek justice in regional and third-country courts. The inter-American system, in particular, has attempted to press the Salvadoran state to provide greater domestic accountability.

El Salvador ratified the American Convention on Human Rights in 1978 and recognised the contentious jurisdiction of the Inter-American Court of Human

Rights on 6 June 1995. The day after the 1989 Jesuit murders, the case was denounced by the region-wide human rights monitoring organisation Americas Watch (now part of Human Rights Watch) to the Inter-American Commission on Human Rights (IACHR). Reporting in December 1999, the IACHR declared the Salvadoran government responsible and called for investigation, punishment, reparations to victims' families, and repeal of the amnesty law (IACHR 1999a). This was not the first time the IACHR had been called on to take a position on events in El Salvador. In a 1994 country report, the Commission declared that regardless of how necessary peace negotiations had been, 'the very sweeping General amnesty law passed by El Salvador's Legislative Assembly constitutes a violation of [its] international obligations'. It went on to list concerns that included the granting of 'reciprocal amnesty' without prior acknowledgement of responsibility, the non-exclusion of crimes against humanity, and the elimination of the possibility of victim compensation through the extinguishing of civil liability (IACHR 1994, chap. II, part 4).

Reporting in 1999 on two specific cases, those of Lucio Parada Cea and Víctor Hernández Vásquez, the IACHR recommended investigation, punishment, and reparations (IACHR 1999b, 1999c). In the Parada Cea case, the Commission called on the Salvadoran state to 'guarantee the petitioners the exercise of the rights guaranteed by the [American] Convention [on Human Rights] to all citizens, despite what is provided for in the General amnesty law for the Consolidation of Peace (decree No. 486). To that end, if need be, it should annul that law *ex-tunc*' (IACHR 1999b, XII, para. 1). A third 1999 report, on the Jesuit case, plus a 2000 report on the Archbishop Romero assassination case, reiterated and echoed those previous recommendations (IACHR 1999a, 2000). In reply, as noted above, the Salvadoran government requested a special 2007 audience at which it defended the amnesty law before the Inter-American Commission.

The Inter-American Court, for its part, issued a 2005 verdict in the case *Serrano-Cruz Sisters v El Salvador*, which resulted in the establishment of the National Commission for the Location of Missing Children (Comisión Nacional de Búsqueda de Niñas y Niños Desaparecidos). The ruling also called for creation of a genetic database and for a national day to commemorate child victims.[24] In 2011, the Court again ruled against El Salvador in the case *Contreras et al. v El Salvador*.[25] On 25 October 2012, the Court pronounced directly for the first time on the status of the amnesty, in the El Mozote case, speaking in forceful terms.[26] The ruling clearly declared the amnesty law to be a violation not only of international norms but also of the peace agreements. The judgment noted that the 2000 constitutionality decision, which supposedly modulated the amnesty, had had no discernible practical effect whatsoever. Compensation payments were ordered in all three judgments (Serrano-Cruz, Contreras, and El Mozote), but to date have only been made in the Serrano-Cruz case. Public admissions of state responsibility, also ordered in all three, were carried out (before the Inter-American Court verdict, in the case of El Mozote). In none of the three cases has the order to investigate and punish those responsible been fulfilled.

Official attitudes to Inter-American Court verdicts nonetheless show a degree of evolution. In 2005, in Serrano-Cruz, the state strenuously opposed the Court's temporal jurisdiction (the crime had been committed in 1982 whereas the Court's contentious jurisdiction was not recognised until 1995). This objection was partly validated by the Court. However, by the time of the Contreras and El Mozote verdicts of 2012, the state did not contest on these grounds. This tacit acknowledgement is a significant change in state attitude to the Court, although there is still some way to go in compliance.

Cases in Spanish domestic courts

Violations stemming from the Salvadoran civil war were also brought before the Spanish courts, using universal jurisdiction and related arguments. As we have seen in other chapters of this book, resort to Spanish courts to adjudicate Latin American atrocity crimes dates back at least to the mid-1990s, when Operation Condor cases for Spanish nationals and other victims in Southern Cone countries were admitted. These led to the detention of former Chilean dictator Augusto Pinochet in London, to other extradition attempts, and to the jailing in Spain of former Argentine navy officer Adolfo Scilingo. Between 2003 and 2005, Spanish court jurisdiction over crimes committed in Chile, Argentina, and Guatemala was challenged, though it was eventually reaffirmed. In 2009, Spanish law was amended to severely limit Spain's interpretation of universal jurisdiction.[27] It is now a legal requirement in Spanish domestic law (rather than, as before, a strategic preference on the part of case-bringers) that alleged crimes demonstrate a traditional jurisdictional connection, such as the involvement of Spanish citizens as victims or perpetrators.

In November 2008, the Spanish Association for Human Rights and the US-based Center for Justice and Accountability (CJA) put forward a case in Spain in association with relatives of some of the victims of the Jesuit massacre. The case is being worked for CJA by Almudena Bernabeu, a Spanish-born lawyer now based at CJA. The Spanish citizenship of five of the six priests helped to keep the case active when other pure universal jurisdiction cases were all but ruled out. On 9 January 2012, Spanish magistrate Eloy Velasco requested that El Salvador extradite 13 retired Salvadoran army officers to Madrid. The Salvadoran Supreme Court rejected this request in May of that year, relying on a now-superseded outright constitutional ban on extradition of nationals. The case is ongoing, however, and those bringing the case hope to reactivate domestic proceedings in El Salvador using the 'extradite or prosecute' principle. In January 2016, Velasco reiterated his extradition request.

CJA also had close contact with Salvadoran exiles in the United States after it became involved, in the first decade of the 2000s, in a series of civil claims brought there against high-level Salvadoran army officers who had retired to Florida. First initiated by the families of the four US churchwomen killed by National Guardsmen in El Salvador in 1980, the series of cases, later brought by survivors in exile, used US domestic legislation (the Torture Victim Protection Act and the Alien Tort Claims Act) in an effort to have the men declared, at least, civilly liable. The results led to successful immigration and deportation proceedings against perpetrators, with former Salvadoran defence minister Carlos Eugenio Vides Casanova, implicated in the churchwomen case, finally being deported from the United States in April 2015.

Reparations

Although the Salvadoran state has seemed to be extremely reluctant to deal with most aspects of past violations, there has been some progress in the field of reparations to victims, at least in the symbolic sphere. Most of the progress has been in response to pressure from NGOs or the inter-American system, though the election of an FMLN government in 2009 also marked an apparent turn towards more spontaneous acknowledgement. In the early post-war years, a compensation plan was established, according to truth commission recommendations, for those left orphaned or disabled.[28] Victims of human rights violations (HRV), however, received less attention than ex-combatants. The National Reconstruction Plan, 1992–96, was supposed to integrate former combatants into the productive system by providing loans and training. A land transfer programme established in rural areas is considered to have been a failure, with low production performance and high rates of abandonment. It is important to keep in mind that reintegration programmes or compensation to former combatants are not the same as reparations to victims.

Neither economic nor symbolic reparations received much attention during the first decade and a half of post-peace accord governments. There was little noticeable change in the symbolic arena until FMLN presidencies began in 2009. The few symbolic gestures that did take place prior to 2009, such as the 2003 installation of a Monument to Memory and Truth in a San Salvador park, were promoted by civil society rather than the state (Lazo Fuentes and Rey Tristán 2011). They do not, in this sense, count as reparations at all. Much of this changed in the Funes administration, which undertook both apologies and practical measures. However, while the state under Funes recognised its responsibility for past official crimes, it was reluctant to address crimes committed by the guerrilla forces. Accordingly, the government did not promote the reinterpretation or annulment of the amnesty law.

Some of the most significant changes under Funes were symbolic. In December 2011, during the 30th commemoration of the El Mozote massacre, President Funes publicly apologised to victims on behalf of the state. Other symbolic gestures include: a posthumous award in 2009 to the murdered Jesuits; a public apology by the president in 2010 for violations carried out by state agents during the war; a government apology in 2010 to the family of Archbishop Romero; and the Salvadoran state's initiatives around the UN's International Day for the Right to the Truth, which takes place annually on 24 March – a date chosen to coincide with the anniversary of Romero's assassination (Lazo Fuentes and Rey Tristán 2011).

With respect to other measures, Funes set in motion the creation of a reparations programme for victims of serious violations during the conflict. An advisory commission, the National Commission for Reparations to Victims of Human Rights Violations during the Internal Armed Conflict, was created by Executive Decree 57 in May 2010 and drew up recommendations for an executive-administered reparations scheme. After a long hiatus, the Programme for Reparations to Victims of Serious Human Rights Violations Occurring in the Context of Internal Armed Conflict was authorised by Decree 204 in October 2013 and established in 2014 under the presidency of Salvador Sánchez Cerén. Its declared aim was to establish a registry of victims under the direction of a five-person board, two of whose members would be victims' representatives. Detailed implementation proposals called for the presentation of quarterly reports. Press reports in July 2014 suggested the programme had begun to function although, as of July 2015, no official reports were yet available.

Table 8.1 shows that actions taken before 2009 were few and were driven mainly by NGOs or decisions of the inter-American system. After 2009, initiatives were more likely to be taken by the government without obvious external prompting, which could be considered progress. However, practical implementation of reparations seems to be lacking to date, although it is too early to evaluate the results of the Reparations Programme in mid-2014.

Table 8.1 An overview of reparations in El Salvador, 1989–2014

Administration	*Date*	*Policy or measure*	*Actor*
20 years of continuous right-wing ARENA party presidencies	1989–2009	Denial of state and armed forces responsibility for human rights violations[a]	State
President Francisco Flores (1999–2004)	2003	Monument to Memory and Truth	NGOs
President Antonio Saca (2004–9)	2007	Day to commemorate children who disappeared during the armed conflict	State, in compliance with Inter-American Court verdict
Left-wing FMLN party (formerly armed opposition) presidencies under President Mauricio Funes (2010–14) and President Sánchez Cerén (2014–)	2009	Posthumous recognition of the Jesuit priests murdered in 1989	State
	2010	Public apology for violations carried out by state agents	State

Table 8.1 (cont.)

Administration	*Date*	*Policy or measure*	*Actor*
Left-wing FMLN party (formerly armed opposition) (*continued*)	2010	Public apology to the family of assassinated archbishop Oscar Romero	State
		Creation of National Commission for the Location of Missing Children	State, in compliance with Inter-American Court verdict
		Creation of National Commission for Reparations to Victims of Human Rights Violations	State
	2011	Salvadoran state participates in UN proposal for International Day for the Right to Truth, to be celebrated on the anniversary of Romero's death	State, prompted by Inter-American Court verdict
		Public apology to relatives of victims of the El Mozote massacre	State
	2012	Public apology in Contreras case	State, in compliance with Inter-American Court verdict
	2013	Creation of full Reparations Programme (operational as of July 2014)	State

a. Classed as a negative measure or counter-measure.

Conclusions

The Salvadoran peace process, initially underwritten by the international community, struggled from the beginning to reconcile the urgent need for peace with the need for some path towards accountability for human rights violations and infractions of international humanitarian law committed during the civil war. A number of obstacles, including but not limited to a lack of real alternation in national government for almost 20 years, made accountability a remote prospect in many of its dimensions. The peace accord signatories, namely ARENA and the FMLN, did agree to establish the truth commission. However, this positive accountability step was undermined by the passage of an exceptionally broad amnesty law at the very moment when the CVES launched its report; this made criminal prosecution for the violations documented by the commission virtually impossible. This 'reciprocal amnesty', as described by the Inter-American Commission on Human Rights in its 1994 report, was explicitly crafted to ensure impunity for both parties to the peace agreement, to their mutual benefit. As these parties have remained dominant in Salvadoran politics, there has been no initiative to modify the amnesty law. The government's reluctance to deal with the past was further demonstrated by its unwillingness to accept the truth commission's findings or implement its recommended reforms and reparations.

Various institutions established to ensure more accountability for past or present violations have been weak in practice and have rarely managed to produce the desired results. The Supreme Court, and the state apparatus in general, seem still to be influenced by partisan dynamics. Pacts between political forces have distorted the institutional reforms implemented after the peace agreements, leaving checks and balances ineffectual when it comes to implementing equality before the law. Early transitional justice in El Salvador was a party-dominated process in which human rights considerations 'all but disappeared from the political agenda' (Sieder 2001, 188; see also Collins 2010, 160).

The situation is complicated by a perceived security emergency in the country, with high levels of 'ordinary' crime. Responses have included public calls for hard-line policing (*la mano dura*) and partial reversal of the demilitarisation that was one of the hard-won achievements of the peace process. Human rights organisations are criticised as being soft on crime. The reality of present-day criminality is undeniable, with El Salvador ranked as one of the most violent societies in the world. According to estimates, the death rate today is at least as high as it was during the civil war.[29] This is used by some to downplay the importance of past crimes and argue the impossibility of investigating them (Cuéllar Martínez 2010, 145). High crime levels coupled with low conviction rates also suggest an overwhelmed judicial system, unlikely to be able to deal adequately with human rights violations, whether past or present.

Political partisanship and lack of judicial independence have been compounded by the absence of strong and unified human rights organisations, a situation confirmed by the authors' field research in El Salvador in 2011 and 2012. Internal difficulties and coordination problems have beset NGOs supporting current litigation over past crimes. This bears out previous studies asserting the relative weakness of these organisations as well as the lack of a tradition of legal activism in the country.[30] Another factor that may have had a negative impact both on accountability and on the quality and diversity of public debate about related matters is the absence of an independent media sector. The mass media in El Salvador are monopolised by influential business groups, mostly aligned with ARENA; in general, they are hostile to human rights issues.

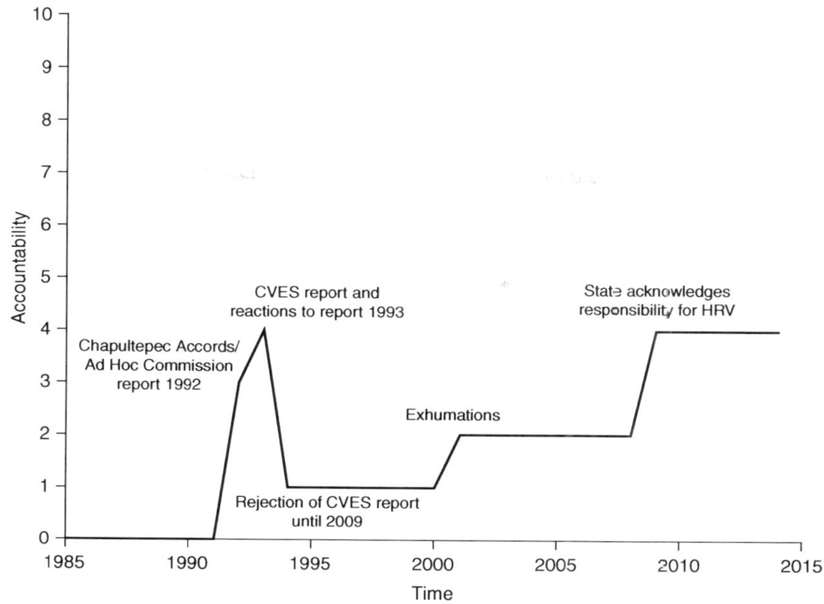

Figure 8.1 El Salvador: the truth dimension of accountability, 1992–2014
Source: Authors' construction, 2015.

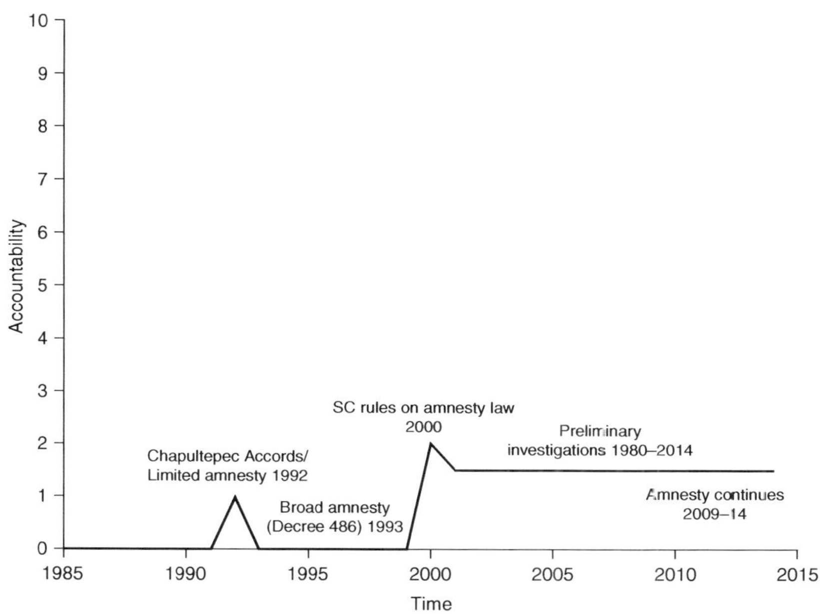

Figure 8.2 El Salvador: the overcoming amnesty dimension of accountability, 1992–2014
Source: Authors' construction, 2015.

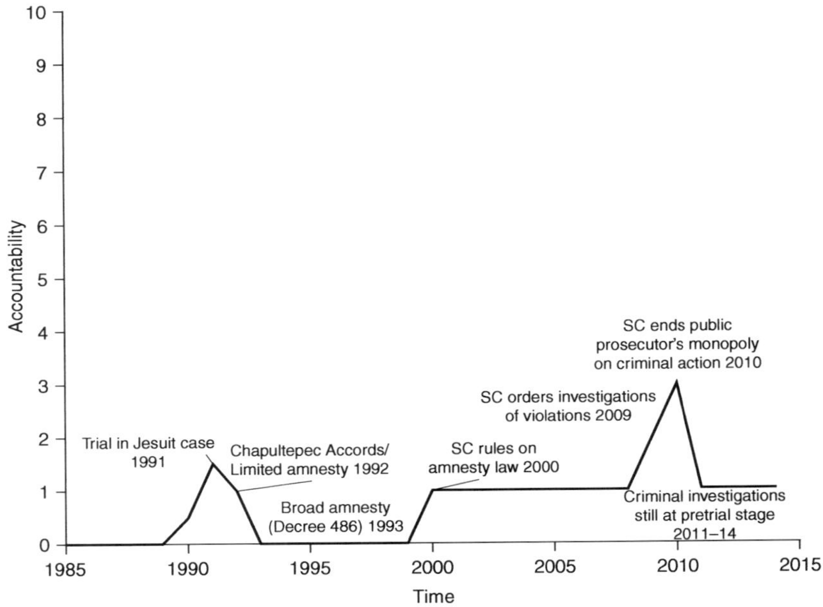

Figure 8.3 El Salvador: the trials dimension of accountability, 1992–2014
Source: Authors' construction, 2015.

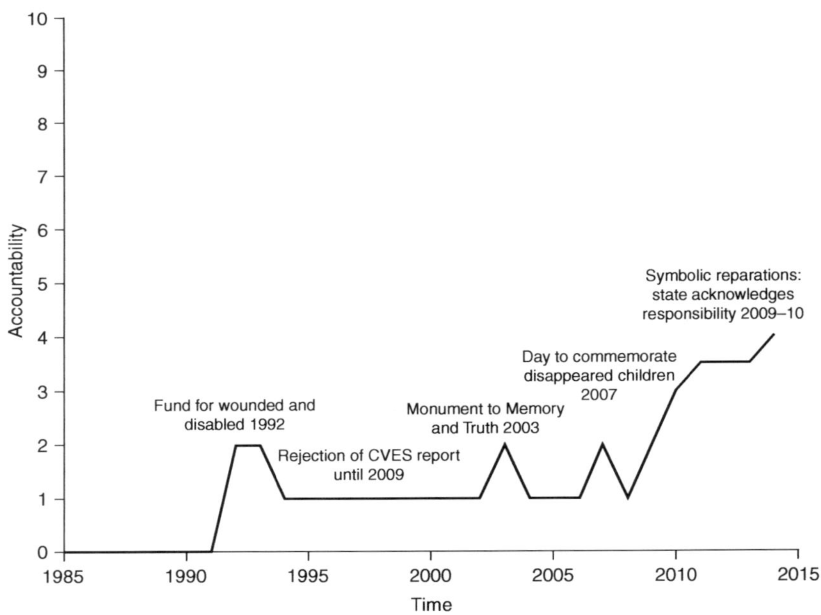

Figure 8.4 El Salvador: the reparations dimension of accountability, 1992–2014
Source: Authors' construction, 2015.

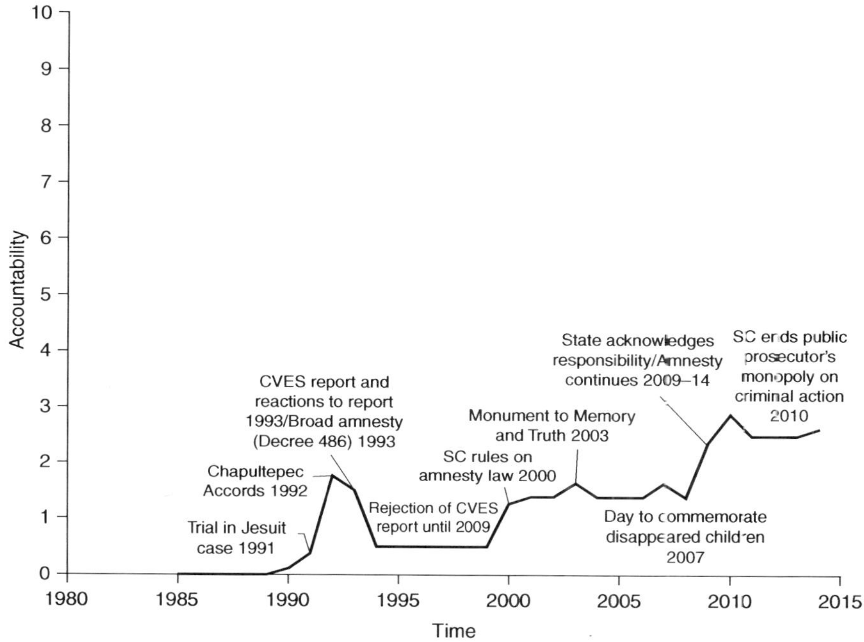

Figure 8.5 El Salvador: overall trend towards accountability, 1992–2014
Source: Authors' construction, 2015.

Overall, we can conclude, as does the United Nations in its human development report, that public participation in El Salvador is largely limited to voting (UNDP 2010). Significantly, there seems to be at least as much, and possibly more, movement on human rights cases in El Salvador outside the country – in third-country courts and the regional human rights system – as in domestic courts. The obstacles to domestic criminal prosecutions include the practical and logistical difficulties common to many post-war settings, notably the absence, loss, or destruction of contemporaneous records and the lack of sufficient evidence of individual, rather than institutional, culpability. Outside settings seem more receptive and, in some cases, are simply more accessible to exiles, overseas NGOs, and well-connected victims' relatives. Some, though not all, of these overseas initiatives are focused on making the domestic system more responsive.

Despite this rather grim picture, there have been persistent, if limited, claims for truth, justice, and reparations, made both domestically and internationally. These have led recently to recognition of state responsibility and at least the promise of new measures, suggesting that President Mauricio Funes's government understood that El Salvador's transitional justice agenda is still relevant. Forward movement domestically on the El Mozote case, as on the recently inaugurated reparations programme may, in time, contribute to a growing focus on transitional justice questions by stimulating greater awareness and wider dissemination of truths about the past.

Notes

* The authors thank Marcos Iglesias, who helped with translation of the first draft of the chapter; Elin Skaar, who provided useful comments on the manuscript; and especially Cath Collins for her expert guidance, patience, and understanding throughout the writing and revision of this chapter.

1 The smallest nation in Latin America by area, El Salvador occupies 20,720 square kilometres on the Pacific coast of Central America, with a population of just over 6 million. While its per capita gross domestic product (GDP) is relatively high compared to its near neighbours, and the World Bank classifies it as a lower-middle-income country, El Salvador, like the rest of Central America, lags ever further behind the South American countries in development indices and suffers sharp internal inequalities and high levels of violence. See IDB (2014) for recent statistics.

2 Bulmer-Thomas (1987, 3, 33) notes that, before the 1930s, 'coffee was king' in El Salvador. As late as 1979, coffee still constituted around 40 per cent of the country's exports, with agriculture as a whole representing 65 per cent of all exports.

3 The 1932 massacre, known as La Matanza, also targeted indigenous people, which is one reason that the indigenous share of the population today is notably lower in El Salvador than in neighbouring countries, especially Guatemala.

4 The armed forces killed thousands of civilian non-combatants in 1979 and 1980, before the armed conflict even officially began. This repression may have blocked an incipient popular insurrection, but it also locked in a determined social base that enabled the armed left to build a highly effective and sustained insurgency, with support in rural poor communities. See Wood (2003) on the diverse social origins of both the guerrilla forces and the opposition to them.

5 The FMLN was formed on 10 October 1980 by five left-wing guerrilla organisations: the Popular Liberation Forces (FPL, in its Spanish acronym); Popular Revolutionary Army (ERP); Armed Forces of Liberation (FAL), aligned with the Communist Party; National Resistance (RN); and Workers' Revolutionary Party (PRTC). In May 1980, most major leftist and centrist popular organisations and political parties formed a broad coalition, the Revolutionary Democratic Front (FDR), which allied itself with the FMLN for the duration of the conflict (Call 2002, 546).

6 1980–90 estimates. By 2014, the estimated population living within the country's borders was 6.4 million, with half again as many Salvadorans living abroad (World Population Review, http://worldpopulationreview.com/). Many of the latter were in the United States, often due to war-related displacement. War also devastated the economy in El Salvador, and some members of the traditional rural elite were forced from the countryside by the relative strength of the guerrillas (Paige 1997).

7 Cristiani was in office from 1989 to 1994. Post-accord presidents were Armando Calderón Sol (ARENA, 1994–99), Francisco Flores (ARENA, 1999–2004), Antonio Saca (ARENA, 2004–9), Mauricio Funes (FMLN, 2009–14), and Salvador Sánchez Cerén (FMLN, 2014–). Funes, previously a well-known TV journalist, formed part of a post-war Frente leadership not directly associated with armed activism. Sánchez Cerén, formerly Funes's vice president, has a much more combative profile as a former guerrilla commander. He won an extremely narrow victory over ARENA in February 2014 with a margin of less than 0.5 per cent of the vote.

8 ARENA was founded by, among others, Roberto D'Aubuisson, a military officer who also operated right-wing death squads in the 1980s and whom the truth commission held responsible for the 1980 assassination of Archbishop Romero (UN 1993).

9 The FMLN performed well in elections even before its 2009 presidential victory, making important gains in the national legislature and in municipal elections. In this sense it represents a successful case of transition from guerrilla movement to political party. However, it did not enjoy a legislative majority during Funes's mandate, a period that also reportedly saw tensions between Funes and his party (Hume 2014, 339).

10 The text of the Chapultepec Accords is available in English on the United States Institute of Peace website, www.usip.org.

11 All quotations from the Commission's final report are from the official English translation (UN 1993), available on the United Nations website.

12 Decree Law 904 of 4 December 1996.

13 The possible exception was made where the date of commission of a crime meant that amnesty of it would violate pre-existing constitutional dispositions. These prevent an incumbent government, such as the one that had overseen the peace accords, from amnestying its own acts. The very existence of such dispositions shows how prevalent self-exculpatory amnesty has been in the country's history.

14 The 12 December 2000 ruling concerns the Jesuit case. See 'Resolución de sobreseimiento de la Jueza Tercera de Paz en el Caso Jesuitas', cited in an extensive case chronology on the Universidad Centroamericana website (IDHUCA 2015).

15 Inter-American Court of Human Rights (I/A Court HR), *Case of the Massacres of El Mozote and Nearby Places v El Salvador*, Judgment of 25 October 2012, para. 2. The case is about 'alleged successive massacres committed between December 11 and 13, 1981, in the context of a military operation by the Atlacatl Battalion, together with other military units, in seven places in the northern part of the department of Morazán, Republic of El Salvador, during which approximately 1,000 people were killed'.

16 The statute of limitations for homicide became ten years. In a situation where international law forbidding a statute of limitations for atrocity crimes is ignored, while retrospective changes in law are permitted as long as they benefit potential defendants, this ruled out at a stroke serious investigation of wartime massacres, most of which were carried out in the early 1980s.

17 Appearing before a legislative committee in March 2013, the Public Prosecutor's Office admitted that it had not been able to keep accurate data on any category of criminal cases since 2010 (Chávez 2013).

18 These organisations are the Catholic Church-sponsored human rights office Tutela Legal, created in 1977 and closed in 2013; the Foundation for the Study of Applied Law (FESPAD), a think tank; the Madeleine Lagadec Centre for the Promotion of Human Rights; Pro-Búsqueda, an association dedicated to the search for missing children; the non-governmental Human Rights Commission of El Salvador (Comisión de Derechos Humanos de El Salvador, CDHES); and IDHUCA, the Human Rights Institute of the Jesuit University. Consulted in late 2012, the Supreme Court declared that no relevant information was available, while the Public Prosecutor's Office simply declined to answer.

19 Such children, orphaned by the killing of their parents or simply lost or abandoned due to forced exile and internal displacement, were often treated as war bounty by the military. Some were pressed into service at military bases; others were given or sold for overseas adoption.

20 In a field research interview carried out in 2011 for the Spanish-funded project Against Impunity, one representative of a committee of former political prisoners explained how exchanges in 2008 and 2009 between the group and human rights professional Carlos Beristain had helped them realise that they were entitled to define themselves

as survivors, with corresponding rights. Beristain, a psychologist of Spanish origin, has also worked extensively in Colombia, Peru, and Guatemala. He is one example of the network of individuals who have made a notable difference to the region's accountability history.

21 The Argentine Forensic Anthropology Team (Equipo Argentino de Antropología Forense, EAAF) was trained by, among others, renowned forensic anthropologist Clyde Snow (see Chapter 3). In January 2013, the Salvadoran Supreme Court convoked regional and international experts to discuss definitive exhumation of victims' remains from El Mozote in order to comply with the 2012 Inter-American Court judgment. The experts included personnel from the EAAF; the International Commission on Missing Persons, based in Bosnia and Herzegovina; the Human Rights Center at the University of California, Berkeley; and the Guatemala Forensic Anthropology Foundation. A first meeting of the international group took place in El Salvador in early 2014 (see Lampros 2014), and work subsequently began under the supervision of the Salvadoran court and the Public Prosecutor's Office. However, in April 2015, relatives working through NGO Tutela Legal obtained a court injunction halting the work on grounds that their rights to participation and information were not being respected (see *Diario Co Latino* 2015).

22 The decisions are dated 26 June 2009, 25 November 2009, and 1 December 2010 (case files 192–2007, 198–2007, and 199–2007, respectively).

23 Constitutional Chamber of the Supreme Court, Judgment of 23 December 2010, Exp. 5-2001/10 and others. The resolution came in response to an unconstitutionality claim filed by a group of citizens against various articles of the Criminal Procedure Code.

24 I/A Court HR, *Case of the Serrano-Cruz Sisters v El Salvador*, Judgment of 1 March 2005. The National Commission for the Location of Missing Children was established by Decree 5 of 15 January 2010 and began operations on 14 March 2011.

25 I/A Court HR, *Case of Contreras et al. v El Salvador*, Judgment of 31 August 2011.

26 I/A Court HR, *Case of the Massacres of El Mozote and Nearby Places v El Salvador*, Judgment of 25 October 2012.

27 Spanish Organic Law of the Judicial Branch, Art 23.4.

28 Legislative Decree 416 of 1992 established the Fund for the Protection of Those Wounded and Disabled as a Result of the Armed Conflict. Article 22 defined beneficiaries as 'Salvadorans disabled as a direct result of the armed conflict in the country; parents who lost their children, and minor or otherwise dependent children who lost their parents' (our translation). Article 23 specified that the pensions were equally available to civilians, members of the armed forces, or former FMLN combatants.

29 The country has the second-highest homicide rate in the world after Honduras, with an annual average of 60.2 homicides per 100,000 inhabitants in 2005–12 (UNODC 2013).

30 According to Popkin (2000), the involvement of the international community in the peace process may have weakened the local human rights community. Cuéllar Martínez (2007), however, suggests that a coherent Salvadoran human rights movement did not exist either before or after the armed confrontation. Moodie (2010) argues that in El Salvador, war crimes are narrated in terms of personal experience rather than as public violence stemming from the conflict, something that involves a separation of individuals from social movements.

References

Buergenthal, Thomas. 1996. 'La Comisión de la Verdad para El Salvador.' In *Estudios especializados de derechos humanos I*, 11–62. San José: Inter-American Institute of Human Rights.

Bulmer-Thomas, Victor. 1987. *The Political Economy of Central America since 1929*. New York: Cambridge University Press.

Call, Charles T. 2002. 'Assessing El Salvador's Transition from Civil War to Peace.' In *Ending Civil Wars: The Implementation of Peace Agreements*, edited by Stephen John Stedman, Donald Rothchild, and Elizabeth M. Cousens, 383–420. Boulder, CO: Lynne Rienner.

Chávez, Suchit. 2013. 'FGR no posee datos actualizados de procesos judiciales.' *La Prensa Gráfica*, 5 March.

Collins, Cath. 2010. *Post-Transitional Justice: Human Rights Trials in Chile and El Salvador*. University Park: Pennsylvania State University Press.

Cuéllar Martínez, Benjamín. 2007. 'El Salvador.' In *Victims Unsilenced: The Inter-American Human Rights System and Transitional Justice in Latin America*, edited by Katya Salazar and Thomas Antkowiak, 33–70. Washington, DC: Due Process of Law Foundation.

——2010. 'El Salvador.' In *Las víctimas y la justicia transicional: ¿Están cumpliendo los Estados latinoamericanos con los estándares internacionales?*, 127–56. Washington, DC: Due Process of Law Foundation.

Diario Co Latino. 2015. 'Juez de Paz suspende exhumaciones en "El Mozote"'. 17 April.

Dunkerley, James. 1982. *The Long War: Dictatorship and Revolution in El Salvador*. London: Junction.

Hume, Mo. 2014. 'El Salvador.' In *Handbook of Central American Governance*, edited by Diego Sánchez-Ancochea and Salvador Martí i Puig, 385–99. New York: Routledge.

IACHR (Inter-American Commission on Human Rights). 1994. *Report on the Situation of Human Rights in El Salvador*. OEA/Ser. L/V/II.85 Doc. 28 rev., 11 February. Washington, DC: OAS.

IACHR (Inter-American Commission on Human Rights). 1999a. *Ignacio Ellacuría SJ et al. v El Salvador*. Report 136/99, Case 10.488, 22 December. Washington, DC: OAS.

IACHR (Inter-American Commission on Human Rights). 1999b. *Lucio Parada Cea et al. v El Salvador*. Report 1/99, Case 10.480, 27 January. Washington, DC: OAS.

IACHR (Inter-American Commission on Human Rights). 1999c. *Víctor Hernández Vásquez v El Salvador*. Report 65/99, Case 10.228, 13 April. Washington, DC: OAS.

IACHR (Inter-American Commission on Human Rights). 2000. *Monsignor Oscar Arnulfo Romero y Galdámez v El Salvador*. Report 37/00, Case 11.481, 13 April. Washington, DC: OAS.

IDB (Inter-American Development Bank). 2014. *Approach Paper: El Salvador, 2009–2014: Country Program Evaluation*. Washington, DC: IDB Office of Evaluation and Oversight.

IDHUCA (Instituto de Derechos Humanos de la Universidad Centroamericana). 2015. *Caso jesuitas*. San Salvador: IDHUCA. http://www.uca.edu.sv/publica/idhuca/jesuitas.html.

Karl, Terry Lynn. 1992. 'El Salvador's Negotiated Revolution.' *Foreign Affairs* 71(2): 147–64.

Lampros, Andrea. 2014. 'Forensic Experts Bolster El Salvador's Intended Investigation of El Mozote.' *Human Rights Center Blog*, University of California, Berkeley, School of Law, 7 February.

Lazo Fuentes, Xiomara, and Eduardo Rey Tristán. 2011. '¿Es la justicia el precio de la paz? Logros y limitaciones en el proceso de paz salvadoreño.' In *Conflicto, memoria y pasados traumáticos: El Salvador contemporáneo*, edited by Eduardo Rey Tristán and Pilar Cagiao Vila, 211–40. Santiago de Compostela, Spain: Universidad de Santiago de Compostela.

Moodie, Ellen. 2010. *El Salvador in the Aftermath of Peace: Crime, Uncertainty, and the Transition to Democracy*. Philadelphia: University of Pennsylvania Press.

Paige, Jeffery M. 1997. *Coffee and Power: Revolution and the Rise of Democracy in Central America.* Cambridge, MA: Harvard University Press.

Popkin, Margaret. 2000. *Peace without Justice: Obstacles to Building the Rule of Law in El Salvador.* University Park: Pennsylvania State University Press.

——2002. *Iniciativas para mejorar la independencia judicial en América Latina: Una perspectiva comparada.* Washington, DC: Due Process of Law Foundation.

Seligson, Mitchell, and Vincent McElhinny. 1996. 'Low-Intensity Warfare, High-Intensity Death: The Demographic Impact of the Wars in El Salvador and Nicaragua.' *Canadian Journal of Latin American and Caribbean Studies* 21(42): 211–41.

Sieder, Rachel. 2001. 'War, Peace, and Memory Politics in Central America.' In *The Politics of Memory: Transitional Justice in Democratizing Societies*, edited by Alexandra Barahona de Brito, Carmen González-Enríquez, and Paloma Aguilar, 161–89. New York: Oxford University Press.

Stanley, William. 1996. *The Protection Racket State: Elite Politics, Military Extortion, and Civil War in El Salvador.* Philadelphia: Temple University Press.

UN (United Nations). 1993. *From Madness to Hope: The 12-Year War in El Salvador: Report of the Commission on the Truth for El Salvador.* Document S/25500, 1 April, official translation. New York: UN Security Council. http://www.un.org/en/ga/search/view_doc.asp?symbol=S/25500.

UNDP (United Nations Development Programme). 2010. *Informe sobre Desarrollo Humano El Salvador 2010: De la pobreza y el consumismo al bienestar de la gente: Propuestas para un nuevo modelo de desarrollo.* San Salvador: UNDP.

UNODC (United Nations Office on Drugs and Crime). 2013. 'UNODC Homicide Statistics 2013.' http://www.unodc.org/gsh/en/data.html.

Valencia Caravantes, Daniel, and Fátima Peña. 2014. 'Así se fraguó la Amnistía.' *El Faro*, 7 April.

Wood, Elisabeth Jean. 2003. *Insurgent Collective Action and Civil War in El Salvador.* Cambridge: Cambridge University Press.

Zamora, Rubén. 2012. 'La Amnistía fue la primera violación de los Acuerdos de Paz.' Interview by Fernando de Dios, *ContraPunto*, 8 January.

Chapter 9

Guatemala

Truth and memory on trial

*Jemima García-Godos and Luis Raúl Salvadó**

On 10 May 2013, a Guatemalan tribunal sentenced former army general Efraín Ríos Montt to 80 years in prison for genocide and crimes against humanity committed 30 years earlier during the country's internal armed conflict. Ríos Montt, Guatemala's *de facto* president from March 1982 until August 1983, became the first former head of state anywhere to be tried and sentenced for core international crimes in a domestic court in his home country. For thousands of victims and their families, for human rights defenders at home and abroad, and for all those seeking accountability for the atrocious crimes committed during the Guatemalan conflict, that sentence was an unprecedented achievement, a symbol of justice in a country uncomfortably used to impunity.

The impression of justice achieved, however, was short-lived. Only ten days later, the Guatemalan Constitutional Court nullified the sentence for Ríos Montt based on what it considered to be procedural failures of the right to due process (FIDH 2013).[1] An attempt to restart the trial in early 2015 was aborted when the defence questioned the neutrality of the new presiding judge. The latest attempt to restart the trial in July 2015 was also intrerrupted.

These dramatic events underscore the elusiveness of judicial accountability in Guatemala for crimes committed during the internal armed conflict.

Almost 20 years have passed since the signing of the peace accords that ended the armed conflict between the government and the armed insurgency led by the Guatemalan National Revolutionary Unity (Unidad Revolucionaria Nacional Guatemalteca, URNG).[2] The accords, signed in 1996, highlighted democracy and inclusion as guiding principles for the future of Guatemala. Today, it is important to evaluate both the degree to which the accords have been implemented and the transformative potential they held and still hold for Guatemalan society. This can be done by examining the various initiatives aimed at consolidating, opposing, or neutralising the commitments in the accords. These initiatives incorporate legal and political processes, originating both from the state and civil society, with local as well as international support.

Prominent among these initiatives are transitional justice mechanisms aimed at achieving either stability for the peace process or accountability for past crimes. This chapter examines the implementation of these mechanisms, including truth commissions, amnesty, prosecutions, and reparations, in order to assess what role transitional justice may have played in fulfilling the accountability agenda embodied in the peace accords. The chapter starts with a brief account of the political context leading up to the accords and a discussion of the ways in which they did or did not incorporate accountability for past human rights violations. The chapter then considers each transitional justice mechanism separately, although their implementation processes, as we will see, are closely interrelated.

The political negotiation of peace, and what came out of it

Guatemala's violent internal conflict was one of the longest in Latin America, lasting for 36 years. At the start of the conflict in 1960, the country was characterised by deep structural inequalities along class and ethnic lines. Economic and political power was concentrated in a landed elite, while the large majority of the population – Ladinos and, especially, indigenous Maya – suffered exclusion and discrimination (CEH 1999). Formally a constitutional democracy, Guatemala was ruled by alternating elected and *de facto* military governments throughout the extended armed conflict. Against the global backdrop of the Cold War, social and popular demands were seen by most of these governments, civilian and military alike, as part of a communist threat.[3]

In the course of the conflict, the Guatemalan people suffered brutal cycles of violence, most notably between 1966 and 1968 and again between 1981 and 1983. These periods were characterised by widespread government repression and a violent counter-insurgency strategy (Falla 1995). During the first cycle, cities and rural areas in the eastern part of Guatemala were most affected. The second cycle was characterised by continuous violence in the urban areas along with a strategic shift of military operations to the Western Highlands, territories densely populated by indigenous Maya. Scorched-earth tactics were systematically applied by the military in hundreds of Mayan villages, their populations massacred or forced to flee. The conflict left over 200,000 people dead and tens of thousands disappeared, with another 1 million people displaced from their homes. Most of the victims were rural and of indigenous Mayan origin (CEH 1999). This deeply scarred Guatemalan society as a whole, altering social relations and affecting social, ethnic, cultural, and political organisation in many ways. While the impact was greatest in the areas where the counter-insurgency doctrine was applied militarily on the ground, the conflict reshaped state institutions as a whole over four decades, intensifying repressive features and increasing existing tensions in state-society relations.

On 29 December 1996, the signing of a final peace accord, the Agreement on a Firm and Lasting Peace, officially ended the internal armed conflict. The signing capped six years of direct negotiations between the Guatemalan government and the armed insurgency, represented by the URNG, under the auspices of the United Nations. The formal starting point for the final accord was the Basic Agreement for the Search for Peace by Political Means, known as the Oslo agreement, of 29 March 1990. From 1994 onward, the peace talks were facilitated by MINUGUA – the United Nations Mission for the Verification of Human Rights and of Compliance with the Commitments of the Comprehensive Agreement on Human Rights in Guatemala. Even after the conclusion of the long and difficult negotiations, however, there remained serious questions about the prospects for a deep institutional, political, and social transformation that would address the structural causes of the armed conflict.

When the peace negotiations started in 1990, both the government and the URNG found themselves in vulnerable positions, allowing the international community to bring pressure to advance the negotiations. Government forces enjoyed significant military advantage, but their brutal counter-insurgency practices had discredited them before significant sectors of national and international public opinion (Vela Castañeda 2011). The URNG was in some disarray, with internal splits over class and ethnicity, divisions accentuated by and perhaps contributing to its military weaknesses. Discontent within the rank and file of the insurgency led to ruptures with the guerrilla high command. Nonetheless, the URNG retained links to the repressed but resilient social and popular movements in the country.[4]

In addition, the insurgency gradually lost popular support in the course of the negotiations, in part because the accords it signed were widely perceived as weak in their response to popular demands for justice. One was the June 1994 agreement that set the terms for the establishment of the Commission for Historical Clarification (Comisión para el Esclarecimiento Histórico, CEH). The accord generated disillusionment within social movements and the human rights sector for its provision that 'the Commission shall not attribute responsibility to any individual in its work, recommendations and report *nor shall these have any judicial aim or effect*' (Operation, para. III, emphasis added).[5] This prefigured the limited possibilities for criminal accountability in the future.[6]

Two other disputed accords were the Agreement on Identity and Rights of Indigenous Peoples (March 1995) and the Agreement on Socio-economic Aspects of the Agrarian Situation (May 1996). With respect to the former, indigenous organisations criticised the fact that central issues such as the right to land and territory were not included. Cojtí Cuxil (2006) argues that the accord was positive insofar as it called for the state to recognise its responsibility for historic discrimination against indigenous peoples. However, negotiators ignored many indigenous demands, including the crucial issue of territorial autonomy. In subsequent years, measures to change the situation of indigenous people would be deemed insufficient, discontinuous, marginal, and purely symbolic (Cojtí Cuxil 2006). Regarding the agreement on agrarian issues, the key issue of land reform – previously a main item on the URNG agenda – was among those that disappeared from the final text. The need for state intervention to remedy the country's highly inequitable land distribution gave way to market-led land reform.

After signing of the final accord in 1996, the insurgency was transformed into a political party, but it failed to develop the strength or secure sufficient alliances to enable it to successfully bring pressure for compliance with the commitments set out in the accords. In the post-conflict period, the URNG was socially and politically weak, its electoral support gradually waning. In the first post-conflict election, in 1999, the URNG, in coalition with other political organisations, received approximately 271,000 votes, or 12.3 per cent. By the 2011 elections, the URNG's support had shrunk to only 2.8 per cent of the vote.[7]

Furthermore, post-conflict governments have shown little interest in seriously supporting the accords in their policy-making, whether because of weakness or indifference or both. The capacity of the state apparatus – with the exception of the army – has been gradually reduced in accordance with neo-liberal tenets, further limiting the possibilities for implementing the peace commitments.[8] It took nine years to pass the Framework Law on the Peace Agreements (Decree 52–2005), which recognised the accords as formal state commitments and established the National Council for Implementation of the Peace Accords (Consejo Nacional para el Cumplimiento de los Acuerdos de Paz, CNAP). Initially considered innovative because of its representative composition, CNAP has kept a very low profile since its creation.[9]

Since the signing of the accords, a new institutional framework has gradually been created in Guatemala, including numerous joint committees, new legislation, and the implementation of several transitional justice mechanisms. These have had varying degrees of success. Holding elections free of fraudulent practices is more common than before: since 1996, Guatemala has had five democratically elected presidents.[10] Respect for civil and political rights has improved when compared to the worst years of the armed conflict. Yet effective and democratic rule of law in Guatemala is still fragile (Schirmer 1999). Social movements and civic organisations continue to denounce violations of fundamental human rights targeted against activists and the population more generally. There has also been a noticeable lag in efforts to guarantee economic, social, and cultural rights. Community and indigenous leaders face enormous difficulties in advancing their claims to territory and natural resources, among other core issues.

On the surface, the process of building formal democratic institutions is advancing. However, as Guy Hermet (2008) cautions, when we speak of democracy, there is frequent confusion between scope and depth. Social, political, economic, and cultural dynamics continue to produce the kinds of inequalities and exclusions that were recognised as the root cause of the armed conflict. This reality is exacerbated by the international economic crisis and by the deterioration of the country's economy, together with the post-conflict surge of gangs, organised crime, and drug trafficking. These illicit activities pose a challenge to the effective presence of the state across the national territory.

Sectors of the power elite and the national political class have repeatedly refused to recognise the need for profound structural reforms to underpin the development of democratic social relations. The long period of armed conflict, preceded by a series of military and civilian dictatorships, impeded the emergence of a democratic culture among broad sectors of the population. Elite intransigence helps explain, in part, apparent citizen disinterest or disenchantment in the post-conflict period, as well as the resurgence of discourse that recalls the central postulates of the Cold War.[11] It is, therefore, not surprising that high levels of impunity and corruption persist in the Guatemalan judicial system, along with the use of violence and coercion against human rights advocates, victims, and survivors (OHCHR 2014).

Truth: the struggles for historical memory

The Guatemalan internal armed conflict has been the subject of much debate. There is no social consensus on what the conflict was about, on the roles of different social and political actors (armed and unarmed), or on how to address the legacy of the past. Throughout the conflict, repressive state measures limited the space for the human rights sector in Guatemala, which nevertheless found much-needed support in Catholic and international human rights networks. In the post-conflict period, the debate on the truth of what happened was ignited by the report, *Guatemala: Nunca más* (*Guatemala: Never Again*), produced by the Catholic Church's Recovery of Historical Memory Project (Proyecto Interdiocesano de Recuperación de la Memoria Histórica, REMHI). The second impetus to this debate was the official truth commission report, *Guatemala: Memoria del silencio* (*Guatemala: Memory of Silence*), produced by the Commission for Historical Clarification under the terms of the Oslo agreement. REMHI made its report public on 24 April 1998; the CEH report was issued the following year, on 25 February 1999.

The idea behind the REMHI project began to take shape when the agreement to establish the CEH was signed in 1994. Many social movements and human rights organisations in Guatemala regarded that agreement with dismay, feeling that it placed too many limits on the CEH's mandate and on the assignment of criminal responsibility for violations committed during the armed conflict. It was in this context that Monsignor Juan Gerardi, a Catholic bishop who was acting director of the Human Rights Office of the Archbishopric of Guatemala, proposed a Church-sponsored truth initiative. It would draw on the experiences of Church interventions in other countries, such as El Salvador, to recover historical truth as a contribution to the peace process.[12] The aim was to produce a report that would set a high standard for quality and depth that the CEH would then be pressured to meet.

These two initiatives differed in their methodologies and operational approach, as well as in the resources available to them in terms of time, budget, and personnel. The REMHI project was conducted over three years by 600–800 bilingual facilitators who collected testimonies from people who had experienced the armed conflict. Almost 6,500 testimonies were recorded and systematised, providing the basis for a four-volume report that focused on the victims and impacts of violence, the types of violence, and the historical context surrounding the conflict. The CEH project, on the other hand, was sponsored by the United Nations and headed by three commissioners, two of them Guatemalans and one non-Guatemalan.

It operated between July 1997 and February 1999, with a professional staff of 100–200 people.

Despite their different contexts and mandates, both truth commissions came to similar conclusions about the armed conflict. Briefly stated, the reports conclude that at least 200,000 people died as a result of the conflict, and 40,000 to 50,000 were forcibly disappeared (CEH 1999; REMHI 1998). Both reports deemed the state to be responsible for the majority of fatal violence committed during the conflict, including numerous massacres and criminal acts targeted mainly against the indigenous population. The CEH report states clearly that the Guatemalan state carried out genocidal practices (*actos de genocidio*) as part of counter-insurgency campaigns against indigenous Mayan populations in a number of districts (CEH 1999, para. 3601).

The most shocking response to the REMHI report came two days after its release, when Bishop Gerardi was assassinated in his home in Guatemala City. The murder remains unsolved, but has been interpreted as a warning against human rights advocacy (Goldman 2007).

In the view of the Guatemalan human rights sector, the government's collaboration with the CEH during the investigation phase undermined the legitimacy and credibility of the upcoming report as an official document that emanated from the peace negotiations.[13] Less than a year after the murder of Bishop Gerardi, the CEH submitted its report to the government and the public in a solemn ceremony during which Gerardi's efforts, and the significant contribution made by the REMHI report, were specifically acknowledged. However, about a week later, the government took out an advertisement in the print media disputing that the CEH report, *Guatemala: Memoria del silencio*, was the official story of the internal armed conflict.

Thus, while setting the record straight in some respects, the REMHI and CEH reports also initiated a struggle over the official memory of the internal armed conflict in Guatemala. This struggle involves, on one hand, relatives' and victims' organisations, human rights organisations, and other civil society actors,[14] and on the other hand, the military and related support groups. Among those who have weighed in with their perspectives are former members of the armed insurgency (Macías 1997; Palma Lau 2010; Porras Castejón 2011), former military officers (Gramajo 1995; Mérida 2010; Ventura Arellano 2012), scholars (Falla 1993; Rosada-Granados 1999; Sabino 2008; Torres-Rivas 2011), and journalists.

Over the past five years, the struggle over historical memory has intensified, and the polarisation of views has become evident in the country's media. In May 2012, the independent Forensic Anthropology Foundation of Guatemala (Fundación de Antropología Forense de Guatemala, FAFG) unearthed the largest mass grave found to date, containing the remains of over 250 people, at a former military base in Cobán, Alta Verapaz. After the discovery, media commentators argued that the state should take responsibility for a systematic exhumations policy, as the country had stubbornly refused to face up to what happened during the conflict

(Gamazo 2012; Font 2012). Articles, columns, and readers' letters followed, taking positions in favour of and against trials involving military personnel.[15]

By September 2012, a pro-military support organisation had been formed. The Association of Relatives and Friends Acting in Solidarity with the Military, known as Familia, held a demonstration in support of officers and generals either charged with, or on trial for, war-era crimes. At the rally, Zury Ríos Sosa, daughter of Ríos Montt, coined a phrase now often used in this debate when she claimed that 'a soldier should not apologize'.[16] Pro-military slogans and placards, including one reading 'There was no genocide in Guatemala' also appeared outside the Ríos Montt genocide trial in 2013. Memoirs giving a self-justifying account of the conflict from an unrepentant military perspective began to appear (AVEMILGUA 2013). Despite the solid evidence of grave human rights violations presented by both the REMHI and CEH reports, and the fact that the CEH spoke explicitly of genocide, the issue of whether the armed forces' actions against indigenous communities during the conflict constituted attempted genocide remains in dispute.

At the local level, the reconstruction of histories and memories of the armed conflict has taken place since the 1990s in a variety of forms, ranging from local exhumation initiatives to collective memory projects (Flores 2001; Huet 2003, 2008; Paniagua, Mezquita, and Martínez 2012). The latter have taken a more formalised shape with the introduction by local communities of 'grievance memorials' (*memoriales de agravio*) as part of the process towards collective reparations implemented by the National Reparations Programme (Programa Nacional de Resarcimiento, PNR). The first grievance memorial was presented to the PNR in 2008 by the community of Cocop, the first Maya Ixil community to suffer a massacre, in 1981. This community was thus also the first to receive collective reparations. However, the community's expectation of full collective reparations remained unfulfilled, as the PNR ceased activities there the same year (CAFCA 2010, 5).

Other rural communities affected by the armed conflict have also taken steps to meticulously organise information, determining facts and dates and setting up detailed lists of victims and material damages. To date, over 70 grievance memorials have been developed by local victims' organisations in the Quiché region and the Ixil Triangle, both among the areas most affected by state violence during the conflict. Communities request comprehensive forms of reparations from the state, including collective, symbolic, and individual measures.[17]

The shadow of amnesty

The Guatemalan experience with amnesty for crimes committed during the armed conflict is based on the National Reconciliation Law (Decree 145–96 of 27 December 1996), whose stated aim was to promote reconciliation among the parties to the armed conflict. It decreed the extinction of criminal liability of direct authors, accomplices, and accessories, whether state or non-state actors, for political and related crimes committed during the armed conflict and until

1996. A notable aspect of this amnesty law is that it does not include core international crimes. Article 8 expressly states that 'the extinction of criminal liability referred to in this Act shall not apply to crimes of genocide, torture and enforced disappearance, as well as those crimes that are not subject to the extinction of criminal liability in accordance with domestic law or international treaties ratified by Guatemala' (our translation).

Guatemala's amnesty law, therefore, is unusual among the cases considered in this book in that it operates within the parameters of international human rights law and humanitarian law. This may be due to the influence of the United Nations during the peace process, as well as the timing of the process itself. By the mid-1990s, the diffusion of international norms regarding accountability for core crimes had started to make blanket amnesties unacceptable to the international community. Given the restrictions established by the amnesty law, legal challenges from Guatemalan victims' and human rights organisations have focused on cases related to the crimes of genocide, torture, and enforced disappearance. This will be addressed in the section on trials below.

Guatemala's various administrations since 1996 have responded unevenly to the state's commitments under the peace agreements. Although new institutions such as the Ombudsman's Office and the Peace Secretariat were established, along with some new public policies, these did not add up to an integrated system capable of building peace and democracy. Many of the agencies and administrative bodies created in accordance with the agreement on the time frame and implementation of the peace accords were established by executive decree rather than through the legislative process.[18] In Guatemala, this implies less institutional strength in terms of continuity and resources. During his term, President Otto Pérez Molina, a former military general and leader of the Patriotic Party (Partido Patriota),[19] proposed changes to the institutions linked to the peace accords, with the stated objective of improving their functioning. There is suspicion among human rights organisations, however, that this may be a veiled attempt at regressive reengineering of these institutions.

Contributing to this climate is a proposal from a senior official to declare a new amnesty law as a prerequisite for a full investigation of what occurred during the armed conflict.[20] The justification given is that many of those who were involved in atrocities are prepared to make revelations about their past actions but are inhibited from doing so by the possibility of facing criminal prosecution. In other words, this logic revives the 'truth for amnesty' or 'truth for impunity' formula that was explicitly rejected at the end of the armed conflict.

Trials: strategic litigation or doing what is possible?

In Guatemala's dysfunctional institutional environment, the road to legal accountability involving criminal prosecutions for past human rights violations has been discontinuous and full of obstacles. Clear pro-impunity tendencies are evident within the justice system. Nevertheless, Guatemala offers examples of the investigation and resolution, with convictions, of a number of emblematic cases.[21] The role of the Inter-American Court of Human Rights has been vital in unblocking some obstacles at the domestic level. Human rights organisations leading legal cases – such as the Mutual Support Group (Grupo de Apoyo Mutuo, GAM), the Centre for Human Rights Legal Action (Centro para la Acción Legal en Derechos Humanos, CALDH), and the Legal Bureau for Human Rights (Bufete Jurídico de Derechos Humanos, BDH) – have become increasingly active in engaging the regional system to try to overcome the absence of proper remedies in domestic courts. The role and impact of the inter-American system will be discussed in more detail below.

The first major impulse leading to judicial processes for past human rights abuses was the delivery of the CEH report in 1999. The report offered a window of opportunity for victims' groups and human rights organisations to put forward claims to establish responsibility for past crimes. The first guilty verdict came the same year, when a former member of a civil defence patrol, a civilian, was sentenced to 220 years in jail.[22] Previous legal changes or developments that allowed the Guatemalan judicial system to pursue such cases included the 1994 incorporation of the crime of enforced disappearance into the Penal Code, as well as a 1996 district appeal court ruling that crimes committed against civilians by members of the armed forces should be tried in ordinary, rather than military, courts. However, the judicial cases brought in 1999 and subsequently have been slowed through repeated use by the defence of *recursos de amparo* (writs of protection), a legal remedy intended to protect individual rights *in extremis*.[23]

It is difficult to establish with accuracy the number of ongoing human rights cases as well as the number of military officers currently on trial in Guatemalan courts for conflict-related acts. A report by the Due Process of Law Foundation, a region-wide non-governmental organisation (NGO), estimated 1,749 open cases in 2010 (DPLF 2010, 169). As we will see below, official figures given by the Public Prosecutor's Office (Ministerio Público), are far below this estimate. According to the office's 2013 annual report, in that year only 11 denunciations were made, and four verdicts delivered, for crimes related to the armed conflict (Ministerio Público 2013, 140).

One feature of the Guatemalan justice sector that has an impact on the outcomes of legal processes is the selection of Supreme Court judges. These judges are appointed by the National Congress from a shortlist developed by a dedicated commission, thus posing several challenges to the independence of senior judges. A similar issue arises with regard to the Constitutional Court: two of its five members are appointed by the other two branches of state (the president and Congress), and a third member is nominated by the Supreme Court. On several occasions, the Supreme Court and, particularly, the Constitutional Court have gone beyond their mandates, intervening to a questionable extent in lower courts' handling of human rights cases involving members of the armed forces. In one widely criticised example, the Constitutional Court took the unprecedented step in 2000 of overturning both first instance and appeal court verdicts in a notorious massacre case (the 1982 Dos Erres case, in which 350 people were killed). The overturning of these verdicts was based on the amnesty provisions of the National Reconciliation Law, even though these do not apply to crimes against humanity.

The Dos Erres case is an example of the many obstacles that victims and relatives face in seeking domestic justice for crimes committed during the Guatemalan armed conflict. As a result, a significant number of such cases have been taken to the inter-American human rights system. Since 1999, the Inter-American Court of Human Rights has issued eight rulings pertaining to the Guatemalan armed conflict, including well-known cases such as Myrna Mack (2003), Maritza Urrutia (2003), Plan de Sánchez (2004), and Dos Erres (2009).[24] In each case, damages were awarded to victims against the state of Guatemala. In December 2009 the Guatemalan Supreme Court (SC) declared Inter-American Court verdicts to be 'self-executing', that is, they must be adopted and implemented by the Guatemalan judicial system without delay.[25]

Human rights organisations, survivors, victims, and their relatives have also considered it necessary and strategic to bring cases before third-country courts. The choice of cases for submission to the regional system or third-country courts is sometimes driven by practical considerations such as citizenship connections or eligibility requirements. Within these limitations, the civil society organisations that advance such cases try to carry out strategic litigation, selecting cases that are considered emblematic or paradigmatic insofar as they are illustrative of many other cases and have the potential to set precedents once a decision is made. In this way the Guatemalan human rights sector is attempting to push cases that open the way for future cases to come.[26]

An important example of strategic litigation in a third country is the universal jurisdiction litigation in Spanish courts that eventually generated the domestic genocide case against Ríos Montt and four co-defendants. The case was initiated by Nobel Peace Prize winner Rigoberta Menchú in 1999 when she presented a claim to the Spanish National Court against Ríos Montt for the crimes of genocide and torture. Although the issue of jurisdiction was initially rejected by Spanish lower chambers and Spain's Supreme Court, these decisions were appealed, and in 2005 the Spanish Constitutional Court concluded that universal jurisdiction applied and that the case could proceed in Spanish courts. Since then, the defendants have presented numerous appeals. International arrest orders have been issued, but only one arrest has been made. In 2007 the Guatemalan Constitutional Court (CC) declared that the Spanish court system did not have jurisdiction to try Guatemalan citizens, thus obstructing, yet again, the course of justice. In spite of these obstacles, the Spanish process continues (FIDH 2013).

Various developments have contributed to the advance of accountability in Guatemala over the past ten years. In 2005, the archives of the former National Police (associated with repression and dissolved a year after the peace accords) were accidentally unearthed after decades of abandonment. Today these records have been transformed into the state-administered Historical Archive of the National Police, with support from the United Nations and international donors. The

Archive has become an extraordinarily useful source for understanding the interconnected operating structures of the police and the army during the conflict.[27] The following year brought the promulgation of the Law on Freedom of Access to Public Information (Legislative Decree 57–2008), which institutionalised access to public records. In 2007 the International Commission against Impunity in Guatemala (Comisión Internacional contra la Impunidad en Guatemala, CICIG) was established, with the mandate to function as an international monitoring body on the rule of law and accountability in Guatemala.[28] It is in this context that the first conviction of a high-ranking officer was issued in 2009 for forced disappearance during the armed conflict in the El Jute case, in Chiquimula (CALDH 2010). This demonstrated, first, that justice extends beyond the rank and file, and second, that domestic courts can deliver convictions.

Cases have also advanced due to the staunch persistence of individuals within the state apparatus who are committed to human rights and the rule of law. In December 2010 the Public Prosecutor's Office came under new administration when Claudia Paz y Paz Bailey was appointed prosecutor general (*fiscal general*) by then president Álvaro Colom.[29] With a background in the non-governmental and human rights sector, she was welcomed by pro-accountability actors, and her role in reshaping the Public Prosecutor's Office cannot be overstated. During her tenure, the overall focus was on improving accountability and combating impunity, both for crimes of the past and for present crimes. Policy changes included tackling organised crime – a major social and political problem in post-conflict Guatemala – through strategic criminal prosecution with an emphasis on the rights and protection of victims and witnesses (Ministerio Público 2012). The prosecution strategy was intended to take account of the large backlog of cases pending in the Guatemalan judicial system, recognising the difficult conditions surrounding justice administration in the country. Shifting away from a case-by-case approach, the strategy focused on targeted identification and investigation of criminal structures, seeking patterns in interconnected cases. The same approach was applied to the Unit for Special Cases from the Internal Armed Conflict, part of the Prosecutor's Office of Human Rights (Fiscalía de Derechos Humanos) at the Public Prosecutor's Office.

Not surprisingly, this change of direction at the Public Prosecutor's Office provoked opposition from military-based organisations such as AVEMILGUA (Asociación de Veteranos Militares de Guatemala) and Familia, which have closed ranks in an uncompromising defensive posture. These two associations have targeted CICIG, the Public Prosecutor's Office, and the Criminal Chamber of the Supreme Court for public criticism, marshalling economic resources and powerful supporters for their vendetta.[30] The case against General Ríos Montt has raised the profile of these organisations and their arguments. The current line of defence for military personnel on trial for crimes committed during the armed conflict is to argue that massacres and extrajudicial killings were committed by both sides but that the state did not undertake practices of genocide.[31] This has raised a new set of challenges for political-legal struggles against impunity.

Furthermore, in the aftermath of the impasse around the Ríos Montt trial, the Constitutional Court took the decision in February 2014 to shorten the mandate of Paz y Paz on grounds of irregularities in her appointment, calling for a new selection committee to find a replacement. The committee excluded Paz y Paz from the list of nominees and Thelma Aldana was appointed the new prosecutor general in May 2014. It remains to be seen whether the advances in accountability made under the leadership of Paz y Paz will be weakened, dismantled, or further developed by the new prosecutor.

The Ríos Montt case

The case against former army general and *de facto* president Efraín Ríos Montt has received much international attention.[32] After being ousted as head of state by a military coup in 1983, Ríos Montt did not disappear from public life. He founded a right-wing party, the Guatemalan Republican Front (Frente Republicano Guatemalteco) in 1989, was elected to Congress in 1990, and served several terms until 2012. During this period he enjoyed parliamentary immunity. He made two unsuccessful bids for the presidency, in 1999 and 2003.

The charges against him date back to 2001, when the Association for Justice and Reconciliation (Asociación Justicia y Reconciliación, AJR), a coalition of communities affected by the conflict, lodged before the public prosecutor a complaint for genocide and crimes against humanity. The complaint named Ríos Montt along with José Mauricio Rodríguez Sánchez, former chief of military intelligence; Oscar Humberto Mejía Víctores, former defence minister; and Héctor Mario López Fuentes, former army chief of staff. The prosecutor's office, however, failed to open investigations, and it was not until 2007 that a lower court admitted the AJR's request that the Ministry of Defence be required to hand over information regarding military operations in the early 1980s. The Ministry continued to ignore the decision until 2009. That same year, army records for Operation Sofia, conducted during the Ríos Montt period, were found by the National Security Archive, a United States-based NGO. This evidence was placed at the disposal of the Spanish court and the domestic courts through case plaintiffs (FIDH 2013, 8).

In June 2011, ten years after the case started, the prosecutor general completed the investigation. On 26 January 2012, only days after his congressional term – and immunity – ended, Ríos Montt was indicted on charges of genocide and crimes against humanity in connection with his 1982–83 term as *de facto* head of state.[33] The judicial process itself started in January 2013 in the Guatemalan Court for High Risk Crimes (Tribunal A de Mayor Riesgo).[34] In the Ríos Montt trial, the initial claimant AJR participates as *querellante adhesivo* (civil party complainant) in support of the prosecution, being represented by two human rights NGOs, CALDH and BJD.

During the proceedings, which started on 19 March 2013, more than 90 survivors presented their testimonies, with terrifying accounts of massacres, forced displacement, torture, and rape. Expert witnesses were also called upon to elaborate on forensic evidence, statistical analysis, operational plans and chain of command in the Guatemalan armed forces, and international law concerning core crimes (Open Society Justice Initiative 2013). The trial was closely followed by national and international media, judicial observers, human rights advocates, and victims' groups around the world.[35] In Guatemala, the trial provoked public demonstrations both for and against accountability (*La Nación* 2013), contesting the issue of whether genocide had or had not occurred. In other words, the struggle for memory continued.

Despite intense use of delaying tactics by the defence, on 10 May 2013, the Court for High Risk Crimes sentenced Ríos Montt to 80 years in prison for genocide and crimes against humanity. The relief and sense of justice of thousands of victims was short-lived, however. On 20 May, the Guatemalan Constitutional Court nullified the sentence, based on allegations of procedural errors that compromised due process. This unprecedented and widely criticised decision effectively rolled back the process to the moment when the alleged procedural failures occurred: 19 April 2013 (Hernández 2013; *El Telégrafo* 2013).[36] This implies that all proceedings that took place after that date will have to be repeated, including the sentencing.

Restarted in early January 2015 after endless wrangling about court composition, the process was almost immediately suspended when the defence charged one of the new judges with bias. In July 2015, Ríos Montt was declared mentally unfit by the National Institute of Forensic Science (a subsidiary of the Public Ministry) and thus unable to stand trial. As of January 2016, it is still uncertain when or whether the process will restart. Clearly, the trial is about much more than the fate of Ríos Montt as an individual; at stake is the struggle for truth and memory, and the acknowledgement that genocide and gross violations of human rights did happen in Guatemala. Survivors, support groups, and human rights organisations follow vigilantly any developments affecting the potential reopening of the trial. Although short-lived, the guilty verdict of 2013 was considered a victory and has given hope to those seeking accountability for past crimes in Guatemala.

Reparations

Addressing the needs of victims has been formally on the agenda since implementation of the peace accords began (Alvarado Pisani 2007). Overall achievements, however, are limited. In 1994, the Global Accord on Human Rights, signed by the Guatemalan government and the URNG, established a state duty to attend to the victims of the internal armed conflict and provide reparations (sec. VIII, para. 1). The mandate of the Commission for Historical Clarification called for the formulation of specific recommendations to preserve the memory of the victims and to favour peace and the observance of human rights and democracy. The CEH's final recommendations, in 1999, included the ambitious National Reparations Programme. Although the 1996 National Reconciliation Law had granted perpetrators limited amnesty from prosecution, it did not waive the right to truth and reparations. This fact, plus the inclusion of reparations measures in both the CEH mandate and the peace accords, has reinforced the demand that the state provide reparations (*resarcimiento*). For many human rights organisations, however, this cannot be done without also addressing amnesty and impunity (Sieder 2001; Crandall 2004).

Implementation of reparations programmes started with pilot projects in 2001. These led to the enactment of Decree AG258 of 2003, which established the National Reparations Commission (Comisión Nacional de Resarcimiento, CNR) and the National Reparations Programme (PNR). The CNR initially included representatives from victims' groups and civil society organisations alongside state representatives. The rules regulating the PNR's functions were first established in 2005, the same year that the CNR reduced the number of representatives to five, from the public sector only. The PNR was reorganised in 2008 and again in 2012, during two different administrations. The institutional shift initiated in 2012 aimed to bring the programme in line with overall social policies introduced by the Otto Pérez Molina government.[37] As of 2014, however, the PNR still did not have a national register of victims. Allocation and entitlement was therefore based on ad hoc registration processes, which have been criticised by user groups and experts for arbitrariness and for placing the burden of proof on victims (Red de Organizaciones 2012).

Assisting victims through reparations has proved to be a challenging task in Guatemala, given institutional uncertainty and limited resources. The institutional and legal basis for reparations rests on governmental decrees (*acuerdos gubernativos*, issued by the executive), not laws passed by the legislature. This makes the implementing agencies (CNR and PNR) vulnerable to recurrent, politically driven changes that add unnecessary pressure to an already fragile structure. For example, since the establishment of the PNR, each presidential administration has introduced changes to the programme, altering the emphasis and forms of interaction with different stakeholders, such as civil society and victims organisations. Between 2008 and 2011, relationships with human rights organisations became closer, as the PNR's leadership at that time was drawn from the human rights sector. This, however, did not necessarily imply a strengthened relationship with indigenous organisations, some of whom are critical of what they consider to be clientelistic practices of the PNR (Red de Organizaciones 2012).

The original aim of the reparations programme in Guatemala was to provide comprehensive reparations in five areas: material restitution (including housing support), economic compensation (individual and collective), cultural reparations, measures to restore the dignity of victims, and psycho-social rehabilitation. Together, these measures were meant to address the collective and ethnic dimensions of the armed conflict. Although the National Reparations Programme, as formulated, includes all these aspects, an overall assessment shows that the PNR has focused its efforts on the implementation of economic compensation, which started in 2006. In 2011, almost 80 per cent of the PNR's funding was allocated to individual economic compensation, while activities to strengthen the dignity of victims received 15 per cent of the budget (PNR 2011). Despite this, only 1,685 individual beneficiaries received economic compensation in 2011 (PNR 2011, 33), with 868 more added in 2012 (PNR 2013, 24). Updated totals are not readily available, although the PNR indicated that, as of the end of 2011, it had registered 52,922 files (*expedientes*) of human rights violations committed during the armed conflict (PNR 2013, 27).[38] Not all human rights violations provide the basis for economic compensation in Guatemala (see below), but the difference between the number of beneficiaries in 2011–12 and the total number of violations registered suggests a mismatch between the scope of potential beneficiaries and the results achieved.

According to Guatemala's Public Policy on Reparations (PNR 2003), victims are defined as all those who have suffered a human rights violation, directly or indirectly, individually or collectively. The violations that provide a basis for reparations are enforced disappearance, extrajudicial execution, physical and psychological torture, forced displacement, forced recruitment of minors, sexual violence, violence against children, and massacres. The economic reparations programme is supposed to give priority to beneficiaries who have permanent disability and thus are not able to support themselves, and to the elderly.

Victims' groups and beneficiaries of the economic compensation programme have raised several criticisms of its implementation. One concerns the relatively small amount of compensation provided. According to current regulations, each recognised family unit can claim compensation for a maximum of two victims or violations, irrespective of whether more family members were victimised or several violations were suffered. The monetary lump sum assigned to a family unit which has suffered the death of a relative is 24,000 quetzales (approximately US$3,100) for the first victim, with an additional 20,000 quetzales (approximately US$2,600) for a second victim. Thus, the maximum a family can receive is around US$5,700. Providing economic reparations at the family-unit level has also generated cultural problems. According to Viaene (2010), the Mayan cosmology to which many surviving families subscribe requires initial steps of direct discussion, negotiation, and agreement between victim and perpetrator as a fundamental stage in repairing harm. This step is not contemplated in the operations of the National Reparations Programme, where compensation is provided through a cheque delivered at a public event. This means of delivery is not in tune with Mayan practices and can even be experienced as a form of revictimisation.

Two aspects of reparations in Guatemala are closely linked to criminal accountability. The first concerns exhumations. Official practice to date has been to leave this task to specialised NGOs and civil society organisations. These organisations, mostly funded by international donors, provide technical and forensic expertise, and sometimes legal advice and psychological counselling as well. The demand to investigate new clandestine burial sites and identify the remains of thousands of victims nonetheless far exceeds existing capacity, despite the commitment and professionalism shown by these institutions.[39] The PNR provides some support at the end of the process, at the reburial stage, although this is considered insufficient by victims' organisations (Red de Organizaciones 2012).

A second aspect concerns the use, for judicial purposes, of information collected by the PNR in the registration process. Current national legislation requires public institutions that obtain knowledge about serious conflict-era crimes to report them to the Public Prosecutor's Office. This duty obviously also applies to the PNR. In 2009, for example, the PNR passed on 3,385 reports (*denuncias*) of human rights violations committed against 5,908 victims during the armed conflict to the public prosecution service in order to initiate criminal investigations (Human Rights Committee 2011, para. 28). It is unclear whether the survivors or relatives directly involved were consulted or had given their consent for this procedure. While the Public Prosecutor's Office has the mandate to initiate such investigations on its own, it is problematic that victims are not properly informed about a process that potentially will involve them.[40]

One final observation is that economic reparations have begun in a relatively expedient way. In the absence of a consolidated victims' register, compensation, like other forms of reparations, has instead been granted on the basis of a PNR database known as the Listado Rápido (Quick List). The lack of a single register has been noted since the first PNR evaluations and still poses a challenge to the fulfilment of the PNR's mission in support of victims and survivors (PNR 2007, 2014).

Conclusions: accountability against all odds

The peace accords that put an end to the internal armed conflict in Guatemala embodied the aspiration for a democratic political project. Accountability for human rights violations during the conflict and redress to victims were understood to be central to the achievement of this aspiration. A simple checklist of the transitional justice mechanisms utilised might give the impression that Guatemala has fulfilled the accountability agenda envisaged in the accords. Such an assessment would be only partly correct. There have been significant, albeit few, advances in transitional justice, notably the publication of two solid truth commission reports, the genocide trial of Ríos Montt, and the implementation of the economic reparations programme. Important tasks remain pending, especially in the area of criminal justice, particularly investigations and exhumations, and in taking a comprehensive approach to reparations.

Although still incomplete, Guatemala's progress in accountability is striking precisely because it has happened against all odds, in a politically hostile and impunity-prone context. This is particularly evident in the current struggle over historical truth. Revisionist forces have questioned the findings of the CEH and REMHI reports while attempting to obstruct trials against perpetrators. The struggle for memory is taking place in the public debate, but also in closed chambers, where judicial authorities have the capacity to promote or block accountability.

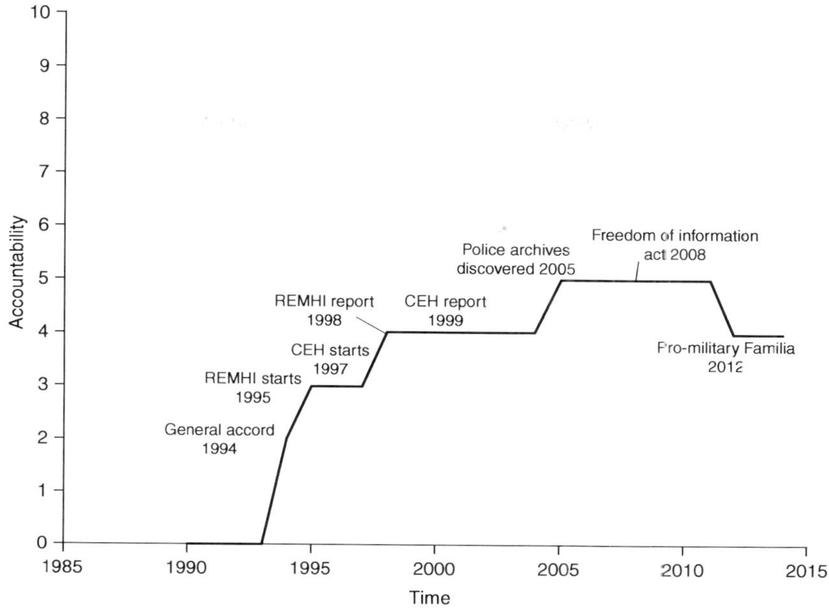

Figure 9.1 Guatemala: the truth dimension of accountability, 1990–2014
Source: Authors' construction, 2015.

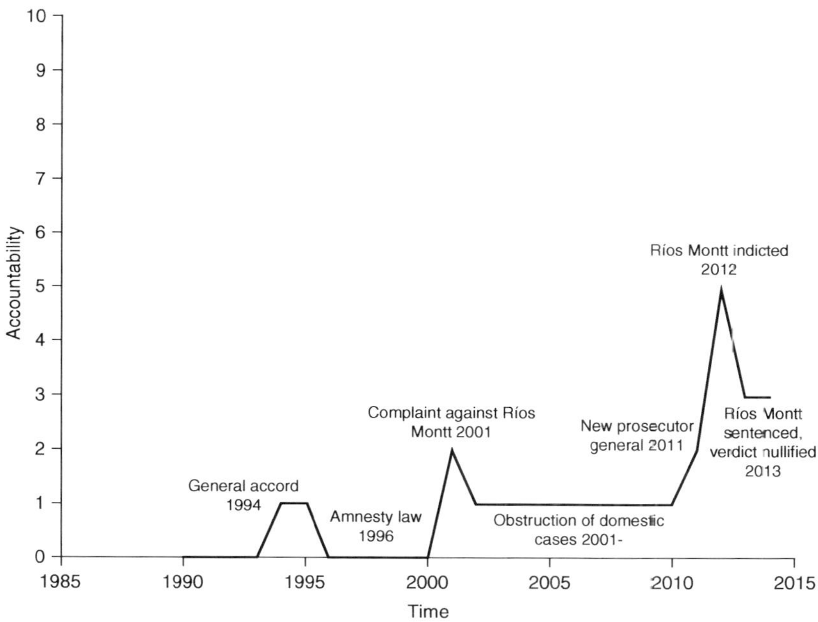

Figure 9.2 Guatemala: the overcoming amnesty dimension of accountability, 1990–2014
Source: Authors' construction, 2015.

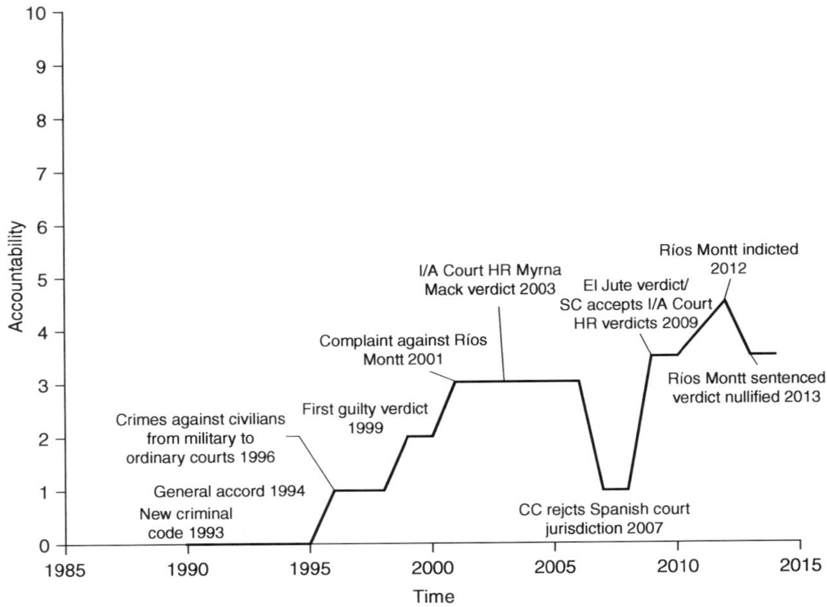

Figure 9.3 Guatemala: the trials dimension of accountability, 1990–2014
Source: Authors' construction, 2015.

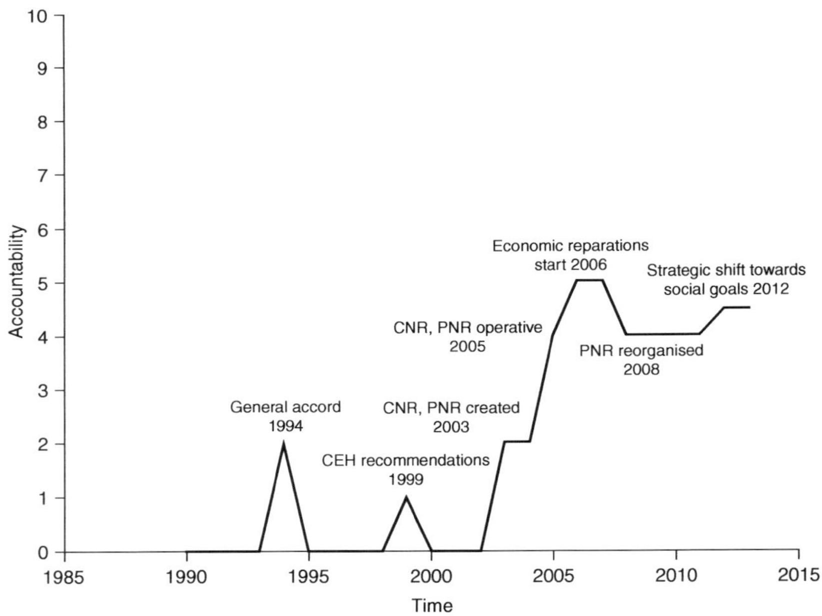

Figure 9.4 Guatemala: the reparations dimension of accountability, 1990–2014
Source: Authors' construction, 2015.

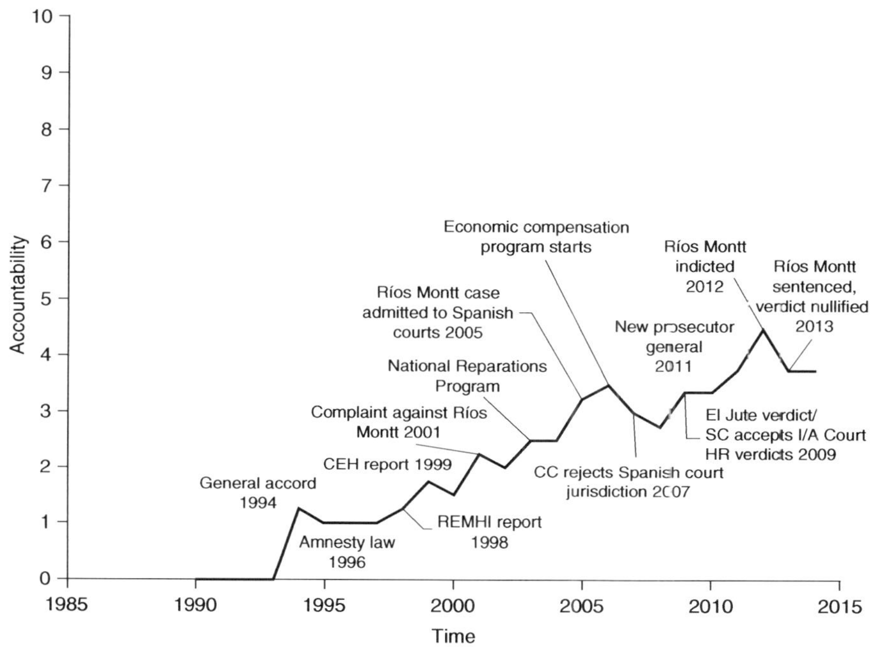

Figure 9.5 Guatemala: overall trend towards accountability, 1990–2014
Source: Authors' construction, 2015.

Advances followed by setbacks are common in Guatemalan institutional and political life and will likely continue. The changes of direction in the Public Prosecutor's Office between 2008 and 2012; the general trends in the National Reparations Programme, if they continue; and above all, the steady commitment of civil society and victims' organisations together provide a measure of hope for more sustained efforts towards accountability and redress.

Notes

* The authors thank Rachael Sieder, Stener Ekern, and Cath Collins for useful comments on earlier drafts of this chapter.

1 The Constitutional Court's ruling (expediente 1904–2013, 20 May 2013), setting forth its arguments in the case, is available in Spanish on the Court's website at http://www.cc.gob.gt/images/DocumentosCC/Exp1904.2013.pdf.

2 Created in 1982, the URNG grouped several Guatemalan insurgent organisations, including the Guerrilla Army of the Poor (EGP), the Revolutionary Organization of the People in Arms (ORPA), the Rebel Armed Forces (FAR), and a faction of the Guatemalan Labour Party (PGT). These groups emerged in the 1960s and 1970s, inspired in part by the Cuban revolution, and sought a radical socialist transformation of Guatemalan society through armed struggle (CEH 1999).

3 The constitution of 1956, in force until 1965, established that all communist activity, whether individual or collective, was punishable (REMHI 1998).
4 Miguel Angel Reyes, interview by authors, April and June 2012. Reyes was a member of one of URNG's member organisations and participated in the URNG advisory team until his resignation in May 1996. All author interviews for this chapter were conducted in Guatemala City.
5 The full name of the accord is the Agreement on the Establishment of the Commission to Clarify Past Human Rights Violations and Acts of Violence that Have Caused The Guatemalan Population to Suffer. English translations of all the Guatemalan accords are available on the United Nations Peacemaker website, http://peacemaker.un.org/.
6 Indeed, these limitations materialised in the National Reconciliation Law of 27 December 1996, discussed later in the chapter.
7 Official election data from Guatemala's Supreme Electoral Tribunal.
8 This can be observed in the dismantlement of the public agricultural sector, among other areas.
9 The CNAP is composed of three members appointed by members of the executive, the legislature, and the judiciary, political parties, and civil society organisations.
10 They are Alvaro Arzú (1996–2000), Alfonso Portillo (2000–4), Óscar Berger (2004–8), Álvaro Colom (2008–12), and Otto Pérez Molina (2012–15), whose term ended abruptly in September 2015 due to corruption charges. Politically, these administrations can be characterised as centre-right to right-wing.
11 Right-wing voices such as that of AVEMILGUA, the belligerent Military Veterans Association of Guatemala, founded in 1995, are increasingly heard in the public debate.
12 Mario Domingo, then director of the Human Rights Office of the Archbishopric of Guatemala, interview by authors, April 2012.
13 For a detailed discussion, see Impunity Watch (2008).
14 Organisations that have played key roles in human rights and/or democratisation efforts include, among others, the Mutual Support Group (GAM), the Centre for Human Rights Legal Action (CALDH), the Legal Bureau for Human Rights (BDH), the Rigoberta Menchú Foundation (FRM), and the Myrna Mack Foundation (FMM).
15 In an opinion piece, journalist Marcela Gereda (2012) took issue with a reader's letter that had praised Ríos Montt 'for saving Guatemala from the guerrillas and for having done good for the country'. Gereda claimed that this view is shared by many in circles close to the military.
16 Quoted in Rodríguez (2012). An article the following day by well-known social commentator Gustavo Berganza (2012) described the march as having been characterised by combative Cold War language and support for impunity.
17 María Eugenia Carrera, interview by authors, April 2012, and Rafael Herrarte, interview by authors, July 2012. Both were programme advisers at the Centre for Forensic Analysis and Applied Sciences (Centro de Análisis Forense y Ciencias Aplicadas, CAFCA), working with victims' organisations and local communities in local memory initiatives.
18 An important exception is the CNAP, discussed earlier, which emanated from the legal framework of the peace accords and was brought into being by Legislative Decree 52–2005.
19 The Patriotic Party obtained 57 out of 158 seats in Congress at the last legislative election in 2012.
20 Antonio Arenales Forno, presidential commissioner for human rights and secretary of peace, has repeatedly raised the idea in statements to local media since his appointment in March 2012.
21 Guatemala's criminal justice system follows a prosecutorial model in which the state, represented by the public prosecutor's office, undertakes investigation and presents

evidence before a judge or group of judges in public proceedings. The judge or judges reach a decision based on evidence presented and debated by defence and prosecuting attorneys. Victims can participate in the process as *querellantes*.

22 Civil defence patrols (*patrullas de autodefensa civil*) were formed by the military during the armed conflict as part of a counter-insurgency strategy to control local villages. Conscripted from civilian rural populations, patrol members were forced to carry out violence against their own and neighbouring communities.

23 Approximately 50 such writs were presented by defence teams on behalf of accused perpetrators during the first decade of the 2000s. Miguel Mörth, lawyer at Bufete Jurídico de Derechos Humanos, interview by authors, 27 April 2012.

24 Details of these cases and an updated list of Inter-American Court (I/A Court HR) verdicts concerning Guatemala can be found on the website of the Presidential Commission for Human Rights (COPREDEH), http://copredeh.gob.gt/index.php?showPage=2403.

25 On 11 December 2009, the Guatemalan Supreme Court established this principle for the Panel Blanca, Niños de la Calle, Bámaca Velásquez, and Carpio Nicolle cases, and by extension for all future verdicts from the Inter-American Court.

26 Miguel Mörth interview, 27 April 2012.

27 According to the Archive's website (http://archivohistoricopn.org/pages/institucion/historia.php), its principal user up to 2011 was the Public Prosecutor's Office, seeking evidence for cases.

28 Creation of such an office was stipulated in the 1994 accord that established the CEH.

29 After being nominated by a selection committee, Paz y Paz was the preferred candidate of human rights organisations. Her appointment followed the removal of the previous Prosecutor General, Conrado Reyes, on charges of corruption.

30 For example, in a column in *El Periódico* on 14 August 2012, Ricardo Méndez Ruiz Valdés attacked the magistrate César Barrientos and prosecutor general Claudia Paz y Paz. Méndez Ruiz, director of the Foundation Against Terrorism (Fundación Contra el Terrorismo), is the son of the interior minister in Ríos Montt's government. In the same edition of the paper, columnist Miguel Albizures commented on Méndez Ruiz's attacks on the prosecutor general made during exhumation processes at the military barracks in Cobán (Méndez Ruiz Valdés 2012; Albizures 2012). Against the backdrop of such public controversy, current president Otto Pérez Molina announced, in February 2015, that the CICIG's mandate might not be renewed. This met with national and international criticism, and the president announced subsequently that Guatemala would request, after all, United Nations support for the continuation of CICIG for two more years.

31 See, for example, a press interview with Antonio Arenales Forno (2012), in which he declared, 'I am outraged that they say there was genocide in Guatemala.'

32 For excellent reviews of the Ríos Montt case and trial, see, among others, FIDH (2013), Open Society Justice Initiative (2013), and the International Justice Monitor site for the Efraín Ríos Montt and Mauricio Rodríguez Sánchez trials (http://www.ijmonitor.org/category/efrain-rios-montt-and-mauricio-rodriguez-sanchez/).

33 The other two co-defendants were detained in 2011, but the charges were later suspended on account of their health.

34 High Risk Courts were established by Decree 21–2009 of the Guatemalan Congress to hear criminal cases that demand increased security measures for those involved, including judges, victims, witnesses, and defendants.

35 See, for example, the websites of Coordinación Genocidio Nunca Más (http://www.paraqueseconozca.blogspot.no/) and the American Society of International Law (especially 'The Rios Montt Genocide Trial in Guatemala', http://www.asil.org/rios-montt-genocide-trial-guatemala).

36 The decision by the Guatemalan Constitutional Court caused condemnation among human rights organisations, scholars, and solidarity groups, both national and

international. Concerns were also expressed by the inter-American human rights system, countries in the region, and the international donor community. Numerous demonstrations and protests were organised both within and outside Guatemala.

37 These social policies focus on improving nutrition, public security, productivity, and competitiveness. The PNR has incorporated these policy changes in its Strategic Institutional Plan 2013–2016, as detailed in its annual reports (PNR 2013, 17, and 2014, 21).

38 In the absence of a national victims' registry in Guatemala, it is not possible to establish with accuracy how many individual victims the 52,922 files actually represent. PNR annual reports do not address that question.

39 Forensic Anthropology Foundation of Guatemala (www.fafg.org) and Centre for Forensic Analysis and Applied Sciences (www.cafcaguatemala.org) have become leading institutions in the field of forensic anthropology at the national and international levels.

40 The same situation arises for the 2,783 files on enforced disappearance transferred by COPREDEH to the Public Prosecutor's Office in 2010. COPREDEH received the files from the CEH Working Group on Enforced Disappearance in 2009. By April 2011, the public prosecutor had initiated investigations on 86 of these files (Human Rights Committee 2011, para. 25).

References

Albizures, Miguel Ángel. 2012. 'Una clara amenaza: Por eso los ataques a la Fiscal.' *El Periódico*, 14 August.

Alvarado Pisani, Jorge. 2007. 'Notas para la genealogía del Programa Nacional de Resarcimiento.' In *La vida no tiene precio: Acciones y omisiones de resarcimiento en Guatemala*, 39–55. Informe Temático del Programa Nacional de Resarcimiento. Guatemala: Magna Terra.

Arenales Forno, Antonio. 2012. 'Me indigna que se afirme que en Guatemala hubo genocidio.' *El Periódico*, 26 February.

AVEMILGUA (Asociación de Veteranos Militares de Guatemala). 2012. *Guatemala bajo asedio: Lo que nunca se ha contado*. Guatemala: AVEMILGUA.

Berganza, Gustavo. 2012. 'Guatemala: La fallida marcha de los militares, lenguaje de la Guerra Fría.' *El Periódico*, 11 September.

CAFCA (Centro de Análisis Forense y Ciencias Aplicadas). 2010. *Análisis del informe del Estado de Guatemala sobre el cumplimiento del Pacto Internacional de Derechos Civiles Políticos realizado por organizaciones de víctimas del enfrentamiento armado interno de Guatemala*. Guatemala: CAFCA.

CALDH (Centro para la Acción Legal en Derechos Humanos). 2010. *Un paso más para hacer visibles a las miles de víctimas que ya no están – primera sentencia por desaparición forzada en Guatemala*. Guatemala: CALDH.

CEH (Comisión para el Esclarecimiento Histórico). 1999. *Guatemala: Memoria del silencio*. Guatemala: CEH. An official English summary of the report is available at http://www.aaas.org/sites/default/files/migrate/uploads/mos_en.pdf.

Cojtí Cuxil, Demetrio. 2006. 'Apreciaciones sobre el cumplimiento del Acuerdo sobre Identidad y Derechos Indígenas (AIDPI).' In 'Diez años después de la firma de la Paz', special issue, *Diálogo* (FLACSO-Guatemala), December.

Crandall, Joanna. 2004. 'Truth Commissions in Guatemala and Peru: Perpetual Impunity and Transitional Justice Compared.' *Peace, Conflict and Development* 4 (April): 1–19.

DPLF (Due Process of Law Foundation). 2010. *Las víctimas y la justicia transicional: ¿Están cumpliendo los Estados latinoamericanos con los estándares internacionales?* Washington, DC: DPLF.

El Telégrafo. 2013. 'Activistas protestan en México contra anulación de sentencia a Ríos Montt.' 28 May.

Falla, Ricardo. 1993. *Masacres de la selva: Ixcán, Guatemala, 1975–1982*. Guatemala: Editorial Universitaria, Universidad de San Carlos.

——1995. *Historia de un gran amor: Recuperación autobiográfica de la experiencia con las Comunidades de Población en Resistencia, Ixcán, Guatemala*. Guatemala: Editorial Universitaria, Universidad de San Carlos.

FIDH (International Federation for Human Rights). 2013. *Genocidio en Guatemala: Ríos Montt culpable*. Paris: FIDH.

Flores, Carlos Y. 2001. *Bajo la cruz: Memoria y dimensión sobrenatural del gran sufrimiento entre los qéqchi' de Alta Verapaz*. Cobán, Guatemala: Centro Ak' Kutan.

Font, Juan Luis. 2012. 'Los aparecidos.' *El Diario*, 9 July.

Gamazo, Carolina. 2012. 'Los fantasmas de Cobán.' *El Diario*, 8 July.

Gereda, Marcela. 2012. 'Efraín el Grande?' *El Periódico*, 16 July.

Goldman, Francisco. 2007. *The Art of Political Murder: Who Killed the Bishop?* New York: Grove Press.

Gramajo, Alejandro. 1995. *De la guerra … a la guerra: La difícil transición política en Guatemala*. Guatemala: Fondo de Cultura Editorial.

Hermet, Guy. 2008. *El invierno de la democracia. Auge y decadencia del gobierno del pueblo*. Barcelona: Los Libros del Lince.

Hernández, Daniel. 2013. 'Protests Follow Judges' Rulings in Guatemalan War Crimes Trial.' *Los Angeles Times*, 19 April.

Huet, Alfonso. 2003. 'La diócesis de la Verapaz y el conflicto armado.' In *Rescatando la memoria del camino: Diócesis de Verapaz 1935–2003*. Cobán, Guatemala: Centro Ak' Kutan.

——2008. *Nos salvó la sagrada selva: La memoria de veinte comunidades Q'eqchi'es que sobrevivieron al genocidio*. Cobán, Guatemala: ADICI Wakliiqo.

Human Rights Committee, International Covenant on Civil and Political Rights. 2011. *Respuestas del Gobierno de Guatemala a la lista de cuestiones (CCPR/C/GTM/Q/3) que deben abordarse al examinar el tercer informe periódico de Guatemala (CCPR/C/GTM/3)*. 7 April. New York: United Nations.

Impunity Watch. 2008. *Recognizing the Past: Challenges to Combat Impunity in Guatemala*. Utrecht, Netherlands: Impunity Watch.

La Nación. 2013. 'Protestan a favor de Efraín Ríos Montt en Guatemala.' 12 May.

Macías, Julio César. 1997. *La guerrilla fue mi camino: Epitafio para César Montes*. Guatemala: Editorial Piedra Santa.

Méndez Ruiz Valdés, Ricardo. 2012. 'Las presiones del magistrado.' *El Periódico*, 14 August.

Mérida, Mario Alfredo. 2010. *La historia negada: Compendio acerca del conflicto armado interno en Guatemala*. Guatemala: printed by author.

Ministerio Público. 2012. *Plan operativo anual 2012 modificado*. Guatemala: Ministerio Público. http://www.mp.gob.gt/wp-content/uploads/2011/06/PROGRAMAS-POA-ANUAL-2012-MODIFICADO.pdf.

——2013. *Memoria de labores 2013*. Guatemala: Ministerio Público.

OHCHR (Office of the United Nations High Commissioner for Human Rights). 2014. *Informe de la Alta Comisionada de las Naciones Unidas para los Derechos Humanos sobre las actividades de su oficina en Guatemala*. Guatemala: OHCHR.

Open Society Justice Initiative. 2013. *Judging a Dictator: The Trial of Guatemala's Ríos Montt.* New York: Open Society Justice Initiative.

Palma Lau, Pedro Pablo. 2010. *Sierra Madre: Paisajes y perfiles de la guerra revolucionaria.* Guatemala: F&G Editores.

Paniagua, Walter, Carlos Mezquita, and Denis Martínez. 2012. *Guatemala Resists Forgetting: Post-Conflict Memory Initiatives.* Utrecht, Netherlands: Impunity Watch.

PNR (Programa Nacional de Resarcimiento). 2003. *Texto el Libro Azul: Política pública de resarcimiento.* Guatemala: PNR.

——2007. *Informe de la evaluación conjunta del PNR y de los programas de apoyo al PNR de GTZ y PNUD.* Guatemala: PNR.

——2011. *Memoria de labores 2011.* Guatemala: PNR.

——2013. *Memoria de labores 2012–2013.* Guatemala: PNR.

——2014. *Memoria de labores 2013–2014.* Guatemala: PNR.

Porras Castejón, Gustavo. 2011. *Las huellas de Guatemala.* Guatemala: F&G Editores.

Red de Organizaciones. 2012. *Situación de la política pública de reparación del estado de Guatemala: Informe alternativo al informe anual del Alto Comisionado de las Naciones Unidas para los Derechos Humanos.* Guatemala: Red de Organizaciones Sociales y Víctimas del Conflicto Armado Interno de Guatemala.

REMHI (Proyecto Interdiocesano de Recuperación de la Memoria Histórica). 1998. *Guatemala: Nunca más.* 4 vols. Guatemala: Oficina de Derechos Humanos del Arzobispado. Abridged edition published in English as *Guatemala: Never Again!* (Maryknoll, NY: Orbis; London: CIIR, 1999).

Rodríguez, Francisco. 2012. 'Zury Ríos: "Un soldado no debe pedir perdón …"' *El Periódico*, 10 September.

Rosada-Granados, Héctor. 1999. *Soldados en el poder: Proyecto militar en Guatemala, 1944–1990.* San José: Fundapem/Utrecht University.

Sabino, Carlos. 2008. *Guatemala, la historia silenciada (1944–1989).* 2 vols. Guatemala: Fondo de Cultura Económica.

Schirmer, Jennifer. 1999. *The Guatemalan Military Project: A Violence Called Democracy.* Philadelphia: University of Pennsylvania Press.

Sieder, Rachel. 2001. 'War, Peace, and Memory Politics in Central America.' In *The Politics of Memory: Transitional Justice in Democratizing Societies*, edited by Alexandra Barahona de Brito, Carmen González-Enríquez, and Paloma Aguilar, 161–89. New York: Oxford University Press.

Torres-Rivas, Edelberto. 2011. *Revoluciones sin cambios revolucionarios: Ensayos sobre la crisis en Centroamérica.* Guatemala: F&G Editores.

Vela Castañeda, Manolo E., ed. 2011. *Guatemala, la infinita historia de las resistencias.* Guatemala: Secretaría de la Paz de la Presidencia de la República.

Ventura Arellano, Víctor Manuel. 2012. *La estrategia fallida: El ocaso de una guerra popular prolongada Guatemala, 1979–2000.* Guatemala: printed by author.

Viaene, Lieselotte. 2010. 'Life Is Priceless: Mayan Q'eqchi' Voices on the Guatemalan National Reparations Program.' *International Journal of Transitional Justice* 4(1): 4–25.

Chapter 10

Peru

Beyond paradigmatic cases

Jemima García-Godos and Félix Reátegui[*]

Peru is distinguished by the dual nature of the transition that took place in 2000: a transition from the internal armed conflict that had gripped the country since 1980, and a transition from authoritarian rule (1992–2000). This twofold process has created challenges as well as opportunities for an accountability and human rights agenda. Peru has made some noteworthy advances, including the Fujimori trials, an exemplary truth commission, and a widely recognised collective reparations programme. Yet proponents of greater accountability still come up against daunting obstacles on a daily basis. Above all, the legacies of the armed conflict and the authoritarian regime continue to shape contemporary politics and institutions. Political supporters of former president Alberto Fujimori are the second-largest group in the Peruvian Congress, while guerrilla cells of the Maoist Sendero Luminoso still carry out sporadic actions in the eastern highlands, ensuring that Peruvians do not take peace for granted. The human rights agenda remains actively contested in the Peruvian political arena and in public debate.

This chapter assesses Peru's experience of accountability for past human rights violations by considering how transitional justice mechanisms have been implemented in the country since 2000. The chapter first presents a brief historical background and several unique features of the Peruvian case. It then examines the four transitional justice mechanisms included in this study – truth-seeking, amnesties, trials, and reparations – and issues arising from their implementation. While Peru is recognised for specific achievements in transitional justice, its experience also illustrates that steady progress towards accountability is still vulnerable to a lack of consensus about the legacy of the past as well as an inconsistent institutional framework regarding human rights.

Understanding the Peruvian case

Peru experienced an internal armed conflict from 1980 until the mid-1990s as a result of the guerrilla war initiated by the Peruvian Communist Party Shining Path (Partido Comunista del Perú Sendero Luminoso, known as PCP-SL or Sendero). The fighting broke out just as Peru was making the transition to democracy after 12 years of military rule. Starting in the southern Andes highlands, the conflict spread gradually as Sendero opened new fronts across the country. Peruvians' experience of conflict thus shows great variations across regions and over time.

In 1982, the civilian government granted political-military powers to the Peruvian armed forces in order to counteract the spread of guerrilla warfare in the highlands. Military violence against civilians peaked in 1983 and 1984, with continuous attacks on the rural population, which was suspected of supporting the guerrillas. Despite the harsh repression of those years, the democratic governments of the 1980s lacked a clear national counter-subversive strategy. Such a strategy only emerged in 1989 within the military. It was endorsed, implemented, and eventually altered by President Fujimori, who was elected in 1990.

The conflict caused the forced displacement of 600,000 people and the death or disappearance of approximately 70,000. 79 per cent of the victims lived in rural areas, 75 per cent spoke Quechua or another indigenous language as their mother tongue, and 68 per cent had low levels of formal education (CVR 2003a, vol. 8, 316). This profile of the victims reflected the discriminatory nature of the violence and the long history of subordination of the indigenous peasant population of Peru.

In September 1992 the leader of the PCP-SL, Abimael Guzmán, was captured along with several other members of the guerrilla high command. By that time, Sendero guerrillas had also been expelled from their original strongholds in the south-central Andes. This was due in large part to the activities of peasant patrols (*comités de autodefensa*), operating independently at first and after 1991 as an integral part of the army's counter-subversive strategy (García-Godos 2008). It is common in Peru to regard the capture of Guzmán as marking the end of the armed conflict, so the period from the mid-1990s onwards is seen as a post-conflict period, or 'period of reconstruction', as it was commonly known in Peru. In spite of this, large areas of the national territory were kept under a state of emergency as late as 1999 due to the sometimes alleged, sometimes real, presence of guerrillas.[1] The government's political and military victory over the Sendero guerrillas is one of the main features of the Peruvian transition to peace, which was also characterised by national ownership of the process and the near absence of disarmament, demobilisation, and reintegration programmes.

In terms of transitional justice, however, the process of transition in Peru dates not from the end of the armed conflict but from the collapse of President Fujimori's regime in 2000, as he was seeking re-election to a third term. The once-popular Fujimori had turned into an authoritarian and corrupt leader with little regard for democratic practices and institutions, the rule of law, and human rights (Burt 2007). Following broad public opposition and demonstrations, and amid a corruption scandal, Fujimori fled Peru in November 2000.

Shortly afterwards, in 2001, a truth commission was established with the mandate to investigate systematic human rights violations committed during the armed conflict by both state agents and guerrilla groups. The Peruvian Truth and Reconciliation Commission (Comisión de la Verdad y Reconciliación, CVR) delivered its final report in August 2003, analysing the causes and consequences of the armed conflict (CVR 2003a). The CVR and its report were controversial from the outset, and public debate has continued to ebb and flow in the years since then, with attacks from critics and expressions of support or demands from human rights advocates. Interpreting the armed conflict remains a central – and contentious – task in Peruvian society today.

Since the fall of the Fujimori regime, Peru has had three democratically elected presidents: Alejandro Toledo (2001–6), Alan García (2006–11), and Ollanta Humala (2011–). The period has been characterised both by sustained economic growth and by social conflict around issues of participation, inequality, and exploitation of natural resources. These issues have dominated the public debate over the past decade, leaving relatively little space for other concerns. In this context, three aspects may be considered vital to understanding the Peruvian experience with accountability for past human rights violations.

First, the Peruvian political process is characterised by the near absence of political parties. This has not always been so, but the economic crisis of the 1980s combined with the crude violence of the internal armed conflict meant the effective dismantling of the political party system (Tanaka 1998). Established parties and loyalties fell apart in Peru's 'lost decade', leaving the political scene to be occupied by independent candidates. Fujimori stood as an independent candidate in the presidential election of 1990, an outsider with no previous political experience or party affiliation. State repression, meanwhile, weakened labour unions and social movements, which were suspected of being infiltrated by the guerrillas. As a result, the system of political representation and interest mediation that had emerged with the return to democracy crumbled. While the neo-liberal policies of the 1990s put an end to the economic crisis, albeit with huge social costs, they did not do much to reconstitute the political arena and address the crisis of representation. Instead, the focus shifted towards individuals, with a diminished role for the state and the public. Today, there is a competitive electoral process in Peru, but congressional representatives have few incentives to establish constituencies based on collective agendas rather than on individual political ambitions.[2]

Second, the openness of the Peruvian judicial system to political influence is a persistent obstacle to accountability. Since the 1980s, several attempts have been made to initiate judicial sector reform, but none has been carried through. Systemic challenges to justice administration affect all levels of the judiciary, from local peace judges to higher tribunals. Judicial independence was perhaps at its most vulnerable during the Fujimori regime, when courts were openly used both to curb political opposition and as a tool of repression. In this context, the role of the inter-American human rights system has been vital in moving judicial processes forward; several cases tried at the regional level have set judicial precedents for Peru and the region.[3] As will be discussed later, the limited achievements in Peruvian courts have come despite, rather than because of, the functioning of judicial institutions.

Third, the human rights sector, despite some notable achievements, shows limited success in mobilising popular and political support for human rights issues and in influencing the political agenda. This, in turn, is closely related to the first two factors, namely limited political representation and a permeable judicial system. The impetus created by the transition itself, by the CVR report in 2003, and by the Fujimori ruling in 2009 has been difficult to sustain. Although there are many victims' organisations, their efforts are often scattered. Moreover, the composition of victims' organisations largely reflects the overall profile of victims of the armed conflict in Peru: poor people from rural areas, with few material resources and little political clout.

Against this backdrop, we examine the trajectory of transitional justice mechanisms in Peru. It should be noted that the term 'transitional justice' is seldom used beyond the realm of human rights organisations in Peru; even among victims' organisations, the term is scarcely heard. This likely reflects the limited mobilisation in favour of accountability and human rights in Peruvian society at large. Nonetheless, it is possible to trace a transitional justice process, beginning in 2001, which has at its centre an official truth-seeking effort by a truth commission, the CVR.

A truth waiting to be told: the Peruvian Truth and Reconciliation Commission

The quest for truth existed from the earliest years of the Peruvian armed conflict. In Ayacucho in the 1980s, the mothers of disappeared persons began to challenge the police and the military, demanding to know the whereabouts of their loved ones. As the families organised, they established close relationships with Peruvian human rights organisations in the search for their relatives.[4] In 1985, in the midst of the armed conflict, the National Human Rights Coordinating Committee (Coordinadora Nacional de Derechos Humanos, known as Coordinadora) was established. The network gathered over 50 smaller organisations of victims' families, peasants, displaced people, religious activists, and human rights advocates (Root 2009).

Although the judiciary received numerous denunciations, investigations were seldom initiated. Even the recognition of victims as subjects of rights was neglected throughout the armed conflict, and the few existing organisations of victims remained weak. Nevertheless, the transitional government offered a window of opportunity to find out what had happened to thousands of Peruvians during the armed conflict.

Peru's truth commission was established in 2001 by the transitional government of President Valentín Paniagua and was confirmed later by elected President Alejandro Toledo. Given the context of the transition, the CVR was authorised by executive decree rather than through legislation by the National Congress. The creation of the CVR was not the result of massive popular demand. Rather, it reflected the strength gained by human rights non-governmental organisations

(NGOs) in negotiations around the transition. These NGOs were vocal in presenting the demands of victims' organisations, and they had strong support from the international community, especially international human rights networks. Looking to similar commissions in other Latin American countries such as Chile, Argentina, and Guatemala, the Peruvian human rights sector proposed a mechanism to initiate a process of accountability for human rights violations committed during the armed conflict and the authoritarian Fujimori regime.

The CVR received a broad mandate: to investigate the crimes and human rights violations committed in the context of violence by both terrorist organisations and state agents; to produce an explanation of the factors that led to violence; to contribute to justice; and to make recommendations for reparations and for institutional reform. However, to fulfil this mission, the CVR received no jurisdictional powers whatsoever. It did receive authorisation to interview victims and others, to demand information from institutions, and to organise public hearings. The period to be investigated was 1980–2000, focusing on violations both by guerrilla groups and by state agents. The CVR's 12 commissioners included respected members of human rights organisations, academia, the Catholic and Protestant churches, as well as a representative of the military. Considered an important part of the transition, the CVR was provided with financial and technical resources to carry out its work.[5]

During its 26 months of operation, the CVR collected 17,000 testimonies of victims and organised 12 public hearings with victims in different regions. It investigated a number of cases in an effort to identify perpetrators, demonstrated that the armed actors had committed crimes against humanity, and proposed a legal framework for prosecution of human rights violations. The Commission estimated that the total number of dead and disappeared persons exceeded 69,000. It identified 24,000 full names of victims, made a list of 8,000 disappeared persons, and identified the existence of 4,644 burial sites, having collected preliminary evidence in 2,200 of them (CVR 2003a, vol. 8, 344). On 28 August 2003, the CVR delivered its final report, which included an in-depth account of the events and a well-documented analysis of the armed conflict in Peru from 1980 to 2000, along with a detailed set of recommendations.[6]

The conclusions of the CVR's final report spoke of a truth waiting to be told:

> Violence fell unequally on different geographical areas and on different social strata in the country. If the ratio of victims to population reported to the TRC [Truth and Reconciliation Commission] with respect to Ayacucho were similar countrywide, the violence would have caused 1,200,000 deaths and disappearances. [...] The TRC has established that the tragedy suffered by the populations of rural Peru, the Andean and jungle regions, Quechua and Ashaninka Peru, the peasant, poor and poorly educated Peru, was neither felt nor taken on as its own by the rest of the country. This reveals, in the TRC's judgment, the veiled racism and scornful attitudes that persist in Peruvian society almost two centuries after its birth as a Republic.[7]

The CVR estimated the number of dead and disappeared at 69,280 – almost three times the official figure of 25,000 that Peruvians had generally accepted. How can the enormous gap between the official figure and the CVR estimate be explained? At the deepest level, the answer is likely to be found in Peruvian society's disregard for the rural indigenous people who made up the majority of the victims. Having long ignored the existence of this subordinated population, the Peruvian state and society found it easy to overlook their deaths (García-Godos 2008). Another groundbreaking conclusion of the CVR was that the PCP-SL guerrillas were the main perpetrators of violence in the Peruvian armed conflict, accounting for 54 per cent of casualties.

Delivery of the final report caused some public controversy, with criticism coming especially from the armed forces and from leaders of the political parties that were in government during the armed conflict. Nonetheless, the CVR's narrative was, overall, well received or at least passively accepted during the first years after its release. The recommendations garnered much attention in political circles, human rights organisations, and the media. They included recommendations in the areas of justice (to create a specialised prosecutions system), reparations (to establish a comprehensive reparations plan), and institutional reform. Although there have been some advances in the fields of justice and reparations, institutional reforms have been completely neglected by all three administrations holding office since 2003.

Since the truth commission's report, several unofficial initiatives have been carried out, mainly by victims' communities with sponsorship and technical assistance from NGOs. A notable example is the memory project developed in Lucanamarca, a peasant community where Sendero Luminoso massacred 69 people in the early 1980s. Typical of such projects, it maintains a friendly but critical dialogue with the CVR's narrative: community members accept the general terms of the CVR's account and analysis but also demand a more accurate rendition of their local history.[8]

At the institutional level, the documentation, statistical data, and visual material generated by the truth commission was passed on to the Ombudsman's Office (Defensoría del Pueblo). It is to be permanently stored and accessed at the Place of Memory (Lugar de la Memoria) in Lima. The initiative to establish an official memory museum in 2008 and 2009 fuelled public debate over historical interpretation of the armed conflict. Nonetheless, a building was erected and the facility opened in 2015.

Recent years have seen a trend towards more hostile questioning of the CVR's findings. As in Guatemala, a struggle for memory has gained momentum in the media, with the participation of different (and in some cases aggressive) stakeholders. They include an organisation of retired army generals, which produced a counter-report to challenge the CVR's version.[9] The emergence of such criticism is at least partly a reaction to the ongoing human rights trials of high-level military officials and former president Fujimori, discussed below. Opponents of the prosecutions and of accountability more generally have opposed any attempt to use the CVR's report to inform state policy-making. They particularly object to bringing the CVR's analysis into the educational system as part of lessons about the country's history.

Amnesties

In Peru today, no amnesty law hinders the investigation and prosecution of human rights violations committed during the armed conflict, but this is a relatively recent situation. Members of the armed forces involved in such violations have been shielded from both investigation and prosecution in a variety of ways, formally as well as *de facto*. To start with the latter, one effective form of protection was provided by conducting judicial processes in military courts instead of in the ordinary judicial system. There have been many successful efforts by the Military Tribunal (Fuero Militar Policial, formerly Consejo Supremo de Justicia Militar) to claim jurisdiction over human rights cases, with results equivalent to an amnesty. As documented by the Coordinadora, 83 human rights cases were initiated by military courts between 1980 and 1992, but only one had reached a guilty verdict (CNDDHH 1996, part II).

De facto impunity was formalised in June 1995 when the pro-Fujimori majority in Congress approved the amnesty law (Law 26479). The move followed the indictments of General Julio Salazar Monroe for 15 extrajudicial executions in the Barrios Altos section of Lima in 1991 and of four members of the paramilitary Colina Group for killings at Lima's La Cantuta University in 1992. The new law provided full immunity from investigation, charges, and even compliance with guilty verdicts to all police and military personnel involved in any form of violent activity 'related to the fight against terrorism' since 1980. As some judges refused to apply the amnesty to ongoing human rights cases under their supervision – including the Barrios Altos case, among others – Congress passed the Interpretive Law (Law 26492) a month later. It established that the amnesty law was not subject to judicial review and that judges were obliged to apply it to all cases.

The amnesty laws evoked public outrage in Peru and were condemned by numerous international organisations (CNDDHH 1996). Ignoring the widespread climate of opposition to amnesty, the Peruvian Supreme Court decided to close the Barrios Altos case in October 1995, pursuant to the new amnesty legislation. Relatives of the Barrios Altos victims then presented a claim to the Inter-American Commission on Human Rights against the application of the amnesty law in the case. This gave rise to the landmark Barrios Altos decision of 2001 by the Inter-American Court of Human Rights, establishing the incompatibility of amnesty legislation with the American Convention on Human Rights. But from 1995 until their nullification in 2001, the amnesty laws closed off all avenues by which to pursue criminal accountability for human rights in domestic courts in Peru – civil and military courts alike.

While the 1995 amnesty laws applied to members of the Peruvian armed forces, earlier Peruvian legislation had provided certain benefits regarding investigation, prosecution, and reduction of sentences to members of the two main guerrilla groups, Sendero Luminoso and Tupac Amaru Revolutionary Movement. In this sense the Repentance Law (Legislative Decree 25499) of November 1992 can be considered a partial amnesty. The law was part of a package of counter-subversive legislation introduced by Fujimori, offering reduction and even annulment of sentences for members of guerrilla groups willing to demobilise and provide information to the authorities about the operations and structures of these groups.

In terms of transitional justice, the Repentance Law bears some similarities to the Colombian Justice and Peace Law, as it provided guerrilla members certain benefits in exchange for their demobilisation and information. This scheme is possibly the closest one gets to a state-sponsored demobilisation process in Peru. The law was effective until November 1994; the number of people registered as *arrepentidos* (repentant) reached several thousand.[10] The majority of the demobilised were Sendero cadres, usually young men from rural areas who had been forced to join guerrilla operations locally (Tapia 1997), although there were also some mid-level militants. Most returned to their localities shortly after providing information to civil and/or military authorities. In retrospect, though the Repentance Law may have contributed to a relatively peaceful demobilisation of guerrilla members and supporters in Peru, the scheme had also a perverse outcome: the need to provide information to avoid prosecution or shorten one's own sentence resulted in many innocent people being accused of belonging to a subversive group. In 1993–94, the years that the law applied, almost 10,000 people were arrested on charges of terrorism and treason, two new crimes specified in the counter-subversive legislation of 1992 (de la Jara Basombrío 2001, 41).

The threat of amnesty is not entirely past in Peru. One last attempt to grant the security forces immunity from prosecution was made during President Alan García's administration in 2010. Legislative Decree 1097 prescribed the foreclosure of cases against military and police personnel when 36 months had passed without reaching a verdict. This decree was challenged by human rights NGOs and many other sectors of society and, in 2011, was declared unconstitutional by the Constitutional Court.[11] More recently, the legal defence team of former president Fujimori has attempted to avoid the fulfilment of court verdicts and prison terms, using the legal concept of pardons (*indultos*).

Human rights prosecutions in Peru: changes and continuities

In order to understand transitional justice prosecutions in Peru, it is necessary first to examine how human rights violations were dealt with before the transition. As we will see, the violations that transitional justice prosecutions have tried to address since 2000 were committed not only during the armed conflict, but also in the course of prosecutions of alleged guerrillas in the 1990s, which violated the right to due process. Building on the work of Rebecca Root (2012), this section considers judicial processes against alleged guerrilla members before and after the transition, processes against perpetrators from the Peruvian armed forces, and the Fujimori trials.

Since the early 1980s, when extrajudicial executions, massacres, and disappearances started to take place in Peru, families of the victims have searched for their loved ones, seeking truth but also criminal justice for the perpetrators of these violations. Many denunciations were made to local courts; some judicial processes were initiated, but few were completed. Two principal factors blocked judicial processes in the 1980s. In the first place, the state of emergency and military control imposed limitations in the areas affected by the armed conflict. As the country became aware of the serious situation in the highlands, the civilian government of President Fernando Belaúnde (1980–85) sent in the armed forces to control Sendero's advance in 1982, subordinating civilian authorities to military command. Often special authorisations were needed from the military authorities to travel to certain areas to investigate or gather evidence. Judicial staff and civil authorities were also fearful of travelling to the countryside to investigate, with or without police protection, as Sendero guerrillas had openly identified them as targets of attack and execution. The indiscriminate repression and violence that took place in the highlands of Ayacucho and Huancavelica in 1983 and 1984 made these the worst years of the armed conflict in terms of number of deaths, massacres, and internal displacements.

A second factor obstructing judicial processes was the issue of jurisdiction over human rights cases for violations committed in areas under a state of emergency. The Accomarca case is a good example. In August 1985, a military patrol killed 62 people in the peasant community of Accomarca, including 26 children. Several survivors of the massacre and other witnesses were killed over the next few weeks. The reports of these acts provoked national repudiation, and an investigative congressional committee was put in place, parallel to a judicial investigation at the local court. The latter led to the indictment of four army officers and the general commander of the armed forces in the emergency area. While both Congress and the local prosecutor agreed that the case belonged in ordinary courts, the military claimed that the case belonged in military courts. The Supreme Court ruled in favour of the military, citing the fact that the violations were committed in an emergency area controlled at the time by the armed forces and not by civilian authorities (CVR 2003b, 166). The case was then tried by a military court, leading to a short prison sentence for the main accused, Telmo Hurtado, not for the crime of murder, but for military disobedience.[12] Based on this precedent, for the remainder of the armed conflict, military jurisdiction over human rights cases implied *de facto* impunity for perpetrators belonging to the armed forces.

It is in this context that victims' relatives and human rights organisations in Peru reached beyond the national jurisdiction to the Inter-American Court to seek justice and accountability (Villarán de la Puente 2007). Beginning with its first verdict in 1991 (*Neira Alegría et al. v Peru*), the jurisprudence of the Inter-American Court has played a key role in setting a standard for the Peruvian judicial system and for the protection of human rights in the country. The Court's decisions have put constant pressure on Peruvian authorities to comply with the country's human rights obligations, provoking open challenges. On several occasions, the Fujimori regime interpreted rulings of the Court as interference in the internal affairs of the country. In July 1999, the Peruvian Government announced its unilateral decision to withdraw the country from the inter-American system, with immediate effect, declaring that the Court lacked competence/jurisdiction over Peruvian cases.

This attempt came as Peru awaited Inter-American Court rulings in two important cases: the Baruch Ivcher case and the Constitutional Court case. Both cases demonstrated the authoritarian character of the Fujimori regime. In the Ivcher case, an Israeli-born businessman, the main shareholder of a privately owned television channel critical of the regime, was politically persecuted and his Peruvian citizenship was revoked. The Constitutional Court case dealt with the arbitrary removal of three members of that court who voted against the legislation which would enable Fujimori to run for election for a third term, in violation of the national constitution.

The Inter-American Court, in a historic pronouncement on 24 September 1999, found the withdrawal of a state inapplicable and ruled that it is up to the Court itself to establish the cases over which it has jurisdiction.[13] Although relations between the inter-American system and Peru have improved since then, Court verdicts have continued to provoke critical reactions on the part of subsequent governments. In terms of compliance, Peru's record has improved substantially (Root 2012).

Judicial processes against alleged guerrilla members before the transition

The Repentance Law, allowing partial amnesties to demobilised guerrillas, was part of a larger framework of counter-subversive legislation introduced by the Fujimori regime in 1992. One of the most notorious aspects of this package was a law placing the crime of terrorism under ordinary jurisdiction by judges whose identities would remain undisclosed (Decree 25475). Another law placed the crime of treason under military jurisdiction, giving rise to summary processes (Decree 25659). At least ten related decrees were introduced between May and November 1992, all of them imposing serious limitations on the right to due process of law. Subsequently, thousands of people were arrested and tried for the crimes of terrorism and treason in both ordinary and military courts, with the faces of the judges covered to protect them from possible vengeance (thus the name *jueces sin rostro* – literally, faceless judges). According to de la Jara Basombrío (2001, 41), based on official figures from the National Registry of Detainees, the number of people detained for terrorism or treason went from 713 in 1992 to 4,222 in 1993 and 5,165 in 1994, the years when the Repentance Law was in place. The total number of detainees for these crimes was 21,795 for the period 1992–2000.

Implementation of the counter-subversive legislation led to a surge of complaints to human rights organisations from families and relatives of the detainees, protesting wrongful detentions. Many of the detainees were tortured to produce confessions or to force them to identify others. Between 1992 and 2000, 6,075 detainees were set free before any judicial process could take place, often having experienced torture and abuse. Of the approximately 15,680 detainees who were tried, more than 60 per cent were released by the courts (de la Jara Basombrío 2001, 31). The indiscriminate character of detentions and the situation of those accused of terrorism or treason and wrongfully detained became one of the most important issues for the human rights movement and victims' organisations in Peru.

As human rights advocates documented more and more cases of wrongful detention, the government established an ad hoc commission to investigate and recommend presidential pardons for some of those who had been sentenced to prison for terrorism or treason. Although this opened some possibilities for release of detainees, the human rights community questioned the use of pardons as the appropriate mechanism. Technically, pardons can be granted to people found guilty, but not to those found innocent of a charge for which they have been wrongfully accused, detained, tried, and sentenced. In Peru, these are known as *inocentes indultados* (pardoned innocents). Between 1996 and 2000, 546 people were 'pardoned' having been wrongfully accused of terrorism (de la Jara Basombrío 2001, 45). The pardon did not necessarily restore the rights of the *inocentes indultados*. Many had been severely harmed, their names had not been cleared, and they were often subject to continuing police harassment and suspicion (Enco Tirado et al. 2006).

The trials against active and proven guerrilla members were equally arbitrary, conducted in military courts without the defendant having the right to a proper defence or legal counsel. The most notorious case was against the top leadership of PCP-SL, including its leader Abimael Guzmán. He was tried and sentenced to life imprisonment in 1992, in a verdict reached only a few days after his arrest. The trial of civilians by Peruvian military courts, independently of the charge or of their actual guilt or innocence, has been contested in several cases by the Inter-American Court.[14]

Criminal accountability after the transition

By the time of the transition, the accountability agenda for human rights violations committed in Peru in the period 1980–2000 was enormous. The Fujimori regime had attempted to remove the country from the inter-American system, the only mechanism of human rights protection available to Peruvians up to that time; fortunately, this effort failed. One of the first things that the transitional government of President Valentín Paniagua did to restore the rule of law was to re-establish Peru's participation in the inter-American system. This, together with the Barrios Altos judgment of 2001 in the Inter-American Court, gave a new impetus to the human rights sector and to a great number of issues and cases not yet addressed by the Peruvian judicial system.

As a direct consequence of the Barrios Altos case, the Peruvian state and the Inter-American Court agreed on a list of 159 cases to be processed and/or reopened to fulfil the effective right to due process (IACHR 2001). These emblematic cases would be advanced by the Public Prosecutor's Office (Ministerio Público) to demonstrate Peru's commitment to human rights and criminal accountability. The development of these cases would be monitored by the Ombudsman's Office. Later, with the release of the CVR final report in 2003, 47 additional cases were presented to the Public Prosecutor's Office, also under the supervision of the ombudsman (Defensoría 2013, 95). The monitoring of this universe of cases by the Ombudsman's Office provides a good indication of overall progress or limitations in criminal accountability, as noted below.

One of the institutional changes that influenced criminal accountability in Peru after the transition was the creation of specialised human rights prosecutors at national and regional levels, in 2002 and 2003 respectively. In addition, a specialised chamber for human rights cases, the National Criminal Court (Sala Penal Nacional), was established in 2004, initially also with regional jurisdictions. A new criminal code (Nuevo Código Procesal Penal) was introduced the same year, to be implemented gradually across the country by 2010.[15] Since 2001, the Constitutional Court has made substantial contributions to criminal accountability in Peru by issuing a large number of rulings regarding human rights violations, right to due process, and the unconstitutionality of both military jurisdiction in human rights cases and the counter-subversive legislation. A ruling in 2003 decided that all judicial processes conducted by military courts and 'faceless judges' during the Fujimori regime were to be started anew. This was indeed an unprecedented measure in Peru. According to Root (2012, 104), by adopting this position the Constitutional Court re-established the control of civilian courts over all cases involving civilians, even those charged with terrorism or treason. These cases have been retried, beginning in 2003, despite fears from some sections of the population that former guerrilla leaders might go free. Abimael Guzmán himself was retried and convicted again in 2004. Other Sendero leaders were also convicted. According to an Ombudsman's Office report, by 2013 the National Criminal Court had issued 891 judgments related to the crime of terrorism, convicting 949 people and acquitting 710 (Defensoría 2013, 121).

A significant victory came in 2006, five years after the initial indictment in the case, when the National Criminal Court issued a guilty verdict for four police officers in the forced disappearance of 22-year-old student Ernesto Castillo Páez in 1990. This was the first judgment for the crime of forced disappearance to be issued in a Peruvian court, and it incorporated elements of international human rights legislation in the evaluation of evidence. This legal victory might have been expected to lead towards a conscious public policy on the issue of forced disappearance or other efforts by national decision makers to address the issue. However, this has not occurred. Although it is believed that more than 15,000 people disappeared as a result of the armed conflict and authoritarian rule, Peru does not yet have a public policy to search for the disappeared (Defensoría 2013, 148).

How far, then, has Peru moved forward towards criminal accountability for human rights violation? Although advances were made in the first years after the transition, there were notable setbacks during the García administration in terms of both political interference in the judicial process and the Court rulings issued in this period.[16] Based on the 194 cases monitored by the Ombudsman's Office since 2001, the results are not very satisfactory.[17] By May 2013, only 32 of the cases had reached a verdict, while 77 had been dismissed (archived). Another 36 were in the preliminary investigation stage, and 32 were in other intermediate stages of the judicial process (Defensoría 2013, 116). Of the 35 verdicts issued in the 32 completed cases, 20 were acquittals, 12 were condemnations, and three were mixed (Defensoría 2013, 122).[18]

In spite of the institutional changes implemented in the early 2000s, human rights prosecutions still tend to be excessively prolonged over time, undermining the rights of victims to truth, justice, and reparations, as well as the right of those indicted to due process (Rivera Paz 2010). Many factors, both structural and institutional, contribute to these delays. For one, the organisation and structure of the judiciary has undergone a number of changes over the past decade, and specialised units have been split, merged, or required to send cases from one jurisdiction to another. In 2005 the judiciary introduced a centralised institutional design for human rights cases, which meant that all such cases in the provinces would be transferred to courts in Lima for investigation and trial. Given that the great majority of violations were committed in the highlands and that most victims and relatives are of poor, rural origin, this centralisation has seriously reduced the ability of families and witnesses to follow and participate in trials. Furthermore, the mandate of specialised units that were originally designed to focus on human rights cases has been constantly expanding since 2005. Today, the National Criminal Court oversees cases of corruption and narcotraffic, illegal mining, money-laundering, social unrest, and more, along with its core responsibility for human rights cases (Defensoría 2013, 112).

Concerning the judicial processes themselves, one important factor obstructing the course of justice is the absence of information needed to identify perpetrators. In a great many cases, the armed forces have been unwilling to provide necessary information about the composition of units deployed during the armed conflict (Defensoría 2013, 127). Proper development of judicial processes has also been hindered by the failure to carry out arrest orders; by limited or non-existent mechanisms of legal support and protection for victims, witnesses, and human rights advocates; and by the reluctance of members of the Peruvian judicial system to recognise and apply relevant national and regional jurisprudence.

The latter aspect in particular has caused national controversy on several occasions, when individual judges disregarded the categorisation of specific crimes by the Inter-American Court or reached mixed verdicts, convicting perpetrators of some crimes but not others. In 2012, presiding judge Javier Villa Stein received widespread criticism when the ruling issued by the permanent chamber over which he presided at the Supreme Court questioned the classification of the

Barrios Altos killings as crimes against humanity. This definition had already been applied by the National Criminal Court, as well as in the Fujimori case.[19] The Villa Stein judgment was rejected by the victims, by the Ombudsman's Office, and by the Supreme Court itself, which overturned the verdict a few months later. Also in 2012, in the case of Los Cuarteles, the incumbent judge questioned the classification of enforced disappearance as a criminal act and dismissed the participation or testimony of relatives as 'biased' in favour of the victim.

In this general context of institutional change and judicial delay, it is extraordinary that the Peruvian judicial system produced one of the most paradigmatic cases of transitional justice in Latin America, the Fujimori trials.

The Fujimori trials

In November 2000, President Fujimori abandoned Peru, seeking refuge in Japan for three years.[20] Attempts by the Peruvian government to have him extradited failed, in spite of the serious charges against him. In November 2005, Fujimori travelled unexpectedly to Chile, where he was arrested by the Chilean authorities at Peru's request. After a lengthy extradition process, the Chilean Supreme Court voted in favour of Fujimori's extradition in September 2007. The former president was sent to Peru to be tried for seven of the 13 charges that the Peruvian authorities had documented against him. The seven charges – two cases of human rights violations and five cases of corruption – represented a substantial reduction from the dozens of charges that were pending against the former president at the start of the extradition negotiations.

Fujimori was sentenced to 25 years in prison for the two cases of human rights violations on 7 April 2009. The verdict by the National Criminal Court marked the end of a 15-month judicial process. The first case concerned the disappearance or killings of 25 people by the paramilitary Colina Group at Barrios Altos and La Cantuta in November 1991 and July 1992. The other case involved several incidents of illegal arrest, kidnapping, and torture in the basement of the headquarters of the Army Intelligence Service (Servicio de Inteligencia del Ejército, SIE). These cases were dealt with in a single process, since they both concerned human rights violations. According to the prosecuting authorities, Fujimori was directly responsible for these atrocities because of the national security policy that allowed the creation of paramilitary groups in order to eradicate guerrilla members. The argument was that Fujimori knew of the existence of the Colina Group, endorsed its methods, and showed little or no willingness to stop the group even though he had the authority to do so.

Initially, the prosecution had difficulties providing material evidence, documents, or testimonies to prove that Fujimori ordered the actions at La Cantuta, Barrios Altos, and the SIE. This changed after January 2008, when several members of the Colina Group were questioned by the Court. Their responses strengthened the prosecution claim that the atrocities had been reported to Fujimori, who had full knowledge of them and approved them. Fujimori's defence argued that the Colina Group was created by the army in secrecy and that the president neither knew about nor accepted the group's actions. The president, they argued, could not stop something that he did not know about.

Fujimori's trial and sentence had great legal significance: it was the first time in history that a former head of state had been extradited to his country of origin to be prosecuted for human rights violations (Burt 2009). In its decision, the Court found Fujimori guilty of the crime of homicide, applying elements of crimes against humanity to address the gravity of the crimes involved (Salmón 2014, 66–67). The judges found sufficient evidence for the existence of a national security policy that allowed systematic violations of human rights, and Fujimori was convicted as the principal person responsible for the crimes committed within the framework of this policy. Against a grim background of weak judicial independence, Fujimori's conviction was considered a test of the Peruvian judicial system. In this particular test the Court, led by Judge César San Martín, succeeded in every way. Subsequent trials against Fujimori on corruption charges have continued since 2009.

The momentum gained by Fujimori's conviction has suffered setbacks over the past years, with several acquittals and few convictions in other human rights cases (Rivera Paz 2012). Nevertheless, in 2014, three new condemnatory verdicts finally incorporated a vital element applied in the Fujimori verdict: the role of military structures in the systematic violation of human rights.[21] There is still much to be done to strengthen accountability for human rights violations in Peru. Understanding how the military and intelligence services operated during the armed conflict, for example, is an essential step towards establishing criminal responsibility in systems with clear chains of command (Rivera Paz 2015). Overall, the prospects for future judicial action remain unclear.

Half-full or half-empty: victims' reparations in Peru

The issue of reparations as a mechanism of transitional justice was introduced in Peru by the CVR. One of the truth commission's objectives was to 'determine the whereabouts, identification, and situation of victims' and to make proposals for 'moral and material redress for victims or their relatives'.[22] Accordingly, the CVR understood reparations as 'an act of justice – individual or collective – and a duty to rebuild what has been harmed. [...] Reparations are understood as instruments of reconciliation, intended to remedy the grave imbalance created by the conflict and affirm a new social pact' (CVR 2003a, vol. 9, 21).

In the decade preceding the CVR, although Inter-American Court rulings had included specific forms of reparations to victims, the topic of broader reparation programmes remained absent from the public debate. The only form of redress for harm suffered by civilians was a compensation scheme developed for members of peasant patrols who sustained casualties during combat. It was established in 1998, in the final years of the Fujimori administration, and basically provided for monetary compensation, known as *indemnización* (García-Godos 2008). Relatively few people benefited from that scheme. There were also other compensation schemes directed to specific groups of people, such as members of the armed forces and police, public officials, and civilian authorities. Support to peasant communities as affected groups was addressed in terms of 'reconstruction'. A national programme in charge of return and reconstruction in areas affected by violence operated between 1995 and 2001 (Programa de Apoyo al Repoblamiento y Desarrollo de Zonas de Emergencia, PAR) (García-Godos 2006).

The CVR brought a significant change, with new emphasis given to victims of the armed conflict. This development came late to Peru in comparison to other transitional countries in Latin America, a region with emblematic experiences of victims' reparations programmes. Even the term 'victim' was not widely used before the CVR, except by human rights organisations. Instead, terms referring to specific violations were applied to groups of people, such as *detenidos desaparecidos* (disappeared detainees) or *desplazados* (displaced persons).

The CVR's final report included a detailed proposal for a comprehensive reparations plan. However, it took two years before the law creating the Comprehensive Reparations Programme (Programa Integral de Reparaciones, PIR) was passed in 2005.[23] Around this time, the concept of victims' rights began to move beyond the realm of human rights organisations and enter mainstream discourse. Reparations were re-envisioned as redress to the victims of the Peruvian armed conflict, irrespective of whether or not they lived in 'areas affected by violence'. An administrative unit to design, implement, and monitor victims' reparations was created in 2004, before the law was passed. This is known as the High-Level Multisectoral Commission (Comisión Multisectorial de Alto Nivel, CMAN).

The law also established the National Registry of Victims (Registro Único de Víctimas, RUV) to be monitored by the Reparations Council (Consejo de Reparaciones, CR). In addition to designing and operating the RUV, the Council develops criteria to determine whether a person or group of people can be accredited as victims. Victim status enables a person or group to be included in the victims' registry and to access benefits under the different reparations programmes. Although the definitions of 'victim' and 'beneficiary' in the law, the rules of procedure, and the registry are relatively broad and inclusive, there is one important exclusion from the status of victim (and thus access to reparations): former members of guerrilla groups. This exclusion points to the political character as well as the limits of transitional justice mechanisms in post-conflict societies (Laplante 2009).

The law envisaged the creation of six reparations programmes, providing benefits to prioritised groups in the areas of health, education, housing, civil rights, symbolic reparations, and collective reparations, as well as other programmes that the CMAN might find appropriate (such as the individual economic reparations programme described below). At the same time, the law called for local and regional governments and civil society to participate in providing reparations as a supplement to the national programmes. One of the first activities of the new institutions for reparations was to set up a common registry of victims' organisations in order to identify counterparts for the purpose of coordination and dialogue. Along with local-level initiatives, this contributed to an upsurge in the number of victims' organisations that were created and registered in 2006–7. Victims were optimistic that their prolonged deprivation and abandonment by the state was coming to an end, and they had high hopes for a response to their long-standing demands. The risk, however, was that they would experience an increased sense of abandonment if the reality did not meet their expectations (Laplante and Theidon 2007).

The Collective Reparations Programme (Programa de Reparaciones Colectivas, PRC) was the first to be implemented, in 2007. Based on needs assessments of local communities affected by the armed conflict, the programme provided financial support for small development projects, often accompanied by a symbolic act to commemorate the victims and survivors. These projects involved basic infrastructure and productive initiatives, but also day care centres, schools, and playgrounds. Some human rights organisations have criticised this type of support on the grounds that such collective reparations are not clearly distinguished from ordinary development projects. They point out that development initiatives are the duty of states under any circumstances, and such projects do not embody the restorative dimension that reparations are meant to fulfil. The PRC was most active until 2011 and was, for a long time, the only reparations programme in operation. According to the Reparations Council, of the 5,697 communities registered as affected by the armed conflict in 2013, just 33 per cent had received collective reparations by that date (Defensoría 2013, 30).

The National Registry of Victims became operational in 2008. By March 2013, the RUV included 182,350 individual victims (59 per cent identified as direct victims, 41 per cent as indirect victims) and 5,597 collective victims (Defensoría 2013, 25). The registration and accreditation processes have required both technical capacity and political commitment. The completion of this registry was considered a precondition for the implementation of programmes focusing on various forms of individual reparations, most notably the Programme for Individual Economic Reparations (Programa de Reparaciones Económicas Individuales, PREI), which became operational in 2011. Though the RUV continues to receive applications for accreditation, access to the PREI was closed to new applicants in 2011, a decision that is being contested by both victims and human rights groups.

The implementation of reparations in Peru has taken place in a context of limited dialogue and interaction between stakeholders (victims and their relatives) and public agencies in charge of the programmes (Rubio Escolar 2013). This is particularly noticeable in the economic reparations programme. Although welcomed by victims' organisations, it has faced serious criticism for the unilateral design of the measures provided. Economic compensation is set at 10,000 nuevos soles (approximately US$3,300) per victim in cases of disappearance, death, sexual violence, or permanent disability. If a victim of disappearance has only one relative entitled to compensation, the full amount will go to that person alone. If the victim left a spouse, children, and parents, the same amount will have to be divided among them (50 per cent for the spouse, 50 per cent for the other beneficiaries).

According to the Reparations Council, there are 82,710 individual beneficiaries entitled to economic compensation, corresponding to 88,559 registered violations (*afectaciones*). By August 2014, economic compensation had been granted for 62 per cent of these violations. In terms of beneficiaries, 54,856 individual beneficiaries received compensation, for an average of 3,359 nuevos soles (approximately US$1,100) per beneficiary. Although the programme is still being implemented, problems have emerged regarding the limited compensation for multiple violations, arbitrary criteria for compensation to certain groups of victims (such as the elderly), and confusion regarding grounds for exclusion from benefits (Defensoría 2014).

There are several possible reasons for the limited role of victims' organisations. It could be argued that the identification of victims as 'target beneficiaries' of policies and administrative programmes restrains their participation as active stakeholders in decision-making processes that concern them. The limited participation may also reflect the socio-economic profile of most victims: indigenous, poor, peasant populations, with limited voice in the public sphere. However, the poverty and marginalisation of the victims was the reason for the prompt initiation of the collective reparations programme. Except for the PREI, the other reparations programmes are still at an initial implementation stage and could eventually entail a larger role for victims' groups and their advocates.

Despite advances in collective and economic reparations, as well as the completion of the victims' registry, a stocktake of reparations programmes in Peru reveals significant issues that are still pending. According to the Ombudsman's Office, the country has yet to address victims' reparations in a comprehensive public policy (Defensoría 2013, 71). Advances in some areas have come at the expense of others, without coherence and coordination between different public agencies. Reparations in the area of education were first implemented in 2013, while housing-related reparations and reparations to restore civil rights have not been developed at all. Some of the measures described as reparations involve benefits that are available, or are supposed to be available, to everyone, irrespective of victim status. The measures offered as health reparations, for instance, make use of a national social programme for access to health services. Yet that programme, available to all Peruvian citizens, cannot be considered as health reparations, as it has not been tailored to the physical and mental health issues of victims. Concerning symbolic reparations, initiatives to restore the memory and dignity of victims were introduced in the collective reparations programme, and a number of memory initiatives have taken place around the country, as noted earlier. Yet these are mainly local efforts, not the result of a coordinated effort to promote symbolic reparations. In sum, the metaphor of the half-full or half-empty glass describes the current status of victims' reparations in Peru.

Conclusions

The legacy of the armed conflict and authoritarian rule in Peru still weighs on the country's political present and future. The transition in 2000 brought a conscious effort on the part of the transitional government to come to terms with the past. The clearest achievement since then has doubtlessly been the CVR and its final report, which set the record straight and attempted to define an accountability agenda for the future. However, as in other countries in the region, we see that the quality of a truth commission's report is no guarantee of the support and follow-up it will receive. While the final report identified the PCP-SL guerrillas as the main perpetrators of human rights violations in Peru, it also documented violations committed by the armed forces with the approval of civilian administrations. The Fujimori regime based its power on the support of the armed forces, and in spite of the transition, the military remained – and remains today – a powerful institution in Peru. Although the amnesty law was lifted in 2001, opening the door for human rights cases to proceed, the armed forces still drag their feet about providing the information prosecutors need to investigate these cases. The

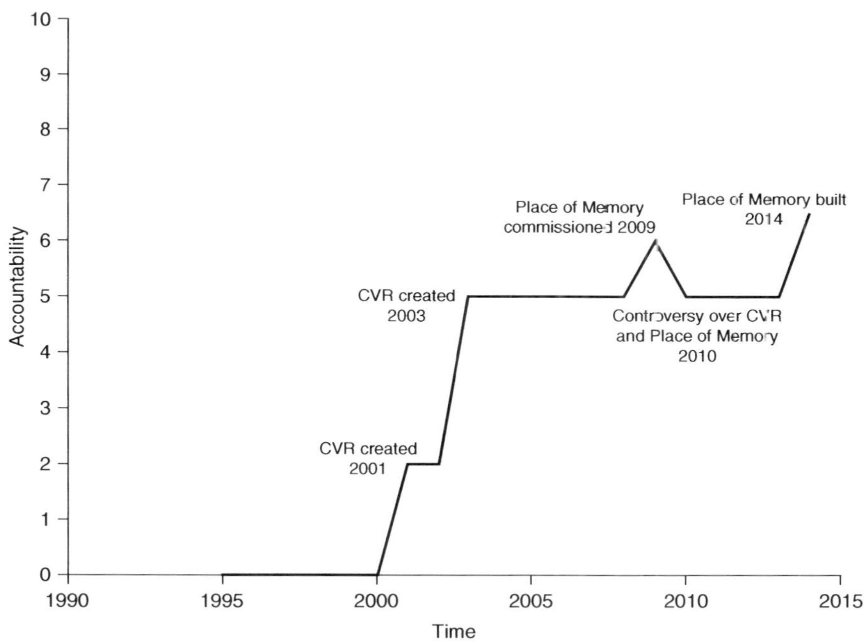

Figure 10.1 Peru: the truth dimension of accountability, 1995–2014
Source: Authors' construction, 2015.

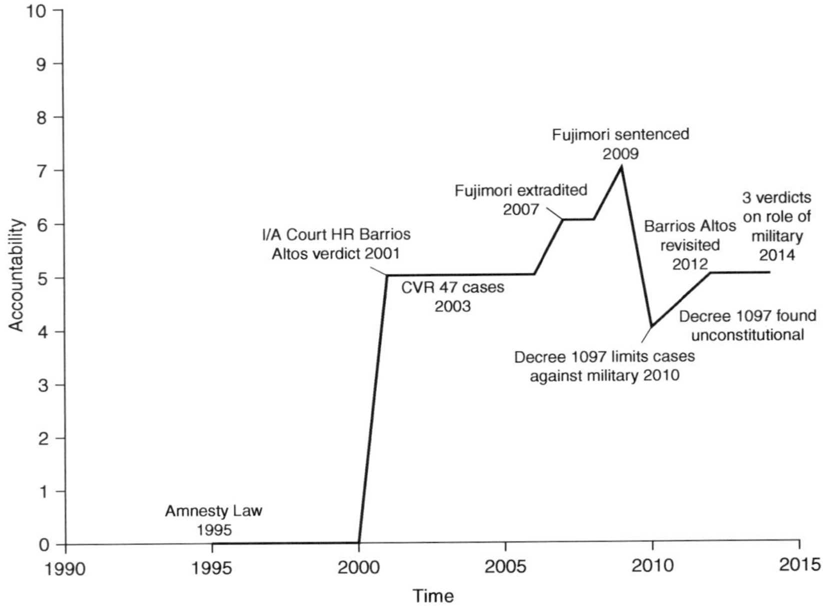

Figure 10.2 Peru: the overcoming amnesty dimension of accountability, 1995–2014
Source: Authors' construction, 2015.

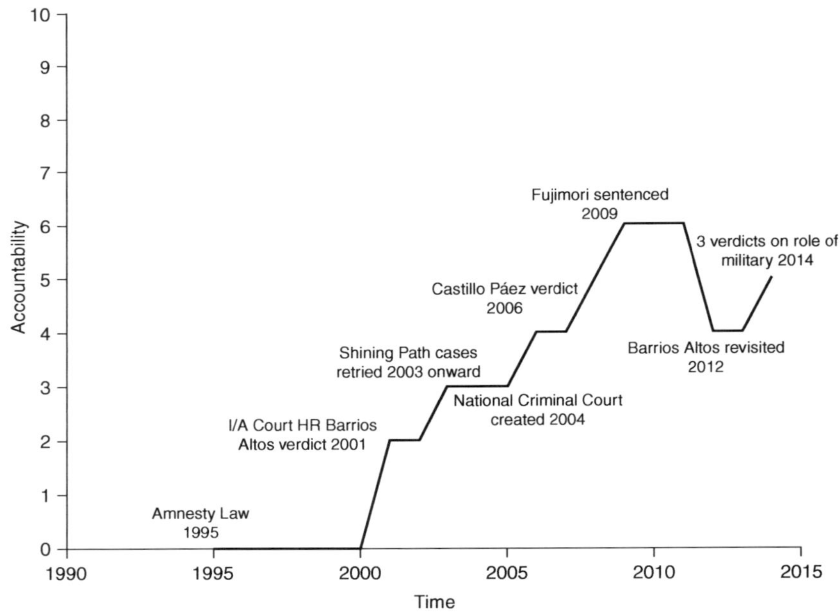

Figure 10.3 Peru: the trials dimension of accountability, 1995–2014
Source: Authors' construction, 2015.

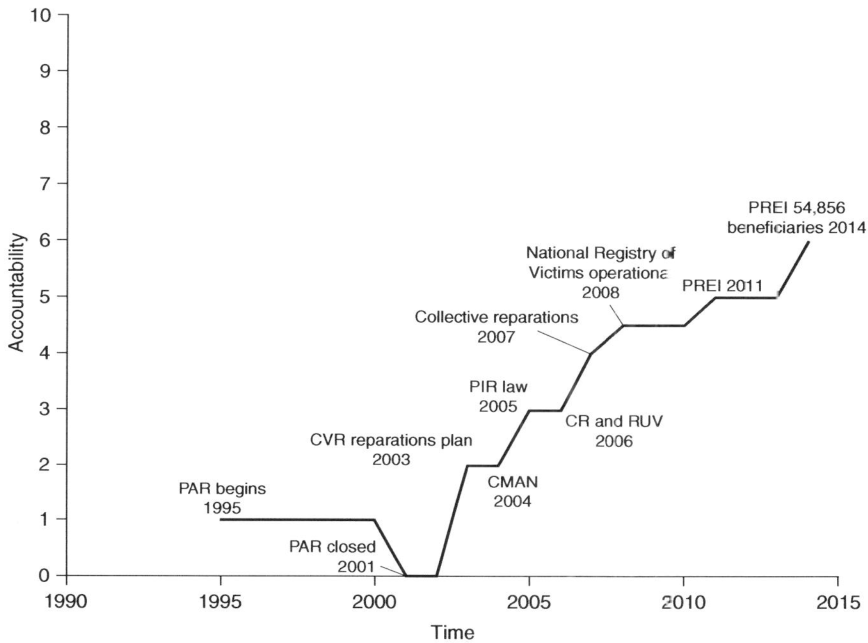

Figure 10.4 Peru: the reparations dimension of accountability, 1995–2014
Source: Authors' construction, 2015.

military also continues to question the veracity of the CVR's final report and the credibility and intentions of the commissioners.

With respect to prosecutions, the Peruvian judicial system has reached some important verdicts, but their significance today does not guarantee that they will be considered and applied as precedents in future cases. Lack of resources imposes an obvious constraint on the judiciary, but an even greater challenge may be the lack of coherence in legal doctrine and its application. The new criminal code introduced in 2004 aimed to secure the right to due process by prioritising oral proceedings and judgments. Yet this has not ensured steady progress, as the various stages of the process are interrupted by lengthy and unpredictable pauses. Judicial processes can thus extend over many years, with negative consequences for victims, survivors, and relatives, as well as defendants.

In the area of reparations, both collective and individual reparations have shown some positive results. Nonetheless, these programmes have not fulfilled their mandates, and victims' expectations for recognition of their rights and of the harm they suffered have not been met. Time is running out, as most victims of the armed conflict in Peru suffered harm in the early 1980s, three decades ago. Reparations, for example, may entitle victims' children to payment for their

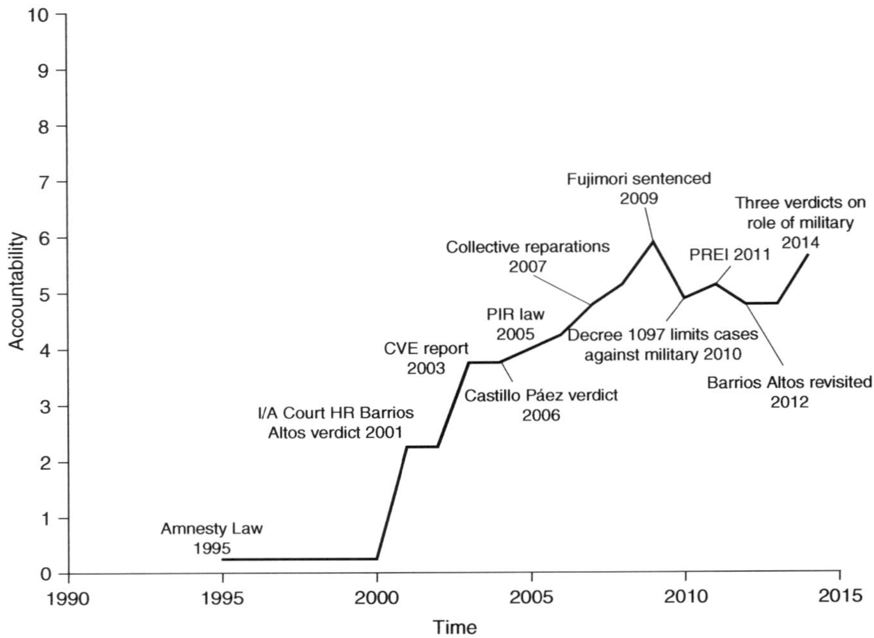

Figure 10.5 **Peru: overall trend towards accountability, 1995–2014**
Source: Authors' construction, 2015.

educational expenses, but the child of a peasant killed in 1984 is today at least 30 years old, probably has a family to support, and has little prospect of being able to return to school. Similarly, physical and mental health services for victims who experienced torture and rape during the armed conflict are coming 20 or 30 years too late. The CVR envisioned reparations as a means to 'remedy the grave imbalance created by the conflict and affirm a new social pact', yet post-transitional governments seem unaware that time is of the essence in the fulfilment of victims' rights.

Internationally, Peru is well known for its impressive and sound truth commission, for the impeccable trials of Fujimori, for its collective reparations programme, and for professionalism in preparing the national victims' registry. These are all examples of advances on the road from impunity towards accountability. Yet, as we have seen, much more needs to be done to build on these achievements.

Notes

* The authors thank Elizabeth Salmón for useful comments on an earlier draft of this chapter.

1 The need for a state of emergency was much debated at the time, as many argued that it was a tactic to limit political opposition to the regime. This might have been the case in some parts of the country, but it was also true that the PCP-SL was still active in other regions. Comrade Feliciano, who took over leadership of the group after the 1992 capture of Abimael Guzmán, was not himself captured until 1999.

2 Peru first attempted to regulate the electoral arena in 2003 with the Law of Political Parties (Law 28094). The law has been modified several times since then.

3 One of the most influential verdicts came in the Castillo Páez case, in which the Inter-American Court of Human Rights (I/A Court HR) established the state's obligation to investigate cases of enforced disappearance even when the identity of the perpetrators had not been established prior to the investigation (*Case of Castillo Páez v Peru*, Reparations and Costs, Judgment of 27 November 1998). An updated list of Inter-American Court verdicts concerning Peru can be found on the Court's website: http://www.corteidh.or.cr/cf/Jurisprudencia2/busqueda_casos_contenciosos.cfm?lang=en.

4 The first victims' organisation in Peru is probably ANFASEP (National Association of Families of the Kidnapped, Detained and Disappeared of Peru), founded in 1983 in Ayacucho, the area most affected by violence.

5 The truth commission was created by Supreme Decree 065-2001-PCM of 4 June 2001, available in Spanish on the CVR website.

6 The nine-volume *Informe final* (CVR 2003a) is available in Spanish on the CVR website at http://cverdad.org.pe/ifinal/, along with an English translation of the report's conclusions.

7 From the CVR's official English translation of the report's General Conclusions (paras. 8–9), available on the CVR website at http://www.cverdad.org.pe/ingles/ifinal/conclusiones.php.

8 See Falconí, Jiménez, and Alfaro (2007). Other locally constructed histories of the armed conflict came from Ayahuanco, Tambo, and Huancavelica.

9 The report, entitled *En honor a la verdad*, was published in 2010 by the Comisión Permanente de Historia del Ejército del Perú, a historical commission of the Peruvian army.

10 Tapia (1997, 81) reports 5,000, Bermúdez (1995) reports 6,759, and the Peruvian Ombudsman's Office (cited in Amnesty International 2003) estimates over 8,300 people participating in the Repentance Law scheme.

11 Judgment 00024-2010-PI/TC, Proceso de inconstitucionalidad contra el Decreto Legislativo No. 1097.

12 Hurtado was later promoted within the military and left Peru when the amnesty law was lifted. He was extradited back to Peru in 2007 and prosecuted in 2011–12. At the end of 2014, the case was still awaiting a verdict.

13 A good summary of that controversy can be found at IACHR (2000, chap. III). See also Dulitzky (1999).

14 See, among others, the judgments in *Loayza Tamayo v Peru* (1997) and *Castillo Petruzzi v Peru* (1999).

15 Peru's criminal justice system is similar to that of Guatemala, following a prosecutorial model in which the state, represented by the Public Prosecutor's Office, undertakes investigations and presents evidence before a judge or group of judges in public, oral proceedings. The judge(s) reach a decision based on evidence presented. Victims can participate in the process as civil parties.

16 Gloria Cano and Carlos Rivera, human rights lawyers, interviews by author, Lima, 10–11 October 2012.

17 The total number of ongoing human rights cases in Peru is not readily available. As of August 2013, the Peruvian judicial system did not have a single, unified registry or database of human rights cases. For useful lists and overviews of ongoing human rights cases, as well as Peruvian jurisprudence, see the report of the Ombudsman's Office (Defensoría 2013, annexes XII and XIII); the website of the Human Rights Trials in Peru Project (http://www.rightsperu.net), with figures updated to September 2012; and the website of the Instituto de Democracia y Derechos Humanos at the Pontificia Universidad Católica del Perú (IDEHPUCP), with a comprehensive list of national jurisprudence (http://idehpucp.pucp.edu.pe/seguimiento/jurisprudencia-nacional/).
18 Another way to assess the status of human rights cases is that presented by Burt (2013, 51). She indicates that, by 2013, the Public Prosecutor's Office had received 2,880 reports of human rights violations committed during the armed conflict. Of these, 48 per cent had been dismissed, 47 per cent were in the preliminary or intermediate investigation stages, and only 2 per cent had reached the trial stage.
19 For an analysis of the implications of the Villa Stein judgment, see Rivera Paz (2012).
20 A detailed account of the Fujimori trials is beyond the scope of this chapter. For excellent reviews and analysis, see Burt (2009) and Salmón (2014).
21 These cases are the disappeared from Universidad Nacional del Centro, the killings of Pucará, and the disappearance of Javier Tineo de la Cruz (Rivera Paz 2015).
22 From the supreme decree establishing the CVR (see note 5). Our translation.
23 Law 28592 was approved on 28 July 2005. The law became effective in 2006 with the approval of its rules of procedure.

References

Amnesty International. 2003. *Peru: The 'Anti-terrorism' Legislation and Its Effects – An Unfinished Business in the Transition to Democracy*. AMR 46/001/2003. London: Amnesty International.

Bermúdez, Alejandro. 1995. 'Los "arrepentidos", una desbandada en Sendero.' *Aceprensa*, 1 February.

Burt, Jo-Marie. 2007. *Political Violence and the Authoritarian State in Peru: Silencing Civil Society*. New York: Palgrave Macmillan.

——2009. 'Guilty as Charged: The Trial of Former Peruvian President Alberto Fujimori for Human Rights Violations.' *International Journal of Transitional Justice* 3(3): 384–405.

——2013. 'Transitional Justice in Post-Conflict Peru: Progress and Setbacks in Accountability Efforts.' *Aportes DPLF*, no. 18: 49–54.

CNDDHH (Coordinadora Nacional de Derechos Humanos). 1996. *Informe sobre la situación de los derechos humanos en el Perú*. Annual report for 1995. Lima: CNDDHH.

Comisión Permanente de Historia del Ejército del Perú. 2010. *En honor a la verdad*. Lima: CPHEP.

CVR (Comisión de la Verdad y Reconciliación). 2003a. *Informe final de la Comisión de la Verdad y Reconciliación*. 9 vols. Lima: CVR. http://www.cverdad.org.pe/ifinal/index.php.

——2003b. 'Las ejecuciones extrajudiciales en Accomarca (1985).' In *Informe final de la Comisión de la Verdad y Reconciliación*, vol. 7. Lima: CVR.

Defensoría. 2013. *A diez años de verdad, justicia y reparación: Avances, retrocesos y desafíos de un proceso inconcluso*. Informe Defensorial 162. Lima: Defensoría del Pueblo.

——2014. *Balance del nivel de cumplimiento del Programa de Reparaciones Económicas Individuales (PREI)*. Informe de Adjuntía 008-2014-ADHPD/DP. Lima: Defensoría del Pueblo.

de la Jara Basombrío, Ernesto. 2001. *Memoria y batallas en nombre de los inocentes: Perú 1992–2001*. Lima: Instituto de Defensa Legal.

Dulitzky, Ariel. 1999. 'El retiro del reconocimiento de la competencia contenciosa de la Corte Interamericana de Derechos Humanos por parte de Perú: Análisis jurídico.' *Pensamiento Constitucional* 6(6): 705–27.

Enco Tirado, Amado, Carlos Rivera Paz, Antonio Salazar García, and Tania Valle Manchego. 2006. *Los requisitoriados por terrorismo ¿quiénes son? ¿Cuántos son? Cumpliendo las recomendaciones de la Comisión de la Verdad.* Lima: Instituto de Defensa Legal.

Falconí, Carola, Edilberto Jiménez, and Giovanni Alfaro. 2007. *Lluqanamarka llaqtanchikpa yuyariynin = Lucanamarca, memorias de nuestro pueblo.* Lima: COMISEDH.

García-Godos, Jemima. 2006. 'Citizenship, Conflict and Reconstruction: A Case-Study of the Effects of Armed Conflict on Peasant-State Relations in Tambo, Peru.' Dr. polit. diss., University of Oslo.

——2008. 'Victim Reparations in the Peruvian Truth Commission and the Challenge of Historical Interpretation.' *International Journal of Transitional Justice* 2(1): 63–82.

IACHR (Inter-American Commission on Human Rights). 2000. *Second Report on the Situation of Human Rights in Peru.* OEA/Ser.L/V/II.106. Washington, DC: OAS.

——2001. Joint press release following meeting with representatives of the government of Peru. Washington, DC: OAS. http://www.cidh.org/Comunicados/English/2001/Peru.htm.

Laplante, Lisa J. 2009. 'The Law of Remedies and the Clean Hands Doctrine: Exclusionary Reparation Policies in Peru's Political Transition.' *American University International Law Review* 23(1): 51–90.

Laplante, Lisa J., and Kimberly Theidon. 2007. 'Truth with Consequences: Justice and Reparations in Post-Truth Commission Peru.' *Human Rights Quarterly* 29(1): 228–50.

Rivera Paz, Carlos. 2010. 'Perú.' In *Las víctimas y la justicia transicional ¿Están cumpliendo los Estados latinoamericanos con los estándares internacionales?*, 191–218. Washington, DC: Due Process of Law Foundation.

——2012. 'La sentencia del caso Barrios Altos: El nuevo instrumento de la impunidad.' *Justicia Viva.* Lima: Instituto de Defensa Legal.

——2015. '2015: Un año decisivo en el sistema de justicia.' *Ideele Revista*, no. 246. Lima: Instituto de Defensa Legal.

Root, Rebecca K. 2009. 'Through the Window of Opportunity: The Transitional Justice Network in Peru.' *Human Rights Quarterly* 31(2): 452–73.

——2012. *Transitional Justice in Peru.* New York: Palgrave Macmillan.

Rubio Escolar, Sinthya. 2013. *La reparación a las víctimas del conflicto armado en Perú: La voz de las víctimas.* Lima: Instituto de Defensa Legal.

Salmón, Elizabeth. 2014. *La condena de Alberto Fujimori y el Derecho internacional de los derechos humanos: Un capítulo fundamental de la lucha contra la impunidad en el Perú.* Bogotá: Universidad Externado de Colombia.

Tanaka, Martín. 1998. *Los espejismos de la democracia: El colapso del sistema de partidos en el Perú, 1980–1995, en perspectiva comparada.* Lima: Instituto de Estudios Peruanos.

Tapia, Carlos. 1997. *Las Fuerzas Armadas y Sendero Luminoso: Dos estrategias y un final.* Lima: Instituto de Estudios Peruanos.

Villarán de la Puente, Susana. 2007. 'Peru.' In *Victims Unsilenced: The Inter-American Human Rights System and Transitional Justice in Latin America*, edited by Katya Salazar and Thomas Antkowiak, 95–126. Washington, DC: Due Process of Law Foundation.

Chapter 11

Colombia

Transitional justice before transition

*Nelson Camilo Sánchez León, Jemima García-Godos, and Catalina Vallejo**

At the turn of the millennium, few would have thought of Colombia as a case study for transitional justice experiences. The country was immersed in a protracted armed conflict marked by numerous atrocities, with millions of internally displaced people. Prospects for peace seemed distant, and for accountability, even more so. Nevertheless, Colombia began a transitional justice process in the mid-2000s, linking the demobilisation of illegal armed groups to the rights of victims – at the same time and through the same legal instrument, the Justice and Peace Law. The law's initial implementation was monitored and partly led by the newly created Commission for Reparation and Reconciliation (Comisión Nacional de Reparación y Reconciliación, CNRR). Other measures followed to address the law's limitations and the demands from victims' organisations.

Today, Colombia illustrates the many challenges involved in seeking accountability for past human rights violations in the context of ongoing conflict and incomplete peace negotiations. These challenges include legal issues (Colombia is the only country in Latin America where the International Criminal Court has opened a preliminary investigation) as well as political and humanitarian considerations. This chapter provides an overview of how transitional justice mechanisms have developed in Colombia over the past decade. It highlights critical issues related to both accountability and impunity that have arisen from the partial implementation of specific measures as an integral part of ongoing peace negotiations for an end to conflict.

The Colombian experience demonstrates that a reconceptualisation of transitional justice is timely and due. On the one hand, the consolidation of normative standards in recent decades means that the peace negotiations in Colombia necessarily differ from those that occurred in Guatemala and El Salvador in the 1980s. On the other hand, the diversity of opposing parties – guerrillas and paramilitaries – and the adoption of transitional measures before the end of the conflict mean that Colombia faces practical and conceptual challenges that are distinct from those affecting its regional neighbours.

Background to the transitional justice process

The current armed conflict in Colombia dates back to 1964, when the first communist guerrilla groups were established: the FARC-EP (Revolutionary Armed Forces of Colombia – People's Army), ELN (National Liberation Army), and EPL (Popular Liberation Army) (Offstein 2003). In the 1970s, these groups were joined by a second wave of guerrillas, most of whom demobilised by 1990. FARC-EP (known as FARC) and ELN remain operative today, the former being the most important guerrilla group in terms of members and operations.

In response to the insurgent violence, businessmen and landowners sponsored the creation of right-wing self-defence groups. In the 1990s, the groups restructured themselves as modern paramilitary forces under the banner United Self-Defence Forces of Colombia (Autodefensas Unidas de Colombia, AUC), developed from a legal framework known as Convivir.[1] Over time, the paramilitary groups consolidated territorial control and started to engage and displace the guerrillas. This was followed by a shift in the balance of power within the paramilitary groups from the original leadership asserted by rural elites to military commanders. The military expansion of the paramilitaries was accompanied by their incursion into formal politics. The areas under their control became strictly regulated, and the official decentralisation process of the 1990s had the unintended effect of tightening their grip on local and regional political institutions. By controlling local constituencies, the paramilitaries also gained access to national politics. The state considered them allies in the anti-guerrilla effort and thus made no objection to their growing military and political power (Duncan 2006; Abdala, González, and González 2008).

President Álvaro Uribe took office in August 2002 pledging to engage in heavy combat against the guerrillas. In December 2002, the AUC declared a unilateral ceasefire, a government precondition for talks with any of the armed groups. Negotiations were formalised on 15 July 2003 with the Santa Fe de Ralito Accord, in which AUC leaders agreed to demobilise fully by the end of 2005.[2] According to official sources, a total of 31,671 members of paramilitary groups had demobilised by August 2006, mostly through collective demobilisation (Alto Comisionado para la Paz 2006).[3]

Although these numbers are impressive, there are continuing reports that armed groups or criminal gangs (*bandas criminales*) are present in various parts of the country, pursuing operations similar to those of the former paramilitaries (OAS 2010; CNRR 2007). Their presence threatens the security of victims and witnesses participating in the transitional justice process, setting clear limits to the effectiveness of protection measures. While these armed groups show diversity in form, structure, membership, and operations, they also share some common features: use of extortion and violence, abuse of power, and links to criminal activities such as drug trafficking. There is also evidence that the groups often operate with the direct or indirect support of local public officials and members of the police and armed forces (CNRR 2007). In what has been dubbed the *parapolítica* scandal, a process of judicial investigation was started in 2006 against 32 (of 102) members of the Colombian Senate on charges of collusion with the former paramilitary groups. This investigation has become an important source of information about the involvement of paramilitary forces in the political arena.

The transitional justice process in Colombia, therefore, is closely intertwined with the negotiation and implementation of peace settlements and the demobilisation of illegal armed groups. These complex processes engage not only the national executive and legislature and the leaders of the armed groups, but also the Colombian judiciary and a wide range of other actors, including civil society groups with a focus on human rights, victims' rights, and peacemaking. International organisations, both inter-governmental and non-governmental, particularly those focused on human rights, peacebuilding, or transitional justice, also influence the debate (García-Godos and Lid 2010).

More than in some other country cases, the transitional justice (TJ) process in Colombia is anchored in the legal system. Colombia has a deeply rooted legalist culture, emphasising the use of legal instruments and judicial processes to regulate most aspects of social, political, and institutional life. As we will see below, TJ in Colombia has been carefully designed and embedded in successive legal instruments, starting with the Justice and Peace Law in 2005 and including, most recently, the Legal Framework for Peace in 2012. The Colombian Constitutional Court is a principal institutional actor in this legalist culture. Through its jurisprudence, the Court has played a key role in the protection of citizens' rights as well as on issues of governance and public policy. The Constitutional Court's oversight, modification, and approval of transitional justice measures has been instrumental in establishing the constitutionality and legitimacy of a TJ agenda.[4]

This agenda occupies a central place in domestic politics. Since the announcement of peace talks in September 2012, the government and the FARC guerrillas have agreed to discuss a six-point agenda: (1) agrarian development; (2) guarantees for the exercise of political opposition and citizen participation; (3) the end of armed conflict; (4) drug trafficking; (5) the rights of the victims of the conflict; and (6) implementation of the agreement. As of January 2016, agreements had been reached on agrarian development, drug trafficking, political participation, and victims' rights. The FARC and the government continue to work towards an accord on the remaining points with a view to concluding a comprehensive peace treaty, supported by the international community, particularly by other Latin American governments.

Notably, there have been disagreements with international bodies such as the Office of the Prosecutor of the International Criminal Court (ICC) regarding justice matters in the accord. There are also doubts as to whether the Inter-American Court of Human Rights will find the formula of prosecuting the most responsible perpetrators of international crimes (rather than all perpetrators) to be in accord with its jurisprudence. Both the ICC prosecutor and the inter-American system have monitored the process closely, but have not provided any substantive and definitive judgment on its compliance with international standards.

Criminal accountability in Colombia: amnesties and trials as a two-pronged strategy

In Colombia, the traditional choice between blanket amnesties and full criminal accountability, as opposite extremes, has been called into question. Although Colombian society rejects the notion of impunity, the consensus view also highlights the risks of implementing excessively punitive transitional measures that would hinder the efforts to reach a negotiated peace (*El País* 2013).

Within Colombia, the question was first raised in general terms: whether the application of punitive standards that were developed mainly to deal with post-dictatorship situations is feasible, or even desirable, during or after transition from armed conflict. Following a regional trend towards hardening punitive standards and prohibiting certain methods of amnesty that perpetuate impunity,[5] academic and political circles in Colombia have recently leaned towards establishing adequate judicial resources for the prosecution of the gravest crimes, even before the end of conflict.

Influence from local and international human rights organisations during the negotiation of the demobilisation framework in the mid-2000s was essential in achieving an absolute prohibition against amnesties for grave human rights violations and infractions of international humanitarian law. Further discussion concentrated on how to determine the mechanisms for prosecution, with the understanding that all such actions as well as all perpetrators of these most serious crimes must be brought to justice.

The legislative process culminated with the passage of Law 975 of 2005, known as the Justice and Peace Law.[6] This served as a framework for the demobilisation of the AUC under a *sui generis* model, referred to as the justice and peace model, for handling of the gravest violations. The law provided, first, that criminal trials as a transitional mechanism should only be used to punish the worst crimes, leaving open the possibility of amnesties or pardons for other crimes committed as a result of the conflict. Second, it introduced a procedure for prioritisation and management of cases under the control of the executive branch. The executive could initiate this process by presenting lists of demobilising individuals to the Attorney General's Office (Fiscalía General de la Nación), to be followed by investigations based on the declarations of demobilising individuals involving serious crimes. Third, in balancing the imperatives of justice and peace, the model prioritised peace over justice only in the proportionality and duration of the sentence, not in attributing responsibility or in the judgment. In other words, contrary to a model of total amnesty, the Justice and Peace Law was generous in the reduction of sentences, but kept the commitment that all of the accused would be liable for punishment by a prison sentence.

With an overwhelming number of potential cases, it was necessary to be selective: the model could not work if every case was to be processed through this system. Accordingly, of the more than 31,000 non-state combatants who laid down their arms by 2006, the policy only applied to those who voluntarily decided to participate, were ready to confess their participation in atrocity crimes, and had no pre-existing, outstanding criminal charges against them. At the time, this included approximately 3,500 people, who were known as *postulados*. The rest of the demobilised – those for whom no charges for atrocity crimes existed at the time – would be reincorporated into society through an amnesty model recognised by the constitution for political offenders. The model relied mostly on the collaboration of ex-combatants because the state had little information on their acts, therefore few judicial investigations and even fewer convictions occurred.

This mechanism, however, faced strong political opposition and legal challenges. First, victims' organisations pointed out that because the state had hardly any information on events that had happened during the conflict, this plan established a sort of hidden amnesty for those combatants who did not confess their crimes. The organisations contended that the state had the duty to investigate each case before granting any type of amnesty or reduced sentence.[7] Second, the political offence provision, which assumed that the paramilitaries had been political offenders, was strongly condemned by the Colombian higher courts. They found that the crime of sedition could not be applied to members of paramilitary groups because they had worked as pro-regime armed actors, not against the system, which is the general understanding of a political offence.[8]

In light of these issues, an additional challenge arose: how to create a mechanism capable of guaranteeing a review of each case in order to prevent atrocious crimes from being ignored, but at the same time, simple enough to avoid overburdening the criminal system to the point of inefficiency. In 2009, the government of President Álvaro Uribe devised a creative procedure based on an ordinary provision of criminal law in the adversarial system. They suggested using prosecutorial discretion to stop criminal proceedings for those cases which, for criminal policy reasons, were not in the interests of justice. Congress then passed a new law, Law 1312 of 2009, which included disarmament in a peace process and provision of reparations to victims as new factors for consideration in the use of prosecutorial discretion. However, the law clarified that prosecutorial discretion could not be invoked in cases considered to be atrocious crimes under international law.

The human rights and victims' organisations that had campaigned against impunity for human rights violations were not fully satisfied by this change. They considered the use of prosecutorial discretion to be an abdication of the state's duty to investigate and prosecute. This would be, in their opinion, a form of disguised amnesty. Using this argument, they brought a case against the legitimacy of the proposal before the Constitutional Court.

The Court ruled in favour of the victims' organisations in a divided decision (Judgment C-936) in 2010. This ruling pushed the state towards full investigation and prosecution of all offences and combatants, an approach that many argued would overemphasise the punitive approach in the transitional process. Furthermore, it triggered a crisis in the demobilisation process, as the initial agreements reached by the government with the demobilised paramilitary groups had not included the prospect of prosecution of all demobilised ex-combatants.[9]

By then, the justice and peace process had been in place for more than five years, but its results were poor. In practical terms, processing thousands of pending cases through the system was virtually impossible. The previous public policy challenge – how to establish an efficient mechanism – was overshadowed by a technical–legal problem: how to interpret the normative standard to allow for a method that did not violate the decision adopted by the Constitutional Court.

Given the tradition of adherence to international standards, the debate did not start, as it had in other countries in the region, with the question of whether or not there was a legal obligation for the state to prosecute the most serious offences. Predominant legal opinion in Colombia accepts the existence of this legal duty. The debate, rather, is over its practical realisation. What is the extent of the duty to investigate and prosecute? Does it automatically include an obligation to consider the option of a prison sentence for those found guilty? If so, what are the applicable sentencing guidelines, and what possibilities exist for using alternative punishment to moderate or exclude incarceration?

There is no clear, universal norm that establishes the scope of the duty to dispense justice. Even in the inter-American system, where the Inter-American Court has been forging a strict regional consensus on the duty to prosecute and punish, it is not clear how this obligation operates in the context of massive violations where, in practice, the state would not be able to successfully prosecute all the perpetrators.

In the Colombian conflict, even if the Colombian state worked with the 'greatest diligence', it would not be able to prosecute all those who potentially bear criminal responsibility.[10] According to official calculations, by 2012, more than 56,000 combatants had demobilised, with as many as 5,000 *postulados* taking part in the justice and peace process. These *postulados* had confessed to 35,430 crimes (*hechos confesados*) and reported 57,131 crimes (*hechos enunciados*), but only 11 verdicts had been issued (CIJP 2012). While the first justice and peace verdict came in 2009, only 33 verdicts had been issued by July 2015. Proceeding at this rate, the justice and peace system would take 99 years to process the people presently subject to it.

Faced with the impracticality of trying and incarcerating so many people, the Colombian Congress designed a new legal instrument based on the distinction between prosecution and carrying out a sentence. The system, which is seen as a contribution to historical truth-finding, utilises a combination of administrative and judicial proceedings set out in Law 1424 of 2010, the Law on the Agreement on Contribution to Historical Truth and Reparations.[11] The mechanism applies to ex-combatants who have committed 'only' the offences of belonging to an armed group and using restricted weapons and uniforms. In order to receive the benefits of the law, these ex-combatants have to contribute, through a non-judicial mechanism, to the reconstruction of historical memory. They must explain the circumstances under which they participated, the structure of the illegal armed group of which they were part, and provide all other details of their participation in the group. They must also pay for the damage caused and perform community service in the region where they have been reincorporated into civilian life.

Next, the competent judicial authority, at the request of the government, orders either the suspension of all arrest warrants issued for the demobilising person or the conditional suspension of sentence enforcement, if the person has already been sentenced and is serving prison time. Once the suspension period of the sentence passes and the individual has satisfied his obligations, the sentence expires.

The Constitutional Court found that this instrument did not violate the state's obligation to provide an effective remedy to victims.[12] According to the Court, Law 1424 did not offer impunity for the actions of demobilising individuals, nor did it offer an unjustified reduction in the duration of the sentences that could be imposed on them. Furthermore, the Court deemed the awarding of liberty-related benefits to be an exercise of the punitive power of the state, given that it always takes place through a judicial proceeding.

This decision, however, did not directly address the problem of an overburdened judicial system. Investigating all acts committed in an armed conflict more than five decades old and processing all ex-combatants has placed great strain on judicial resources. Indeed, it would take the system about 526 years to process all ex-combatants using the proceedings set out in Law 1424. To begin with, the punitive standard remains higher than the international standard because the Colombian model entails the investigation and prosecution of ex-combatants even for crimes that international norms consider amnestiable (though such persons may not serve the complete sentence). Moreover, in accordance with the decision of the Constitutional Court, all combatants who have committed atrocious crimes will have to be investigated, prosecuted, and punished. Yet how those investigations will be completed has not been determined; the number of cases currently known exceeds the capacities of the system (as demonstrated by the justice and peace process). Furthermore, the Court has closed the door on the option of giving concessions to the major leaders of armed groups. It ruled that, given their leadership roles, commanders should be held responsible for their crimes, as either perpetrators or participants.

The large number of victims also presents its own challenges: how to guarantee that the process of accountability will not just exist on paper, but instead will foster the social and collective healing that the victims request. If the norms are not applied effectively, the hardening of the legal standard and the insistence on pursuing a growing number of objectives could lead to greater social frustration and inhibit the achievement of transitional objectives such as effective criminal accountability, recognition of victims, and reconciliation. In light of this concern, after 2010, the government coalition in Congress introduced proposals to relax the model of total punitive justice in favour of accepting restrictions in practice, while seeking to present incentives for negotiating the end of the conflict with armed actors who remain in the fight. Although the fundamental rationale of this strategy is not new, it has led to fierce debates between different sectors of society.[13]

Recent legal reforms have given more consideration to institutional capacities and established a more holistic system of transitional justice. In 2012, the Colombian Congress enacted Law 1592, which aims to remedy bureaucratic problems in the original Justice and Peace Law. Law 1592 requires that prosecutorial efforts be directed towards those 'most responsible' for serious crimes and provides mechanisms for selection and prioritisation of cases on this basis. The argument for these mechanisms proceeds as follows: when the number of cases is substantial, or even overwhelming, the system needs to define clear and transparent rules to establish which cases the authorities will investigate and prosecute first and which cases they will dismiss.[14] If the system does not include those mechanisms explicitly, then the prioritisation and selection will take place anyway, but in an unsystematic and non-transparent manner. In such a scenario the easiest cases to investigate, even if they are of less importance to society, will be the first to be solved. This contributes very little to an exhaustive exercise of historical truth-seeking or to reconstruction of the patterns of atrocities.

Also enacted in 2012 was the Legal Framework for Peace, a constitutional reform providing transitional justice measures. This would help to bring an end to the armed conflict, while also ensuring 'the rights of victims to truth, justice, and reparation'. The Legal Framework for Peace sets basic rules and standards for future negotiations with armed groups that cannot be modified by Congress or the courts (as was the case with the demobilisation of paramilitary groups). This framework spurred the FARC to enter into peace talks with the government in Havana in 2012.

Colombia, then, has not followed the path of its Latin American peers who declared a blanket amnesty from the start. Instead, it has started with a punitive approach based on investigation, prosecution, and sentencing. This model, however, does not necessarily entail massive prosecutions or ensure accountability, as the justice and peace cases to date have shown. Constraints during the implementation phase of the justice and peace process can have an even greater impact than judicial restrictions deriving from an amnesty law.

In this sense, Colombia seems to be moving in the direction of a reduced punitive system. The result may be described as a model of 'accountability pardon', in which concessions are made regarding criminal responsibility in exchange for total confession of atrocious crimes and some degree of reparation.[15] At the start of the process, these concessions were understood to be limited to reduced prison sentences. The current framework includes trials that permit (a) total commutation of the prison sentence for lesser offences, and (b) prioritisation and selection of cases for grave crimes. In such a model, both trials and individual and conditional amnesties play a role in the accountability process.

In an era when the consolidation of international standards impedes blanket amnesties, the search for a negotiated peace is not easy; it is filled with legal complexities that may provide loopholes for avoiding accountability. The Colombian formulas are under the scrutiny of international bodies, notably the Inter-American Court of Human Rights and the International Criminal Court. Experience shows, however, that in contexts such as Colombia, international standards should not be allowed to impede negotiations by blocking benefits or concessions for those who lay down their weapons. Such standards may still be useful in excluding solutions that block access to justice and nullify the rights of victims.

Truth-finding efforts: the 'broken mirror' approach

Truth-finding is a difficult task after an armed conflict has ended. When it takes place during a continuing armed conflict, as in Colombia, it is even more daunting. While other countries have emphasised centralised truth-finding efforts led by truth commissions, Colombia's approach is multifocal. It can be seen as putting together the pieces of a broken mirror, fragment by fragment.[16] Such an approach combines official and unofficial efforts, using both judicial and historical methods, to seek a plurality of coexisting and often conflicting truths.

Several factors account for the emergence of this approach. First, the presence of various groups of armed actors, each with a corresponding set of victims, allows for the existence of multiple narratives on wrongdoings and suffering. Second, the Colombian transitional process began with trials (against demobilised paramilitaries and guerrillas) and an institutional body (the CNRR), both envisaged as sources as truth. Third, these official efforts have been accompanied by unofficial truth-finding initiatives carried out by civil society organisations (ICTJ 2009). A relatively recent development is the inclusion of a 'right to truth' in transitional legislation, as truth and memory efforts have come to be understood as essential in preventing repetition of gross human rights violations.[17] This has led to the allocation of public funds for memory initiatives and historical research, among other initiatives.

Legal developments around truth and memory

According to the Justice and Peace Law, victims have the right to know the truth about the crimes committed by non-state armed groups and the whereabouts of kidnapped and forcibly disappeared persons. The law established the National Commission for Reparation and Reconciliation with the mandate to contribute to the construction of historical truth about armed groups and armed conflict (Sánchez and Uprimny Yepes 2011). To this end, in 2005, the CNRR created the Historical Memory Group (Grupo de Memoria Histórica, GMH). Its task was to document the history of the Colombian armed conflict, focusing on its structural origins and dynamics. It did so with a victim-oriented perspective, highlighting the many voices and local histories that reveal experiences of the conflict (García-Godos 2012). The GMH undertook strategic research on emblematic cases, publishing them as individual volumes and broadly disseminating results through different media.[18] Although the GMH had some similarities to truth commissions in the region, it was considered an interim or preliminary body, with a different mandate (García-Godos 2012).

Additional legislation mandating clarification of the truth is found in Law 1424 of 2010. This law applies to demobilised persons who were not implicated in atrocious crimes and thus were exempt from the justice and peace process. They are required, however, to contribute to historical memory by explaining the circumstances of their participation (Sánchez and Uprimny Yepes 2011).

The enactment of Law 1448 of 2011, known as the Victims' Law, marked a further milestone.[19] Under its provisions, the CNRR ceased to exist. So did the GMH, which was transformed into the National Centre for Historical Memory (Centro Nacional de Memoria Histórica, CNMH).

Historical and judicial truths

The National Centre for Historical Memory was constituted in 2011 as a public body, both non-judicial and non-punitive in nature. It is funded by the state, although it has full financial and administrative autonomy. According to the Victims' Law, the CNMH was created to 'collect and recover all the documentary material, oral testimony and any other means regarding the violations of rights of victims of the armed conflict' (Art 147). The information collected is to be made available to both the general public and the academic community. Alongside this, there will be museum activities and educational events to enrich knowledge of Colombia's social and political history. The CNMH inherited the GMH's mandate to produce and disseminate a comprehensive report on the armed conflict in Colombia, identifying reasons for the emergence and evolution of the different armed groups and providing accounts of the violence based on victims' testimonies.[20] It has expanded this role to include documentation and recounting of past human rights violations on a long-term basis (CNMH 2012).

According to historian Gonzalo Sánchez (2012), director of the CNMH, the process of memory construction is grounded in respect for human dignity.[21] In seeking to articulate the multiple and often differing narratives of victims, the CNMH is guided by inclusive and pluralistic principles, based on the assumption that there is no one unquestionable truth about Colombia's armed conflict. Rather, there exist myriad perspectives that should be respected and voiced, even when they contradict each other.[22]

While historical truth is pieced together by historians and others in civil society, judicial truth emerges as the sum of individual stories told selectively by offenders during the trials process. According to one source, the justice and peace trials clearly contributed to public acknowledgement of extensive paramilitary involvement in the armed conflict and of the human rights violations committed by paramilitary groups.[23] The trials also contributed, to some extent, to the exposure of economic and political structures that enabled this systematic paramilitary violence. Although the process suffered a serious blow in 2008 with the extradition of 14 paramilitary leaders to the United States on drug-related charges, the proceedings have continued and have yielded a growing trove of information for both judicial and historical enquiries.

Nonetheless, according to political scientist Iván Orozco Abad, a former member of the Historical Memory Group, judicial truth has structural limitations. In particular, it can oversimplify the roles of parties to the conflict, thereby impeding understanding of complex truths about the past. Criminal trials need to make clear distinctions between the roles of perpetrator and victim. 'Judicial truth creates pure images of villains and heroes, reproducing images of responsibility and suffering in a black-white manner, not allowing for grey zones or complex roles within the armed political conflict.'[24] In this sense, Orozco says, some of the trials of paramilitaries in Colombia tended to obliterate individual identities, either demonising perpetrators or sanctifying victims.

This limitation of judicial truth, Orozco asserts, is particularly significant in a post-conflict (rather than post-dictatorship) context. In general, post-dictatorship justice is compatible with a clear distribution of responsibilities and a sharp distinction between guilty perpetrator and innocent victim, with respective monopolies on barbarism and suffering. It focuses on the responsibility of the state, with victims assumed to be powerless before the state's repressive machinery. In transitions from internal armed conflict, on the other hand, the roles of victim and perpetrator may be blurred in some (though not all) cases. For instance, some of those responsible for displacement and land dispossession in Colombia could themselves have been victims of displacement in the past. Likewise, some victims could have supported the actions of either guerrilla or paramilitary armed groups. In cases of protracted war, the monopoly on barbarism and suffering, and the distinction between victims and perpetrators becomes even less clear. To capture these nuances, Orozco introduced the concept of 'complex victims' into the debate on transition in Colombia.[25]

Courtroom trials, moreover, provide a problematic venue for unveiling the truth about systematic human rights violations and the structures enabling them. For one thing, when a victim's acceptance of some responsibility in the hostilities is considered self-incriminating, attorneys may advise the victim to stop his or her narrative. In other cases, the Court may silence perpetrators who describe themselves as heroes and saviours of the nation because their narratives are considered justifications of crime (*apología al delito*) (FIDH 2007, 59). To the extent that information about other crimes revealed in court is not processed prior to a new, separate, investigation, it cannot be disputed. Finally, it is unclear whose task it is to integrate all the disparate fragments of information coming out of the justice and peace process in order to reveal complex patterns of abuse.

Comparing the merits of historical and judicial truth, Judge Uldi Teresa Jiménez points out that researchers can use strategies in the truth-seeking process that judges cannot. For instance, they can use confidential sources or ask for contextual information that might not be relevant to the specific case in trial. 'Historians have far fewer restrictions than judges when examining the structures behind massive violations of human rights, partly because the judicial truth is derived entirely from what is said in open court, which must be specifically relevant to the case and based on the concrete evidence brought by the prosecutor.'[26]

Although historical and judicial truth efforts have different roles and different limitations, the two can be understood as being complementary rather than incompatible. Judge Jiménez comments, 'We have often invited the CNMH to the trials to participate and inform us on their investigations of the cases.'[27] Gonzalo Sánchez (2012), the CNMH director, points out that carrying out memory work can reveal the realities hidden behind legal formulations, especially experiences of suffering. A potential obstacle to such work, however, is the risk that historians may be sued for the content of their reports.[28] The Victims' Law therefore included a specific exception for members of the CNMH, ensuring that they cannot be subject to litigation for their findings.

The Legal Framework for Peace tried to remedy the deficiencies of the model that was adopted in the justice and peace process by advocating complementary judicial and historical truth-seeking efforts. Once the guerrillas demobilise, a truth commission will be created with the goal of providing a nuanced global understanding of systematic violence by the different armed actors and its impact on the population. Though it could be argued that it is too early to construct the full truth of the armed conflict, since it has not ended, that is not an adequate justification for refraining from interim efforts. The rationale behind the current work of the CNMH is that victims of the demobilised factions should not have to renounce their right to truth and memory because of pending negotiations, uncertain peace agendas, and blurred promises of an end to the conflict.[29]

Victims' reparations

The enactment of the Justice and Peace Law in 2005 marked the beginning of the process for reparations in Colombia. In practice, however, implementation is only now taking place, through enforcement of the Victims' Law of 2011. Since the conflict is ongoing, security, rule of law, and respect for human rights are either still precarious or non-existent in some areas of the country. The result is a constant flow of new victims and/or revictimisation.

The Justice and Peace Law made explicit recognition of victims' rights based on the principle of comprehensive reparations (*reparación integral*). It sought to provide victims with both material and symbolic forms of reparation, as well as 'satisfaction' and guarantees of non-repetition, following the United Nations (UN) Basic Principles and Guidelines on victims' reparations.[30] However, the law envisaged the provision of victims' reparations as the result of a judicial process, with clear limitations discussed below. Another feature of the law was that the definition of victim did not include anyone whose rights had been violated by members of the armed forces. This provision, which was sanctioned by the Constitutional Court, was vigorously contested by human rights groups and was later dropped under the terms of the Victims' Law.

By March 2012, 386,069 victims had been registered through the justice and peace process – about half of them by the Justice and Peace Unit in the Attorney

General's Office, and the rest by other public agencies such as the National Registrar or the CNRR (CIJP 2012). Within this framework, reparations to victims are to be provided by the individual victimiser after a guilty verdict has been issued. If a victim is unable to identify his or her victimiser, then reparations will be provided from the Reparations Fund, which includes assets provided by the *postulados* when they join the justice and peace process. The form and size of reparations in each case is decided through a special hearing known as *incidente de reparación*, in which victims put forward reparations claims to be heard by the judge. The first reparations hearing took place in 2010. By December 2012, only 14 cases had reached a verdict and only 11 had proceeded to a reparations hearing (FGN 2012; CIJP 2012). The judicial path to reparations has proven to be extraordinarily lengthy and has been heavily criticised by victims' groups, and both human rights and other civil society organisations.

Partly as a response to such criticism, the government established an administrative reparations programme in 2008.[31] The administrative path to reparations demands a much lower threshold of evidence than the judicial path. It is thus a more favourable option for those who cannot identify or are afraid to confront their victimisers, those who do not have financial resources to bring their claims before the justice and peace courts, and those who were victims of organisations other than paramilitary groups (but not including state agents). In this programme, the state assumes the task of compensating the victims of armed conflict based on a principle of solidarity. According to Colombian authorities, this solidarity compensation (*indemnización solidaria*) does not imply any form of state responsibility for the crimes that victims may have experienced; it is merely recognition of the difficult situation they face. This interpretation of solidarity has, not surprisingly, been challenged by victims' organisations and other civil society actors.[32]

Administrative reparations only provide monetary compensation for crimes committed against individuals; they do not include compensation for damage to property.[33] Compensation varies depending on the nature of the crime, ranging from 27 to 40 times the national basic monthly salary, to be paid as a lump sum. The presidential agency Acción Social (now Department for Social Prosperity, DPS), which is also in charge of the Reparations Fund, was initially mandated to establish and implement the administrative reparations programme. Registration for this programme did not exclude victims from seeking reparations from their victimisers through the judicial process. The original registration period for this programme lasted two years, from April 2008 until April 2010. According to official figures, 331,604 applications had been received by the close of registration. By October 2010, 20,837 families had received monetary compensation through the administrative reparations programme (Acción Social 2010).[34]

Victims' reparations, as envisaged by the Justice and Peace Law, also included the development of collective reparation initiatives, aimed at restoring citizens' rights and the rule of law, particularly in those regions of the country most affected by the armed conflict. Throughout its mandate, the CNRR sought to promote victims' rights and a victim-oriented perspective in the various components of the Colombian transitional justice scheme. Working through its extensive regional networks and in cooperation with public institutions at both regional and local levels, the CNRR succeeded in putting the rights of victims on the national public agenda. With the entry into force of the Victims' Law, the CNRR ceased to exist and a new institutional apparatus took over the task of reparations, as described in the next section.

The fact that both judicial and administrative reparations programmes focused on individual monetary compensation opened up a debate about the nature and aim of reparations. Should reparations merely restore the victim to his or her former condition, possibly one of poverty, marginalisation, and vulnerability, or should they attempt to improve the victim's situation, including access to civil rights and civil liberties? This second alternative is termed transformative reparations (*reparación transformadora*). These are reparations that aim not only to remedy the harm to individual victims, but also to transform the socio-structural conditions that fostered armed conflict and human rights violations in the first place.[35]

In a country such as Colombia, where social inequalities and regional disparities are deeply entrenched, the debate about transformative reparations is not merely academic. At its core are questions about how to distinguish between retributive and distributive justice and how to integrate them – or not – in a transitional justice agenda. From this angle, we can consider Colombia's TJ process as a window of opportunity for working towards distributive justice objectives, as this would arguably support peacebuilding processes in the long term. In part, these arguments have been acknowledged and incorporated in the Victims' Law of 2011, as described below.

The Victims' Law: strengthening victims' rights

By 2010, despite CNRR's efforts, no comprehensive reparation programme extending beyond monetary compensation was in place. A first legislative proposal focusing explicitly on victims' rights and reparations was developed by civil society and presented to Congress in 2008 by a group of parliamentarians. Despite much national and international attention, the proposal was dismissed the following year.[36]

In August 2010, just weeks after assuming power, President Juan Manuel Santos forwarded a proposal to Congress promising to address 'the pending debt' the country owed victims of the armed conflict. Shortly after, a separate proposal on land restitution was merged with this legislation, placing the issue of internal displacement at the centre of a national reparations programme. Outreach activities by the CNRR and civil society organisations, congressional debates, and wide media coverage promoted public discussion of the legislation, which was approved by Congress on 1 June 2011. It was signed into law on 10 June as Law 1448, widely known as the 'Victims' Law'.

The legislation has been welcomed by broad sectors of Colombian society, including victims' organisations, for its emphasis on victims' rights and on land and property restitution (*Semana* 2011). Significantly, the law recognises as 'victims' not only those harmed by illegal armed groups, such as paramilitaries and guerrillas, but also those victimised by the Colombian police and armed forces. Reparations can be claimed for physical, material, and psychological harm since 1985, while land and property restitution applies to losses occurring since 1991. Although the law does not affect judicial processes implemented under the Justice and Peace Law, it has significantly reduced, in favour of the victim, the threshold of proof to access reparations, much as the administrative reparations programme did. The necessary regulations to implement the law were passed in late 2011.[37]

The Victims' Law established new institutions for developing and implementing a national reparations programme that includes compensation, restitution, rehabilitation, satisfaction, and guarantees of non-repetition, forms of reparations set forth in the UN Basic Principles. The new institutions include two specialised units for reparations and land restitution, a national registry of victims, a national system for victims' reparations, a national registry for usurped lands, and a centre for historical memory. The new Unit for Victim Reparations (Unidad para la Atención y Reparación Integral a las Víctimas) is placed in the Department for Social Prosperity (DPS 2012). The Land Restitution Unit (Unidad de Restitución de Tierras) operates out of 21 offices across the country (Ministerio de Agricultura 2013).

The situation of internally displaced persons (IDPs) and land and property restitution are extremely complex issues in Colombia, for technical and administrative reasons and because of the strong economic and political interests at stake. While protection of the rights of IDPs came to the government's attention in 1997, the Constitutional Court declared the IDP situation 'unconstitutional' in Decision T-025 of 2004, prompting urgent state action with regard to both humanitarian assistance and property restitution. The coexistence of several forms of property and tenure, incomplete cadastral records, parallel registration systems, multiple registrations, and claims to the same property both concurrently and over time are among the many factors affecting implementation. Coercive practices of land expropriation and usurpation are often legalised through formal and judicial channels. The task is complicated by the presence of strong economic actors and activities on disputed lands (Gutiérrez Sanín 2010). In addition, security challenges both to returning populations and to community leaders making restitution claims threaten progress in implementing these measures.[38]

The new institutions created by the Victims' Law have developed special procedures adjusted to the extraordinary character of transitional justice in Colombia, especially in light of the ongoing conflict and the large number of victims. Unfulfilled expectations and broken promises may damage the fragile trust emerging between the state and victims of the Colombian armed conflict.

Conclusions

Transitional justice in Colombia is a work in progress, one rendered particularly complex by the continuing conflict. Policy makers must comply with legal mandates but must also consider the impact of their actions on the ongoing peace and demobilisation negotiations. The number of victims and crimes continues to grow.

Security and stability in the country remain tenuous, creating additional obstacles for the implementation of transitional justice mechanisms. In the case of land restitution, many of those who lost their land in the conflict have received death threats; some have been killed. Even if some people do succeed in returning to their land, they may be victimised again.

The conflict is now more than five decades old. This creates enormous practical issues for the agencies charged with implementing TJ mechanisms. A key problem is the large numbers of both perpetrators and victims. The Colombian judiciary cannot realistically investigate and prosecute hundreds of thousands of conflict-related crimes. Nor will the state be able to find individualised remedies for the millions of victims.

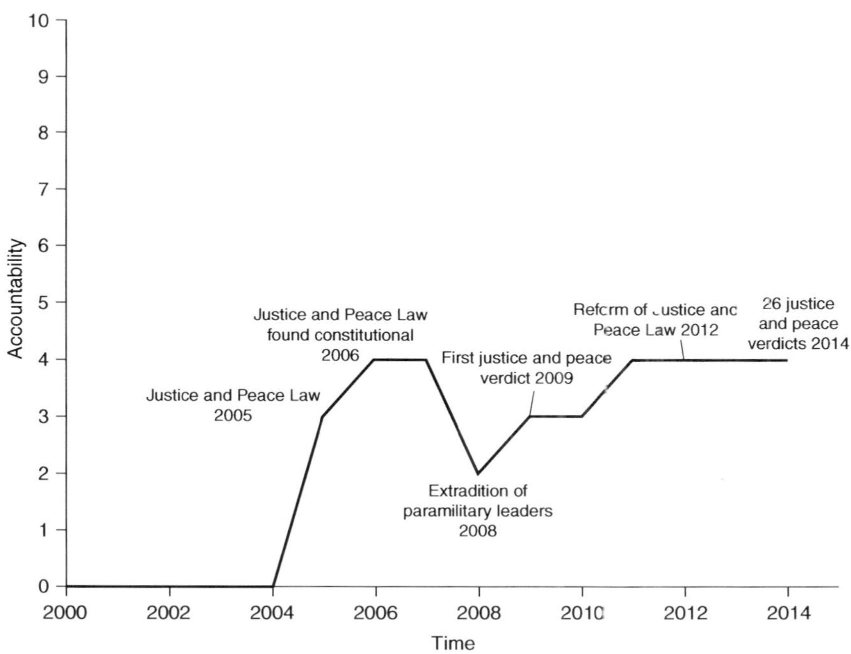

Figure 11.1 Colombia: the overcoming amnesty and trials dimensions of accountability, 2000–2014

Source: Authors' construction, 2015.

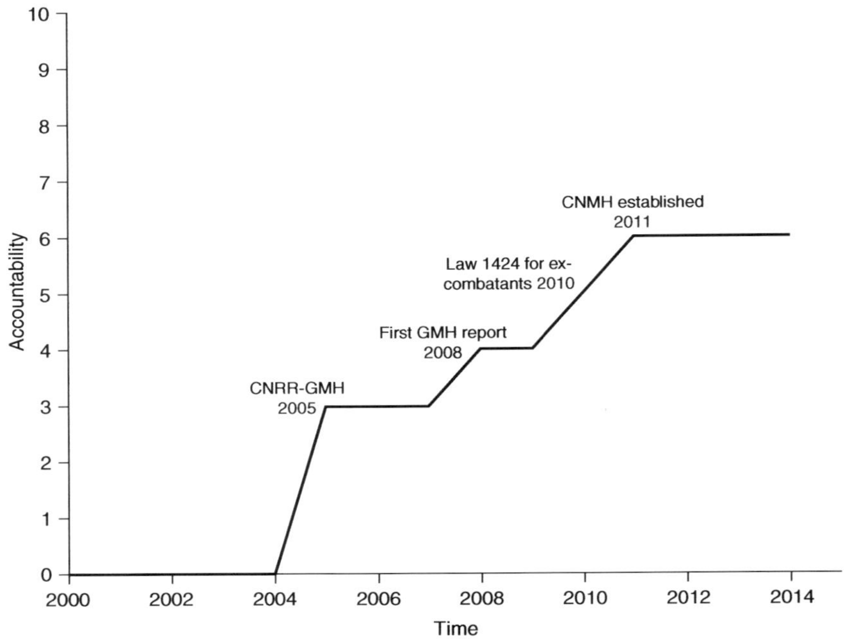

Figure 11.2 Colombia: the truth dimension of accountability, 2000–2014
Source: Authors' construction, 2015.

The Colombian Constitutional Court and the Inter-American Court of Human Rights have both issued rulings calling for more punitive measures in Colombia. Such rulings provide grounds to challenge non-punitive transitional justice mechanisms. Even so, Colombia is not required to take an extreme punitive stance, that is, take to court all perpetrators for all types of violations, something that would be impossible in practice. The Inter-American Court stressed the need for Colombia to use 'the greatest diligence' in investigating and prosecuting crimes and those who are 'most responsible' for criminal violations. In a context of limited resources, this should be taken to mean that Colombia can deal with those who are less culpable through non-judicial means. This view was recently endorsed by the Constitutional Court, when it ruled that the principles guiding the Legal Framework for Peace are in accordance with the constitution.

Colombia's legislature has already laid out some mechanisms that must be incorporated in Colombia's TJ agenda, including the creation of a truth commission after the violence finally ends.[39] In the current context, however, the cessation of violence is the first and highest priority.

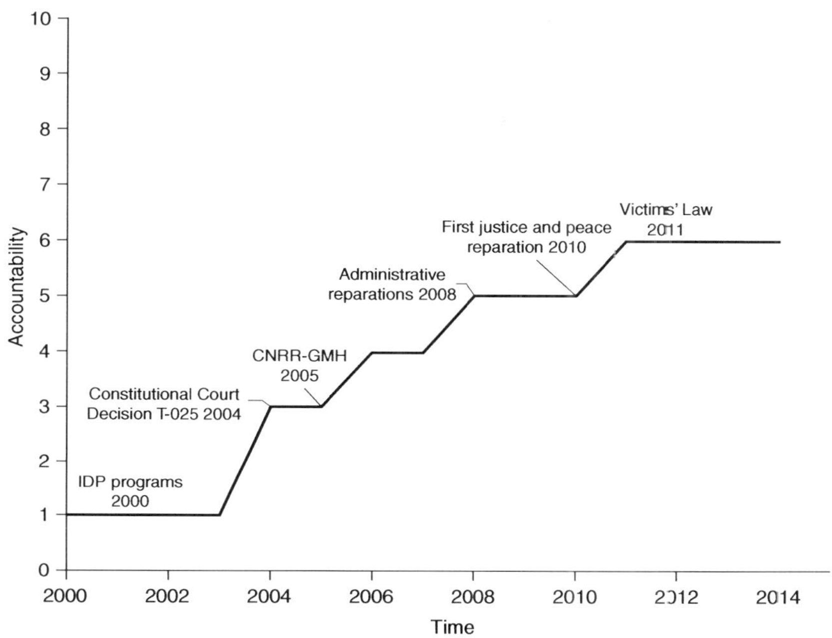

Figure 11.3 Colombia: the reparations dimension of accountability, 2000–2014
Source: Authors' construction, 2015.

As of 2015, talks are continuing between the government and FARC in Havana. With a six-point agenda, the two sides appear determined to take an holistic approach, not settling for piecemeal agreements. A comprehensive agreement between the state and FARC, if and when it is reached, will spread confidence in the country's institutions. This, in turn, will help the government bring stability throughout the country and move into a post-conflict stage, when transitional justice will have to contend with many and varying claims.

Colombia is unique in Latin America in taking significant steps towards transitional justice before the end of a protracted conflict. To date, however, the aims of the country's ambitious TJ process have been achieved only in part. Despite strong advances in the legislative arena, implementation remains hobbled by the huge scope of the task and by the continuing conflict. However, the impact cannot be assessed by numbers alone. Colombia's experience illustrates the urgent need to reconceptualise transitional justice theory and practice. If the negotiations succeed, Colombia may eventually join other Latin American countries in pursuing transitional justice *after* conflict has ended and the country has made a transition to peace.

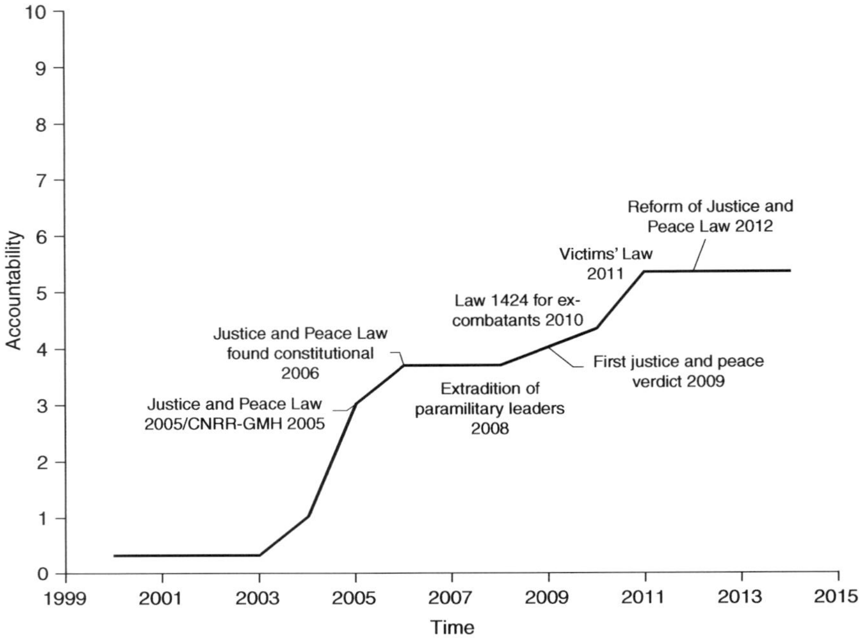

Figure 11.4 Colombia: overall trend towards accountability, 2000–2014
Source: Authors' construction, 2015.

Notes

* The authors thank Clara Sandoval-Villalba, and anonymous reviewers for valuable comments on this chapter.

1 Convivir was established by Decree 356 of 1994, which 'establishes a statute for vigilance and private security' (our translation). Unless otherwise stated, all translations of Colombian laws and legal texts are provided by the chapter authors.
2 The text of the Acuerdo de Santa Fe de Ralito is available in Spanish on ReliefWeb, http://reliefweb.int.
3 The number of demobilised combatants rose to 56,000 by 2012 (CIJP 2012).
4 The Colombian Commission of Jurists filed a case at the Colombian Constitutional Court questioning the constitutionality of the Justice and Peace Law. After extensive deliberations, the Court announced its Ruling C-370 in 2006, finding the overall law to be constitutional, although particular aspects of it were considered unconstitutional, thus needed to be interpreted and implemented differently.
5 By 2005, the inter-American human rights system, as well as several national tribunals, had already ruled to prohibit blanket amnesties and self-amnesties and had asserted a state obligation to combat impunity. See Inter-American Court of Human Rights (I/A Court HR), *Case of Barrios Altos v Peru*, Judgment of 14 March 2001, and *Case of Almonacid Arellano et al. v Chile*, Judgment of 26 September 2006. The Inter-American Court had also issued several decisions establishing the responsibility of the Colombian

state and criticising impunity for human rights violations. It has not, however, explicitly addressed the issue of the legal international standing of the Colombian transitional justice measures.

6 An unofficial English translation of the law can be found on the Verdad Abierta website, https://www.verdadabierta.com/documentos/justicia-y-paz/general-1/352-ley-975-de-justicia-y-paz-version-en-ingles.

7 The Colombian Commission of Jurists fiercely opposed the procedure for the laying down of arms authorised by Decree 128 of 2003 (CCJ 2005). For an overview of the procedures, see IACHR (2004).

8 An exhaustive analysis of the Constitutional Court's arguments can be found in MAPP/OEA (2011).

9 Since the adoption of the justice and peace model, several paramilitary leaders have called the prosecution measures 'a betrayal of the agreements'. In their view, the agreements reached with the government did not contemplate hardening of the punitive standard in Congress or the decision of the Courts (*El Universal* 2009).

10 When there is an obligation to investigate, the Inter-American Court expects the state to proceed with the 'greatest diligence'. I/A Court HR, *Case of the Massacres of El Mozote and Nearby Places v El Salvador*, Judgment of October 25, 2012, para. 319.

11 Law 1424 of 2010 'establishes measures of transitional justice to guarantee truth, justice, and reparation to the victims of demobilised individuals belonging to illegal armed groups, and grants legal benefits and other dispositions'.

12 The case was presented by the Colombian Commission of Jurists and supported by a number of human rights and victims' organisations, which indicates that the fight against impunity is still a central priority on the agenda of these organisations.

13 For an exhaustive legal argument against this model, see the letter from José Miguel Vivanco on behalf of Human Rights Watch to the presidents of the Colombian Senate and House of Representatives, 1 May 2012. The letter is available on the Human Rights Watch website, http://www.hrw.org/news/2012/05/01/colombia-correct-serious-flaws-transitional-justice-bill.

14 Criteria presented as possible bases for prioritisation and selection include gravity, public interest, representativity of the case or of the suspect, viability, and capacity, among others (Bergsmo and Saffon 2011).

15 Rodrigo Uprimny (2006) defines the concept of 'accountability pardons' as those transitional justice models where benefits, such as sentence reduction or individual amnesties, are granted in exchange for true efforts to secure the rights of victims.

16 We thank Rodrigo Uprimny for suggesting this metaphor to us.

17 Law 975 of 2005, Law 1448 of 2011, and the 2012 Legal Framework for Peace all recognise the right to truth.

18 The first GMH report, *Trujillo: Una tragedia que no cesa*, was published in 2008. This report, along with those on the El Salado, La Rochela, Bojaya, and Segovia cases, among others, is available on the website of the National Centre for Historical Memory, http://www.centrodememoriahistorica.gov.co/en/reports.

19 Law 1448 of 2011, the Victims and Land Restitution Law, 'establishes measures to address, support, and provide comprehensive reparations to the victims of the internal armed conflict'.

20 Decree 4153 of 2011 'establishes the creation of the Centre for Historical Memory and other measures'.

21 Gonzalo Sánchez, director of the CNMH, in comments at the event 'El deber de la memoria: Conversación con Félix Reátegui', Feria del Libro de Bogotá (Bogotá International Bookfair), 26 April 2012.

22 Iván Orozco Abad, political science professor at Universidad de Los Andes and former member of the Historical Memory Group, interview by authors, 18 April 2012. All author interviews for this chapter were conducted in Bogotá.

23 Juan Fernando Cristo, Colombian senator, member of the Colombian Liberal Party, and proponent of the Victims' Law, interview by authors, 18 April 2012.
24 Iván Orozco Abad interview, 18 April 2012.
25 Ibid. Orozco is citing Bouris (2007).
26 Judge Uldi Teresa Jiménez of the Superior Court of Bogotá, Justice and Peace Division, interview by authors, 17 April 2012.
27 Ibid.
28 For example, members of the GMH were accused of defamation based on information contained in the *La Rochela* case report (G. Sánchez 2012).
29 Juan Fernando Cristo interview, 18 April 2012.
30 United Nations Basic Principles and Guidelines on the Right to a Remedy and Reparation for Victims of Gross Violations of International Human Rights Law and Serious Violations of International Humanitarian Law, adopted by General Assembly resolution 60/147 of 16 December 2005.
31 Decree 1290 of 2008, 'Programme for individual reparations through administrative means'.
32 On the difference between solidarity and responsibility as the basis for victims' reparations, see N. Sánchez (2009).
33 The Justice and Peace Law applies to all types of criminal acts penalised in the national penal code, without mentioning any specific type of crime. Damage to property is addressed indirectly by way of restitution, identified in the law as a form of victims' reparations. The administrative reparations decree, on the contrary, enumerates the types of crimes considered for monetary compensation, including internal displacement (Decree 1290, Art 5).
34 The number of individual applications processed and approved for compensation by 2010 is not available; the only indicator made public is the number of families that received compensation, along with the amount of money disbursed.
35 On the transformative potential of reparations in the Colombian context, see Uprimny and Saffon (2009).
36 On the debates around the proposal (044/08), see N. Sánchez (2009).
37 An updated list of decrees regulating Law 1448 can be found on the Unit for Victim Reparations website, http://www.unidadvictimas.gov.co/index.php/en/normativa.
38 Several community leaders have been killed during restitution processes or after the returns have been completed (CODHES 2011).
39 Judgment C-579/13 of 28 August 2013.

References

Abdala, Yamile, Darío González, and Eliza González. 2008. *Tierra, oro y conflictos*. Bogotá: INDEPAZ.

Acción Social. 2010. 'Pagos reparación individual vía administrativa.' Bogotá: Acción Social, Subdirección de Atención a Víctimas de la Violencia.

Alto Comisionado para la Paz. 2006. *Proceso de paz con las autodefensas: Informe ejecutivo*. Bogotá: Presidencia de Colombia.

Bergsmo, Morten, and María Paula Saffon. 2011. 'Enfrentando una fila de atrocidades pasadas: ¿Cómo seleccionar y priorizar casos de crímenes internacionales nucleares?' In *Selección y priorización como estrategia de persecución en los casos de crímenes internacionales: Un estudio comparado*, edited by Kai Ambos, 23–112. Bogotá: GIZ.

Bouris, Erica. 2007. *Complex Political Victims*. Bloomfield, CT: Kumarian.

CCJ (Comisión Colombiana de Juristas). 2005. *Sin paz y sin justicia: Aprobada ley de impunidad en Colombia.* Boletín número 6. Bogotá: CCJ.

CIJP (Comité Interinstitucional de Justicia y Paz). 2012. *Informe anual matriz.* Bogotá: Ministerio del Justicia y del Derecho.

CNMH (Centro Nacional de Memoria Histórica). 2012. 'Del grupo de memoria histórica al centro de memoria histórica.' *Noticias CNMH,* 1 March.

CNRR (Comisión Nacional de Reparación y Reconciliación). 2007. *Disidentes, rearmados y emergentes: ¿Bandas criminales o tercera generación paramilitar?* Bogotá: CNRR.

CODHES (Consultoría para los Derechos Humanos y el Desplazamiento). 2011. *¿Consolidación de qué? Informe sobre desplazamiento, conflicto armado y derechos humanos en Colombia en 2010.* CODHES Informa, no. 77. Bogotá: CODHES.

DPS (Departamento para la Prosperidad Social). 2012. 'La entidad: Antecedentes.' Bogotá: DPS.

Duncan, Gustavo. 2006. *Los señores de la guerra: De paramilitares, mafiosos y autodefensas en Colombia.* Bogotá: Planeta.

El País. 2013 'Según encuesta, el 34% de los colombianos apoya el proceso de paz.' 5 December.

El Universal. 2009. 'Ex paramilitar alias "El Alemán", se siente traicionado por Uribe.' 24 August.

FGN (Fiscalía General de la Nación). 2012. *Estadísticas Unidad Nacional de Fiscalías para la Justicia y Paz.* 1 December. Bogotá: FGN. http://www.fiscalia.gov.co/jyp/unidad-de-justicia-y-paz/.

FIDH (International Federation for Human Rights). 2007. 'La desmovilización paramilitar: En los caminos de la Corte Penal Internacional.' http://www.fidh.org/La-desmovilizacion-paramilitar-en.

García-Godos, Jemima. 2012. 'Colombia: Accountability and DDR in the Pursuit of Peace?' In *Transitional Justice and Peacebuilding on the Ground: Victims and Ex-combatants,* edited by Chandra Lekha Sriram, Jemima García-Godos, Johanna Herman, and Olga Martin-Ortega, 219–38. New York: Routledge.

García-Godos, Jemima, and Knut Andreas O. Lid. 2010. 'Transitional Justice and Victims' Rights before the End of a Conflict: The Unusual Case of Colombia.' *Journal of Latin American Studies* 42(3): 487–516.

GMH (Grupo de Memoria Histórica). 2008. *Trujillo: Una tragedia que no cesa.* Bogotá: GMH.

Gutiérrez Sanín, Francisco. 2010. 'Land and Property Rights in Colombia – Change and Continuity.' *Nordic Journal of Human Rights* 28(2): 230–61.

IACHR (Inter-American Commission on Human Rights). 2004. *Informe sobre el proceso de desmovilización en Colombia.* OEA/Ser.L/V/II.120. Washington, DC: OAS.

ICTJ (International Center for Transitional Justice). 2009. *Recordar en conflicto: Iniciativas no oficiales de memoria en Colombia.* Bogotá: ICTJ.

MAPP/OEA (Misión de Apoyo al Proceso de Paz en Colombia). 2011. *Diagnóstico de Justicia y Paz en el marco de la justicia transicional en Colombia.* Bogotá: MAPP/OEA.

Ministerio de Agricultura. 2013. *Unidad de Restitución de Tierras 2013.* Bogotá: Ministerio de Agricultura.

OAS (Organization of American States). 2010. *Décimo cuarto informe trimestral del Secretario General de la OEA al Consejo Permanente sobre la Misión de Apoyo al Proceso de Paz en Colombia (MAPP/OEA).* Washington, DC: OAS.

Offstein, Norman. 2003. 'An Historical Review and Analysis of Colombian Guerrilla Movements: FARC, ELN and EPL.' *Desarrollo y Sociedad*, no. 52: 99–142.

Sánchez, Gonzalo. 2012. Keynote speech at seminar 'La Memoria Histórica', Biblioteca Pública Piloto, Cátedra DEMOPAZ, Medellín, 31 May.

Sánchez, Nelson Camilo. 2009. '¿Perder es ganar un poco? Avances y frustraciones de la discusión del Estatuto de Víctimas en Colombia.' In *Reparar en Colombia: Los dilemas en contexto de conflicto, pobreza y exclusión*, edited by Catalina Díaz Gómez, Nelson Camilo Sánchez, and Rodrigo Uprimny Yepes, 623–718. Bogotá: ICTJ/Dejusticia.

Sánchez, Nelson Camilo, and Rodrigo Uprimny Yepes. 2011. 'Colombia: Transitional Justice without Transition? The Colombian Experience in the Implementation of Transition Measures.' In *Contribution of Truth, Justice, and Reparation Policies to Latin American Democracies*. San José: Inter-American Institute of Human Rights.

Semana. 2011. 'Ley de Víctimas: Un paso histórico.' 28 May.

Uprimny, Rodrigo. 2006. 'Las enseñanzas del análisis comparado: Procesos transicionales, formas de justicia transicional y el caso colombiano.' In *¿Justicia transicional sin transición? Reflexiones sobre verdad, justicia y reparación para Colombia*, edited by Rodrigo Uprimny, 17–44. Bogotá: Dejusticia.

Uprimny, Rodrigo, and María Paula Saffon. 2009. 'Reparaciones transformadoras, justicia distributiva y profundización democrática.' In *Reparar en Colombia: Los dilemas en contexto de conflicto, pobreza y exclusión*, edited by Catalina Díaz Gómez, Nelson Camilo Sánchez, and Rodrigo Uprimny Yepes, 31–69. Bogotá: ICTJ/Dejusticia.

Chapter 12

Conclusions

The uneven road towards accountability in Latin America

*Elin Skaar, Cath Collins, and Jemima García-Godos**

This book has traced trajectories from impunity towards accountability for past human rights violations in nine Latin American countries. Chapter 1 outlined our intentions in embarking on this project: to document and help to explain the significantly changed, but still extremely uneven, state of affairs in present-day Latin America regarding accountability for past political violence. We have attempted to overcome both the methodological weakness of single-case studies (lack of generalisability) and the limitations of large-*n* studies (insufficient attention to context) by tracing accountability trajectories over time in a medium-size set of related countries. We divided the countries into three groups based on type of transition, including post-authoritarian, post-conflict, and (in one case) ongoing conflict. Taken together, the nine cases suggest the range of accountability outcomes that may emerge with the passage of time.

Chapter 2 set out the shared framework that our country case authors used to guide empirical study of the evolution and impact of state policy and other drivers of TJ in four areas: truth-finding, trials, amnesty, and reparations. Country chapters then combined rich in-depth analysis with numerical year-by-year accountability scores for each of the four TJ mechanisms. In this concluding chapter we discuss findings and summarise comparative judgments for the nine countries, using cross-country graphs and 'accountability triangles' as visual aids. We assess the overall trends and patterns discernible in the country trajectories and consider factors that may help explain the differences between them.

We have seen how a set of rights, or at least rights claims, has developed in the wake of widespread state-sponsored or state-tolerated violations of human rights and humanitarian law. The rights to truth, justice, and reparations, grounded and sometimes spelled out in international principles and instruments of law, are today generally supported and promoted by the United Nations system and, in particular, by the inter-American system of human rights protection. This growing body of international and regional thinking about rights lies at the core of our analysis. Our country cases with early transitions have helped shape international doctrine and practice, while also being influenced by it. Some later cases, particularly Colombia, where violence is ongoing, were and are notably influenced by current international precepts.

We define accountability as going beyond formal criminal justice to include *an explicit acknowledgement by the state that grave human rights violations have taken place and that the state was involved in or responsible for them*. Means of accountability can include, but are not limited to, the *recovery and diffusion of truth, criminal prosecution, reparations, and efforts to guarantee non-repetition*. The study attempts to gauge to what extent truth, justice, and reparations-seeking processes have jointly contributed to higher levels of accountability in particular settings.

Towards this end, the nine country chapters empirically document each society's progress from impunity for past human rights violations, committed during military rule or during periods of internal armed conflict, towards accountability. Each chapter examines four transitional justice mechanisms (TJMs): truth-seeking efforts (especially truth commissions), trials, amnesties, and reparations. There is substantial variation between the nine countries in the deployment of these measures and in how profound the shift towards accountability has been. In this concluding chapter, we examine these differences and consider some factors that may help account for them.

Main cross-country findings

No Latin American country comprehensively addressed human rights violations committed by prior regimes at the point of transition towards democracy or peace. Yet all the countries studied in this volume have tried to deal with these violations during the period since transition through transitional justice mechanisms. The timing varies considerably, however. Whereas the transition to democracy in Argentina took place 35 years ago, the Colombian transition is still under way and incomplete. We therefore speak of two types of time: actual time elapsed between the beginning of transition and the implementation of TJMs, and 'world time', that is, the historical regional and international context within which conflicts occurred, transitions began, and TJ dynamics have played out (Skaar and Wiebelhaus-Brahm 2013). Countries undergoing a political transition in the early 1980s did so in a dramatically different international and regional context from that surrounding Colombia's ongoing peace process in 2015. The coexistence of these differing cases within a single region offers a unique opportunity to observe the interaction of regional human rights institutions and prevailing human rights norms and discourse – themselves in constant flux – with domestic transitional justice decisions and activities.

All countries examined in this volume had, by the end of 2014, implemented three or more of the TJMs investigated. Only Brazil and El Salvador had not had any significant trials for past human rights violations; only Colombia did not have a formal truth commission; and only Paraguay had not, at some time, adopted an amnesty law. This relative similarity in levels of TJM adoption, when the entire period between the time of transition and the end of 2014 is considered, might lead some to expect a corresponding similarity in present-day accountability levels. However, our empirical findings strongly suggest that there is substantial variation in accountability achievements. We hypothesised in Chapter 2 that the combination, timing, sequencing, and quality of TJMs might matter for accountability. In this section we explore the extent to which the case studies support these hypotheses.

Combinations, timing, and sequencing of TJMs

We hypothesised that the passage of time would, on balance, work in favour of accountability. We further argued that certain combinations of TJMs are likely to be more conducive to accountability than others. Using a scale from low to high to represent the impunity–accountability spectrum, we rated 16 possible combinations of the four TJMs: truth commissions (TC, here used as shorthand for all truth-finding activities), trials (T), reparations (R), and amnesties (A).[1]

Table 12.1 shows the combinations of TJMs used by the nine countries during the first five years after transition (T1) and those implemented in subsequent years, in the post-transition phase to 2014, the year when data collection ended (T2).[2] Starting at the top row of the table, we expect the *lowest level* of accountability in a country that has amnesty laws precluding criminal prosecution and no other TJ measure to compensate for this legally induced impunity. We expect the *highest level* of accountability in countries that have trials, truth commissions, and reparations – and no amnesty laws obstructing trials (bottom row). Expected accountability levels for all other combinations of TJMs fall somewhere between these two end points of the scale. It should be emphasised that these are *expected* levels: the full potential of each combination to contribute to accountability depends on the seriousness, depth, and perseverance with which each measure is implemented.

Table 12.1 displays two interesting patterns. First, it shows that *some combinations of TJMs are more common than others*. Eight of the 16 combinations do not occur at all in our nine cases, as shown by the empty cells: amnesty only (A); no measures; amnesty plus trials (A+T); reparations only (R); truth commission only (TC); truth commission plus reparations (TC+R); reparations plus trials (R+T); and truth commission plus trials (TC+T). The most common combinations in T1 were amnesty plus truth commission (A+TC, two cases) and amnesty plus reparations plus truth commission (A+R+TC, two cases). The most common combination in T2 was the three pro-accountability measures: truth commissions, reparations, and trials, without amnesty (TC+R+T, four cases). These findings may suggest that, at least in the Americas, early amnesties have not always derailed demands for other TJMs. Truth commissions and reparations, rather than being a distraction from formal justice, may have served as a stepping stone towards challenges to early amnesties and the later emergence of trials.[3]

Second, in line with our assumption about the importance of time, Table 12.1 shows that *expected accountability levels have increased for all countries between the initial transition period (T1) and the post-transition period (T2)*, if one considers only the number and combination of TJMs. During T1, no country deployed all three anti-impunity measures (TC, T, R) without amnesty, the combination with the

Table 12.1 Expected levels of accountability based on combination and timing of TJMs

Overall expected accountability level, low to high	*Combination of TJMs*	*T1 (first five years after transition)*	*T2 (five years after transition until end 2014)*
Lowest level ↑	A (amnesty only)		
	Nothing		
	A+R	Brazil	
	A+TC	El Salvador Peru	
	A+T		
	R		
	TC		
	T	Paraguay	
	A+R+TC	Uruguay Chile	Brazil El Salvador
	A+R+T	Colombia[a]	Colombia
	A+TC+T	Guatemala	
	TC+R		
	R+T		
	TC+T		
	A+R+TC+T	Argentina	Guatemala Chile
↓ Highest level	TC+R+T		Paraguay Peru Uruguay Argentina

a. Colombia is, for all practical purposes, still in transition, so strictly speaking it has no T2. However, since we consider that Colombia's first TJM was implemented in 2005, we have designated the period from 2010 to 2014 as T2 for comparative purposes.

highest accountability rating. amnesty laws were almost universal during T1, present in all countries except Paraguay. Only Argentina deployed all four measures together, the second-highest-rated combination. During T2, five years or more after transition, we see that every country has moved further towards the accountability end of the scale, as each of the nine countries has adopted additional TJMs during that period. By T2, moreover, amnesty has faded from the scene in three countries – Peru, Argentina, and Uruguay – while remaining absent in Paraguay. Amnesty is still present in Guatemala and Chile, but has been constrained within the limits prescribed by international law. This suggests that amnesty laws may have been used primarily to ease the transition to democracy, or to secure peace agreements in situations of internal armed conflict, later becoming more dispensable. This is in line with scholarly arguments that amnesty may be a necessary evil (Freeman 2009) and that appropriately limited amnesties may coexist alongside other forms of accountability mechanisms (Mallinder 2008; Olsen, Payne, and Reiter 2010).

Sequencing of TJMs, an issue mentioned in our theoretical framing as possibly influential (Dancy and Wiebelhaus-Brahm 2015), does not emerge from the country studies as a variable to which any particular pattern is attached. The fact that trials have most often come chronologically after TCs admits many potential explanations other than simple causality. None of our country authors draw a straight line between truth commission revelations and subsequent judicial action. The legal status and take-up of TC results are key here, and these can only be assessed accurately at the level of empirical nuance that the country chapters allow. Similarly, reparations have sometimes occurred independently of truth-telling initiatives. No lessons can be derived here about how such things ought to be done. A final point about sequencing is that with the possible exception of Colombia, we see little sign of conscious, official TJ strategy or planning in which states deliberately introduce measures one at a time. In the eight countries with longer TJ trajectories, *de facto* sequencing appears to have been driven mainly by civil society demand, external pressures, or happenstance rather than by state planning. None of our country authors describes a situation of coherent, sustained TJ policy direction over time. It appears, in other words, that many Latin American states have not yet come to terms with the observable reality that the horizons of transitional justice are much longer than was initially thought.

Quality of TJMs implemented and accountability levels

Going briefly back to Table 12.1, we see that the country with the highest level of expected accountability at the end of T1 was Argentina. By the end of T2, in 2014, Argentina had eliminated amnesty and had been joined by three more countries, Paraguay, Peru, and Uruguay, in having the combination of truth commissions, reparations, and trials (TC+R+T) with no amnesty – the combination with the highest expected accountability rating. Yet there are substantial real-life differences between these four countries with regard to actual accountability scores. At least part of the explanation lies in the quality and implementation of TJMs.

We measured the quality of TJMs by assessing to what extent a given TJM has contributed (or not) to overall accountability in a given country in a defined period. Based on empirical analysis of historical events and guided by a common set of questions (see Appendix 2), authors qualitatively assessed the impact on accountability of measures actually taken in truth, justice, reparations, and amnesty in each country. The results are represented, for heuristic and comparative purposes, on a numeric scale from 0 to 10, where 0 is the lowest and 10 the highest possible score. Accountability scores are assigned to the country on each dimension for each year from the beginning of T1 through 2014. The 2014 scores for each dimension are then averaged to produce an overall country score, as shown in Table 12.2.

Comparing the results of Table 12.2 with those based solely on the number and combination of measures deployed (Table 12.1) strengthens our contention

Table 12.2 Accountability scores for nine Latin American countries, 2014

Country	*Overall accountability score*[a]	*Truth*	*Trials*	*Overcoming amnesty*[b]	*Reparations*
Argentina	9.0	7.5	9.0	10.0	8.0
Chile	8.0	8.5	7.5	6.5	8.5
Uruguay	6.0	6.0	5.0	7.0	5.5
Peru	6.0	6.5	5.0	5.0	6.0
Colombia	5.5	6.0	4.0	NA[c]	6.0
Guatemala	4.0	4.0	3.5	3.0	4.5
Paraguay	4.0	5.0	3.0	NA[d]	3.0
Brazil	3.5	5.5	0.5	1.0	7.0
El Salvador	3.0	4.0	1.0	1.5	4.0

a. The general accountability scores represent a simple mathematical average of the scores given to the four TJMs – truth, trials, (overcoming) amnesty, and reparations – rounded up to the nearest half point (0.5). For Colombia (for which we present amnesty and justice dimensions combined) and Paraguay (which does not have an amnesty law), we have registered the amnesty data as 'not available' instead of adding the value 0 for each of the years to the data set. This to distinguish the countries with blanket amnesty laws (which would receive a 0 on our accountability scale) from those with no amnesty laws. This means that the average accountability score for Colombia and Paraguay = the scores for (T+TC+R) divided by 3, not (T+TC+R+A) divided by 4 as for the other seven countries.

b. Amnesty has a negative effect on accountability, moving a country closer to the impunity end of the scale. However, it is represented here as a positive value, expressing how far a country has progressed in limiting or overcoming amnesty by 2014.

c. Colombia has had a quasi-judicial process combined with a reduced sentencing formula. For this reason the authors opted to treat justice and amnesty together in the Colombia chapter.

d. Paraguay is the only country in our sample that did not pass an amnesty law.

Source: Authors, based on summary of accountability scores in each of the nine country chapters.

that quality is more important than quantity in determining which country has had more, or more complete, transitional justice. We see substantial variation in accountability achievements even between countries that have employed the same number and combination of TJ mechanisms. Guatemala and Chile, which by 2014 had implemented the same combination of truth-finding, trials, and reparations along with (now limited) amnesty, have very different overall scores of 4.0 and 8.0, respectively. Noticeable variation in overall accountability scores also exists between the four countries that, in 2014, shared the same combination of the three pro-accountability mechanisms (TC+T+R) with no amnesty. One of these four countries, Paraguay, has the third-lowest overall accountability score of all nine cases, while another, Argentina, has the highest.

To further explain the discrepancies between expected and actual accountability ratings, the next section details how the nine countries fare when we compare their achievements on each of the three pro-accountability TJ dimensions (truth-finding, trials, and reparations).

Cross-country comparisons of accountability achievements in 2014

To provide a visual, cross-country comparison of the different TJ trajectories, we have created what we call an accountability triangle for each country.[4] The triangle includes three vectors, each of which captures a specific positive dimension of accountability: one vector for trials (T), one vector for truth commissions and other truth-finding measures (TC), and one vector for reparations (R).[5]

The *length* of each vector, from the centre of the triangle to a corner, corresponds to the level of accountability recorded for the TJM in question at the end of 2014 (see Table 12.2). For example, if a country received a score of 8.0 for truth-finding (TC), 4.0 for trials (T), and 5.0 for reparations (R) for 2014, these are the numerical values used to construct the triangle. The *size/area* of the triangle denotes the country's total level of accountability for past human rights violations at the end of 2014. A country with a full score on all three dimensions (10/10/10) would have the largest possible triangle, while a country with low scores on all dimensions (for example, 1/1/1) would have a much smaller triangle. The *shape* of the triangle indicates the areas where advances in accountability have been concentrated. Equivalent developments produce equilateral triangles, while developments concentrated in one or two dimensions produce scalene or isosceles triangles. Figure 12.1 displays accountability triangles for the nine countries.

We can divide the triangles in Figure 12.1 into different categories depending on their size and shape. With respect to *size*, the countries fall into three categories: (a) large triangles (high accountability) for Argentina and Chile; (b) medium-size triangles (medium accountability) for Uruguay, Peru, and Colombia; and (c) small triangles (low accountability) for Guatemala, Paraguay, Brazil, and El Salvador.

Here we can make three general observations. First, the five post-authoritarian countries in the sample (the Southern Cone countries plus Brazil) do not fall into a single category. The type of political violence (authoritarian repression or internal armed conflict) does not, in other words, seem to be a determinant of T2 accountability. Although three of the post-authoritarian countries display the highest current accountability levels, the third, Uruguay, is matched in overall score by Peru, a hybrid case. The remaining post-authoritarian countries, Brazil and Paraguay, are outstripped by Colombia, a conflict country. Brazil is also outdone by Guatemala, one of the two classic post-conflict settings in the study. Brazil's lack of meaningful trials continues to hold it back, although it has made progress in reparations and, more recently, in truth. There are undoubtedly multiple explanations for these uneven outcomes among the post-authoritarian countries.

Second, the pattern in Figure 12.1 clearly rules out intensity and magnitude of violence as a lasting or preponderant independent variable.[6] Brazil and Paraguay, each of which suffered well below 1,000 acknowledged killings or disappearances, have low accountability scores, whereas Uruguay, also with a relatively small number of fatal victims, has a high score. Uruguay, in fact, falls into the same

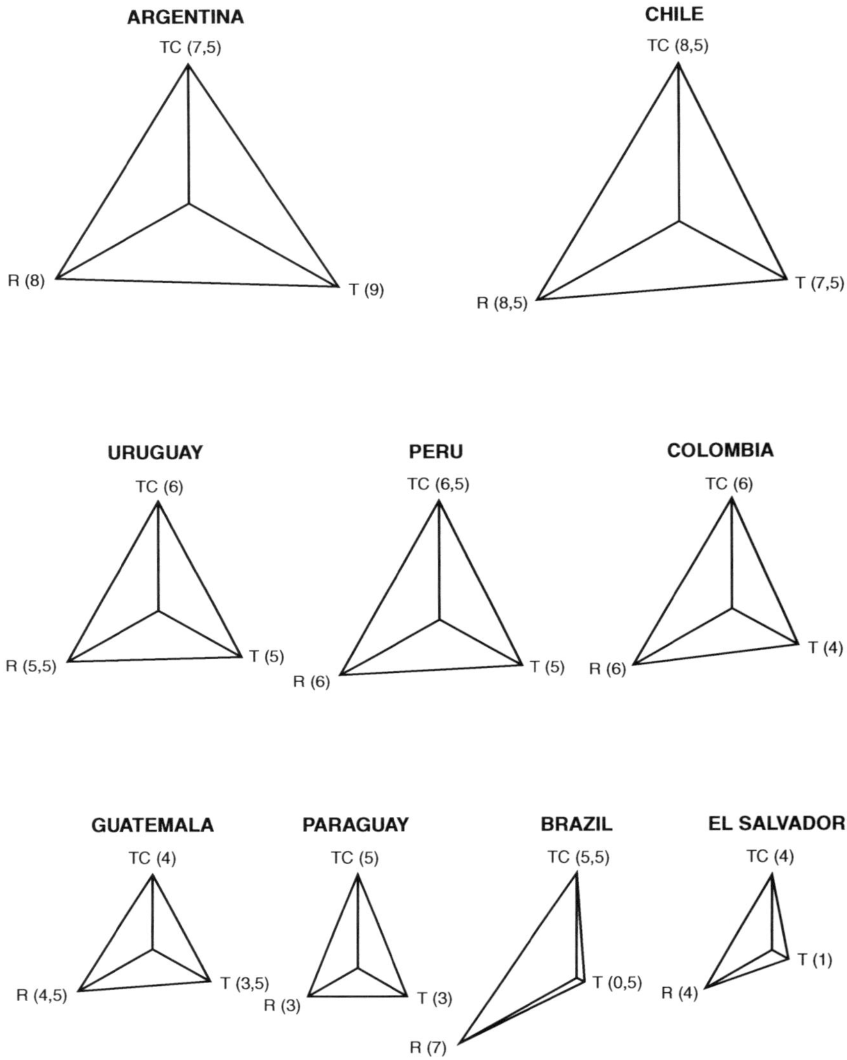

Figure 12.1 Accountability triangles for nine Latin American countries, 2014
Source: Authors' construction.

category as Colombia, the country with the most prolonged and lethal pattern of repression.

Third, there is the issue of 'international time' as it affects accountability levels. In the case of Colombia, regional and international actors, including the International Criminal Court, have explicitly added to the ever-growing list of TJ obligations that the inter-American system also now embraces. Guatemala's amnesty, meanwhile, is the most recently passed amnesty law that is still intact. It is also the only law that incorporated internationally mandated exceptions from the beginning, increasing its legitimacy and limiting its impunity-promoting potential. International time, with the associated gradual construction of blanket amnesty as unacceptable, seems to be at work here.

When we group the accountability triangles according to *shape*, they fall into two categories. Equilateral triangles have roughly the same accountability scores on the three TJ dimensions evaluated, with a variation of 1.5 points or less between maximum and minimum scores across the three vectors. This category includes Argentina, Chile, Uruguay, Peru, and Guatemala. Irregularly shaped triangles have variations of 2 points or more between maximum and minimum; this category contains Colombia, Paraguay, Brazil, and El Salvador. Most of the countries in the second category have lopsided triangles skewed towards reparations and truth. Two have small or marginal achievements on the trials dimension (Brazil and El Salvador). Their similar patterns, however, were produced in quite different ways. In El Salvador, the government steered away from trials after the peace agreement was signed for reasons of stability and the shared interests of the former warring parties; this initial skewed TJ pattern was not disturbed by significant later innovation. In Brazil, very little was done at transition on any TJ dimension. The current skewing is caused by recent (T2) change in two dimensions, not yet matched by positive changes in the third.

It is interesting to note that with the sole exception of Argentina, the justice dimension, as represented by the quantity and quality of trials, continues to underperform both the other dimensions, even though it is generally in the area of criminal justice that most recent (T2) change has occurred. In other words, if we had drawn country triangles earlier, at end T1, they would have had shapes more closely resembling those currently produced by El Salvador and Brazil, with a short trials vector. Trials scores have increased significantly during T2 for all countries, but have still not reached parity with other dimensions. The exception to this pattern is Argentina, the only country whose trial score now exceeds its scores for truth commissions and reparations. Note that Paraguay's still quite low score of 3.0 for trials is now matched by a 3.0 in reparations.

The discussion so far has been based mainly on comparative snapshots for 2014. We now turn our attention to TJ trajectories over time, tracing movements back and forth between impunity and accountability for the nine countries on each of the four accountability dimensions, this time including amnesties.

Accountability changes across countries over time

This section presents five summary graphs, one for each of the four dimensions of accountability plus one showing overall trends. Each graph plots the trajectories of all nine countries based on graphs in the country chapters. It should be kept in mind that these graphs represent chapter authors' assessments of how much particular TJMs have contributed to accountability or impunity on a year-by-year basis. These assessments, while informed by in-depth knowledge and guided by a common set of questions (Appendix 2), have an inescapably subjective component.

The truth-finding dimension of accountability

Figure 12.2 shows a clear movement from impunity towards accountability in the area of truth-finding for all nine countries. Truth dimension scores in 2014 range from a high of 8.5 for Chile, with its two official truth commissions and other interim measures, to a low of 4.0 for El Salvador, where an early truth commission was not followed up by later official efforts. Progress has been step-wise rather than linear in most countries. Backsliding, while rare, has occurred in several countries, where official indifference to or denial of truth commission reports has negated the acknowledgement function of state-backed truth recovery.

Chile and Argentina emerge with the highest truth scores, as both had significant state-sponsored truth commissions with some official follow-up. Peru's well-regarded truth commission puts it in third place.

In-depth country analysis, however, shows that only some of the accountability achievements in the truth dimension are the result of formal truth commissions. Our first unexpected finding is that Colombia, with no formal truth

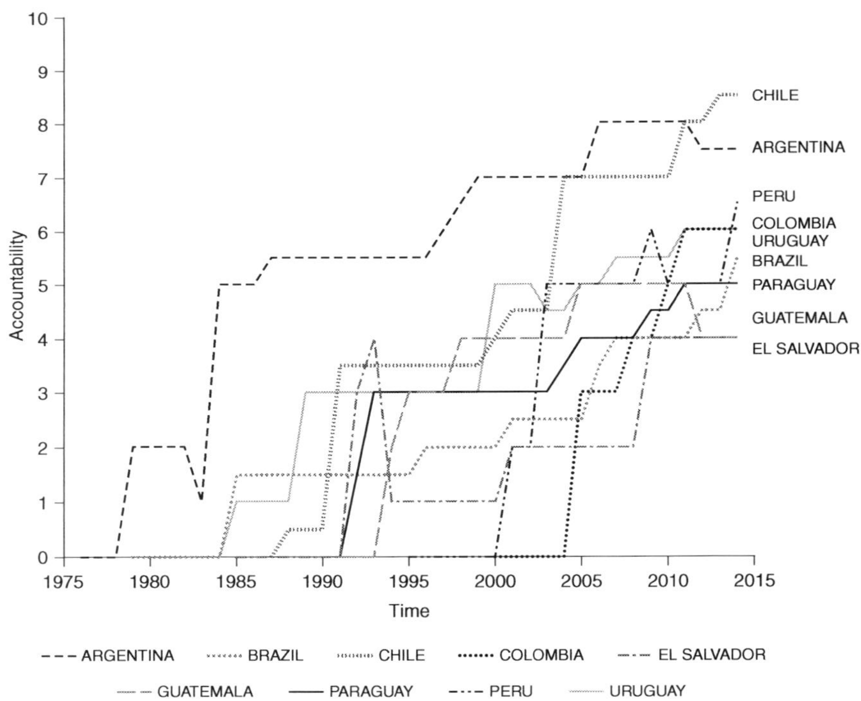

Figure 12.2 The truth dimension of accountability over time for nine Latin American countries

Source: Authors' construction, 2015.

commission to date, scores higher in this dimension than do five of the countries in our sample that have had state-sponsored truth commissions. This may reflect the weaknesses and limitations of many official truth commissions, along with the significant amount of truth-finding work already undertaken by the Colombian state (see Chapter 11). A second unexpected finding is that Brazil, with a very recent TC, scores higher than countries with earlier TCs, particularly those where follow-up has been seriously lacking despite supposedly binding recommendations (e.g. El Salvador). Though it is too soon to tell how good the follow-up of Brazil's commission will be, other aspects of the Brazilian experience boost the country's truth score. These include the acknowledgement function of the Amnesty Commission, the mixed state-civil society commission on deaths and disappearances (precursor to the TC), and the grassroots momentum created around the 2014 state-sponsored truth commission (see Chapter 5). This example shows that truth-finding activities other than TCs can also matter. It also suggests that more recent truth commissions may have learned some positive lessons from the shortcomings of earlier TCs in the region.

The country chapters also demonstrate the importance of non-state truth activities and commissions. Brazil's Nunca Mais project, the Recovery of Historical Memory Project (REMHI) in Guatemala, and the investigation by SERPAJ (Peace and Justice Service) in Uruguay were milestones in their respective countries. These point to the importance of non-governmental entities, notably the Catholic Church, in Latin American truth-finding. Other official and unofficial measures that have contributed to the truth dimension of accountability include memorials, museums, exhumations, recovery of abducted children, court cases (including 'truth trials'), and oral history initiatives.

The trials dimension of accountability

Several scholars have argued that a 'justice cascade', with increased propensity for the prosecution of grave human rights crimes, has swept the world and Latin America in particular over the past decade or two (Lutz and Sikkink 2001; Sikkink 2011). Our findings certainly ratify a major expansion of criminal justice activity in Latin America since the turn of the millennium, but the contributions made by the nine countries to this development are very uneven (Figure 12.3). While Argentina's extensive current trials give it an accountability score of 9.0, closely followed by Chile at 7.5, Brazil and El Salvador, with intact, active, amnesty laws and few, if any, successful prosecutions, score only 1.0 and 1.5 respectively. Such a wide range, in a region with increasing pro-prosecution pressure at the level of the inter-American system, suggests that the justice cascade remains strongly conditioned by national contexts. Key factors include the quality of criminal justice structures and the strength of social demands for accountability which, in turn, may be heightened by a demonstration effect when neighbouring countries undertake active criminal prosecutions.

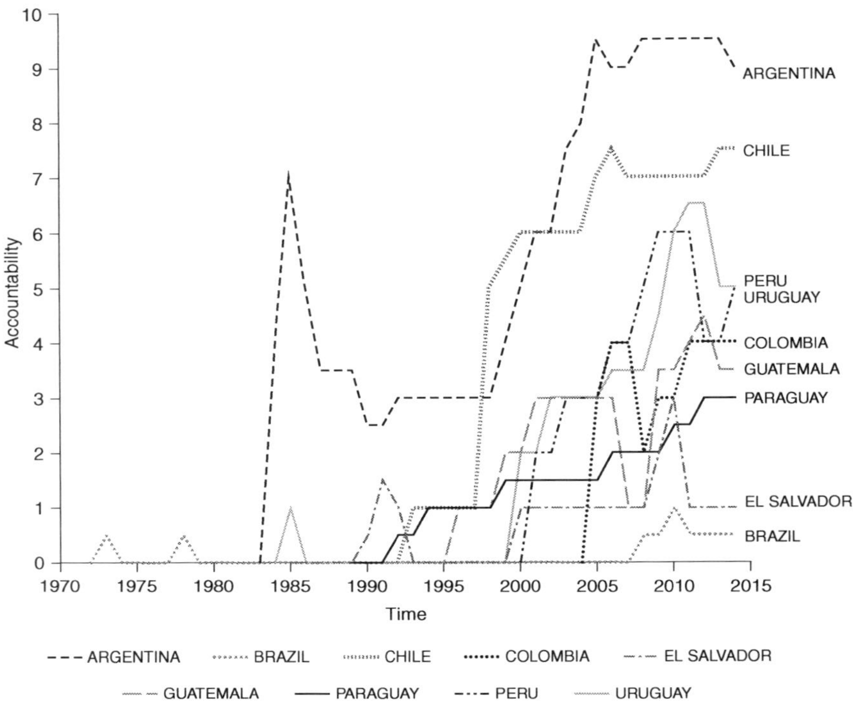

Figure 12.3 The trials dimension of accountability over time for nine Latin American countries
Source: Authors' construction, 2015.

This demonstration effect may be strongest in the former Operation Condor countries, where domestic trials held in one country increasingly involve citizens of other countries and/or generate extradition and information requests. However, current levels of trial activity vary even among the Condor countries. Brazil and Paraguay's lower scores have various possible explanations. For Paraguay, weaknesses and deficiencies in the whole judicial system undoubtedly weigh heavily. In Brazil, there has simply been no political will to revisit violations of the past through criminal justice. Brazil and Paraguay also share relatively low ratios of fatal to survived repressive violence. Torture, notoriously difficult to prosecute under prevailing national law at the time of these offences, was more prevalent in these two countries. While this is also true of Uruguay, the higher per capita rate of death and disappearance in its small population gave the repression greater visibility there – certainly when compared to Brazil – and may have prompted more noticeable change in the Uruguayan case.

Tracking backwards in time, we know that the almost universal deployment or preservation of amnesty at transition impeded early criminal justice. The sole early exception, the Argentine Juntas Trial in 1985, produced a backlash that helped cement widespread toleration of early impunity. Figure 12.3 shows that the justice field became newly active in the late 1990s, in Chile and elsewhere. This supports the view that the 1998 Pinochet arrest had ripple effects beyond, as well as within, Chile's borders, in part by reviving relatives' and survivors' demands for action against former regime figures. Another catalyst for domestic trials in various countries was provided by multiple attempts in European courts to try Argentine, Chilean, Guatemalan, and Salvadoran nationals, among others, for past crimes (Roht-Arriaza 2005).

Finally, we can observe that for many of our countries (Uruguay, Peru, Guatemala, El Salvador, and Brazil) advances in the trials dimension do not indicate a continuous movement towards greater accountability. The Fujimori trials in Peru and the Ríos Montt trial in Guatemala received institutional support, but it was not sustained and did not provide a basis for moving forward with other prosecutions. Consistent institutional support is needed to extend criminal accountability beyond a few high-profile cases.

The amnesty dimension of accountability

Amnesty was the most widely used TJ measure in Latin America before, during, and after transition. It has often been seen as a tool for facilitating democratic transitions or peace negotiations. Offering the military or combatants some measure of immunity or impunity has been a standard way of getting them to the negotiating table (El Salvador, Guatemala, Colombia) or persuading them to initiate or tolerate democratic elections (Chile, Uruguay, Brazil).

While some scholars treat amnesties as the antithesis of accountability, in this volume they are seen as one more transitional justice mechanism, albeit one generally exercising a pull towards impunity. An amnesty adopted to speed elections or get warring parties to lay down arms does not inevitably prevent prosecution of the gravest offences. Thus it need not, if it is appropriately limited, contradict precepts of international human rights law or humanitarian law. Our country studies display different types of amnesty, from limited or partial – respecting the duty to prosecute the most grievous crimes – to extensive or 'blanket' amnesty. Self-amnesty, where the party introducing the law stands to benefit exclusively or disproportionately from it, can be either extensive or limited, but its legitimacy is precarious in either case. As the El Salvador case shows, some Latin American states have long-standing laws regulating such practices; this testifies to a long tradition of using amnesties and pardons to manage political tensions.

In the historical period covered by this book, the choice of blanket or partial amnesty does not seem to depend on regime type, type of political violence, or even transition type. The two most extensive blanket amnesties occurred in one military authoritarian setting (Chile) and one post-conflict setting (El Salvador). Almost all other amnesties were limited to some extent, with certain categories of persons or crimes excluded (for instance, Uruguay's law excluded civilians and the crime of forced disappearance of adults and minors). Most of the amnesties discussed here excluded certain ordinary or economic crimes from their reach, leaving loopholes later exploited by accountability activists (as in Argentina, Chile, and Uruguay).

The question of whether amnesty laws passed or reaffirmed by democratically elected authorities have a special status has arisen particularly in regard to Uruguay and El Salvador. In understanding popular perceptions of amnesty, it is useful to remember that repressive regimes also conceded occasional amnesties or pardons for political prisoners and other opponents. This means that amnesty was not invariably associated with perpetrator impunity. Brazil's amnesty law is in a category of its own, portrayed by the authoritarian regime as falling into this second, pro-prisoner, category while, in practice, used by the regime as a self-amnesty. The two Central American post-conflict amnesties demonstrate the related effects of international involvement and a changing regional and international ethos: while the United Nations was involved as a broker in both peace processes, only the later process, Guatemala's, made any concession to international prohibitions on amnesty for core atrocity crimes. Perpetrators' perceptions of the need for legal protection, and their capacity to impose their wishes, also, of course, had an effect: Paraguay never passed an amnesty law, principally because this suited the faction that gained the upper hand in the country's palace coup.

Overall amnesty trends are displayed in Figure 12.4. Partly or wholly successful challenges to amnesty, which produce an uptick in a country's 'overcoming amnesty' line, can be understood as a combination of two factors: (a) the extent to which the original drafting of amnesty laws permitted investigation or prosecution of certain crimes, and (b) the later emergence (or not) of effective demand – domestic and international – for change or reinterpretation of the amnesty law. The strongest challenges, in Argentina and Uruguay, produced legislative annulment or derogation. However, the experiences of Chile and Guatemala show that prosecutions can still occur around the edges of amnesty, while Peru and Paraguay make clear that the absence of amnesty does not automatically ensure prosecutions.

Most of the formal amnesty laws in our nine countries have seen their impunity-producing effects diminished or abolished over time through political and judicial attrition. Argentina's complete annulment of its two amnesty laws earned it a full score of 10 on the overcoming amnesty dimension by 2014, while Brazil and El Salvador remained at the other end of the scale. The outcome of ongoing efforts to make Brazil comply with the Inter-American Court of Human Rights verdict in the Araguaia case, and of a renewed challenge to the constitutionality of El Salvador's amnesty in the country's Supreme Court (see Chapters 5 and 8), will determine whether there is any immediate prospect of movement at this bottom end of the scale. A final point is that where amnesty still has not

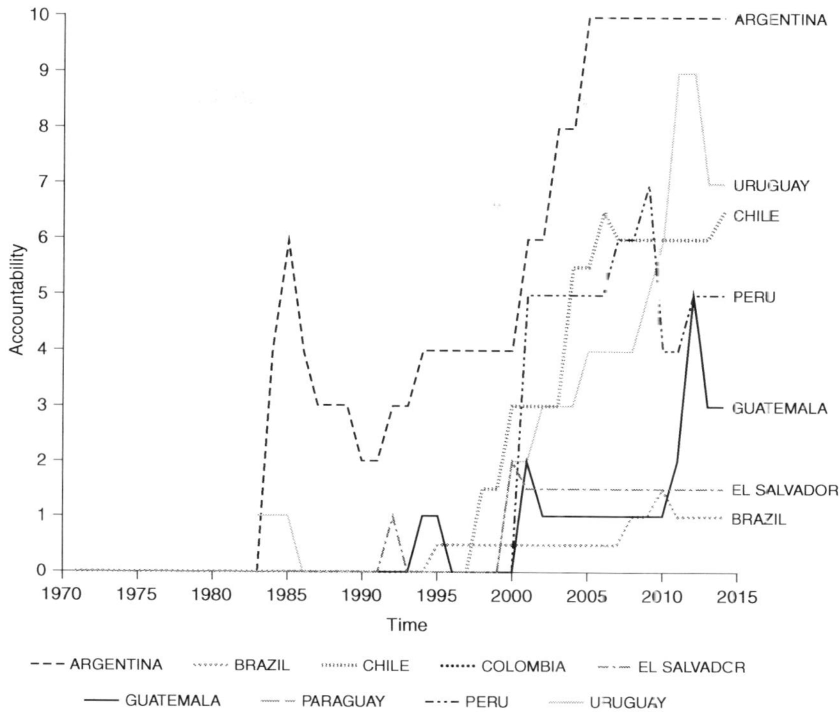

Figure 12.4 The overcoming amnesty dimension of accountability over time for seven Latin American countries
Source: Authors' construction, 2015.

shifted, it remains the immediate focus of much pro-accountability legal activism. Where amnesty was never or is no longer the main impediment, as in Peru, Guatemala, Chile, and Paraguay, activism focuses on overcoming practical and political obstacles to prosecutions.

The reparations dimension of accountability

Compared to trials and amnesty laws, reparations may be less politically contentious, since they can, in theory, be managed directly by new state authorities without directly impinging on perpetrators. We might accordingly expect greater and/or more consistent advances in the reparations dimension of accountability, but this proves only partly true.[7] Although the spread (range) of 2014 scores on the reparations dimension was narrower than the spread on the other three dimensions,[8] reparations scores overall are relatively low: only in Brazil did reparations

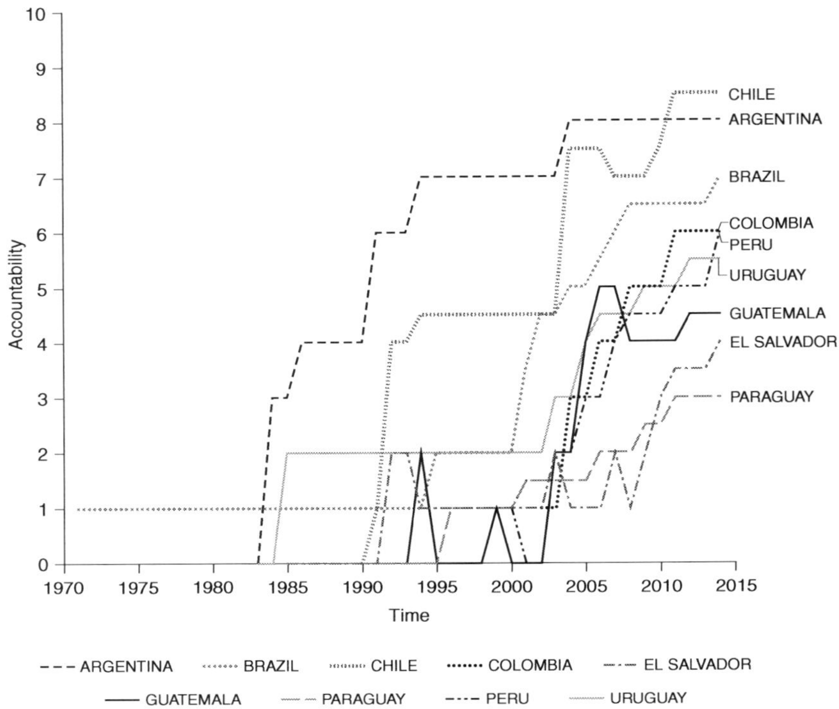

Figure 12.5 **The reparations dimension of accountability over time for nine Latin American countries**

Source: Authors' construction, 2015.

outperform all other accountability dimensions (see Table 12.2). Of the nine countries, only Brazil could be described as having a reparations-driven transitional justice trajectory (see Abrão and Torelly 2012).

Reparations have been implemented most frequently through administrative programmes, often initiated as a result of truth commission recommendations (although Chile, Colombia, Brazil, and Paraguay all introduced at least some reparations before holding a TC). In our case studies, the mere creation of a legal framework for reparations programmes did not guarantee timely follow-through; years often went by before programmes were up and running (see Figure 12.5). Delays were caused not only by budget limitations but also by contestation. Controversies arose over the definition of beneficiaries (Uruguay and Chile), where the onus of proof should lie (Brazil), and the types of measures to be taken (Peru). Particularly where victims were numerous, the genuine administrative challenge of providing individual reparations was sometimes complicated by the absence of national registers (El Salvador, Guatemala) or by the later addition of new programmes made available to categories of victims not included in initial registers or truth commission victim lists. In these circumstances, doubt was cast on the purpose of disbursements made in the name of reparations, as in Guatemala (see Chapter 9).

Within administrative programmes, the most usual specific measure was individual economic (monetary) compensation, although collective reparations were also attempted in Peru and Guatemala. Peru undertook collective reparations through local development projects, while the Guatemalan state mainly supported memorialisation. Symbolic reparations of this kind, involving the financing and promotion of commemorations, memory sites, and museums, became increasingly common in the nine countries, reaching beyond victims and relatives to the general public. Prominent examples include museums and memory sites in Argentina, Chile, Uruguay, and Paraguay. Peru's museum has had a troubled history; other initiatives, too, have triggered counter-commemorations and 'wars' of symbolism (see also Hite 2012).

Reparations involve economic and political commitments that countries are not always prepared to make. Post-conflict processes have tended to emphasise demobilisation and other measures aimed at former combatants. In this regard, the success of victims' organisations in Colombia in gaining space for reparations to be addressed during peace negotiations is a unique achievement. This example and the qualitative country analyses in other chapters suggest that the presence or emergence of a strong and vocal victims' or survivors' lobby represents virtually the only circumstance under which reparations for victims are comprehensively considered early on, or improved significantly over time.

These varied initiatives, reactions, and obstacles, together with a growing tendency for the Inter-American Commission and Court to include both economic and symbolic reparations measures in their country-specific recommendations and rulings, suggest that reparations have now become established in Latin America as an important dimension of accountability.

Overall accountability trends

Figure 12.6 compares overall transitional justice trajectories for the nine countries, including, where relevant, TJM activity that started before initiation of transition.[9] The general trend graphs for each country are computed as a mathematical average of scores for the four TJMs in question (truth-finding, trials, amnesties, and reparations). Argentina's emerges as the most complete transitional justice experience in the region to date, closely followed by Chile and then by Uruguay and Peru.

Three principal observations emerge from this comparison of overall trajectories. First, although some countries made more progress than others, *accountability levels were higher for each country in 2014 than at the beginning of transition, regardless of the date of T1.*

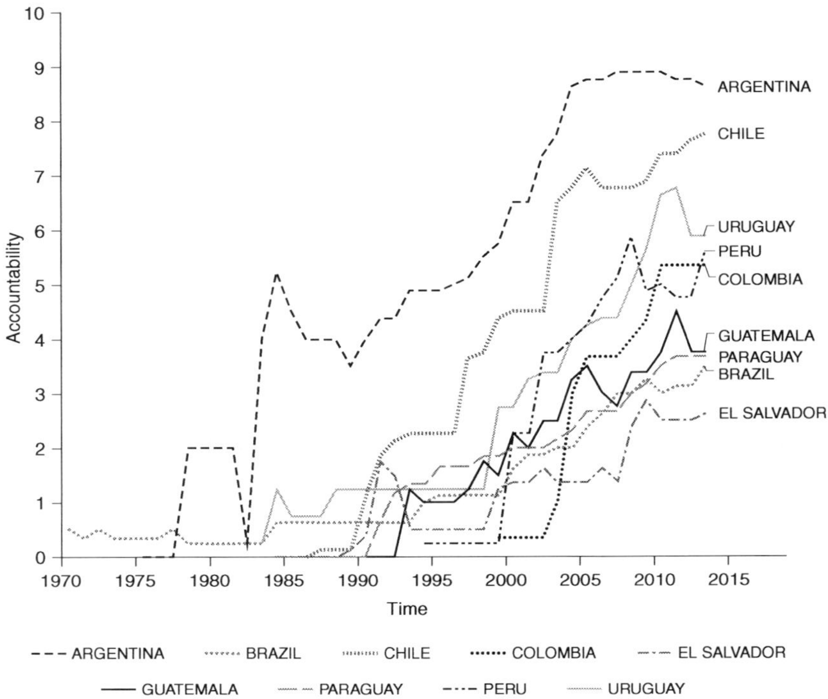

Figure 12.6 **General accountability trends over time for nine Latin American countries**
Source: Authors' construction, 2015.

Second, *movement between impunity and accountability is a non-linear process*. This is seen perhaps most clearly in the case of Argentina, where an early peak in trial activity, in 1985, was followed by backlash and temporary reversal. Other countries as well have experienced setbacks, that is, moments or periods when impunity, rather than accountability, was strengthened, as designated by downward movement of graph lines. Flat portions of a country's line can denote stagnation, the absence of innovation or change or, more frequently, operation within a single period of positive and negative accountability trends that cancel each other out.

Third, Figure 12.6 demonstrates that *the most marked shift from impunity towards accountability has taken place in Latin America since the turn of the millennium*. The next section considers some of the interrelated reasons behind this upsurge in transitional justice efforts.

Political and institutional factors shaping the accountability trajectories

It may be tempting to look for an economic explanation for the cross-country variations outlined above. The countries with more complete TJ experiences include some of the richer countries in the sample, namely Argentina, Chile, and Uruguay. The absence of widespread poverty may free citizens, and indeed authorities, to dedicate more time and energy to issues such as justice and reparations. Nonetheless, Brazil, a regional economic giant, has a relatively low accountability score, despite spending considerable sums on reparations. Mere material wealth is clearly not a sufficient predictor of levels of transitional justice activity. We need other explanations.

Political will has been crucial in all countries examined here. Political preferences for or against accountability weigh heavily in explaining how much, and in what direction, a particular government is willing to push a transitional justice agenda and allocate resources for it. Argentina stands out as the country with the most explicit pro-accountability transitional justice policy as of 2015. The influence of governing elites is particularly noticeable with respect to amnesties because the presidentialist emphasis of most Latin American political systems makes it the prerogative of the executive branch to initiate legislative limitation, or to modify or annul amnesty laws. Nonetheless, judicial branches with a modicum of autonomy can exercise high levels of discretion through interpretation of amnesty laws. In this case, executive control will be restricted to efforts to steer judicial outcomes, for instance by appointing a pliant chief public prosecutor or judges sympathetic to the government's TJ preferences. Implementation of reparations and truth commission follow-up are also good indicators of the presence or absence of political commitment, as they generally require active policy innovation or renewal of budgets.

Political will reflects a government's moral and political commitment to human rights principles as they apply to past crimes. Beyond this, it is shaped by societal factors, including civil society pressures, the relative importance voters place on TJ issues, and countervailing pressures from former perpetrators and their supporters. A government may also be concerned with its international reputation in the human rights field.[10]

Positive political will, though essential, is not sufficient. A second key factor is the changing *role of the military*. In the early years of Argentina's and Chile's transitions, the desire of the first democratically elected presidents to push for prosecution was severely curbed by continuing military influence and threats to derail the democratisation process. In other countries, military pressure or continuing ties between the military and the new democratic government were so strong that no initial push to prosecute materialised (Uruguay, Brazil, Paraguay). As the military has gradually been reformed and/or brought under civilian control in those countries where it was the main perpetrator of violations, military pressure to defend impunity has either lessened or become less central to the formulation of transitional justice policy preferences.[11]

Whereas a strong military influence over democratic politics has often had a decidedly negative effect on accountability focused change, *a strong and vibrant civil society* has been key in placing or keeping transitional justice on the political agenda. Groups within civil society can, of course, hold a range of views, both pro- and anti-accountability. Specific pro-accountability actors, both individuals and non-governmental organisations, have nonetheless been active in demanding truth, justice, and reparations in each of our nine countries. They have submitted evidence to truth commissions and courts, mobilised nationally, (sub)regionally, and internationally, and activated the inter-American system by means of individual petitions. Countries with a history of strong human rights networks, and/or generally buoyant traditions of grassroots political organising, have been at an advantage when compared to Paraguay, the Central American countries, or to some extent Peru, where clientelistic or patronage politics have historically weakened autonomous civil society.

Independent courts, and judges and prosecutors willing to bring and hear cases, have been crucial for the trials dimension of accountability. The independence of courts and judges is affected by long historical and professional trends, and more recently by judicial reforms carried out across the region in the 1990s and 2000s. Courts and judges have increasingly responded more favourably than before – and sometimes more favourably than other branches of state – to regional and international pressures to comply with the contents of human rights instruments and the judgments or recommendations of the inter-American system. The Fujimori trials in Peru are a prime example of this. Unsurprisingly, countries with well-established state bureaucracies (Argentina, Chile, Uruguay) or a strongly legalistic culture (Colombia) have generally seen more activity in the criminal justice dimension of accountability than have countries with historically weak or captured court systems (El Salvador, Guatemala, Paraguay).

We have seen that the *inter-American human rights system* has become an important regional transitional justice actor.[12] Specific Inter-American Court rulings have required steadily more of states in regard to meeting societal and victims' rights to effective remedy, encompassing justice, truth, and reparations. Adverse rulings against a number of our countries, as detailed in the country chapters, have been obtained by domestic case-bringers, who are also active in pushing for subsequent compliance. These rulings have become a new source of jurisprudence for domestic judges within and beyond the target state. These judges are increasingly called upon to rule in novel issue areas, including crimes against humanity and joint criminal enterprise. Regional non-governmental organisations such as the Due Process of Law Foundation have assisted by promoting awareness of regional developments, and jurisprudence, among case-bringers and judges.

Hillebrecht (2012) nonetheless points out that the inter-American system has limited direct powers of enforcement. In practice, the degree of state compliance with Inter-American Court rulings has varied substantially across our nine countries, supporting Haglund's contention that 'the decision to respect rights ultimately lies with the executive, [and] executive decision-making on rights-related policy plays a major role in the effectiveness of the court' (2015, 2). Executive and judicial compliance in the Gelman case against Uruguay (2011) and the Barrios Altos case against Peru (2001) shows how Court judgments can have a positive accountability effect. Perhaps the principal illustration of generalised non-compliance in our sample is El Salvador, whose adverse Court rulings in 2005, 2011, and 2012 – the latter declaring the 1993 General amnesty law in violation of international norms and of the Salvadoran peace agreements – have to date had no discernible effect. Thus, just as we concluded that quality assessment rather than simple counting of TJMs offered the best insight into accountability progress, we also conclude that actual take-up of Court rulings – whether by the target state or another – is at least as significant as the number or content of verdicts.

When these considerations about political will, civil-military relations, judicial independence, and the regional human rights climate are combined with the insights about international time, timing, and sequencing discussed at the beginning of this chapter, we begin to see how upward trends and occasional dips in overall country trajectories may have come about. Two additional factors are worthy of mention. First, countries with recent or ongoing transitions (Peru and Colombia) have transitioned in a regional context with a strong pro-accountability ethos and have an accumulation of regional and international experiences to learn from. Second, particular events such as the Pinochet arrest in 1998 in the United Kingdom transcend domestic frontiers and can create region-wide effects, in this case notably increasing pro-trials pressure from victims and relatives.

This effect is one contributor to a noticeable accountability spike around the year 2000, which has evened off or turned slightly negative in recent years for some countries. This may reflect the exhaustion of the potential and/or impetus for some TJMs in some countries. Human rights organisations may have changed their priorities, while some states continue to have other pressing issues including high homicide rates and impunity rates for common crimes (Guatemala and El Salvador). Finally, the flattening of trend lines in the overcoming amnesty graphs (El Salvador, Brazil) or even negative trends (Uruguay and Guatemala) suggest that challenges to amnesty laws are encountering pushback (see Figure 12.4).

Concluding remarks

While recent scholarly works have explored the impact of transitional justice on broader goals such as democratic consolidation and peace, this study has simply asked how four transitional justice mechanisms together have contributed to or obstructed accountability for human rights violations committed by authoritarian regimes or during internal armed conflict. In so doing, we have also aimed to demonstrate why accountability is best understood across a range of dimensions, rather than solely or principally in relation to criminal prosecution.

A relatively high overall accountability score, such as those the authors assign to Argentina and Chile, requires at least some advance in each of the four dimensions of truth-finding, trials, challenge to amnesty, and reparations. Low overall scores could be the outcome of little or no movement across the board, but we find they have instead resulted from skewed trajectories in which advances in truth and/or reparations have not been matched by progress in trials or the overcoming of amnesty.

An important finding is that the mere presence or absence of amnesty laws is not what tips the balance against or in favour of pro-accountability change, as illustrated by the cases of Paraguay and Chile.[13] *De jure* amnesty, by galvanising human rights organisations, victims' and relatives' associations, and other pro-accountability actors and by raising awareness among judges and prosecutors, has probably been constructive on balance in catalysing other accountability advances. The key lies in clarifying the quite varied types of amnesty laws and their nuanced real-world effects. Such insights may be of assistance to Colombia, faced with the challenge of imagining a transitional justice future in a context within which full accountability and absolute impunity are probably equally unlikely.

Notes

* We are grateful to Catalina Smulovitz and Eric Wiebelhaus-Brahm for valuable comments on this chapter. We also thank Leigh Payne for comments on an earlier version.

1 As detailed in Chapter 2, four combinations use only one TJM (A only, TC only, T only, R only). One of these (A only) is, in fact, negative for accountability since it moves a country closer to impunity. Six combinations use two TJMs (A+TC, A+R, A+T, TC+R, TC+T, R+T); four combinations use three TJMs (A+R+TC, A+TC+T, A+R+T, TC+R+T); and one combination uses all four TJMs (A+R+TC+T). An additional scenario deploys no TJMs at all. We evaluated the expected positive contributions of TJMs to accountability in the following order: T>TC>R>A, meaning that trials contribute most and amnesties least (in fact, negatively) to accountability. This provides the order of combinations displayed in Table 12.2 in terms of expected accountability outcomes (see Chapter 2 for details).

2 This makes T2 a period of highly variable length, spanning little more than a year in some cases and more than three decades in others. The point is to differentiate between TJMs implemented immediately after transition, when political tensions are running high, and TJMs begun during the later post-transition period when accountability may become gradually less contentious (though that does not always happen). The fact that TJMs can be implemented either concurrently or sequentially within each period is not captured in this table.

3 We thank Eric Wiebelhaus-Brahm for pointing this out.

4 We thank Catalina Smulovitz for fruitful discussions on the conceptualisation of an accountability triangle. Other authors, too, have found the triangle motif useful for

presenting cross-country data on three dimensions; see, for example, Brinks and Gauri (2008).

5 In constructing the triangles, we have temporarily set aside the amnesty dimension. T adequately represents the current justice dimension inasmuch as the trials situation at a given moment represents the outcome of the dynamic interplay between the justice imperative and the legal space defined by amnesty laws.

6 Magnitude of violence is reflected in the number of dead, detained-disappeared, and displaced (see Chapter 1, Table 1.3).

7 Greater consistency might be expected because stagnation and backward movement on the other dimensions are often caused by overt resistance and opposition.

8 The difference between the lowest and highest scores assigned to any country for each of the four dimensions in 2014 was only 4.0 for reparations, compared to 4.5 for truth, 8.0 for trials, and 9.0 for amnesty (see Table 12.2).

9 For Colombia, in effect still in transition, the timeline starts in 2000 for comparative purposes only. The Colombian transitional justice process started in 2005 (see Chapter 11).

10 For discussion of how governments react to pressure to comply with Inter-American Court rulings, see Haglund (2015) and Hillebrecht (2012).

11 For a general treatment of civil-military relations in the region, see Pion-Berlin (2001).

12 See the work of Hillebrecht (2012) and of Natalia Saltalamacchia, Sandra Borda, and others in the Inter-American Human Rights Network report (2014).

13 See also Olsen, Payne and Reiter (2010) and Mallinder (2008).

References

Abrão, Paulo, and Marcelo Torelly. 2012. 'Resistance to Change: Brazil's Persistent Amnesty and Its Alternatives for Truth and Justice.' In *Amnesty in the Age of Human Rights Accountability: Comparative and International Perspectives*, edited by Francesca Lessa and Leigh A. Payne, 152–81. New York: Cambridge University Press.

Brinks, Daniel M., and Varun Gauri. 2008. 'A New Policy Landscape: Legalizing Social and Economic Rights in the Developing World.' In *Courting Social Justice: Judicial Enforcement of Social and Economic Rights in the Developing World*, 303–52. New York: Cambridge University Press.

Dancy, Geoff, and Eric Wiebelhaus-Brahm. 2015. 'Timing, Sequencing, and Transitional Justice Impact: A Qualitative Comparative Analysis of Latin America.' *Human Rights Review* 16(4): 321–42.

Freeman, Mark. 2009. *Necessary Evils: Amnesties and the Search for Justice*. New York: Cambridge University Press.

Haglund, Jillienne. 2015. 'Generating Executive Implementation Incentives: Civil Society and the Effectiveness of the Inter-American Court of Human Rights.' Paper prepared for 2015 annual meeting of the American Political Science Association, San Francisco, 3–6 September.

Hillebrecht, Courtney. 2012. 'The Domestic Mechanisms of Compliance with International Human Rights Law: Case Studies from the Inter-American Human Rights System.' *Human Rights Quarterly* 34(4): 959–85.

Hite, Katherine. 2012. *Politics and the Art of Commemoration: Memorials to Struggle in Latin America and Spain*. Abingdon, UK: Routledge.

Inter-American Human Rights Network. 2014. *Assessing the Impact of the Inter-American Human Rights System*. Report on workshop sponsored by Instituto Tecnológico Autónomo de México and Instituto de Investigaciones Jurídicas (UNAM), 10–11 October.

Lutz, Ellen, and Kathryn Sikkink. 2001. 'The Justice Cascade: The Evolution and Impact of Foreign Human Rights Trials.' *Chicago Journal of International Law* 2(1): 1–33.

Mallinder, Louise. 2008. *Amnesty, Human Rights and Political Transitions: Bridging the Peace and Justice Divide*. Portland, OR: Hart.

Olsen, Tricia D., Leigh A. Payne, and Andrew G. Reiter. 2010. *Transitional Justice in Balance: Comparing Processes, Weighing Efficacy*. Washington, DC: United States Institute of Peace Press.

Pion-Berlin, David, ed. 2001. *Civil-Military Relations in Latin America: New International Perspectives*. Chapel Hill: University of North Carolina Press.

Roht-Arriaza, Naomi. 2005. *The Pinochet Effect: Transnational Justice in the Age of Human Rights*. Philadelphia: University of Pennsylvania Press.

Sikkink, Kathryn. 2011. *The Justice Cascade: How Human Rights Prosecutions Are Changing World Politics*. New York: W.W. Norton.

Skaar, Elin, and Eric Wiebelhaus-Brahm. 2013. 'Drivers of Justice after Violent Conflict: An Introduction.' In 'Drivers of Justice,' edited by Elin Skaar and Astri Suhrke, special issue, *Nordic Journal of Human Rights* 31(2): 119–26.

Appendix 1: Impunity and accountability factors

Table A.1 Power holders and institutions that may affect impunity and accountability

Factor	*Impunity*	*Accountability*
Power distribution at moment of transition and over time	Little or no political replacement. Former authoritarians retain strong influence and secure exit guarantees by threatening authoritarian reversal or renewed violence. Power-sharing between former combatants, all of whom were implicated in atrocities and therefore have a shared interest in installing and preserving amnesty. Incoming authorities open to accountability but subject to veto players (economic and other elites) who oppose accountability.	Political alternation: authoritarian regime or combatant state is replaced by incoming political authorities not directly implicated in previous atrocities. Former authoritarians and previous combatants implicated in atrocities have limited or no residual political influence or veto power. May include transition by collapse (outgoing regime militarily, economically, or otherwise discredited). Negotiated or supervised replacement: international supervision or underwriting of transitional arrangements that requires minimum levels of HR and TJ compliance.
Role of military and police in formal political arrangements (where military/police were involved in atrocities)	Military/police retain strong formal or *de facto* political influence and are committed to defending former repressive actions. High command from periods of repression or political violence are not renewed or replaced. Military/police have high levels of formal and economic autonomy from civilian political institutions. Military justice system is allowed to deal with cases of alleged atrocity.	Subordination of military to civilian rule where civilian politicians have an interest in accountability. Reduced military influence in the political sphere: downsizing, geopolitical realignment, abandonment of National Security Doctrine. Military reform through generational replacement or modernisation (e.g. because of desire to participate in peacekeeping operations, for which minimum HR requirements apply).

Table A.1 (cont.)

Factor	*Impunity*	*Accountability*
Influence of other actors	High continuity in public administration. Majority public opinion and main sources of domestic political support are hostile or indifferent to accountability pressures.	Lustration, vetting, or gradual (generational) replacement of high-level civil servants and security forces personnel, and/or explicit recognition and repudiation by existing personnel of previous atrocities. Majority public opinion and/or minority activist groups with access to external support create political incentives for pro-accountability change.

Table A.2 Policies and prevailing norms that may affect impunity and accountability

Factor	*Impunity*	*Accountability*
Government and public policy discourse about past atrocities	Widespread official and public denial or justification of past atrocities. Calls for 'turning the page' on grounds that dealing more vigorously with the past will hinder reconciliation. Calls for understanding and forgiveness (in Latin America, often couched in Christian religious imagery and language and supported by ecclesiastical authorities). Ambiguous or evasive language about past atrocities; reluctance to assign specific or differential responsibility. Notion that both sides are equally to blame is known in Latin America as *la teoría de los dos demonios* (theory of the two demons).	Unequivocal social and official repudiation of past atrocities. Full accountability seen by new authorities as necessary for establishment of rule of law. Explicit commitment to overturning amnesty provisions. Commitment to a new social pact with state-citizen relationship recast on the basis of rights. Incoming authorities have HR issues central in their campaign and manifesto promises.

Table A.2 (*cont.*)

Factor	*Impunity*	*Accountability*
International environment	Prevalence of National Security Doctrine and/or War on Terror ideology. Close/strategic allies are sceptical of or hostile to TJ or international HR law. Regional multilateral HR institutions are non-existent or have little leverage over the country in question. Economic, military, or political dependence on anti-HR or anti-TJ entities.	Post-World War II evolution of norms away from impunity (reflected in creation of International Criminal Court, etc.). Close/strategic allies are committed to TJ and international HR law. Regional multilateral institutions have leverage and norm convergence around HR. Economic, military, or political dependence on pro-HR or pro-TJ entities.
Government and justice sector response to international environment	Absent or limited compliance with international HR norms and with decisions by regional/ international courts and institutions.	High or increasing levels of compliance with international HR norms and with decisions by regional/ international courts and institutions.

Table A.3 Legal–institutional factors that may affect impunity and accountability

Factor	*Impunity*	*Accountability*
Constitutional and institutional reform	Lack of constitutional/ institutional reform.	New constitution, and/or reform of previously compromised or collusive institutions, to improve democratic responsiveness and/ or respect for rights.
Justice sector	Formal justice system historically weak, institutionally underdeveloped, and/or lacking popular legitimacy or confidence of elites. Justice system previously instrumentalised by authoritarian regime or by one side in internal conflict in order to shield perpetrators.	Formal justice system historically strong, enjoying popular legitimacy and confidence of elites. High degrees of judicial independence, at both court level and level of individual judges.

Table A.3 (*cont.*)

Factor	*Impunity*	*Accountability*
Justice sector	Absent or limited justice sector reform, including personnel replacement; or reforms that deliberately or incidentally impede continuity of pre-reform investigations. Inquisitorial system maintained.	Substantial judicial reform, including generational change in key judicial figures and/or changes in their receptivity to accountability claims. Modernisation and technical change, especially strengthened police investigative and/or forensic capacity. Change from inquisitorial to adversarial system. (This shift took place in much of Latin America in the 1990s. Its effects are, in theory, indeterminate for accountability, as attitudes of new state prosecutors can vary. In practice, it is usually accompanied by strengthening of compliance with international standards.)
Creation of permanent human rights infrastructure	TJ and HR issues dealt with ad hoc and sporadically by mainstream institutions or political authorities, with little continuity.	Creation of dedicated TJ or HR entities with institutional solidity and public access (e.g. through an ombudsperson).

Table A.4 Other factors that may affect impunity and accountability

Factor	*Impunity*	*Accountability*
Level of continuing violence (political violence or common crime)	Persistence or irruptions of specific political violence (by state and/or non-state actors) may derail or inhibit TJMs. High or rising levels of common crime may reinforce authoritarian nostalgia, discredit HR discourse, lead to calls for hard-line policing (*la mano dura*), and discourage reform/reduction of security forces.	Steep fall in levels of political violence. Moderate or stable levels of common crime. Demobilisation or explicit abandonment of armed tactics by non-state combatants.

Table A.4 (cont.)

Factor	*Impunity*	*Accountability*
Civil society HR organising	Low levels of HR organising by civil society actors; civil society HR organising drops due to less urgent situation and/or loss of external support and funding. HR movement intentionally sidelined by incoming political forces.	Presence of significant number of civil society HR groups interested in deepening TJ actions. Groups acquire high traction or visibility through judicialisation and/or strategic domestic, regional, and international alliances. Incoming political forces receptive to demands from HR movement.
Demand for accountability	Limited demands by survivors/ relatives for accountability due to desire to move on, absence of trust in judicial system, small numbers of survivors, fatalism or indifference as to likelihood of success, and fear of reprisal.	Strong demands for accountability. 'Demand inflation' may be based on earlier achievements or on demonstration effects of events in other countries (e.g. the 'Pinochet effect').
Profile of victims	Victims are predominantly rural, poor, or otherwise excluded groups with little organisational experience, few resources, and few external connections. Weak/unorganised exile community.	Victims are predominantly urban and middle class with organisational experience, access to resources, and strong national and/or international networks. Motivated, vocal, and organised exile community.
Proportion of population affected by fatal violence	Fatal violence affected a small sector of the population, such as a minority ethnic, religious, or political group, leading to invisibility. Fatal violence was widespread, affecting all sectors of the population, with so many deaths that accountability is not seen as feasible.	Fatal violence at levels that impede invisibility but do not paralyse demand for accountability or possible response.
Life-cycle issues	Perpetrators, victims, and their relatives may want to leave the past behind and allow the next generation to escape the legacy of violence.	Towards the ends of their lives, some survivors or victims' relatives may want a last push to obtain closure. Some perpetrators may acquire a confessional impulse.

Table A.4 (cont.)

Factor	*Impunity*	*Accountability*
Public sympathy for former authoritarians or combatants	High levels of residual support for outgoing authoritarians or for one or both parties to the civil conflict.	Low levels of residual support for outgoing authoritarians or for one or both parties to the civil conflict.
	Low levels of social repudiation of past violence, with absent or muted repudiation by new authorities.	High levels of social repudiation of past violence, including clear repudiation by new authorities.
	Heroic myths: romantic portrayals of past violence by participants, media, or other influential actors.	Absence of heroic myths: past violence not portrayed in favourable terms by participants, media, or other influential actors.
	Discontent with current political or economic situation: authoritarian nostalgia and/or calls for radical or violent change.	Level of economic and social stability permitting attention to and financing of unresolved TJ legacy questions.
Global networks	Restricted or censored citizen access to global networks of information, documentation, and HR organisations.	Ample citizen access to and participation in global networks of information, documentation, and HR organisations (although former combatants and authoritarians can also be strengthened by network opportunities).
	No legislation mandates transparency or access to information.	Legislation on transparency and access to information is in place and enforced.
Unexpected and/or external events	Political unrest; new social or political violence such as assassination of a major political figure; major economic crisis; security emergency (including rise of organised crime and other illegitimate power-holding).	Revelations, accidental and otherwise, leading to new demands (e.g. discovery of Paraguay Terror Archive in 1992, scheduled US State Department declassifications, Pinochet arrest).

Note: HR = human rights; TJ = transitional justice; TJM = transitional justice mechanism.

Appendix 2: Guiding questions and evaluation of specific TJMs

Tables A.5 to A.8 present four sets of questions pertaining to the four transitional justice mechanisms (TJMs) – truth-finding, trials, amnesties, and reparations – addressed in this volume. These questions guided the country chapter authors in their research and analysis and helped them assess to what extent each of the TJMs has contributed to accountability (or, in the case of amnesties, to impunity). Note that this is not a questionnaire presented to informants, but a set of research questions for the authors' use. The answers to these questions (no/somewhat/yes) were gathered from written sources as well as interviews. Overall assessments of TJMs are portrayed in the country chapters in rich textual analysis, not in numerical terms.

To facilitate cross-country analysis, however, the authors also used the questions below to summarise and synthesise their analysis in graphs depicting the trajectory of each of the TJMs in each country over time. This process used a numerical scale running from 0 (complete impunity) to 10 (full accountability). As a rough guide, no = 0 points, somewhat = 0.5 point, and yes = 1 point. For example, if many of the questions pertaining to a given country's truth commission can be answered 'yes', it suggests that this truth commission has contributed more to accountability than a truth commission for which most of the answers to the questions are 'no'. We would stress that this is not mathematics: there is a fair amount of subjective evaluation going into the overall assessment of the contribution of each TJM to accountability.

Table A.5 Research questions on truth-telling and accountability

Question	*No/little accountability*	*Some accountability*	*More accountability*
Was a truth commission (TC) set up by the government?	No		Yes
Were the TC members highly respected?	No	Somewhat	Yes
Did the TC mandate cover the main crimes and main period during which crimes were committed?	No	Somewhat	Yes
Did the TC have adequate resources to carry out its work?	No	Somewhat	Yes
Did the TC complete its work and issue a report?	No	Somewhat	Yes
Was the report endorsed by the government?	No	Somewhat	Yes
Was the report widely disseminated in a language accessible to most victims?	No	Somewhat	Yes
Did the report receive a favourable public reception?	No	Somewhat	Yes
Have recommendations made by the TC in its report been implemented by the government?	No	Somewhat	Yes
Have other truth-finding measures (other than a TC) been implemented by the state?	No		Yes
Has the Inter-American Court ruled against the state and ordered the state to act on its obligation to fulfil victims' right to truth?	No		Yes
If so, did the government comply with this ruling?	No	Somewhat	Yes

Table A.6 Research questions on reparations and accountability

Question	*No/little accountability*	*Some accountability*	*More accountability*
Does the government have a reparations plan?	No		Yes
Has the government initiated economic reparations?	No	Somewhat	Yes
If so, have adequate resources been allocated?	No	Somewhat	Yes
Are economic reparations generally perceived as true reparations? (i.e. not just an extension of development programmes or social security measures)	No	Somewhat	Yes
Has a victims' registry been set up?	No	Yes, but incomplete	Yes
Has a special body been set up to administer/implement the reparations?	No	Planned, but not yet in place	Yes
Has the government made symbolic reparations?	No	Some	Yes
Has the government officially apologised for past atrocities committed by the state?	No	Yes, but reluctantly	Yes
Has the Inter-American Court ruled against the state and ordered the state to pay individual or collective reparations?	No		Yes
If so, did the government comply with this ruling?	No	Somewhat	Yes

Table A.7 Research questions on trials and accountability

Question	*No/little accountability*	*Some accountability*	*More accountability*
Have national trials been held for past human rights violations?	No	Attempts made	Yes
Has the number of trials been high?	No	Somewhat	Yes
Have high-level officials been held to account for human rights violations?	No	Somewhat	Yes
Have verdicts been issued?	No	Some	Yes
Have sentences been imposed where defendants have been found guilty?	No	Somewhat	Yes
Have sentences and prison conditions been in line with people's general perception of fairness?	No	Somewhat	Yes
Have trials generally been perceived as free and fair?	No	Somewhat	Yes
Have judges and prosecutors faced external pressure or threats during their work?	Yes	Some	No
Have trials against nationals for human rights violations been conducted in foreign courts?	No	Yes	
Has the Inter-American Court ruled against the state for human rights violations?	No		Yes
If so, did the government comply with this ruling?	No	Somewhat	Yes

Table A.8 Research questions on amnesty laws and accountability

Question	*No/little accountability*	*Some accountability*	*More accountability*
Is there an amnesty law on the books, or has there been one in recent years?	Yes		No
Is it a self-amnesty law passed by the military?	Yes	No	
Is it a blanket amnesty law?	Yes	No	
Is it a partial amnesty law?		Yes	
Does the amnesty law exclude certain crimes?		Yes	
Was the amnesty adopted to facilitate the transition?		Yes	
Has the amnesty law been challenged in national courts?	No	Yes, but unsuccessfully	Yes
Has the amnesty law been challenged politically?	No	Yes, but unsuccessfully	Yes
Is the amnesty law compatible with international human rights law?	No	Yes	
Has the amnesty law been annulled domestically?	No	Attempted	Yes
Has the Inter-American Court ruled against the state and declared the amnesty law in violation of international law and international obligations of the state?	No		Yes
If so, did the government comply with this ruling?	No	Somewhat	Yes

Index